this
book
is
taBoo

An Introduction to
Linguistics through Swearing

Randall Eggert

University of Utah

PUBLISHER'S NOTE: *The views, opinion, positions and language contained herein are those of the author and do not represent those of the publisher, its management or owners.*

Cover images © Shutterstock, Inc.

For France,
For Salomé

Judged merely as reading matter, the following work . . .
is abominably, incredibly obscene, and the compiler begs
that anyone will lay this book down who is not prepared to look
at all social phenomena with the dispassionate eye of the
anthropologist and the student of abnormal psychology.

—Allen Read

I'll start with a warning. If you are easily offended by cuss words, this book is not for you. Because this book is about taboo language, there are plenty of quotes and examples that include offensive language. I imagine even the most jaded readers will find some examples offensive—I know I do. So if you don't have the stomach for it, close the book. Put it back on the shelf. Walk away.

Are you still with me? Good. We're about to embark on a fascinating tour of language. Quick—think of the foulest, most disgusting, most offensive word you can. Got it? Now, would you ever use that word? By use, I mean would you ever say it to somebody and mean it? Some of you might, given the right circumstances. Others of you would never use the word. Personally, I wouldn't.

Now that I've got you in the right frame of mind, flipping through your mental index of bad words, let's talk about what this book is. It is, first and foremost, an introduction to linguistics. So what is linguistics? I'm glad you asked.

Whenever I'm introduced to somebody for the first time and they find out I'm a linguist, their first response is, "So you must speak a lot of languages?" I typically mumble a little and say something about how I've studied a few languages, but I really don't speak any of them well. They get embarrassed because they thought they knew what a linguist was but were apparently wrong. And I get embarrassed because I have a job nobody understands. When I was a graduate student, one of my professors got so tired of having to explain what a linguist is that he came up with the following definition: "Linguists are the only people who know shit about language" (Rich Janda, pers. comm.). It's not a helpful definition, but it makes Rich feel better, mostly because he gets to say "shit."

In my opinion, the best definition of linguistics is "the scientific study of language." The definition is good, but it requires explanation. First, I should note that we say "language" not "languages." This is kind of like how psychology is the study of the mind, not individual minds. Of course, language—the human ability to communicate using a complex sign system—is too abstract to study directly, so we approach it indirectly by studying individual languages, just as psychologists approach the mind by studying individual minds.

Mark Twain quotes
(collected from http://www.twainquotes.com/Profanity.html, accessed 8/13/2010):

The idea that no gentleman ever swears is all wrong. He can swear and still be a gentleman if he does it in a nice and benevolent and affectionate way.
—Private and Public Morals speech, 1906

There ought to be a room in every house to swear in. It's dangerous to have to repress an emotion like that.
—Mark Twain, a Biography

Under certain circumstances, urgent circumstances, desperate circumstances, profanity provides a relief denied even to prayer.
—Mark Twain, a Biography

When you're mad, count four; when you're very mad, swear! But most of us don't wait to count four! at least I don't!
—quoted in A Lifetime with Mark Twain: The Memories of Katy Leary

He didn't utter a word, but he exuded mute blasphemy from every pore.
—Autobiography of Mark Twain (bowling alley story)

We begin to swear before we can talk.
—Following the Equator

I should also explain what I mean by "scientific study." Linguistics isn't a "hard" science like chemistry or physics; however, it is still a science in that linguists use the scientific method. First, you define a question. Second, you observe phenomena related to the question. Third, you speculate (hypothesize) about an answer to the question. Fourth, you collect data (perform a study or experiment) in order to test your answer. Fifth, you analyze the data and evaluate whether they support or contradict the answer. Throughout this book you'll be asked to follow the scientific method in order to acquire more and more knowledge about dirty words.

So why do linguists study language? For the same reason so many scholars study their various subjects: we want to understand ourselves. We are a narcissistic species; humans are interested in humans. Human language is unique in the world—no other species has the ability to communicate at even close to the level of complexity that we can. This makes language a window into the human mind. Since we can't simply enter the mind and poke around, we need windows.

Quotes Continued:

Let us swear while we may, for in Heaven it will not be allowed.
—Notebook, 1898

If I cannot swear in heaven I shall not stay there.
—Notebook, 1898

The Victorian-era physicist and philosopher John Tyndall said of his friend Herbert Spencer: "He'd be a much nicer fellow if he had a good swear now and then" (quoted in Mencken 1918, 43).

Okay, but I still need to explain why we're studying bad language in this book. Well, why not? You have to start somewhere, and, as it turns out, taboo language tells us a great deal about humans. Besides, it's a lot of fun. Also, it turns out that there's a lot to learn about swearing and less research into it than you might think. As Jay (1992, 112) points out, swear words have not been included in most studies on word usage. Just as there's a taboo on using swear words, there's been an academic taboo on studying them. But, as Read (1977, 5) puts it: "A sociologist does not refuse to study certain criminals on the ground that they are too perverted or too dastardly; surely a student of language is even less warranted in refusing to consider certain four-letter words because they are too 'nasty' or too 'dirty'."

I started studying the linguistics of swearing in earnest about five years ago when we proposed the Bad Words and Taboo Terms class at the University of Utah. Like so many great ideas, the genesis of the class was notes on a napkin. As I remember it, four linguistics professors were sharing a pitcher of beer, brainstorming about what gets students interested in linguistics. Swearing came up, somebody suggested a whole class could be taught on the subject, and somehow I ended up being tasked with proposing the class. I've now taught it for four years, often twice a year.

According to Montagu (1967, 330-331), George Washington was known as quite a swearer, and Mencken (1918, 13) says that Washington "knew far more profanity than Scripture, and used and enjoyed it more."

I began writing this book because I couldn't find a satisfactory text for my students; some books were too intellectual and required too much background knowledge, and some were too infantile and lacked substance. I hope to have met a happy medium between intellectual and infantile. I'm sure I haven't succeeded entirely—in my scholarly zeal I sometimes get lost in details, and sometimes I'm prone to silliness. Forgive me my authorial sins.

OK? Let's get started.

REFERENCES

Jay, Timothy. 1992. *Cursing in America: A Psycholinguistic Study of Dirty Language in the Courts, in the Movies, in the Schoolyards, and on the Streets.* Philadelphia: John Benjamins.

Mencken, H.L. 1918. *A book of Calumny* [first published as *Damn*]. New York: Alfred A. Knopf.

Montagu, Ashley. 1967. *The Anatomy of Swearing.* New York: The Macmillan Company.

Read, Allen. 1977. *Classic American Graffiti: Lexical Evidence from Folk Epigraphy in Western North America.* Waukesha, WI: Maledicta Press.

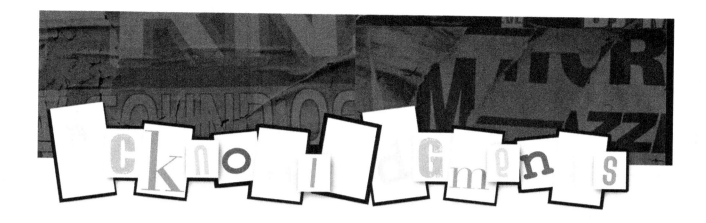

First, I wish to thank all of the students who have taken my Bad Words and Taboo Terms class at the University of Utah. Their curiosity and intellectual passion have inspired this book.

Next, thanks to all the guest lecturers who have contributed to Bad Words and Taboo Terms. Their help with the class aided me in many ways, and the research they did for their lectures has made its way into these pages. I have tried to credit them whenever I borrowed an idea or a fact wholesale from their lectures. But ideas are shaped intangibly as well, polished by those they come in contact with; without the free exchange of ideas I have enjoyed with my colleagues, this book would have been far different, far inferior. In alphabetical order, the guest lecturers have been: Bill Allred, David Bean, Lyle Campbell, Aniko Csirmaz, Marianna DiPaolo, Randall Gess, Rachel Hayes-Harb, David Iannucci, Jeff Metcalf, Maurico Mixco, Holly Mullen, Mike Place, Steve Sternfeld, Nate Vooge, and Sue Wurtzburg. Thanks also go to my chair, Ed Rubin, for his support of the class over the years. Ed, Randall, and Nate shared the pitcher over which the sketch for the class was first drawn.

Thank you to my friends at the Salt Lake Community Writing Center who have read drafts of chapters and given valuable feedback. I especially wish to thank the following readers: Dave Bastian, John Boles, Homer Conder, Kathleen Koprowski, and Jim Rosinus.

Finally, my biggest and most loving thanks go to my wife, France, for her support and love and for being a sounding board over the years.

1. TABOOS

Before we begin, let's get into the history of the word *taboo.* Knowing its history isn't necessary for understanding the ideas we'll be discussing—it may not even be useful. But being a linguist, I'm a word geek, and I just can't help myself. Several Pacific island languages have related words, including Polynesian and Maori (*tapu*), Hawaiian (*kapu*) and Melanesian (*tambu* or *tabu*), but we got the word from the Tongan *tabu,* meaning 'forbidden' (OED). Captain Cook brought it into our language after his 1773 voyage to the island nation of Tonga, where he observed that many practices, especially food-related, were forbidden. For us today, simply put, a **taboo** is a forbidden behavior.

Examples of taboos from American society: dropping your pants in public, picking your nose, staring, cracking your knuckles, leaving your cell phone on during a movie, eating with your mouth open, belching, coughing without covering your mouth, giving hugs to strangers. Do people still do these things? You bet. In fact, I'd wager you've done several of them yourself. There are also stronger taboos, ones I hope you've never done: murder, rape, armed robbery, driving a Hummer. My point is there are lots of behaviors that society censors, and they aren't created equally.

Not only are some taboos stronger or weaker, they also differ from culture to culture. Whenever we talk about some behavior being taboo, we have to frame it in terms of people, place, and time; after all, taboos are conventions, and what is taboo in one community may not be in another. Among many religious cultures there are food taboos; for example, Muslims and Jews don't eat pork, and Hindus don't eat beef. Some taboos are surprising or even bizarre by our standards. In Thailand, I was told never to sit with my legs pointing at somebody, nor should I touch a child's head. In Hungary, a friend informed me that toasts can be done with wine or hard alcohol, but never with beer. In many countries, you should never eat with the left hand. Public displays of affection are taboo in some societies (as they were in my high school's halls—that taboo came from the principal, not the students). In some cultures it is taboo for men to dance with women. In Saudi Arabia, it is taboo for women to appear in public without a headscarf, while wearing a head scarf is taboo in France's schools. In Germany it is taboo to hold your arm up at a 45-degree angle. In India, one should not compliment a baby. In LaVerkin, Utah it is taboo to do activities for the United Nations.

Now that we've defined taboo, we'll turn to **taboo language**. This is the cover term we'll use for any sort of linguistic taboo. The most common type of taboo language is **taboo words**. We could say that taboo words are linguistic expressions that are forbidden—unfortunately, this definition may be too broad (as we'll see in a moment). As we go, we'll refine our understanding of the term.

1.1 Taboo Words

Lots of synonyms exist for taboo words: bad words, naughty words, dirty words, swear words, four-letter words, foul words, curse words, cuss words, bathroom language, locker room talk, etc. My personal favorite dates back to around 1250: Shit worde[1] (Hughes 1991, 58). Although I usually stick with "taboo words" (or "taboo expressions/terms"), for variety, I sometimes use one or another of the above forms.

There are two words I'm more picky about: **profanity** and **obscenity**. These terms I prefer to use to describe subtypes of taboo words. Profanity I use for religious taboo words, and obscenity for sexual taboo words. Other categories include **scatology**, taboo words for bodily effluvia; **slurs**, insulting names, often based on ethnicity, religion, race, gender, or sexuality, but also characteristics like intelligence, height, or deformity; **faunality,** taboo words derived from names for animals; **mortology**, linguistic taboos relating to death; and **appellity,** taboos on proper names.[2] These categories give us the following taxonomy:

- **Taboo Words**
  - **Profanity:** religious words (*God, hell, damn, Jesus*)
  - **Obscenity:** sexual words (*fuck, tits, cock*)
  - **Scatology:** bathroom words (*shit, piss, asshole*)
  - **Slurs:** insulting names (*bastard, kike, nigger, fag, retard*)
  - **Faunality:** animal words (*bitch, pussy, ass, coon*)
  - **Mortology:** death words (*die, cancer*)
  - **Appellity:** proper names (*dick, johnson, fanny*)

The taxonomy is meant as a useful set of terms to distinguish different types of taboo language. It is not meant as a scientific classification (on par with, say, a biological taxonomy). Also, the way I define the terms is not necessarily the way others do. The FCC, for example, gives a secular definition of profanity: "including language so grossly offensive to members of the public who actually hear it as to amount to a nuisance." And Jay (1992) presents an altogether different taxonomy, leaving off some categories (e.g., faunality, mortology, and appellity), while making some finer distinctions than we do, for example, distinguishing profanity (disrespecting religious topics) from blasphemy (attacking a religion or a deity). He also gives a more specific definition for taboo and a less specific one for obscenity: "While taboo restricts what speakers do, obscenity functions to protect listeners from harmful language" (Jay 1992, 5).

I should emphasize that the categories are not meant to be categorical (where a term must fit in one and only one category). Many taboo terms overlap categories (e.g., *cock* belongs in obscenity, scatology, and faunality); many slurs draw from the other categories (e.g., *shithead, motherfucker, bitch*); and virtuoso swearers are fond of mixing categories (e.g., *holy shit, fucking hell, god-damn son of a bitch*). Furthermore it's possible that some taboo terms are unclassifiable, and we may find with further investigation that we should include other categories. Still, the list is not a bad start.

It's important to note what should not be included in the list. There are words like *ain't* or *irregardless* that some people think of as "bad," but not in the same sense we mean. If you say "ain't" or "irregardless," it may reflect badly on you, but not in the same way as if you say "fuck" or "shit" (see Chapter 2). With taboo words,

---

[1] *Worde* used to be the plural form for *word*.
[2] I made up the terms *faunality*, *mortology*, and *appellity*. As far as I can tell, there are no terms for taboos on animal words, death-related terms, or names, yet these are common in many languages (see Chapter 10).

some will feel you have harmed yourself or the people around you. In today's society, the harm is rarely taken to be physical, but there was a time when it was thought that words could cause real harm ("a plague on your house")—hence the term "curse" words (see Section 4.1.2). Taboo words have the power to offend like no other words in the language.

In Section 3 we explore the categories from this taxonomy in more depth.

1.2 Taboo of Word vs. Taboo of Thing

Looking at the taxonomy of taboo words, we can see that many taboo words refer to taboo things or behaviors (e.g., sex, defecation, death). For example, given society's feelings about sex, it's not surprising that sex terms are taboo. Thus, we might think these words are taboo because of what they refer to. However, it's not so simple.

Read (1977:9) poses the following interesting question: "Is it possible for a word to be obscene by nature, in and of itself?" His answer is no. "The determinant of obscenity lies not in words or things, but in the attitudes that people have towards these words and things." He concludes that for something to be obscene it first has to be forbidden or made taboo. In our terms, for a word to count as obscenity, it has to be taboo.

It is not enough for the referent of a word to be taboo to make the word taboo. "[T]aboo of word is a phenomenon altogether separate from taboo of thing" (Read 1977, 10). After all, there are words that mean the same thing, where one is taboo and the other is not, for example, *piss ~ urinate, shit ~ defecate, fuck ~ fornicate, nigger ~ African American, cunt ~ vagina.* So, Read asks, "How is this sense of taboo implanted?" He blames our upbringing:

> Obviously enough, it is the result of training in early childhood, of experiences during the impressionable age, springing from the hushed awe that surrounds these words, the refusal of information concerning them, or the punishment meted out for an inadvertent use of them. There develops a neurosis so ingrained that the will is well-nigh powerless against it. Even when we come to know that there is not a proper basis for the feeling, we are prompted by motivations so deeply planted that we have the reactions in spite of our intellect. (1977, 10–11)

Although Read's analysis was not backed up by empirical evidence, he was probably accurate to a large degree, as we'll find in Chapters 11 and 12.

It seems to me we have a need for certain words to be forbidden. From a young age, we understand and expect that some words are off-limits. What's more, we are aware the ban is arbitrary, not simply based on the referent, because the fact is sometimes we have to talk about taboo things. As Read (1977, 11) puts it, "The fact that only certain words are so regarded [as taboo] is attributable to the patterning tendency in man: if certain objects are arbitrarily designated as scapegoats, then the remainder may be approached without fear."

1.3 Breaking Taboos

Often, when I discuss taboos on words with people, somebody points out that the words can't be forbidden since people use them all the time. True enough. On the other hand, speeding in your car is forbidden, isn't it? We have to be careful to recognize that just because something's taboo, doesn't mean it's entirely avoided. Read (1977, 12) puts the conundrum well:

> But why should not verbal taboo be self-defeating? If a word is never spoken, would it not soon be forgotten? At least would not a new generation be unaware of it? But here we come to a quirk in human psychology. Instead of responding to the taboo in the normal fashion, by avoiding such words, some people respond to it by a re-doubled use of the words. They wish to feel the thrill of doing the forbidden, to express the jangled state of their nerves, or to clothe an insult by what they feel are fitting terms.

Read distinguishes between an "inverted taboo" and actually breaking a taboo. An inverted taboo is when a person uses a taboo word for the "thrill" of using it. On the other hand, he argues that "[t]he only way that a taboo can be actually broken is to use a word unemotionally in its simple literal sense" (1977, 13). The closest that Read can see to somebody actually breaking the taboo is D.H. Lawrence's *Lady Chatterly's Lover,* where the characters freely and without shame use *fuck* and *cunt* with their original meanings. Here's a famous passage from Chapter 12:

> "What is cunt?" she said.
>
> "An' doesn't ter know? Cunt! It's thee down theer; an' what I get when I'm i'side thee, and what tha gets when I'm i'side thee; it's a' as it is, all on't."
>
> "All on't," she teased. "Cunt! It's like fuck then."
>
> "Nay nay! Fuck's only what you do. animals fuck. But cunt's a lot more than that. It's thee, dost see: an' tha'rt a lot besides an animal, aren't ter?—even ter fuck? Cunt! Eh, that's the beauty o' thee, lass!" (Lawrence 1968, 191)

Read's distinction between "actually" breaking a taboo and inverting the taboo isn't, in my mind, all that useful. The fact is if you use a taboo word you've broken a taboo. A more interesting question is why people break taboos—we'll be approaching that question from different angles throughout this book.

Also, we need to keep in mind, as we observed earlier, that context plays a role. It's less taboo to break the taboo of using taboo words in some contexts than others. We'll talk more about that in Chapter 14. And, of course, we need to recognize that some people are more likely to break taboos than others—some of this has to do with the person's personality and some to do with their background (sex, age, social class, race, etc.). We'll discuss how social background affects swearing more in Chapter 13.

1.4   Tabooness

As we observed at the beginning of this chapter, taboos are socially determined. Therefore, which words are taboo depends on the time, place, and community: *bloody* is taboo in the United Kingdom, but not the United States; *zounds* used to be taboo but isn't now; and *punk* is taboo among male prisoners in the United States. Also, a word may be taboo in one context but not in another: for example, *pee-pee* is a fine word to use with a kindergartener asking to be excused but not with a high school student. That said, I contend that for any given community, words can be ranked according to their **tabooness,** irrespective of context.

Jay (1992, 37) estimates that most adults use sixty to seventy different types of taboo expressions, and by the age of ten most children use thirty to forty. Children understand quite early that some words are taboo. Jay (1992, 24) reports asking a couple two-year-old boys if they knew any bad language with one responding, "I know *goddamn it,* but he knows *son of a bitch!*" When my nephew, Jakob, was about three he looked at me with horror when I said the word *kill.* "That's a bad word," he said. It turns out his parents had thought he was too violent in his playing and forbid him from saying *kill.* A couple days later, I saw him stamping his feet in the backyard and asked what he was doing. He said, "I'm dying ants."

> Two six-year-olds discussing "bad things to do": "[N]ever say *red hell* to a bull or he will charge you . . ." (reported in Jay 1992, 24).

Jay (1992, 25) writes that "early name calling is based on the recognition of a discrepancy between 'normal' kids and deviants in addition to those unresolved tensions about sex and elimination that each brings to school." So we see that from early on children use invectives, invectives derived from slurs, obscenity, and scatology.

Of course what qualifies as taboo changes over time. What we considered "bad" as a child may not be so bad when we grow up; for example, in kindergarten, a number of us were under the misapprehension that "the f-word" was *fart,* which we considered to be a scandalous word. Also, what our grandparents think is really taboo may not correspond with what we think is really taboo. As Hughes (1991, 263) puts it: "The word-field of swearing is . . . in constant flux, as older terms of weight and force are trivialized, to be replaced by modish newcomers." It seems that each generation is shocked by the swearing of the subsequent generations; this dates at least to the fifteenth century, when many lamented the trend or fashion of swearing (Hughes 1991, 61–62).

Granting that different generations and different communities have different standards for what is or is not taboo, let's engage a bit in a fiction that linguists call the **ideal speaker.** The ideal speaker is a hypothetical person who we imagine represents the average speaker of a language. Of course, we know there's lots of variation between speakers (just imagine a conversation between a taxi driver from London, a surfer from California, a miner from Kentucky, and a philosophy professor from Australia). There's even variation between speakers from the same community (identical twins speak differently). Nonetheless, to get stuff done in linguistics, sometimes we have to ignore differences.

For any speech community, we can imagine an ideal speaker. For that speaker, some words are neutral, some are taboo. Of the taboo words, the speaker will consider some more taboo than others. Let's imagine that this ideal speaker were to rate each word on a scale from 1 to 7 for how taboo it is, where 1 is a neutral (non-taboo) word and 7 is the most ridiculously taboo word the speaker knows. These ratings, we'll call a word's **tabooness.**

Now, how does this ideal speaker know to rate *fornication* relatively low on the scale (probably 1 or 2) and *fuck* relatively high (probably 4 or 5)? Well, it comes from society, right? We learn what's taboo simply by navigating through our daily lives. And this is exactly the same way we learn how to speak in the first place. Just as we know "hello" is said when meeting somebody and "goodbye" when leaving them; and we know it's "I'm hungry" not "I have hunger"; and we know to refer to ourselves with *I* or *we,* not *you, he, she,* or *they;* we know that *fuck* is a worse word than *fornicate.* By being a member of a speech community, we know what's forbidden in that community.

Putting this idea of tabooness to the test, the Spring 2010 students of Bad Words and Taboo Terms at the University of Utah conducted a **tabooness survey.** They distributed written questionnaires with a list of words and sentences to 260 participants and asked them to assign a tabooness rating from 1 to 7 to each word/sentence. Participants were told to rate the words and sentences not by their own standards, but by their community's standards. In theory, if we could get a good enough sample of different speakers, we could construct the tabooness ratings for an ideal speaker of American English. Students aimed to get a wide cross-section of American English speakers, but, as you can imagine, Utahans are disproportionately represented in the sample. The survey should be seen as a work-in-progress, but I will present some of the preliminary results in this chapter and in subsequent chapters (especially Chapter 13). I will subsequently refer to it as the Tabooness Survey.

Other similar studies have been conducted, which I will discuss in more depth in Chapter 13. One massive study was done by the United Kingdom's Advertising Standards Authority (ASA 2000).

1.5   *Taboo Language Beyond Mere Words*

Taboo language is not restricted to words, however. There are not only taboos against which words we can say, but also on which topics we can discuss. For example, even if you avoid taboo words, it's still taboo to discuss your sex life or your bathroom-related problems. As was demonstrated at the University of Utah in 2002, it's taboo for professors or TAs to ask students to identify their religion; a group of students petitioned for the suspension of a political science TA after he asked the LDS students in class to raise their hands (*Daily Utah Chronicle* 2002). There are also language taboos associated with how we address others: in Germany, you must not address strangers, elders, and people with authority over you with *du,* the informal 'you'; in the United States, you must not use a person's first name unless you are on "a first-name basis" with them. When I moved to Hungary to teach English after graduating from college, I learned that Americans have a taboo against discussing money; I learned this because strangers kept asking me how much I made, and I realized how uncomfortable I was with the question.[3]

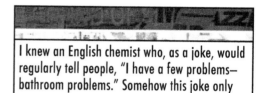

I knew an English chemist who, as a joke, would regularly tell people, "I have a few problems—bathroom problems." Somehow this joke only works with a British accent.

2   CLASSES OF TABOO WORDS

In essence, the words that are taboo in a language refer to behavior or things that have strong emotional resonance for us.[4] That emotional resonance may be awe, disgust, fear, titillation. . . . Although the categories are not mutually exclusive, and although after more investigation we may need to expand the list, classifying taboo

---

[3] After repeatedly being asked this question at a party, I mentioned it to a Hungarian friend. She was surprised that I would take offense and said that it was just a way of breaking the ice, similar to asking a college student "What's your major?"

[4] Though as we observed in Section 1.2, not every word that refers to such behaviors or things is taboo.

words can help us create order and better understand linguistic taboos. In Section 1.1 I presented a taxonomy of taboo words, reproduced here:

- **Taboo Words**
  - **Profanity:** religious words (*God, hell, damn, Jesus*)
  - **Obscenity:** sexual words (*fuck, tits, cock*)
  - **Scatology:** bathroom words (*shit, piss, asshole*)
  - **Slurs:** insulting names (*bastard, kike, nigger, fag, retard*)
  - **Faunality:** animal words (*bitch, pussy, ass, coon*)
  - **Mortology:** death words (*die, cancer*)
  - **Appellity:** proper names (*dick, johnson, fanny*)

In this section, we look at each category in more depth.

2.1 *Profanity*

Profanity is complicated because most of the words in it are not taboo in and of themselves. For example, *Jesus* is not taboo when used in an orthodox way, as in (1), but is when it is used as an exclamation (see Section 4.2.2), as in (2):

1. Jesus is considered a prophet by Muslims.
2. Jesus, you walk fast!⁵

Because most words in this category have non-profane uses, it is challenging to rate them for tabooness. For this reason, when conducting the Tabooness Survey, we did not include profanity in the list of words. Instead, we asked participants to rate sentences that could only be interpreted as orthodox (e.g., (3–6)) or profane (e.g., (7–10)).

3. Hell is where the devil lives.
4. She believes in God.
5. Jesus Christ had disciples.
6. God damned him.
7. What the hell are you doing?
8. I swear to God, I laughed my head off.
9. Jesus Christ that plate is hot!
10. Hot Damn!

Most people gave the orthodox uses of *hell, God,* and *Jesus* (*Christ*) a tabooness rating of 1 (median score).⁶ Interestingly, *damn* is somewhat more taboo when used in its classic sense, as in (6), which received an average score of 3.2 (median score of 3), than when used as an exclamation, as in (10), which received an average score of 2.3 (median score of 2).⁷ Profane uses of *hell* and *God* received weakly taboo ratings of, on average, 2 to 2.5, while (9) received an average rating of 3.8 (median score of 3).

In today's English, thinking of that ideal speaker (see Section 1.4), profanity is only weakly taboo. Of course, there are communities of English speakers where it is more strongly taboo—for example, an outspoken student in my Bad Words and Taboo Terms class, a woman who did not blush when talking about obscenity like *fuck* or *cunt*, explained during class discussion that she could not bring herself to even say or write profane expressions with "the g-word" in them.

---

⁵ I suppose that (2) would not be profanity if it were addressed to Jesus Angel Garcia, the Spanish race-walker.
⁶ The average score is always somewhat above 1. Surprisingly, one person gave (4) a 6, and one person gave (5) a 7, the highest rating. These may have been transcription errors when tabulating the data.
⁷ "Damn it!" received roughly the same ratings as "Hot Damn!".

Historically in English, profanity was a much stronger taboo than it is today. In the Middle ages, profanity was seen as literally re-wounding Christ (Hughes 1991, 60–61). Even just a century ago, profanity would have been considered more taboo than it is today, although by then obscenity was becoming a bigger taboo (see Chapter 7). In the late nineteenth century early twentieth century, *hell* was the word of choice to express strong emotions (kind of like *fuck* is today). Mencken (1962, 661), following Merryweather (1931), lists the following *hell* expressions divided into fourteen classes:

> During a recent production of the play *Sylvia* in Salt Lake City, one of the actors refused to utter lines where the name of her "lord and savior" was used profanely (Brooke Bartlett pers. comm.). The playwright had given explicit instructions about which lines of obscenity could or could not be changed, but it had apparently not occurred to him to give similar instructions about profanity.

- *Hell* as "the equivalent of negative adverbs," or as an intensifier thereof, as in *the hell you say* and *like hell I will.*

- As a super-superlative, as in *colder than hell.*

- As an adverb of all work, as in *run like hell* and *hate like hell.*

- As an intensifier of questions, as in *what the hell?, who the hell?, where in hell?,* etc.

- As an intensifier of asseverations, as in *hell, yes!*

- As an intensifier of qualities, as in *to be hell on,* and *hell of a price.*

- As an indicator of intensified experience, as in *hell of a time, get the hell,* and *to beat hell.*

- In a more or less literal sense, as in *wouldn't it be hell?, go to hell, the hell with, hell on wheels, hell to pay, like a snowball in hell, till hell freezes over,* and *to beat hell.*

- As a synonym for uproar or turmoil, as in *to raise hell, to give him hell,* and *hell is loose.*

- As a verb, as in *to hell around.*

- As an adjective, as in a *hellish hurry* and *hell-bent.*

- In combination with other nouns, as in *hell's bells, hell and red niggers, hell and high-water, hell and Maria, hell-raiser, hell-diver, hell-bender,* and *hell-to-breakfast.*

- In derivatives, as in *hellion, hell-cat,* and *heller.*

- As a simple expletive, as in *Oh, hell.*

Today, many of my students say that profanity barely feels like swearing at all. It can be heard regularly on network television. Indeed, the FCC's definitions of restricted speech center on obscenity and scatology, not on profanity.[8] However, in other languages, profanity still carries with it a strong sense of tabooness (see Chapter 10).

2.2 *Obscenity*

Terms for sex and sex organs make up a large part of our taboo word vocabulary. They are often adapted for new purposes, for example, as slurs (see Sections 2.4 and 4.3) and to express strong emotions (see Section 4.2). Obscene terms also tend to overlap with scatological terms: our sex organs serve a double purpose in that they're also used in evacuating urine; ejaculate is simultaneously obscene because it's part of sex and scatological because it's part of our bodily effluvia; even terms like *asshole,* which is obviously—and primarily—involved in evacuation, can take on obscene meanings in the right context. As I noted before, these classes are not meant to be categorical; terms can comfortably fit in more than one class. In this section, I focus on terms that get their tabooness from their sexual meaning.

As Hughes (1991, 166) puts it, "The mainstream of American swearing is more concerned with obscenity than with profanity." Since at least the end of the eighteenth century, Americans have been squeamish with sex terms. At one point, even *leg* was considered an obscene word in American English (see Chapter 7). *Condom* was taboo until the 1980s AIDS pandemic brought it into advertising (Hughes 1991, 161).

---

[8] I am using these terms according to the definitions given in section 1, not the FCC's definitions; the FCC defines these terms far differently than we do.

Of course, it's not just Americans who use obscenity. Read (1977, 11) quotes from Roth (1897, 184) describing swearing in Mitakoodi, a native language of Australia:

> Foul language is very commonly made use of under circumstances of contempt, derision, or anger: the foulness does not, however, consist so much in the actual thoughts conveyed as in the particular words employed, there being both a decent and indecent vocabulary to describe the particular region, the generative organs, which are then usually drawn attention to. Thus in the Mitakoodi language, *me-ne* is the 'society' term for vulva and nothing is thought of its utterance before a company of people, while *koon-ja*, *puk-kil*, or *yel-ma-rung-o*, all names for the same part, are most blackguardly words to use.

Just as sexual terms are used in Mitakoodi "under circumstances of contempt, derision, or anger," we find the same phenomenon in English. Imagine a person dropping a heavy object on their foot; they're likely to shout, "Fuck!" It is doubtful, however, that the person has sex on their mind at that moment. We discuss this semantic weakening (or "semantic bleaching") in more depth in Chapters 4, 7, and 14. For now, I just want to note that where *hell* was the workhorse of American swearing at the beginning of the twentieth century, *fuck* became the workhorse by the final quarter of the century. Here are just a few examples culled from the Internet:[9]

11. Wake The Fuck Up Coffee, 1 1b.

    [product sold by Hot Sauce World]

    (http://www.hotsauceworld.com/wafuupco1l.html, accessed 8/10/2010)

12. I . . . I . . . I don't fucking know what the fuck this fucking thing the fuck is!

    (http://www.fupenguin.com/2009/08/slow-burn-cuteness-silent-killer.html, accessed 8/10/2010)

13. He's such a fuck up!

    (http://perezhilton.com/2010-07-09-jon-gosselin-misspells-girlfriends-name-on-tattoo, accessed 8/10/10)

14. I think plenty of Americans here would be more than happy to give their opinion on something they know less than fuckall about . . .

    (http://metatalk.metafilter.com/14458/Electionfilter, accessed, 8/10/2010)

15. I found this lesser-known movie on a list of best films in the so-called "mindfuck" genre.

    (http://bokononist87.blogspot.com/, accessed 8/10/2010)

16. Sweet fucking lord! This is great!

    (http://www.dreadcentral.com/news/35246/the-original-a-nightmare-elm-street-coming-blu-ray, accessed 8/10/2010)

17. Jesus H fuck this is not a good day to LoL

    (http://forum.leaguecraft.com/showthread.php?tid=9403, accessed 8/10/2010)

I'll list as many uses of *fuck* as I can, but I'm sure I've missed some:

- *fuck*   intransitive verb meaning 'fornicate': *They fucked.*
- *fuck*   transitive verb meaning 'perform sexual intercourse': *He fucked her.*
- *fuck*   count noun meaning 'sexual intercourse': *How about a fuck?*
- *fuck*   count noun meaning 'sexual partner': *She's a lousy fuck.*
- *fuck*   count noun meaning 'obnoxious person': *He's such a fuck.*
- *fuck*   count noun used with *not give* to mean 'not care': *She doesn't give a fuck about her job.*
- *fuck*   exclamation of strong emotion: *Fuck!*
- *fuck*   emphatic used in comparatives: *It's tougher than fuck to find parking here.*

---

[9] By the way, I don't recommend doing a Google search on *fuck*. I had to weed through some website descriptions that even without pictures were damaging to my retinas.

- *fuck*   quasi-imperative used to disparage someone or something (see Chapter 9): *Fuck you and the horse you rode in on.*
- *fuck*   emphatic used with *yes* or *no: Fuck yes!*
- *as fuck*   emphatic used with predicate adjectives: *This class is cool as fuck.*
- *fuck off*   intransitive verb meaning 'go away': *I wish she'd just fuck off.*
- *fuck up*   transitive verb meaning 'break': *He fucked up my car.*
- *fuck up*   transitive verb meaning 'make drunk': *Gin can really fuck you up.*
- *fuck up*   count noun meaning 'incompetent person': *She's a fuck up.*
- *fuck with*   transitive verb meaning 'meddle with': *Don't fuck with my stereo.*
- *fuck around*   intransitive verb meaning 'do nothing': *Some kids were just fucking around.*
- *fuck over*   transitive verb meaning 'wrong': *His company fucked him over.*
- *the fuck*   emphatic used with *wh*-questions: *Who the fuck let the dog in?*
- *the fuck*   emphatic used in some imperatives: *Hurry the fuck up!*
- *the fuck*   used at the beginning of a sentence to express incredulity at what somebody else has just said: *The fuck you did.*
- *a fuck of a*   emphatic mostly used with lot: *He's a fuck of a lot smarter than he looks.*

Of course, this list doesn't include derived forms (e.g., *fucking, fucker, fucked up*) nor compound forms (e.g., *mindfuck, fuckall, clusterfuck*) nor the infix-*fucking*- (e.g., *unbefuckinglievable*, see Chapter 8).

Fuck isn't unique. The meanings of sexual terms often shift and change over time. Hughes (1991, 254) gives many examples of how unstable they can be. *Bugger*, from the French word for 'Bulgarian,' meant 'heretic' in the fourteenth century and subsequently meant 'sodomite' or 'practicer of bestiality' (sixteenth century) and 'fellow' (eighteenth century).[10] *Fanny* means 'vagina' in the UK and 'butt' in the U.S. *Frig* originally meant 'masturbate' (sixteenth century) but came to mean 'copulate' by the eighteenth century. *Prat* was a word for 'butt' originally (sixteenth century), then 'vagina' (nineteenth century), and by the 1960s 'idiot'. During the fourteenth century, *tail* could mean either 'butt', 'vagina', or 'penis'. *Punk* originally meant 'whore' (sixteenth century), but in the early twentieth century it meant 'young man or boy who is the partner of an older man' and then 'worthless fellow'. We can add onto Hughes' observations about *punk*, noting that in mainstream society it retains its meaning of 'worthless fellow' or 'hoodlum' (with perhaps some connotations to punk music), and it's common for friends to refer to each other as "punk"; however, in a class discussion, a student observed that when she jokingly said to her brother, who had just been released from prison, "Hey, punk," he grew angry and told her *punk* was a very bad word in prison, where it still retains its homosexual meaning.

Terms for sex organs are common today and seem to have lost some of their tabooness. For example, most people see *dick* as only moderately taboo—interestingly, on the Tabooness Survey *dick* and *penis* had the same median rating of 3, though the average ratings were 3.5 and 2.7, respectively. Of course, because body part terms are also used as slurs, it can be difficult to get an accurate rating without a context, which is why we included sentences in addition to words. Consider the sentences in Table 1.1 and their tabooness ratings from the Tabooness Survey on page 10.

All of the terms for male genitalia got an average rating of between 3.0 and 3.5. Similarly, the term for female secondary sex organs, *tits,* got a rating of 3.3. Terms for female genitalia are more taboo than male; here, *pussy* was rated 3.8 and *cunt* 5.3. In isolation, *pussy* and *cunt* were each rated slightly higher, 3.9 and 5.7 respectively, but this was a general trend for all words (for some reason participants tended to rate words in isolation higher than sentences containing the same words). In contrast, the clinical term *vagina* was rated 2.6 (about the same as *penis*). Interestingly, participants viewed the clinical term *clitoris* as more taboo, rating it 3.2. I find this interesting especially because there is no commonly used taboo word for 'clitoris'—*clit* may be the closest we've got.

---

[10] In England today, *bugger* is used as a verb for 'sodomize' as well as a noun and is found in many expressions: "You bugger!", "The bugger!", "Bugger off!", "Bugger you!", "Bugger!", "Bugger it!", "to bugger about" (cf. Hughes 1991, 31).

Table 1.1		
Tabooness Ratings for Body Part Terms		
Sentence	*Mean Tabooness*	*Median Tabooness*
He's a man, so he has a prick.	3.0	3
He's a man, so he has a dick.	3.1	3
He's a man, so he has a cock.	3.5	3
She's a woman, so she has tits.	3.3	3
She's a woman, so she has a pussy.	3.8	4
She's a woman, so she has a cunt.	5.3	6

Back to *fuck.* To satisfy your curiosity, the tabooness rating was 5.4 (median of 6). We discuss *fuck* in context in Section 4.

2.3 Scatology

Terms for nearly anything that we excrete from our bodies are candidates for taboo words in some language or another: feces, urine, ejaculate, vomit, saliva, perspiration, blood, menses. The one exception may be tears, for which no language is known to have a term that is taboo (Lyle Campbell pers. comm.). It's not surprising that bodily effluvia should lead to taboos—they're gross. We like to keep our distance from them and try not to be contaminated by them. Indeed, the more gross the more taboo the taboo words are likely to be. We can do a simple test along these lines: list all the bodily effluvia you can think of and rank them according to which ones you would least like to come into accidental contact with. Allan and Burridge did a study where they asked students and staff at several Australian universities to rank how revolting the different body byproducts were; based on their study here are the effluvia in order from most revolting to least (Allan and Burridge 1991, 163):

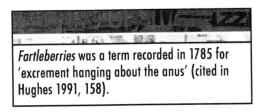

Fartleberries was a term recorded in 1785 for 'excrement hanging about the anus' (cited in Hughes 1991, 158).

- feces, vomit
- urine, semen
- menstrual blood[11]
- fart, snot
- pus
- spit
- belched breath
- skin parings
- sweat
- nail parings
- breath
- blood from a wound
- hair clippings
- breast milk
- tears

For most people, feces is grosser than urine. And *shit* is more taboo than *piss;* on the Tabooness Survey *shit* had an average rating of 3.0, while *piss* had an average rating of 2.4. Moreover, four subjects (out of 87) ranked *shit*

---

[11] Not surprisingly, men found menses more revolting than women. See Chapter 10 for more on language taboos associated with menstruation.

a 6 or a 7, while no subjects (out of 89) ranked *piss* above 5. For many people, ejaculate is even grosser than feces, and unsurprisingly, *cum* ranked higher than *shit*: 3.9, with 18 subjects (out of 87) ranking it above 5.

Scatology may be the earliest swearing that children acquire; according to Jay (1992, 73), children, beginning at the end of their second year, use terms associated with toilet training to express anger: *pee pee, poop head, ka ka, wiener, bum bum, tinkler.* However, Allan and Burridge (2006, 173) point out that infants and animals are not repulsed by feces and other effluvia; children learn to be disgusted by their by-products through toilet training.

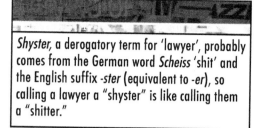

Shyster, a derogatory term for 'lawyer', probably comes from the German word *Scheiss* 'shit' and the English suffix *-ster* (equivalent to *-er*), so calling a lawyer a "shyster" is like calling them a "shitter."

As we grow into adults we acquire a robust disgust for things that come out of our bodies, especially feces. Pinker (2007) notes that it is not coincidental that the substance that carries the most disease is also the one that is most disgusting to us. Just as feces can infect us, we think the word *shit* can contaminate us. But this is a strange leap, isn't it? How do we go from the substance being disgusting to the word for the substance being taboo? As Allan and Burridge (2006, 40) put it, "There are no rational grounds to accept that a 'dirty word' like *shit* should be treated in the same way as we treat faecal matter. But we can admit that the connotations of taboo terms are contaminated by the taboo topics which they denote." Similarly, Jay (2000, 200) writes, "Feces represents the universal disgust item, and any substance or thought associated with feces, or other disgusting body products (e.g., snot, pus, scabs), becomes contaminated too."

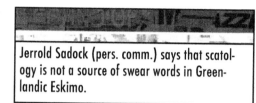

Jerrold Sadock (pers. comm.) says that scatology is not a source of swear words in Greenlandic Eskimo.

The referent of the word contaminates the word, but why do the words hold such power for us? Some scholars describe this as a type of "word magic" (see Section 4.1.2 and Chapter 10 for more on word magic), a superstitious belief in the magical power of words: the word becomes "dirty" by its association with the substance and then "soils" our minds when we hear it. While superstition may be part of it, I think there's a more rational process as well. Pinker (2007, 345–346) sheds some light on this: "The strongest component of the disgust reaction is a desire not to eat or touch the offending substance. But it's also disgusting to *think* about effluvia, together with the body parts and activities that excrete them, and because of the involuntariness of speech perception, it's unpleasant to hear the words for them." In other words, the way we're wired, when we hear or read the word *shit* we can't help but think of the substance (see Chapter 12), and the substance makes us disgusted.

Like *fuck*, *shit* is a workhorse in modern American swearing.[12] As I did for *fuck*, I culled the internet for uses:

18. He [Tsinghua University principal Mr. Gu Binglin] indicated straightforwardly that the university education system is in effect "pouring shit into the students minds."

    (http://www.chinasmack.com/2008/stories/china-universities-pouring-shit-into-students-minds.html, accessed 8/11/2010)

19. Congratulations girl, you just made my shit list.

    (http://amatorian.livejournal.com/, accessed 8/11/2010)

20. Come to think of it alot of my stupid worries come from procrastinating on things so I should just get my shit together.

    (http://www.takeshimiyazawa.com/archives/2006_06_01_archive.html, accessed 8/11/2010)

21. I wouldn't tell the family what to do and yes, children do speak @ funerals and shit but damn, she on live television, the web, and some other shit.

    (http://nahright.com/news/2009/07/07/video-chali-2na-ft-talib-kweli-lock-shit-down/, accessed 8/11/2010)

---

[12] The original working title for my Bad Words and Taboo Terms class was Fuck and Shit Class because somehow every conversation about taboo language eventually turns to these two words. We opted for the more sober title, however, because we didn't want to contaminate unsuspecting students' minds as they read the class schedule.

22. Typical Chicago chick, obnoxious and fug but still thinks she's the shit.

(http://www.dlisted.com/node/38300, accessed 8/11/2010)

Several websites give "shitlists" meant to explain various philosophical and religious -isms using the word *shit*. The following examples come from the Sceptic Files (http://www.skepticfiles.org/atheist/shitlist.htm, accessed 8/11/2010):

- Agnosticism: What is this shit?
- Atheism: I don't believe this shit.
- Baptist Fundamentalism: Shit happens because the Bible says so.
- Buddhism: Shit happens.
- Catholicism: If shit happens, you deserved it.
- Descartes: I shit therefore I am.
- Empiricism: Shit only happens if I see it happen.
- Hinduism: This shit happened before.
- Islam: If shit happens, it is the will of Allah.
- Judaism: Why does shit always happen to us?
- Nihilism: Everything is shit.
- Protestantism: Let shit happen to someone else.
- Secular Humanism: Shit happens, but there's a rational explanation.
- Unitarianism: There's only one shit, but you can have it happen any way you want.
- Utilitarianism: Do that which generates the greatest shit for the greatest number.

I'll list as many uses of *shit* as I can. I'm sure you can think of some I've missed, and, like with *fuck*, I have left off derived forms (e.g., *shitty, shitter, shitless*) and compound forms (e.g., *bullshit, shithead, shit-for-brains*):

•	*shit*	verb meaning 'defecate': *Don't shit so close to the campsite.*
•	*shit*	transitive verb meaning 'deceive': *Are you shitting me?*
•	*shit*	reflexive verb meaning 'be surprised': *When he finds out, he'll shit himself.*
•	*shit*	non-count noun meaning 'feces': *There's shit all over the dog park.*
•	*shit*	count noun meaning 'feces': *She has to take a shit.*
•	*shit*	non-count noun meaning 'drugs': *He always has good shit to smoke.*
•	*shit*	generic non-count noun substituting for almost anything: *Let me just put this shit in my locker.*
•	*shit*	count noun meaning 'obnoxious person': *He's such a shit.*
•	*shit*	exclamation of strong emotion: *Shit!*
•	*shit*	emphatic used with *yes*: *Shit yes.*
•	*the shit*	something or somebody who is very good: *This book is the shit.*
•	*the shit hit the fan*	idiom meaning 'the situation turned bad': *When she saw my tattoo, the shit hit the fan.*
•	*up shit creek*	idiom meaning 'to be in a bad situation': *If I don't pass this class I'm up shit creek.*
•	*shit on a shingle*	non-count noun meaning 'chipped beef on toast with gravy': *At summer camp we ate shit on a shingle every other day.*
•	*shoot the shit*	idiom meaning 'chat': *When we get together, we just shoot the shit.*

- *talk shit*   idiom meaning 'say something uncalled for': *If you talk shit, you've got to expect people will get pissed.*

- *shit fire*   exclamation of strong emotion: *Shit fire!*[13]

- *one's shit together*   used with *get/have*, meaning 'put/have one's life in order': *He can take care of himself—he's got his shit together.*

- *shit bricks*   idiom meaning 'be angry': *When she sees my grades, she'll shit bricks.*

- *tough shit*   idiom meaning roughly 'who cares?': *So you need to get glasses, tough shit.*

- *shit happens*   idiom meaning 'that's life': *You totaled my car? Oh well, shit happens.*

- *eat shit*   general expression of disparagement often used with *and die: Eat shit!*

- *no shit?*   expression of surprise: *You're getting married? No shit?*

Jay (1992, 165) suggests that scatological terms are rarely used positively, and he takes this as an indication of how offensive we find the associated body parts and processes. However, there are at least three prominent uses of *shit* in the list provided that are clearly positive: to say that something or somebody is "the shit" is a high compliment, as is to say that something (particularly marijuana) is "good shit," and, as an emphatic, *shit* seems more common with an affirmative than a negative, *shit yes* vs. *shit no* (compare to *fuck* and *hell*, which are equally comfortable with *yes* and *no*). There are also several neutral uses of *shit*, such as *shooting the shit, get one's shit together,* and the generic *shit* that substitutes for almost any noun.

As with obscenity, scatological terms often are adapted for use as slurs. They also frequently have their core meaning change, as we saw with *shit* and has happened with *piss. Piss off* has two meanings: in American English, it is a verb meaning 'anger', and in British English, it is used as a weaker equivalent to *fuck off. Pissed,* as well, has two meanings: in American English, it is an adjective meaning 'angry', and in British English, it is an adjective meaning 'drunk'.[14]

2.4   Slurs

Slurs are often drawn from other classes of taboo words: profanity (e.g., *devil*), obscenity (e.g., *motherfucker, dick, cunt, cocksucker*), scatology (e.g., *shithead, asshole*), faunality (e.g., *bitch, ass*). In Chapter 13 we look at slurs for men and women in some depth. In this section, however, we focus on racial and ethnic slurs, in particular, *nigger.*

Slurs have been with us a long time. As Hughes (1991, 50) observes: "Hatred of strangers appears to be an ingrained feeling which has been verbally impacted for centuries." Hughes lists some common slurs for "others," distinguishing between general terms that can be used for any group of foreigners and specific terms that refer to a particular group (see Table 1.2 on page 14).

Sometimes, given the right context, even standard terms can be used and perceived as slurs. Hughes (1991, 126) quotes a defendant in a 1915 Middlesex Police Court as saying "He called me a German and other filthy names." We discuss the tendency to derogate terms for others more in Chapter 7.

In today's English, slurs are probably the most taboo category of all. In the Tabooness Survey, *nigger* and *cunt* had the highest average tabooness ratings: 5.6 and 5.7, respectively (median scores of 6).[15] Now you might be quick to point out that *cunt* also belongs to obscenity. True. However, when we look beyond the words to how the words are used, the Tabooness Survey shows us that when it's used as an obscenity as in (23), *cunt* has an average rating of 5.3, but when it's used as a slur as in (24), it has an average rating of 5.8 (both had a median score of 6).[16]

23. She's a woman, so she has a cunt.

24. She's a cunt.

---

[13] My friend's mother used to say, "Shit fire and save matches," which I guess makes it an imperative of sorts.

[14] An English guy I met while I was studying abroad in Vienna informed me that he was going to go out to some bars that night and "get pissed." Initially, I thought this must be a British custom: go to bars and pick fights—after all, I'd heard about so-called "football hooligans."

[15] The next highest was *fuck*, with 5.4. No other words had an average rating above 5.

[16] No other sentences ranked above a 5 average on the survey, though no sentence included the word *nigger*.

	General Terms	*Specific Terms*
TABLE 1.2		
The Semantic Field of Xenophobia (Hughes 1991, 27)		
Anglo-Saxon	Heathen	
1500	Infidel, Paynim	
1550		Bugger, Turk, Greek, Coolie
1600	Savage, Alien, Intruder, Interloper, Barbarian, Foreigner	Blackamoor, Ethiop, Jew, Tartar
1650		Bogtrotter
1700		Vandal, Goth, Macaroni, Dago
1750		Hottentot, Yankee, Cracker, Frog
1800	Native	Kaffir, Nigger, Coon, Frenchy, Wi-wi, Sheeny
1850		Greaser, Gringo, Canuck, Sambo, Jap, Yid, Mick, Limey
1900		Kike, Hun, Chink, Wop, Boche, Fritz, Jerry, Kraut, Pom, Wog, Spic, Eyetie, Ofay, Spaghetti, Wetback, Nip, Gook, Anglo
1950		Slant, Slope, Munt, Honkie, Paki

It may be relatively recent that these words have become the most taboo in our society (see Chapters 7 and 15). In a 1972 study, *tits* had a higher mean tabooness rating than *nigger*, and *fuck* had a higher one than *cunt*; in a 1978 study, *douche-bag* had a higher rating than *nigger*, and *motherfucker*, the highest-rated word, had a higher one than *cunt*, the second highest-rated word (Jay 1992).

Today it is unacceptable for people to say racist things, even if they have racist thoughts. "Heightened awareness and increased unpopularity of racism have, furthermore, had the effect of self-censorship, driving the more emotive or critical words underground or out of use" (Hughes 1991, 128). For example, in Cockney rhyming slang, where a rhymed word or phrase stands in for another (usually taboo) term (see Chapter 6 for more), there are a lot of coded ways of referencing slurs. These are demonstrated in Table 1.3 on page 15.

In the rest of this section we discuss one of the most hot-button terms in the English language: *nigger*. Following, is an example of how the term can be used to abuse another person taken from a description of an event in Ruleville, Mississippi reported in *Encounter*, November 1965 (p. 95; quoted in Hughes 1991, 246):

> [The two highway patrolmen] stood me against the wall. "You a nigger or a nigra?" one asked. "A Negro," I said. The other hit me across the mouth. Then he asked, "You a nigger or a nigra?" "A Negro," I said again. The first punched me hard on the ear, and I fell down. They took me by the shirt and arm, and they pulled me up. I could feel two teeth were loose. The first patrolman asked me again, "You a nigger or a nigra?" I looked at their faces, and I knew what they wanted me to do.
>
> "A nigger," I said. Then they smiled, because it was what they wanted to hear.

Hughes (1991) traces *nigger* back to 1800 (p. 127) and suggests it was originally just a term for color (pp. 239–240). However, Asim (2007, 10–11) traces it back further, suggesting it derived from *Niger* and may have been first used as a slur as far back as the late sixteenth century. He notes further that the neutral word *Negro* dates back as far as 1555, so other forms (*nigger, niger, negur, negar*) are reasonably assumed to be derogatory. Asim quotes Ignatius Sancho, an Afro-British writer, writing in 1766: "I am one of those whom the vulgar and illiberal call 'Negurs'" (11).

TABLE 1.3		
Codes for Foreigners and Aliens in Rhyming Slang (Hughes 1991, 136)		
Long Version	*Short Version*	*Disguised Term*
Army tanks		Yanks
Bubble and squeak	Bubble	Greek
Egg and spoon		Coon
Five to two	Five	Jew
Flour mixer		Shikse
Four by two		Jew
Front wheel skid		Yid
Ham shank		Yank
Harvest moon		Coon
Kangaroo		Jew
Lucozade		Spade
Razor blade		Spade
Sausage roll		Pole
Septic tank	Septic	Yank
Silvery spoon		Coon
Tea pot/Saucepan lid		Yid
Tiddly-wink		Chink

Today, most Americans agree that *nigger* is highly offensive and highly taboo. There is, however, a controversy about a related word, *nigga*. In an art-poster, Carl Pope wrote the following message:

African-Americans, Negroes, Blacks

And Post-Blacks All Agree:

THE USE OF THE

"A"

INSTEAD OF THE

"ER"

CHANGES

EVERYTHING!

Pope's poster is part of a series meant to be provocative. The statement, itself, is not accurate insofar as there is a lot of debate within the African American community as to whether *nigga* should be any less taboo than *nigger* (see Asim 2007 for an extensive discussion). Asim points out that "racist whites have used 'nigga' nearly as often as they've used 'nigger'" (224). During an April 2008 lecture in Salt Lake City, Utah, Asim explained one reason he does not use either word: while being interviewed on a talk radio show, Asim took a call from a man who said some of his friends had been lynched and he didn't want the last word his friends heard to ever leave his own lips.

Nevertheless, many African Americans consider *nigga* (not *nigger*) acceptable when used by African Americans (see Chapter 14 for more on non-negative uses of slurs) but not when used by whites. *Nigga* is used extensively by black rap artists and black comics, but it is frowned upon when used by white rappers and comics. Chris Rock has a seven-minute-long comedy routine about the question "Can white people say 'nigga'?", to which "the correct answer is 'not really.'"[17] We discuss issues of who can and cannot say certain words in more depth in Chapter 15.

---

[17] Much of the routine is spent explaining an absurd and highly entertaining exception.

Much of the issue surrounding *nigger* stems from the history of Blacks in America, in particular—but not restricted to—the history of slavery (again, see Asim 2007 for discussion). We should note that slurs for whites are not nearly as taboo or offensive as slurs for African Americans. Asim (2007, 206) quotes from a 1975 *Saturday Night Live* skit in which Chevy Chase and Richard Pryor exchange escalating slurs:

CHASE: "Jungle Bunny!"

PRYOR: "Honky."

CHASE: "Spade!"

PRYOR: "Honky-honky!"

CHASE: "Nigger!"

PRYOR: "Deeead Honky."

Part of the point here is there is no slur for whites equivalent to *nigger*. Several white comedians, most notably Mike Birbiglia, have done routines where they imagine *cracker* (or *cracka*) being used among whites like *nigga* is among African Americans:

Because a lot of Black comics use the N-word, I like to use the C-word, like "Me and my cracker friends were driving down the street in my Volvo station wagon when I say, 'Hey cracker, have some Sun Chips,' and he says, 'Not till we get to the picnic, cracker,' and I say, 'Cracker, please!' and he says, 'Cracker, what?'"

Then I said that at a show and this Black guy comes up to me after the show and he's like, "Great show, cracker." And I was like "Actually, you can't call me a cracker, only we can call each other cracker." (Mike Birbiglia, "Crackers")

Part of the reason that *nigger* is so much stronger than *honky* or *cracker* has to do with who holds power in society. Slurs for discriminated people tend to be more taboo and more offensive than slurs for privileged people (compare *retard* to *egghead* or *nerd*). We discuss a similar phenomenon in Chapter 13 when we compare slurs for males to slurs for females (you can guess which tend to be more offensive).

2.5   Faunality

I don't have a lot to say about this category in this chapter (see Chapter 10 for more). Contemporary English does not use animal terms to a great degree, though some of our terms are derived from animal terms: *cock, ass, pussy, bitch, coon.* In today's society, I expect many people no longer associate these terms with the animals they originally referred to. That is to say, today they derive their tabooness from their associations to obscenity or slurs, not from animals. Those terms that still derive their power from their reference to animals (e.g., *pig, dog, monkey, cow*) are only slightly taboo. In some contemporary languages, animal terms are used frequently and productively as terms of abuse. For example, in French to call somebody "une vache Espagnol" ('a Spanish cow') is a fairly strong insult (meaning that the person speaks French with a bad accent).

In some languages, there is a taboo against saying the names of certain (typically dangerous) animals (see Chapter 10). In fact, our word *bear* originally (thousands of years ago) came from a word meaning 'brown'; because people weren't supposed to say the actual name for 'bear' they would refer to "the brown one." In Slavic languages, the word for 'bear' comes from 'honey eater'.

2.6   Mortology

Death and dying are uncomfortable topics. People don't like to just come out and say them, so you hear people saying things like, "Fluffy went to a better place" or "Fluffy's in heaven" or "Fluffy passed away." Even our words *die* and *death* originated as euphemisms:

"One can often observe people avoiding unpleasant words, such as *die, death*—these words in pre-Germanic replaced the Primitive Indo-European term represented by Latin *morī* 'to die'. . ." (Bloomfield 1933, 401). Montagu (1967, 16) describes how some Australian Aborigines are known to call out the name of a deceased relative when in pain—this is based on a taboo against saying the name of a deceased person for a long period following their death.

Our language is chock full of ways of talking about death and dying without using the words. Mencken (1962) collected expressions for 'to die', 'death', 'dead', 'to kill', and 'to be executed'; most of them were somewhat humorous—we often make light of those things that trouble us the most. In Table 1.4, we have Mencken's facetious substitutes, and in Table 1.5 (on page 18) we have the more serious euphemistic substitutes.

TABLE 1.4			
Facetious Substitutes for Death and Dying (Mencken 1962)			
'To Die'	*'Death' and 'Dead'*	*'To Kill'*	*'To Be Executed'*
to croak	the blow off	to take for a ride	to fry
to kick the bucket	the one-way ticket	to put on the spot	to take a hot squat
to peg out	the wind-up	to put the finger on	to walk the last mile
to pass in one's checks	the fade-out	to bump off	to be topped
to go under	the finish	to wipe out	to be gassed
to kick	the last call	to rub out	
to go West	the pay-off		
to blow off	checked out		
to fade out	done for		
to kick off	finished		
to bite the dust	gone under		
to fan out	down and out		
to flunk out	washed up		
to fold			
to get the ax			
to hop off			
to go off the deep end			
to lose the decision			
to pass out			
to pass out of the picture			
to poop out			
to pop off			
to shove off			
to shuffle off			
to shoot the works			
to slough off			

TABLE 1.5			
Euphemistic Substitutes for Death and Dying (Mencken 1962)			
'Dead'	'Buried'	'Death'	'Grave'
breathed his last	laid to rest	the Grim Reaper	narrow home
gathered to his fathers	consigned to the earth	the Destroying Angel	long home
laid down his burdens	gone to join his fathers	the Pale Horseman	
gone to rest	resting in peace		
called home			
sleeping the long sleep			
passed to his reward			
gone ahead			
gone to his reward			

If you look through obituaries, you're likely to find plenty of other euphemisms. In war-time, we prefer terms like *casualties* and *collateral damage* to *deaths*. We tend to avoid terms for fatal diseases. For example, *AIDS* is a word often avoided (see Allan and Burridge 2006), and people really don't like to talk about cancer. Pinker (2007, 343) notes that *a long illness* in obituaries is usually a euphemism for *cancer*. Burridge and Allan (2006, 64–65) quote the following passage from Cassileth and Hamilton (1979, 242):

> Family members look intently at the physician as he speaks. "scan . . . cytology . . . report . . . primary site . . . malignant tumor . . . adenocarcinoma . . . metastasis . . ." Brows furrow as the family continues to hear: "excision . . . chemotherapy . . . contraindicated . . . radiotherapy . . . palliative . . . any questions?" "Yes" responds the family member, "Can you tell yet whether he has cancer and will he get well?"

Jeff Metcalf has written an outrageously funny play called *A Slight Discomfort* about his experiences with prostate cancer (see www.aslightdiscomfort.com). Originally, Metcalf wrote the play for National Public Radio, but he soon learned his text would not be allowed on the air due to concerns about FCC fines (Metcalf pers. comm.). But from Metcalf's point of view, you can't talk about prostate cancer without violating taboos (e.g., how do you talk about prostates without mentioning penises?).[18] The biggest taboo Metcalf violates, I believe, is talking about cancer at all—especially, with a sense of humor. On the other hand, as we saw with the facetious terms for 'death' and 'dying', humor is often a way to deal with taboo topics, and in the end the play works mostly because it is humorous.

2.7 Appellity

Like faunality, this is not a very productive category in modern English. We have a few taboo words derived from names (e.g., *fanny, dick*), but this is not a productive process in English. These probably begin as euphemisms and become taboo over time (see Chapter 7 on the euphemism treadmill). There are taboos of usage in our society; for example, we should not call certain people (our parents, teachers, professors, etc.) by their first names. However, such restrictions on usage don't lead to the names themselves being taboo (just because your professor's first name is Susan doesn't mean you can't refer to your friend, Susan, by her name).

In some languages, however, names do become taboo. We discussed this briefly in Section 2.8, where in some Australian languages there is a taboo on uttering the name of a deceased person (see Allan and Burridge 2006 for discussion). Such taboos are transferred to all people with this name—they have to find a new name.

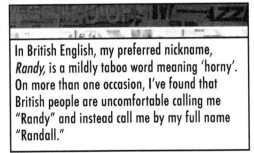

In British English, my preferred nickname, *Randy*, is a mildly taboo word meaning 'horny'. On more than one occasion, I've found that British people are uncomfortable calling me "Randy" and instead call me by my full name "Randall."

---

[18] The play was eventually picked up by the Salt Lake Acting Company and has been shown across the country as well as abroad.

It gets even more complicated because the names of people often come from common nouns, so speakers have to invent new words too; this would be like if somebody named Grant died, we would have to find a word to replace *grant*. In Chapter 10, we discuss naming taboos in Ancient Chinese.

3   SWEARING

Some scholars distinguish between the following verbs: **swear, curse, cuss.** Traditionally, swearing was a religious oath, but it came to also mean taking such an oath without the necessary religious conviction. Cursing was also associated with religion, an invocation for a higher power to cause harm to somebody. *Cussing* was simply an alternative (vulgar) pronunciation of *cursing*. In this book, I use the verbs *swear* and *cuss* interchangeably, and I don't restrict their usage to religious taboos. I also use the noun forms (**swearing** and **cussing**) interchangeably to describe the usage of taboo words in general. *Curse* and *cursing* I generally reserve for a type of swearing, that of wishing harm on somebody.

Just as we classified taboo words into a taxonomy, we can also classify types of swearing. First, we'll make a three-way distinction between **propositional, emotive,** and **invective** swearing. **Propositional swearing** is when taboo terms are used with their original force and meaning. **Emotive swearing** is when taboo terms are used purely for their emotional power, without any propositional meaning. And **invective swearing** is when taboo terms are used to malign or insult others (or oneself).

Within propositional swearing we have **oath-making, cursing,** and **denotative** swearing. People swear, often invoking deities, to guarantee their word, as in (25).

25. I swear to tell the truth, the whole truth, and nothing but the truth, so help me God.

This, itself, is not taboo, but when folks make oaths "loosely," without the proper conviction, as in (26), it weakens the power of oaths for others, so that is considered taboo, especially in earlier times when oaths were taken very seriously (Hughes 1991).

26. I swear to God I nearly laughed myself to death.

Cursing is when we call for harm to happen to another. Sometimes a higher power is called upon:

27. May God damn you to Hell!

Sometimes not:

28. A plague upon your house!

And sometimes it can be in the form of a command:

29. Eat shit and die!

Denotative swearing covers all the other areas of propositional swearing—that is, when we use taboo words in a sentence with the literal meaning intact, as in (30–31).

30. The toilet backed up and now the bathroom floor is all shitty.
31. I can't go into my dorm room because my roommate is fucking her boyfriend again.

Under emotive swearing, we have **emphatic** and **exclamatory** swearing. Emphatic swearing is when a taboo word loses its original meaning and is used only to add emotion to a statement, as in (32–33).

32. I wish my landlord would replace the shitty floors in my apartment.
33. My roommate's with her fucking boyfriend again.
34. What the hell are you talking about?

Exclamatory swearing is when we use a taboo word to emotionally respond to some event, thought, or thing, as in (35–37).

35. Oh my God!
36. Fuckin' A!
37. Shit!

Invectives demean or insult, so it's natural that slurs are a major part of this type of swearing, especially in **name-calling:**

38. You bastard/bitch/shit-for-brains!

39. Cracker motherfucker!

Slurs can also be used as **pejoratives.** While name-calling is insulting somebody to their face, pejoratives refer to people in the third-person, as in (40–41).

40. Fags, kikes, spics, and niggers are ruining this country.

41. Look at that piece of ass.

Virtually all slurs used in name-calling can also be used pejoratively, but not all pejoratives work in name-calling. For example, *piece of ass* in (41) is pejorative, but it would seem odd to call somebody a "piece of ass" to their face. Also within invectives are **maledictives,** sort of a catchall for other forms of verbal abuse:

One difficulty with pejoratives is that people don't always agree on whether something is insulting or not. In class discussions for my Bad Words and Taboo Terms class, *milf* ('mother I'd like to fuck') has come up; most males say it's meant as a compliment, while many females say it's offensive.

42. Piss off!

43. Fuck that shit!

44. The hell with your rules!

These subdivisions give us the following taxonomy:

- Swearing
  - Propositional
    - Oath-making
    - Cursing
    - Denotative
  - Emotive
    - Emphatic
    - Exclamatory
  - Invective
    - Name-calling
    - Pejorative
    - Maledictive

We investigate each of these types in more depth in Section 4.

4. CLASSES OF SWEARING

Just as we discussed the different categories of taboo words in Section 2, we now discuss the different categories of taboo word usage.

4.1 Propositional

In Chapter 4, we discuss the three aspects of a word's meaning, one of which is the propositional (informative) meaning (along with the emotional and social aspects). We've already seen that the meaning of a taboo word can shift and change, and, moreover, its use can be extended to a staggering variety of new purposes, from a generic stand-in, to an emphatic, to an insult, etc. We saw this, especially, with the long lists of uses for *fuck* and *shit.* By propositional swearing, we mean using a swear word in a sentence so that it affects the overall propositional meaning; from a logician's point of view, this means that the taboo word contributes to the truth value of the sentence (i.e., the word is essential for determining whether the entire statement is true or false). This often means using the words with their literal meaning, for example, *fuck* to mean 'fornicate', *shit* to mean 'defecate' or 'feces', *cock* to mean 'penis', and *bitch* to mean 'unpleasant woman'. (Note that we don't mean using the words with their "original" meaning; using *cock* to mean 'rooster' or *bitch* to mean 'female dog' is not swearing.[19]) In addition, we consider figurative and idiomatic uses of swear words to be propositional; for example, (45–47) can be "translated" into non-taboo sentences:

45. He's fucked up.

    'he's drunk'

46. She's full of shit.

    'she's telling lies'

47. I'm so pissed off.

    'I'm so angry'

Within the class of propositional swearing, we have oath-making, cursing, and denotative swearing.

4.1.1 Oath-Making

Oath-making is the oldest form of swearing in English (see Chapter 7). As we discussed in Section 3, if you sincerely make an oath, this is not generally considered swearing (in the taboo sense of the word). In the Ten Commandments, God exhorts his followers: "Do not misuse my name. I am the Lord your God, and I will punish anyone who misuses my name" (Exodus 20:7). However, some Christians view any form of oath-making taboo because Jesus is reported saying:

> You know that our ancestors were told, "Don't use the Lord's name to make a promise unless you are going to keep it." But I tell you not to swear by anything when you make a promise! Heaven is God's throne, so don't swear by heaven. The earth is God's footstool, so don't swear by the earth. Jerusalem is the city of the great king, so don't swear by it. Don't swear by your own head. You cannot make one hair white or black. When you make a promise, say only "Yes" or "No." Anything else comes from the devil.
>
> (Matthew 5:33–37)

Pinker (2007) describes why oaths had the power they did and why there were prohibitions against using religion to seal them. Imagine you lived some thousand years ago and you make a promise—say, to return money you've borrowed, to supply goods in the future in exchange for immediate compensation, or to be faithful to a leader—why should anybody believe you? Today, we'd sign a contract that has legal consequences if broken, but in the olden days all we had was a person's word. So people sealed their words by calling on a higher power: *As God is my witness, May God strike me dead if I'm lying, God blind me.*

> Such oaths, of course, would have been more credible in an era in which people thought that God listened to their entreaties and had the power to carry them out. At the same time, every time someone reneges on an oath and is not punished by the big guy upstairs, it casts doubt on his existence, his potency, or at the very least how carefully he's paying attention. The earthly representatives of God would just as soon preserve the belief that he does listen and act in matters of importance, and so are unhappy about people diluting the brand by invoking God as the muscle behind their small-time deals. Hence the proscriptions against taking the name of the Lord in vain. (Pinker 2007, 341)

All that said, early oaths in English did not resort to higher powers so much as a person's honor (Hughes 1991). For example, in early epic poetry, such as *Beowulf,* a man's oath is taken very seriously. During the eighth century, the laws of Ine said, "He who kills a thief may declare with an oath that he slew him as a guilty man . . ." (quoted in Hughes 1991, 44). In a society like this, where honor is so important, we can see why making an empty oath would be extremely taboo, and we can imagine that anybody who lightly made an oath would be ostracized.

---

[19] Original meaning is a fuzzy concept anyways. After all, how far back in time do we trace a word to find out its original meaning—see Chapter 7 for more on the history of swear words.

Today, we are far more skeptical of a person's word, but the vestiges of oaths remain, even when they are said frivolously. A search on the Internet offers up these gems:

48. I swear to god monkeys behind computers are approving apps.

   (http://www.9to5mac.com/chatisfaction-hits-the-app-store, accessed 8/12/2010)

49. Tell me I did not just see a trailer for a movie that is *I swear to god* CHARLIE'S ANGELS meets HERO by the director of THE TRANSPORTER, featuring, apparently, Holly Valance putting on her bra via kung-fu.

   (http://www.warrenellis.com/?p=1557, accessed 8/12/2010)

50. i swear to god i want to marry my dvr.

   (http://lorenblogs.tumblr.com/, accessed 8/12/2010)

51. Some day, as God is my witness, I will stamp out the disgusting and redundant construction "that being said."

   (http://www.pajiba.com/trade_news/hbo-orders-up-animated-version-of-the-ricky-gervais-show-podcast.php, accessed 8/12/2010)

4.1.2 Cursing

When we curse somebody we state a wish for harm to come to them. There is a superstitious element to most cursing (word magic): by vocally wishing harm, we cause harm. Perhaps the most explicit reference to such a belief is found in the following charm: "I chant a charm of victory, I bear a rod of victory/ Word-victory, work-victory" (cited in Hughes 1991, 39). One of my favorite curses is from the seventeenth century in which you wish someone "to suffer a blow over the snout with a French faggot-stick[20]," which meant, 'to lose one's nose to the pox' (Hughes 1991, 132).

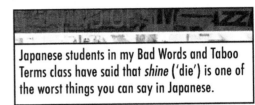

Japanese students in my Bad Words and Taboo Terms class have said that *shine* ('die') is one of the worst things you can say in Japanese.

Plagues have been a big source of curses in English history. For example, the famous line from *Romeo and Juliet:* "A plague o' both your houses." Hughes (1991) demonstrates in Table 1.6 that our various words for 'plague' all came to be used as curses (imprecations).

TABLE 1.6		
The Semantic Correlatives of the Plague and the Pox (Hughes 1991, 190)		
Literal Sense	*Word*	*Imprecatory Sense*
1303	pestilence	1386
1350	pocky	1598
1398	pestilential	1531
1542	pestiferous	1458
1548	plague	1566
1550	pox	1588
1568	pest	1570
1604	plaguey	1574

Interestingly, the imprecatory uses of *pestiferous* and *plaguey* predate their literal uses, which Hughes takes to mean that "the plague became such a fashionable topic in swearing that the emotive use became dominant" (190). We talk more about emotive swearing in Section 4.2.

---

[20] Of course, this was long before *faggot* achieved its present status as a slur for male homosexuals (that usage began in the early twentieth century).

The primary plague we've had in contemporary times is AIDS, but Hughes (1991) comments that, unlike earlier epidemics, AIDS has had virtually no impact on swearing. This may not be entirely true, however; note the (ironic) use of it on *The AV Club's* message board, where commentators often wish "canceraids" on each other, as in, (52), written by a poster who was annoyed by the previous posts on a thread:

52. CANCERAIDS FOR ALL !!!!!!!!!!!!!!!!!!!!!!!!!!!!!

(http://www.avclub.com/articles/tv-in-a-bottle-19-great-tv-episodes-largely-confin,42284/, accessed 6/24/2010)

In fact, it seems that *canceraids* may now simply mean 'bad' to some speakers, as in (53).

53. Speed dating: delicious happy or canceraids?

(from a question posted to the website *Penny Arcade,* http://forums.penny-arcade.com/showthread.php?t=107315, accessed 6/24/2010)

Of course the classic English curse is simple and to the point: *Damn you!* or *God damn you!*

4.1.3 Denotative Swearing

As we've discussed, obscene and scatological words are taboo because of their association with a taboo thing or taboo behavior. But we've also seen that taboo words are especially likely to shift meaning. We might imagine that obscene or scatological words would be most taboo when they are used denotatively—that is, with their sexual or effluvial meaning intact. In Tables 1.7 and 1.8, we compare denotative uses of *fuck* and *shit* with some of their idiomatic or figurative uses. The tabooness ratings come from the Tabooness Survey.

TABLE 1.7			
Tabooness Ratings for Denotative and Idiomatic/Figurative Uses of *Fuck*			
	Sentence	*Average Tabooness*	*Median Tabooness*
Denotative	He fucked her.	4.9	5
	He's fucking her.	4.8	5
	They fucked last night.	4.6	5
Idiomatic/Figurative	I fucked up my philosophy test.	3.9	4
	She was fucked up after four beers.	3.8	4
	They're going to fuck him up.	4.6	5
	He fucked her over.	4.4	4

TABLE 1.8			
Tabooness Ratings for Denotative and Idiomatic/Figurative Uses of *Shit*			
	Sentence	*Average Tabooness*	*Median Tabooness*
Denotative	My dog shit on the floor.	3.0	3
	There was shit in the toilet.	2.9	3
	I have to take a shit.	3.5	3
Idiomatic/Figurative	You're in deep shit.	3.3	3
	This room looks like shit.	2.8	3
	She's full of shit.	3.3	3
	My car is a piece of shit.	2.7	3
	That shit is amazing.	3.2	3
	He's trying to get his shit together.	3.1	3
	Grab your shit, let's go.	2.9	3
	This paper is the shit.	2.5	2

The first thing we notice comparing *fuck* with *shit* is that the former is more taboo than the latter. When we look at the median values in Table 1.7, an interesting pattern emerges that we don't see in Table 1.8: on the whole, the denotative sentences with *fuck* are more taboo (median value of 5) than the idiomatic/figurative ones (median value of 4). The one exception is the sentence with *fuck up* meaning 'beat up'. In contrast, the median values for *shit* in both the denotative sentences and the idiomatic/figurative sentences were 3, with only one exception—*the shit* meaning 'very good'.[21] In Sections 4.2 and 4.3, we'll compare the denotative values with emotive and invective uses, respectively.

4.2   Emotive

In Chapter 4, we discuss the emotional aspect of meaning in more depth. Many words in a language have emotions attached to them without being taboo—for example, *love, rape, beautiful, stingy, foul, wretched, awesome.* However, swear words have more emotional charge than any other words. So it's not surprising that we sometimes swear for no other reason than to release emotion. As Jay (2000, 51) puts it, "We express emotions through cursing[22] to soothe ourselves and to communicate information about our emotional states to listeners." We swear to express practically any emotion from surprise to fear, from elation to disappointment, from pain to bliss, and from serenity to anger. When we swear emotively we communicate to our hearers the strength of our emotions (Jay 2000, 52). The stronger the taboo, the stronger the emotion.

According to Jay (2002), we especially swear to express anger. In a study that Jay conducted at a summer camp, he found that campers used *fuck* exclusively to express anger or frustration, and the same goes for *shit*[23] (Jay 1992, 68–69). This use of swearing to express anger may actually be a good thing. As Jay points out, in most cases when anger turns to aggression, the aggression is verbal, not physical (108). Swearing may be like a pressure valve, allowing enough pent up anger to escape that we don't resort to physical violence.

We separate emotive swearing into two classes: emphatics and exclamations. The first are used roughly like we use the adverbs *really* or *very,* only the taboo emphatics resonate more emotionally. Emphatics, along with propositional swearing, belong to what Jay (2000) classifies as **strategic** swearing. This is where we consciously choose to swear in order to best communicate our message. Exclamations, short outbursts of taboo words triggered by a strong emotional reaction, are classified by Jay as **automatic swearing.** This is less conscious. We discuss this distinction more in Chapter 12.

4.2.1   Emphatics

As we saw in Section 2.2, *fuck* is often used emphatically. This is especially common with the form *fucking* (cf. Chapters 8 and 9). In Table 1.9, we compare the emphatic uses of *fuck* with its denotative uses.

TABLE 1.9			
Tabooness Ratings for Denotative and Emphatic Uses of *Fuck*			
	Sentence	*Average Tabooness*	*Median Tabooness*
Denotative	He fucked her.	4.9	5
	He's fucking her.	4.8	5
	They fucked last night.	4.6	5
Emphatic	I fucking hate mornings.	3.9	4
	That was fanfuckingtastic.	4.3	4

Like we saw with the idiomatic/figurative uses, the emphatic uses of *fuck* were rated as less taboo than the denotative uses.

---

[21] In Chapter 7, I speculate that positive uses of taboo words are less taboo than negative uses.

[22] Note, Jay uses *cursing* the same way we use *swearing.*

[23] Except *holy shit*, which was used for surprise.

In Chapter 15, we discuss a famous case involving Bono, the lead singer for U2, where in accepting an award on live TV, he said, "This is really fucking brilliant!" Initially, the FCC decided this was not a violation of their policy rules because he did not use *fuck* denotatively; this opinion was later overruled by higher-ups in the FCC.

4.2.2 Exclamations

In the heat of the moment, when we're really stirred up emotionally, we often let loose a swear word. A group of jocks in my high school could regularly be heard in the lunch room shouting, "Fucking woo-hoo!" When in severe pain, most of us let loose a string of naughty words (we discuss why in Chapter 12). When shocked, scared, dismayed, elated, or whatever, we swear. Most swear words lend themselves to exclamations, especially those from the categories of profanity, obscenity, and scatology—for some reason slurs don't seem to lend themselves as well to exclamations, though I have heard people shout "Son of a bitch!" or "Bastard!" when angry or disappointed without it being directed at anybody in particular. Today, *fuck* and *shit* are our most common exclamations.

We did not include many exclamations on the Tabooness Survey because the tone of voice and the context is so important for determining what emotion is being expressed. We can, however, compare one example for *fuck* and one for *shit* (see Tables 1.10 and 1.11).

TABLE 1.10			
Tabooness Ratings for Denotative and Exclamatory Uses of *Fuck*			
	Sentence	Average Tabooness	Median Tabooness
denotative	He fucked her.	4.9	5
	He's fucking her.	4.8	5
	They fucked last night.	4.6	5
exclamatory	Fuck yeah!	4.3	4

TABLE 1.11			
Tabooness Ratings for Denotative and Exclamatory Uses of *Shit*			
	Sentence	Average Tabooness	Median Tabooness
denotative	My dog shit on the floor.	3.0	3
	There was shit in the toilet.	2.9	3
	I have to take a shit.	3.5	3
exclamatory	Shit, that hurt.	2.6	2

In both cases, the denotative uses are considered more taboo than the exclamatory use (medians of 5 and 4, respectively, for *fuck*, and 3 and 2 for *shit*). This is not surprising. People tend to give us leeway when we're under the influence of strong emotions.

4.3 Invective

Although I, myself, swear infrequently, swearing doesn't bother me much and I'm rarely shocked by it. I used to speculate about what would really shock me until, in the summer of 2002, I heard some kids, probably about twelve years old, "talking smack"—mostly pretty banal stuff about beating each other in some game (*fuck* and its variants were used)—and one of them said, "I'm going to take you down like the Twin Towers." I'm not sure the kid really understood what he was saying, but I'll admit it got my heart racing and made me angry.

The heart racing and anger are at the heart of a lot of swearing, especially invectives, where the purpose is to insult or diminish somebody or something. Ritualized insulting is a common and popular practice around the world, and it usually involves taboo words. Jay (1992, 24) observes that "words take on the power of weapons to their users."

Flyting is an ancient tradition of verbal sparring, where "combatants" swap insults (see Chapter 7 for examples). Hughes (1991, 47) describes flyting:

> Although the language is often gross, even grotesque and astonishingly scatological, there is also a certain element of play. Skill in barbed insult, dexterity in the wounding phrase, is very much a part of heroic language of the North, where the complexity of word-play reaches astonishing proportions in skaldic verse, which was delivered *ex tempore*. It is the verbal equivalent of virtuoso sword-play. The existence of this acceptable convention of insult in such a restrained linguistic régime suggests that it was a species of safety-valve . . .

A similar ritual can be found in African American communities with a game called "The Dozens" or "Sounding." You probably know a variant of this game involving "Your Mama" jokes, which, of course, are not restricted to jokes about mothers. Abrahams (1962, 209–210) describes the process of sounding as follows:

> One insults a member of another's family; others in the group make disapproving sounds to spur on the coming exchange. The one who has been insulted feels at this point that he must reply with a slur on the protagonist's family which is clever enough to defend his honor (and therefore that of his family). This, of course, leads the other (once again, due more to pressure from the crowd than actual insult) to make further jabs. This can proceed until everyone is bored with the whole affair, until one hits the other (fairly rare), or until some other subject comes up that interrupts the proceedings (the usual state of affairs).

Both Abrahams (1962) and Labov (1972) emphasize the formulaic aspects of sounding; Abrahams shows that many sounding insults are rhymed and Labov shows how the insults follow set syntactic structures. One of the "rules" is that the insults have to be absurd; if one of the players gets too personal and hits too close to reality with one of the jokes, the game ends and the insults become real (Labov 1972). Battle rap (where rappers extemporaneously exchange poetic insults set to a beat) is probably an outgrowth of sounding.

Another common type of ritualized insulting is "talking trash/smack" before or during a game or contest. Nate Vooge (pers. comm.) tells me this is particularly common on the chatboards during online gaming. In December 2005, Smith (2006) recorded all the taboo words he heard used during 33.9 hours of playing Halo 2 (an online multiplayer game). Smith calculated that he heard racial, sexual, or homosexual invectives on average 4.25 times per hour (he explains that these were just the ones he could hear—what you hear in the game is dependant on your proximity to other players).

I distinguish between three types of invectives: name-calling, where you insult a person to their face using a slur; pejoratives, where you use a slur in the third person; and maledictives, where you use taboo expressions to insult or diminish another.

4.3.1 Name-Calling

Calling people names is an obvious way to insult them, and it is one of the earliest types of insults we learn. Jay (1992, 25–26) gives the following taxonomy of children's name-calling (examples are mine):

- Name-calling
  - **Physical peculiarities and appearance**
    - *fatso, bubble-butt, four-eyes, pencil-neck*
  - **Real or imagined mental traits**
    - *dummy, idiot, space cadet, airhead, retard, dumb-ass*
  - **Social Relationships**
    - *bully, nark, brown-noser, teacher's pet*
  - **A parody on the child's name**
    - *Rick the prick, Gary-fairy, Susie-floozy, Deloras~Delorass*

- Weakness of the body or spirit
  - *chicken, coward, pussy, wimp, wuss, cry-baby*
- Social deviations
  - *whore, slut, fag, queer, homo, dyke, lesbo*
- Animal names
  - *pig, dog, cow, chicken, ass, bitch*
- Ethnic slurs
  - *nigger, kike, wop, spic, chink, greaser, wetback, cracker*
- Body parts
  - *dick, pussy, cock, cunt, asshole, prick*
- Body processes and products
  - *fart, poop, shit, piss, booger*

Most such name-calling relies on an "us vs. them" mentality. "[W]hen members of an out-group are labeled and targeted, also operating is a sense of in-group solidarity for the non-target group doing the name calling" (Jay 1992, 27).

We talked extensively about slurs in Section 2.4, and we will come back to them in later chapters (notably, Chapters 7, 13, 14, and 15). Name-calling can be one of the most offensive speech acts a speaker can perform. On the other hand, name-calling can also be done affectionately (see Chapter 14).

4.3.2 Pejoratives

As we've done in Sections 4.1 and 4.2, we'll compare uses of *fuck* and *shit* used denotatively with pejorative uses (see Tables 1.12 and 1.13).

TABLE 1.12			
Tabooness Ratings for Denotative and Pejorative Uses of *Fuck*			
	Sentence	*Average Tabooness*	*Median Tabooness*
denotative	He fucked her.	4.9	5
	He's fucking her.	4.8	5
	They fucked last night.	4.6	5
pejorative	He's a motherfucker.	4.9	5
	He's a funny motherfucker.	4.5	4

TABLE 1.13			
Tabooness Ratings for Denotative and Pejorative Uses of *Shit*			
	Sentence	*Average Tabooness*	*Median Tabooness*
denotative	My dog shit on the floor.	3.0	3
	There was shit in the toilet.	2.9	3
	I have to take a shit.	3.5	3
Pejorative	That little shit broke my stereo.	3.2	3

In these tables, we see that pejorative uses of *fuck* and *shit* tend to have roughly the same tabooness as denotative uses (medians of 5 for *fuck* and 3 for *shit*). However, we see a contrast between *motherfucker* used negatively and *motherfucker* used affectionately, which only received a median of 4.

Using *nigger* as a pejorative is especially taboo (at least for whites), and it has been for some time. When Stephen A. Douglas, a presidential hopeful, used *nigger* during a speech to the Senate in 1854, he was told, "Douglas, no man will ever be President of the United States who spells *Negro* with two *g*'s" (quoted in Goodwin 2005, 163). When telephone conversations between a ranting Mel Gibson and his former girlfriend Oksana Grigorieva were released to the public, most of the immediate press reaction focused on one sentence where he used *nigger*: "You look like a fucking pig in heat, and if you get raped by a pack of niggers, it will be your fault." What's especially amazing about this focus is that Gibson repeatedly calls Grigorieva "cunt," and he threatens to kill her, not to mention blaming the victim in a hypothetical gang-rape (cf. Churchwell 2010 for discussion).

4.3.3 Maledictives

Our final type of swearing is maledictives, which is a grab-bag for the various ways we insult people or things using taboo words. This category overlaps with cursing, but it tends to be more general and less focused on wishing harm. Obvious examples are seen in (54–60).

54. Fuck you.
55. Go to hell.
56. Go fuck yourself.
57. The hell with that.
58. Fuck that shit.
59. Bite me.
60. Kiss my ass.

In Chapter 9 we talk extensively about the quasi-imperative *fuck,* as in (54).

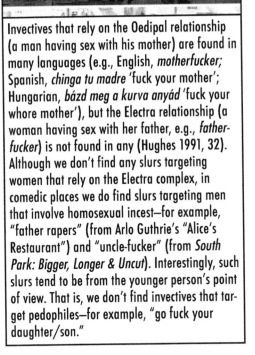

Invectives that rely on the Oedipal relationship (a man having sex with his mother) are found in many languages (e.g., English, *motherfucker;* Spanish, *chinga tu madre* 'fuck your mother'; Hungarian, *bázd meg a kurva anyád* 'fuck your whore mother'), but the Electra relationship (a woman having sex with her father, e.g., *father-fucker*) is not found in any (Hughes 1991, 32). Although we don't find any slurs targeting women that rely on the Electra complex, in comedic places we do find slurs targeting men that involve homosexual incest—for example, "father rapers" (from Arlo Guthrie's "Alice's Restaurant") and "uncle-fucker" (from *South Park: Bigger, Longer & Uncut*). Interestingly, such slurs tend to be from the younger person's point of view. That is, we don't find invectives that target pedophiles—for example, "go fuck your daughter/son."

5   ORGANIZATION OF THE BOOK

I've tried to organize this book so that most chapters are independent. The first part, **The Bawdy Basics,** comprises four chapters (Chapters 2–5); these should be read first and in order. The second part, **The Dirty Details,** comprises ten chapters (Chapters 6–15), which can be read in any order. Unfortunately, some concepts in these chapters may be introduced more than once. I believe such redundancy is a fair trade-off for allowing readers (and instructors) to jump around and investigate ideas in any order they feel like.

At the end of each chapter, I have included exercises. These exercises are intended to get you to think. They are open-ended and have no single correct answer. In many cases, you are asked to solve a problem by performing your own mini-study. These are real problems, ones that haven't been solved conclusively, yet. Maybe you'll come up with a great study and a convincing analysis. Maybe you'll become famous (by linguistics standards).

Part I: The Bawdy Basics

Chapter 2, Grammar, Grammar, Grammar, discusses different ways of defining grammar, ultimately focusing on the only reasonable way to approach it (the linguistic way).

Chapter 3, "If You Say 'Jehovah' Once More . . .": The Use/Mention Distinction, discusses an important distinction in language: that of using a linguistic expression versus mentioning it.

Chapter 4, So Then She's Like, "What's Language For?": The Informative, Emotional, and Social Functions of Language, discusses gossip. It also discusses language evolution. And the functions of language. And emotions. And sociability in general. And linguistic meaning.

Chapter 5, Do Swear Words "Just Sound Bad?": The Arbitrariness of Language, discusses the sounds of language, how we produce them, and how they are connected to meaning. (By the way, the answer to the question in the title of this chapter is, "No.")

Part II: The Dirty Details

Chapter 6, X-phemisms: The Good, the Bad, and the Straight, is about euphemisms, dysphemisms, and orthophemisms.

Chapter 7, *Fornicating Under Consent of the King vs. *Pug:* Historical Swearing, talks about the history of English swearing, how swear words change over time, the etymology of swear words, and where *fuck* came from (hint: it's not an acronym).

Chapter 8, Morphofreakingphonology, is about English infixation and prosody. Is it interesting? Absofreakinglutely.

Chapter 9, Taboo Sentence Structures, looks at the grammar behind *fuck* and *fucking.* Among other things, we discuss why "fuck me" should not always be taken as an invitation.

Chapter 10, Tabernacles, Names, Menses, Animals, and Mothers-in-Law: Cross-Cultural Taboos, is about . . . Well, doesn't the title say it all?

Chapter 11, Learning to Swear in a Second Language, investigates the differences between the way we learn and process taboo words in our native language versus in another language. It also talks about Monopoly money.

Chapter 12, This is Your Brain on Taboo Words: Psychoswearing, looks at linguistic taboos and the brain. You'll also learn a cool word: *coprolalia.*

Chapter 13, Socio-Swearing: Do Men do it More than Women?, discusses the swearing habits of females and males.

Chapter 14, "When You Call Me That, Smile": Context, looks at how the situation in which a taboo word is uttered can affect how it is interpreted. Also it ponders whether college students eat feces or not.

Chapter 15, Deleting Expletives, is about #@%! censorship.

REFERENCES

Allan, Keith, and Kate Burridge. 1991. *Euphemism and Dysphemism: Language Used as Shield and Weapon.* New York: Oxford University Press.

Allan, Keith, and Kate Burridge. 2006. *Forbidden Words: Taboo and the Censoring of Language.* Cambridge: Cambridge University Press.

ASA. 2000. Delete Expletives? *http://www.asa.org.uk/Resource-Centre/Reports-and-surveys.aspx* (accessed 8/13/2010).

Asim, Jabari. 2007. *The N Word: Who Can Say it, Who Shouldn't, and Why.* New York: Houghton Mifflin.

Bloomfield, Leonard. 1933. *Language.* New York: Hold, Rinehard and Winston.

Cassileth, Barrie R., and Jane Hamilton. 1979. The family with cancer. In *The Cancer Patient: Social and Medical Aspects of Care,* ed. Peter A. Cassileth, 233–249. Philadelphia: Lea & Febiger.

Churchwell, Sarah. 2010. Mel Gibson: Racism isn't even the Half of it. *The New Statesman,* July 14, 2010.

Daily Utah Chronicle. 2002. Comments Offend Some LDS Students. April 10, 2002. http://www.dailyutahchronicle.com/news/1.366903 (accessed 12/10/08).

FCC. Frequently Asked Questions. http://www.fcc.gov/eb/oip/FAQ.html#TheLaw (accessed 8/9/2010).

Goodwin, Doris Kearns. 2005. *Team of Rivals: The Political Genius of Abraham Lincoln.* New York: Simon and Schuster.

Hughes, Geoffrey. 1991. *Swearing: A Social History of Foul Language, Oaths, and Profanity in English.* Oxford: Blackwell.

Jay, Timothy. 1992. *Cursing in America: A Psycholinguistic Study of Dirty Language in the Courts, in the Movies, in the Schoolyards, and on the Streets.* Philadelphia: John Benjamins.

Jay, Timothy. 2000. *Why We Curse: A Neuro-Psycho-Social Theory of Speech.* Philadelphia: John Benjamins.

Labov, William. 1972. *Language in the Innercity: Studies in the Black English Vernacular.* Philadelphia: University of Pennsylvania Press.

Lawrence, D.H. 1968. *Lady Chatterley's Lover.* New York: Bantam Books.

Mencken, H.L. 1918. *A book of Calumny* [first published as *Damn*]. New York: Alfred A. Knopf.

Mencken, H.L. 1962. *Supplement One: The American Language.* New York: Alfred A. Knopf.

Merryweather, L.W. 1931. *Hell. American Speech,* August: 433–435.

Montagu, Ashley. 1967. *The Anatomy of Swearing.* New York: The Macmillan Company.

OED. *Oxford English Dictionary.* Online edition.

Pinker, Stephen. 2007. *The Stuff of Thought: Language as a Window into Human Nature.* New York: Penguin Group.

Read, Allen. 1934. An Obscenity Symbol. *American Speech* 19(4): 264–278.

Read, Allen. 1977. *Classic American Graffiti: Lexical Evidence from Folk Epigraphy in Western North America.* Waukesha, WI: Maledicta Press.

Roth, Walter E. 1897. *Ethnological Studies among the North-West-Central Queensland Aborigines.* Brisbane.

Smith, Josh. 2006. Frequency of Profanity in Halo 2. http://www.imjosh.com/2006/02/08/frequency-of-profanity-in-halo-2/ (accessed 12/17/2007).

The Bawdy Basics

Part I

2

chapter

Grammar, Grammar, Grammar

1. UGH

What's your first reaction when you hear the word *grammar?* Most people yawn, shudder, or say, "Ugh." Linguists salivate. Well, maybe not salivate, but linguists really, really like grammar.

So are linguists weird? Perhaps. But before you judge, understand that what linguists have in mind when they think of grammar is different from what most people do. In fact, you could say the word *grammar* is polysemous (but only say that if you're not afraid of sounding pretentious).

There are three types of grammar we will be concerned with: **mental grammar, descriptive grammar,** and **prescriptive grammar.**

1.1 Mental Grammar

Anybody who can speak a language has a grammar of that language stored in their brain; we call this a mental grammar. If you are reading this (and obviously you are), I can safely conclude you have a mental grammar for English stored in your head, kind of like Adobe Reader or Java on your computer hard drive. Take a moment and see if you can find your mental grammar. No? Try doing a search—mentally type in the words "mental grammar." Still nothing? I swear it's in there.

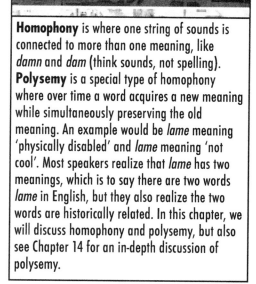

Homophony is where one string of sounds is connected to more than one meaning, like *damn* and *dam* (think sounds, not spelling). **Polysemy** is a special type of homophony where over time a word acquires a new meaning while simultaneously preserving the old meaning. An example would be *lame* meaning 'physically disabled' and *lame* meaning 'not cool'. Most speakers realize that *lame* has two meanings, which is to say there are two words *lame* in English, but they also realize the two words are historically related. In this chapter, we will discuss homophony and polysemy, but also see Chapter 14 for an in-depth discussion of polysemy.

Okay, in truth, we can't find our mental grammars. They're hidden deep in our subconscious. There are lots of things we have the ability to do without being consciously aware of how we do it (e.g., walking, knitting, piano playing, skiing, painting a picture, whistling a tune, eating a sandwich). If you were conscious of what you were doing as you did these things, you would have trouble doing them. Next time you're eating a sandwich, try to identify all the coordinated movements involved: the hand's, the lips', the jaw's, the tongue's, the pharynx's. . . .[1] Subconsciously, you know exactly what you need to do to eat, walk, whistle, etc., but it takes special effort to bring this knowledge to the conscious level; and chances are that even if you try, you'll never fully grasp everything that goes into it. For example, even though most engineers can walk, so far none have designed a robot that can fully imitate the way a human walks.

So if a mental grammar is only found inside the black box of a speaker's subconscious, what evidence do we have it exists? That's easy. How do you prove you have the ability to whistle a tune? Whistle a tune. How do you prove you have a mental grammar for English? Carry on a conversation in English. We call the ability to do something **competence,** and we call the actual doing of that thing **performance.** You can only demonstrate competence through performance.

In the case of language, competence is manifested in a mental grammar. A mental grammar comprises the knowledge necessary for constructing and understanding language. It also helps us determine what is a possible construction and what isn't. Consider the following invented words:

1. grod
2. rltaf
3. slimp
4. potm

Most any English speaker will tell you that (1) and (3) are possible words, but (2) and (4) are not. Now consider the following words:

5. unpickable
6. unpossible
7. Ultraman
8. Manultra

Although my spell-checker disliked all of (5–8), (5) and (7) are perfectly fine English words: (5) describes a lock that cannot be picked and (7) is the English translation of Japanese superhero *Urutora Shirīzu*. Note that (8) would never have been the translation for the superhero, and (6) is an impossible word because of *impossible.* Now consider these sentences:

9. The dog watched the president of France play ping-pong.
10. The president of France watched the dog play ping-pong.
11. The dog watched the of France president play ping-pong.
12. The dog play the president of France watched ping-pong.
13. The the of play watched dog ping-pong France president.
14. Dog watch France president play ping-pong.

I doubt you've ever before read the exact sentence in (9); however, you can recognize that it's a fine English sentence. Although more absurd, (10) is also fine. (11–13), which use the same words as (9–10), are stinky sentences. You might be able to understand (14), but you'd also say that it's not really English.

These intuitions that we have about how sounds combine to form words (1–4), how subword units[2] combine to form words (5–8), and how words combine to form sentences all come from our mental grammars. We are not taught our native language, the language that we begin learning shortly after birth; rather, we acquire it naturally, similar to how we learn to eat. We subconsciously process the language input (people talking around or to

---

[1] You'll find that this isn't the most pleasant way to eat. If it's a really good sandwich, hold off and do it another time.
[2] We call these morphemes. We'll talk more about them in Chapter 8.

us), classify it, and generalize from it. Nobody had to teach you how to determine whether (1–8) were possible words or (9–14) were possible sentences. Your parents or teachers never said to you, "Now, remember never put more than one *the* at the beginning of a sentence." We can see this especially when it comes to swearing. I think it's safe to say your teachers never instructed you on the grammar of swearing (and yes, there is a grammar of swearing), yet you can evaluate that (15–17) are grammatical, while (18–20) are not.[3]

15. Alafuckingbama
16. What the hell do you want me to do with this book?
17. I told you to fuck off!
18. *Alafuckingska.
19. *Which the hell book are you talking about?
20. *I told you to fuck you!

Note the asterisks in front of (18–20). Linguists use asterisks to mark sentences that are **ungrammatical**.[4] When linguists say something is "ungrammatical," they mean it in a specific way, namely, a linguistic expression that is not acceptable according to a speaker's mental grammar. Grammarians (note the distinction—linguists are not grammarians) often use ungrammatical in a different sense, which we return to when we discuss prescriptive grammar.

1.2 Descriptive Grammar

A basic assumption of linguistics is that a language is an internally coherent system, like, say, algebra or chess. The mental grammar of a language defines the system of that language in the same way that axioms define an algebra or rules define chess. Accordingly, we assume a mental grammar consists largely of rules. If a construction violates any of the rules of the grammar, it is considered ungrammatical. The grammatical system of any language turns out to be surprisingly complex. It may seem strange at first how complex the system is, seeing that your average five-year-old has command of it. On the other hand, our subconscious minds are capable of performing incredibly complex tasks. For example, most of us can catch a lobbed ball; however, if you've ever studied calculus, you know how complicated it is to calculate the arc of a trajectory.

Even though folks have tossed balls for millennia, we were only able to consciously calculate the trajectory in the early eighteenth century. As I said earlier, the subconscious mind is a black box. We can't simply open a person's skull, peer inside, and find the grammar (though it might be fun to try). Instead, we have to work inductively, following the scientific method.

The scientific method always begins with data, so let's talk about the nature of linguistic data. We gather our data from speakers of the language under consideration. More specifically, from native speakers. We focus on native speakers because we can be sure that they have acquired the complete system of the language, while nonnative speakers (people who acquired the language later in life, usually as a second language) may have gaps in their grammars.

There are two types of linguistic data: naturally occurring and invented. Naturally occurring data are examples that native speakers actually said (or wrote). Invented data are examples that a linguist has made up.

Naturally occurring data can be gathered in various ways. A linguist could tape-record a conversation or conduct an interview. A linguist could gather data from published sources: a large collection of such data is called a corpus. Sometimes linguists collect data in a natural setting, and sometimes in a laboratory. The advantage of naturally occurring data is they are "authentic," a speaker really produced the linguistic construction. A disadvantage is we have little control over the data; we may be interested in a particular phenomenon but not find relevant examples.

Invented examples, such as those given in (1–20), are useful because they allow us to focus on the phenomena we are most interested in. However, it's not enough to simply invent an example. I could invent a French

---

[3] We discuss examples like (15) and (18) in Chapter 8. We briefly return to *hell* constructions (e.g., (16) and (19)) in Chapter 11, and we discuss the imperative *fuck* (e.g., (17) and (20)) in Chapter 9.

[4] Now that we've established the convention, you can go back to (1–14) and place an asterisk in front of the ungrammatical examples. Go on, do it. It'll be fun.

sentence (e.g., (21)), but it doesn't count as data. It only counts as data when paired with native speaker intuitions (and I'm not anywhere near a native speaker of French).

21. Enculer tu putin merde.

By native speaker intuitions, we mean judgments by one or more native speakers (preferably more than one) as to whether the construction is grammatical or not. We've already touched on one advantage of invented examples, namely that they allow us to concentrate on the relevant data without having to sift through a lot of irrelevant stuff. Another advantage is that invented examples can include negative data (i.e., ungrammatical examples). A corpus of naturally occurring data presumably only includes grammatical examples (aside from false starts, typos, and slips of the tongue).

From the data, we begin making hypotheses. Our hypotheses take the shape of rules for generating grammatical sentences (and not ungrammatical ones). A system of such rules leads to a descriptive grammar of a language. There are three tests for the adequacy of a descriptive grammar:

A descriptive grammar of Language X must:

i) generate all grammatical sentences of X

ii) generate no ungrammatical sentences of X

iii) mirror the mental grammar of X

Test (i) asks whether the descriptive grammar can generate all the grammatical sentences of a language; if the descriptive grammar fails Test (i), it is said to undergenerate. Test (ii) asks whether it can generate only the grammatical sentences of a language; if it fails Test (ii), it is said to overgenerate. At this point in the science of linguistics, we have yet to produce a descriptive grammar for any human language that can pass either of these tests. That's okay—that means there's job security in linguistics.

The primary purpose for developing a descriptive grammar is to better understand how our minds work. In other words, we develop a descriptive grammar in order to have a model for a mental grammar (which, remember, we can't actually see). This leads us to Test (iii): whether it adequately reflects the nature of the mental grammar. This is, of course, the most difficult test, one that is subject to both theoretical and empirical arguments. Although for many linguists, this is the most interesting aspect of studying language, it is not one we will be able to devote much space to in this book. Before you can begin debating the nature of a mental grammar, you really have to have an adequate descriptive grammar (adequacy is relative; adequate does not mean it fully passes Tests i and ii).

1.3 Prescriptive Grammar

When most people get that grimace on their faces at the word *grammar*, it's because they're thinking of prescriptive grammar. Specifically, they're thinking of such esoterica as "use *whom* when applicable," "don't split infinitives," "don't end a sentence with a preposition," "say 'you and I . . .' not 'you and me . . . ,'" "*ain't* is not a word," "it's pronounced 'library' not 'libary,'" etc. In all these cases, the goal of the prescriptive grammar is to get speakers to speak in a way grammarians have declared is "correct." In other words, the prescriptive grammarian has prescribed how we should speak and anything that diverges from their version of the language is "ungrammatical" (not in the sense that we linguists use the word, though).

Sometimes, the prescription is designed to get us to speak a more old-fashioned version of the language, as is the case for *whom*, as in (22–25):

22. Whom are you criticizing? [correct]

23. Who are you criticizing? [incorrect]

24. Whom is criticizing you? [incorrect]

25. Who is criticizing you? [correct]

The pattern used to be rather consistent in earlier forms of English, where *who* was reserved for sentential subjects and *whom* for sentential objects (a pattern seen consistently today with *he/him* and *they/them*). Today, *whom* has fallen out of favor and is reserved for formal writing and persnickety speakers.

Other prescriptive rules, such as not splitting infinitives, were simply invented whole-cloth. As Safire (1992) observes: "Only the cultural elite goes out of its way to avoid inserting an adverb between the leaves of an infinitive." This rule never fully caught on. It was invented primarily because some snooty grammarian decided sentences like (26–27) were bad.

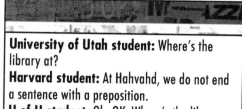

A **split infinitive** is when you take an infinitive verb (*to* + verb), such as *to piss*, and insert an adverb or a preposition phrase or whatnot between the *to* and the verb, such as *to loudly piss*. Grammarians don't want you to tell others "to loudly piss"; they'd rather you told them "loudly to piss" or "to piss loudly".

26. To boldly go where no one has gone before. (*Star Trek: The Next Generation*)

27. Remember to never split infinitives (Safire 1979, cited in Richoux 2002)

But why are these bad? Well, it used to be that intellectuals thought Latin was the perfect language, and wherever English diverged from Latin, it was inferior. You can't split a Latin infinitive, seeing that it's just one word, so this hypothetical grammarian decided we shouldn't split infinitives in English, even though it's something we are able to easily do, seeing that ours is two words (*to* + verb).

University of Utah student: Where's the library at?
Harvard student: At Hahvahd, we do not end a sentence with a preposition.
U of U student: Oh, OK. Where's the library at, asshole?

The prescription against ending sentences with prepositions was also invented whole-cloth. In most languages it's not possible to strand prepositions, but stranded prepositions are something that the English mental grammar seems quite happy with. Many people have ridiculed this prescriptive rule; in what is probably an apocryphal anecdote, Winston Churchill decried stranded prepositions as "the sort of English up with which I will not put."

Of course, a linguist could tell you that the humor in the sentence credited to Churchill comes from the fact that *up* is not, in fact, acting as a preposition in this sentence. Sometimes what appear to be prepositions in English are actually verb particles. One way we can see the difference is that, in questions, prepositions *can* be stranded, while verb particles *must* be stranded. In (28a) we can interpret the sentence in two ways (the most obvious being the telephone book way), while (28b) can only be interpreted in a gynecological or proctological way.

28. a. Who(m) are you looking up?

   b. Up who(m) are you looking?

Our final two examples of prescriptive rules are really ways of distinguishing between a more formal (standard) form of English and more colloquial (non-standard) forms. As children, we're repeatedly taught not to say sentences like (29a) but instead sentences like (29b).

29. a. Me and Pat went to the park.

   b. Pat and I went to the park.

The idea is that if you were to get rid of *and Pat*, you would use *I* not *me* (I doubt you would say, "Me went to the park."). Interestingly, it's mostly the educated who make the inverse of this "mistake." I'm confident that if you listen closely enough, you'll catch a professor (maybe even me) saying (30a) instead of the correct (30b).[5]

30. a. Between you and I . . .

   b. Between you and me . . .

Most educated people don't use *ain't*, unless they're being ironic, but it's nonsense to say *ain't* ain't a word. If so, how is it that English speakers all understand *ain't* perfectly well? It would be more precise, descriptively, to say it is a word not typically used in the standard variety of English.

---

[5] You can tell 30b is the correct form because if you substitute "you and I/me" with a single pronoun (viz. *we/us*) you get the object form, not the subject form: "between us" not "between we."

Prescriptive grammar relates to taboo words in an obvious way: we are told they should never be used. This injunction is a prescriptive rule par excellence. It is, in fact, a proscription (note that many prescriptive rules are proscriptive).

From the earlier discussion about the goals of linguistics, it should be clear that linguists are primarily concerned with mental grammars and descriptive grammars and have little scholarly concern for prescriptive grammars. This is not to say linguists never pay attention to prescriptive grammar; linguists, like all language users, come in many stripes: some are more conservative and believe people should follow prescriptive rules, while others are more liberal and don't really give a crap. The same goes for taboos. While most all linguists recognize they are a natural part of language, not all linguists use them. Just as it is a linguistic fact that many English users say "ain't," strand prepositions, split infinitives, and fail to use *whom,* it is a linguistic fact that language users swear. Therefore, as linguists, we study that aspect of language, the prescriptivists be damned.

2 MODULES OF GRAMMAR

As discussed, grammars (both descriptive and mental) are complicated, far more intricate than, say, chess. To make things more manageable, we can divide a grammar into different parts, which we call modules.[6] We divide our study of grammar into the following modules:

- **Phonology,** the study of the sound system of language.
- **Morphology,** the study of the meaningful "atoms" of language and how they combine to form words.
- **Syntax,** the study of how words combine to form phrases, and phrases combine to form sentences.
- **Semantics,** the study of the meaning of words, phrases, and sentences.

2.1 Phonology

Intuitively, we know each language has a different set of sounds to work with, kind of like how different painters work with different palettes. This fact, in itself, is not so remarkable. What's more interesting to linguists is that the palette of sounds a given language has forms a system. Within this system, we call the sounds **phonemes.** Each phoneme is discrete,[7] which means that it is identifiably distinct from all other phonemes in the system. That is to say English /t/ is a phoneme because it is not /d/ or /p/ or /s/ or /o/ . . . and vice versa.

On the other hand, there are different ways to pronounce /t/. Say the word *tits.* Say it loud. Come on, do it. This word has two tokens of the phoneme /t/. But listen closely. The two sounds aren't the same. You can demonstrate the difference by holding a strip of paper a half-inch from your lips. Say the word again. Notice how the paper flaps when you say it. Now take off the first /t/ and say *its.* This time the paper doesn't flap. What gives? They're both /t/, aren't they? Of course. But sometimes /t/ just doesn't feel like making paper flap.

The blue of the sky is different from the blue of the sea is different from the blue of the eyes of that really sexy person you had a crush on in high school. But they're all blue, right? Because they're not green or yellow or red. Phonemes come in different hues (which we call **allophones**), but as long as the differences don't lead to different meanings, then they're not relevant to the language's sound system. In fact, normal people (by normal people I mean people who have no background in linguistics) don't even realize that the first and third sounds of *tits* are different—and in terms of the grammar, they're not.

Sometimes it's useful to show the actual physical sounds (phones) of a word to contrast them with the abstract phonemes that make up the word in our grammar. For that reason, we have a convention to distinguish between a phonemic representation of a sound and the physical (phonetic) representation. We represent phonemes with slashes—for example, /tɪts/—and phones with square brackets—for example, [tʰɪts]. In Chapter 5, we discuss phonetics and the phonetic alphabet.

---

[6] The modular approach to grammar is not only a practical decision; there are some theoretical arguments regarding Test (iii), too.

[7] Discrete does not mean that a phoneme is good at keeping secrets and only picks its nose when nobody's looking—you're thinking of *discreet.*

2.2 Morphology

The word *motherfucker* is clearly divisible into three parts: *mother, fuck, -er.* The smallest meaningful parts of a word, we call **morphemes.** Note that these parts aren't combined haphazardly. You don't get just any combination (see 31.a–f):

31. a. *fuckermother

    b. *erfuckmother

    c. *fuckmotherer

    d. *ermotherfuck

    e. *mothererfuck

Intuitively, we sense that *motherfucker* is a combination of *mother* and *fucker* and that *fucker* is a combination of *fuck* and *–er.* We can represent this diagrammatically in a tree (Figure 2.1).[8]

Morphemes come in two stripes: **free** and **bound.** Free morphemes can stand on their own as words, such as *rat, bastard, shit, damn, cock.* Bound morphemes are like parasites: they have to attach to another morpheme to survive. Examples are *-ing, -ation, -s.* You can take two free morphemes and form a new word, such as *rat-bastard.* Or you can take a free morpheme and attach a bound morpheme, such as *shitting, damnation, cocks.* Bound morphemes are sometimes called affixes, and they come in three stripes: **suffixes, prefixes,** and **infixes.** We've already seen three suffixes in action (*-ing, -ation, -s*). Examples of prefixes are *re-, un-, pre-,* giving us such words as *refuck*[9], *unfuck*[10], and *prefuck*[11]. Infixes are more common in some other languages than they are in English, but we've still got a few, and most of them are taboo. We'll discuss them in Chapter 8.

2.3 Syntax

Sentences are composed of words, for example, (32):

32. My dog shit on the carpet.

It's obvious there are rules for how the words are ordered. What may not be as obvious is that sentences aren't just linear sequences of words. Sentences are structured vertically and horizontally. (32) can be diagrammed as in Figure 2.2.

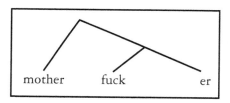

FIGURE 2.1. *Morphological representation of* motherfucker.

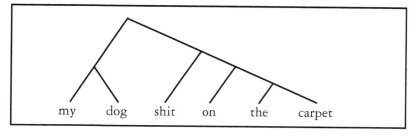

FIGURE 2.2. *Hierarchical structure of (32).*

---

[8] Linguists like trees—you'll see a lot of them in this book.

[9] "I refucked my knee in the basketball game" (http://www.urbandictionary.com/define.php?term=refuck, accessed 7/2/08).

[10] "You best unfuck your attitude" (http://www.urbandictionary.com/define.php?term=unfuck, accessed 7/2/08).

[11] "[T]he reason why A&F clothing is so comfortable is because they prefuck up your clothes, with holes and tears and grease and shit" (http://drummin-foo.livejournal.com/60347.html, accessed 7/2/08).

There are four identifiable units in this sentence: i) *my dog,* ii) *shit on the carpet,* iii) *on the carpet,* iv) *the carpet.* These units are called phrases. We don't have time here to go into the methods for discovering the full structure in Figure 2.2, but we can focus on just one phrase: *my dog.* We can tell these two words form a unit because we can replace it with a single word (e.g., *He shit on the carpet*). Also it can stand on its own (e.g., *Who shit on the carpet? My dog*). You can even conjoin it with another similar phrase (e.g., *My dog and my child shit on the carpet*). What's more, *the carpet* forms a phrase of the same type. We can see this because any word or words that can grammatically replace *my dog* can also replace *the carpet* (see 33–38).[12]

33. He shit on my dog.

34. My child shit on my dog.

35. The fat police officer with the monobrow shit on my dog.

36. My dog shit on him.

37. My dog shit on my child.

38. My dog shit on the fat police officer with the monobrow.

In fact, we can even interchange *my dog* and *the carpet.*

39. The carpet shit on my dog.

It doesn't matter that (39) makes absolutely no sense. Syntax doesn't have to make sense. Even if (39) is absurd, we can all tell that it's grammatical.

2.4 Semantics

In the previous section, I noted that syntax doesn't have to make sense. In fact, we could say that syntax is a meaningless study. Meaning belongs to semantics. We can look at linguistic meaning on two levels: **lexical** and **compositional.** Lexical semantics studies meaning at the level of words (or morphemes). Compositional semantics studies meaning at the level of phrases and sentences.

We'll focus on lexical semantics. One place to begin is to look at meanings in terms of sets and subsets. For example, we can start with the word *human.* This word denotes a set, namely all those people in the world we call human.[13] The set of humans is a subset of other sets (e.g., animals and mammals). And we can divide humans into subsets (e.g., men, women, girls, and boys). A subset of men are bastards and a subset of women are bitches. We can diagram this as in Figure 2.3.

The relationships between the words can be described with two terms: **hypernym** and **hyponym.** Take the word *man.* A hypernym of *man* is any word that denotes a superset of the set denoted by 'man'. Given Figure 2.3, *man* has *human* and *animal* as hypernyms (all men are humans, and all men are animals; some but not all humans are men, and some but not all animals are men). A hyponym of *man* is any word that denotes a subset of the set denoted by 'man'. Given Figure 2.3, *man* has *bastard* as a hyponym (some but not all men are bastards; all bastards are men).

During his travels studying bathroom graffiti in 1928, Allen Read found at least three different meanings for *ass*: 'buttocks', 'anus', and 'vagina' (Read 1977[D2]: 30-32).

Now, some women believe all men are bastards and some men believe all women are bitches. You could make the case that for such people *man* and *bastard* are synonyms and *woman* and *bitch* are synonyms.[14] **Synonyms** are two words that denote the same set.

---

[12] It might seem that pronouns are an exception to this observation (e.g., *My dog shit on he*). However, they are not an exception if we accept that each pronoun has two forms (*I/me, she/her, he/him, they/them, we/us*), a bit like /t/ can have more than one allophone.

[13] What? You think this is circular? Yeah, well, so's your old man.

[14] My tongue's in my cheek here. As we'll see in Chapter 4, there's more to meaning than denotation.

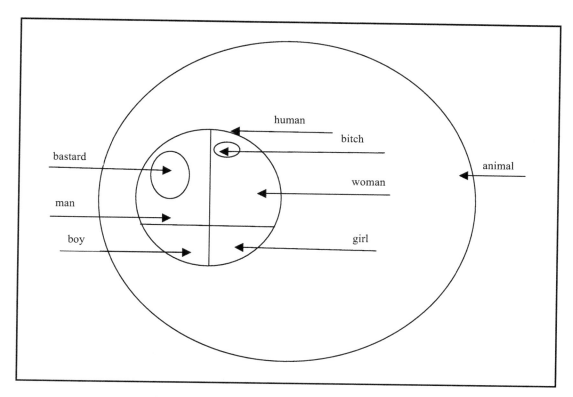

FIGURE 2.3. *Venn diagrams for* human *(not to scale)*.

Sometimes two words sound exactly the same, but they mean different things, for example, *damn* and *dam* (it is irrelevant that they are spelled differently, since you can't hear how a word is spelled and we all learn to speak before we learn to read—here's my mantra: **spelling is irrelevant**). Such words are **homophones.** Homophones are the inverse of synonyms: one sound-form, two meanings vs. two sound-forms, one meaning.

A subcategory of homophony is **polysemy.** With polysemy, there's still one sound-form and two meanings; however, there's an intuitive relationship between the two words. For example, *bastard* has two meanings: i) 'an illegitimate son'; ii) 'a despicable man'. As Herman Jolly puts it in his song *Gin Kicks In,* "Just 'cause your mom and dad got wed doesn't mean that you can't be a bastard." *Bastard* has two meanings, but we can see that one meaning derived from the other. In Chapter 14 we discuss polysemy in more depth.

Just as we have to recognize that one sound form may have more than one meaning (i.e., words can be homophonous or even polysemous), we have to recognize that taboo words get used in lots and lots and lots of different ways (we discussed this in Chapter 1 and we'll discuss it more in Chapter 4). We also have to recognize that people may not agree on the meanings of words. In Chapter 7, we see that taboo words often have multiple meanings during their lifespans. In Chapter 13, we'll see that men and women may not agree on the meanings of certain slurs; for example, common words like *slut, stud, milf, slimeball,* and *manwhore* may have different meanings for the different sexes.

3 THE LEXICON

The **lexicon** is not a module of grammar; within the system of language it plays a complementary[15] and essential role to the grammar. The lexicon is the database for the system. It is, first and foremost, the list of words and morphemes of the language, but it is more than that. For each word or morpheme in the language there is an

---

[15] No, it doesn't say nice things about the grammar—that's complimentary.

entry in the lexicon, and each entry provides vital information for each module. For example, let's consider the entry for *shit*.

> *shit*
>
> Phonology: /ʃɪt/
>
> Morphology: free morpheme
>
> Syntax: count noun
>
> Semantics: 'solid waste evacuated from an animal's rectum'

Shit is highly polysemous, so there will be different entries for each of its senses (e.g., one for the verb meaning 'to defecate'; one for the verb meaning 'to kid'; one for the idiomatic use as in, *You're the shit;* one for idiomatic use in *I don't give a shit,* etc.).

4.   CONCLUSION

In this chapter, we haven't really addressed taboo language so much as we've established a framework for talking about it. In the coming chapters, we'll talk a good deal about the grammar of taboo language, both mental and descriptive. Occasionally, I may mention prescriptive grammar, too. When I simply say "grammar," however, understand it to mean either mental or descriptive—usually the context will indicate which is meant, though sometimes the distinction won't affect the point being made; when we talk about prescriptive grammar, I'll always be specific.

Within grammar, we've established four modules: phonology, morphology, syntax, and semantics. In future chapters, we'll address these different areas; for example, Chapter 8 looks at the infix *-fucking-*, as in *fanfuckingtastic,* which requires us to understand the nature of morphology and phonology, and in Chapter 9 we question whether *Fuck you!* is the same kind of sentence as *Fuck yourself!,* and this requires us to understand syntax.

The main point I want you to take away: languages are best described as systems of rules. These systems are complex but describable. And taboo words and expressions are just as much a part of these systems as any other words and expressions.

REFERENCES

Coyne, James C., Richard C. Sherman, and Karen O'Brien. 1978. Expletives and Woman's Place. *Sex Roles* 4: 827–35.

OED. Entry for *motherfucker. Oxford English Dictionary.* Online edition.

Read, Allen. 1977. *Classic American Graffiti: Lexical Evidence from Folk Epigraphy in Western North America.* Waukesha, WI: Maledicta Press.

Richoux, Donna. 2002. Humorous Rules for Writing ("Fumblerules," "Perverse Rules," etc.). http://alt-usage-english.org/humorousrules.html (accessed 8/21/08).

Safire, William. 1979. "On Language." *New York Times,* October 7, 1979.

Safire, William. 1992. "But Who Won on Language?" *New York Times,* October 25, 1992. http://query.nytimes.com/gst/fullpage.html?res= 9E0CE5D61539F936A15753C1A964958260 (accessed June 18, 2008).

1. Let's say your friend doesn't believe you when you tell her that there is a grammar to swearing. How would you convince her?

2. Are there prescriptive rules associated with swearing beyond the proscription, "Don't!"?

3. Let's say your grandparents are shocked (shocked!) that you are taking a class on swearing. What arguments could you give to show that studying swear words can be beneficial?

3

"If You Say 'Jehovah' Once More..."

The Use/Mention Distinction

1 USE, MENTION, MENTION, AND MENTION

If somebody were to say (1) to you, you would probably find it at least mildly offensive.

1. Shut up!

But it can't be the words that are offensive, since the following sentences are not at all offensive.

2. *Shut up* is a phrasal verb.
3. He said to her, "Shut up!"
4. *Kus* is the Hungarian word for 'shut up'.

Philosophers and linguists call the difference between (1) and (2–4) the **use/mention distinction**. In (1) the phrase *shut up* is used, but in (2–4) the same phrase is mentioned. Any word can be **used**, and any word can be **mentioned**. I can use *dog,* as in (5), or I can mention it, as in (6–7).

5. I have a dog.
6. *Dog* is not a four-letter word.

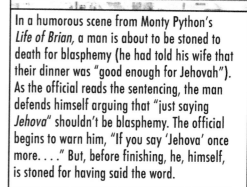

In a humorous scene from Monty Python's *Life of Brian,* a man is about to be stoned to death for blasphemy (he had told his wife that their dinner was "good enough for Jehovah"). As the official reads the sentencing, the man defends himself arguing that "just saying *Jehova*" shouldn't be blasphemy. The official begins to warn him, "If you say 'Jehova' once more...." But, before finishing, he, himself, is stoned for having said the word.

7. I wrote in (5), "I have a dog."

8. What's the Spanish word for 'dog'?

By saying "the use/mention distinction" we make it sound like there's only one distinction, but there are really at least three, each one notated differently, as you've probably already observed (if you haven't already observed that, why don't you go ahead and do so now). Use is use, and I take it for granted that you know how to use *shut up* and *dog* as well as the four-letter words we'll be coming to shortly. But mention ain't just mention—there is **mention qua word**, **mention qua quotation**, and **mention qua meaning**.

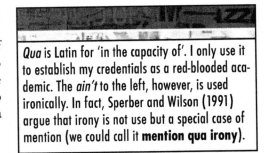

Qua is Latin for 'in the capacity of'. I only use it to establish my credentials as a red-blooded academic. The *ain't* to the left, however, is used ironically. In fact, Sperber and Wilson (1991) argue that irony is not use but a special case of mention (we could call it **mention qua irony**).

1.1 Mention Qua Word

Mention qua word is what linguists usually mean when they say, "the use/mention distinction"; it is a meta-level of language, where we talk about language. We can talk about all sorts of characteristics of a word—its sound, spelling, part-of-speech, formality, offensiveness, euphony, etc. When we mention a word qua word, we put it in italics, so nobody will get confused and think we're using it. For example in (9) the word *dog* is mentioned qua word.

9. An example of faunality is *dog,* a slur meaning 'an unattractive woman'.

One way of recognizing mention qua word is that you can usually put "the word" in front of the mentioned word, as in (9').

9'. An example of faunality is the word *dog,* a slur meaning 'an unattractive woman'.

1.2 Mention Qua Quotation

Mention qua quotation is when you mention a word (or words) spoken at another time. Unsurprisingly, we represent quoted words with quotation marks.[1] The quotation doesn't have to refer to an expression that was uttered in the past (as (3) and (5) presumably do); the quote can be hypothetical, as in (10).

10. Next time just say to him, "Shut up, dog."

In Chapter 15, we'll discuss how the media and the law deal with taboo words when they are mentioned qua quotation.

In the preface of Chaucer's *The Canterbury Tales*, he apologizes for his language, asking the reader to forgive him, and explaining,

"Whoso shal telle a tale after a man
He moote reherce as ny as ever he kan
Everich a word, if it be in his charge
Al speke he never so rudeliche and large,
Or ellis he moot telle his tale untreue . . ."

'Whoever shall tell a tale after a man, he must repeat as near as he can every word, if it be in his charge, although he speaks ever so rudely and freely, or else he must tell his tale untruly'.

(Quoted in Hughes 1991, 63, translation mine.)

1.3 Mention Qua Meaning

Mention qua meaning is, in my experience, the most difficult to grasp. Like with mention qua word, it is meta-language. We are talking about meaning, which is a level or module of grammar.[2] You might say that in this sense there is little, if any, difference between mention qua word and mention qua meaning, seeing that meaning is just as much an aspect of a word as part-of-speech, euphony, or formality. The difference is that when we speak of mention qua meaning the word is mentioned not as itself but as a representation of its meaning, divorced from any particular language. To

---

[1] Brits use single quotes for mention qua quotation. Silly Brits.

[2] For more on meaning, see the discussions on semantics (Chapters 2 and 4), the theory of signs (end of Chapter 5), denotation (Chapter 6), and pragmatics (Chapter 14).

illustrate this, I chose examples where an English word was used to represent the meaning of foreign words in (4) and (8). However (11) is just as much an example of mention qua meaning.

11. What's a five letter word for 'female dog'?

We use single quotes (or inverted commas) to represent mention qua meaning.[3]

2 MENTION AND SWEARING

So what the fuck's this all got to do with cussing?[4] Well, consider (12–15); in (12) *fuck* is used, but in (13–14) it is mentioned.

12. Fuck off!
13. *Fuck* is a bad word.
14. Did you just say, "Fuck the use/mention distinction"?
15. *Bazd meg ezt a kurva kutyát* is Hungarian for 'fuck this fucking dog'.

Now, perhaps you are one of those libertines who are not in the least offended by (13–15); however, I'm sure you realize that many people would be and that many conservatines would choose alternatives to *fuck*, even when they are not using the word, but (merely) mentioning it (cf. 13'–15').

13'. The f-word is a bad word.
14'. Did you just say, "F the use/mention distinction"?
15'. *Bazd meg ezt a kurva kutyát* is Hungarian for 'f*** this f***ing dog'.

In fact, the use/mention distinction is a pretty good test for determining if a word is taboo. If a word retains its power to offend even when it is mentioned, then it is a taboo word. Compare (13–15) with (2–4), where we have a phrase that is potentially offensive when used, but not when it is mentioned. *Shut up* is not a taboo expression; however, telling a person to shut up may be taboo in certain circumstances.

Offensiveness is subjective, of course, which makes the test posited in the previous paragraph less empirical than we might wish. Perhaps a better way to approach this is to observe the responses that offensiveness can trigger. A well-known approach to taboo words is to have people read a word list aloud. Included in the list are neutral words like *shut, dog, Hungarian, say, word,* etc.; positive words like *good, love, beautiful, praise,* etc.; negative words like *bad, ugly, insult, politician,* etc.; and taboo words like *shit, fuck, bitch, damn,* etc. What we find is that people will read through the list at a constant rate as long as the words are from one of the first three categories, but when they reach the taboo words there is a measurable time delay. That is, they pause slightly before they say the taboo words. (See Chapter 12 for discussion of similar experiments.)

An even more sophisticated version of this test involves attaching electrodes to people's fingers in order to measure conductivity: when we have an emotional response to something our skin conducts electricity better. In this test, subjects are shown one word at a time on a computer screen (they don't have to read the words aloud), and their skin conductivity is measured. The conductivity might be slightly more for positive words like *love* or negative words like *ugly* when compared to neutral words like *word;* however, the taboo words cause the greatest amount of conductivity, and the greater the taboo the greater the conductivity. In this regard, the test can not only be used to determine which words in a language are taboo, but also to rank the level of tabooness. (See Chapters 11 and 12 for more on experiments like this.)

To a lesser degree, the low-tech test in which the subjects' reading speed is measured can also help us to discover the level of tabooness. I'm referring here to the fact that many subjects will refuse to even utter some of the taboo words. In fact, there are two English words that a significant percentage of subjects will refuse to utter at all when given such a test. Think for a moment. What do you guess those words are? Don't read ahead! Okay, you've thought of them? Now read ahead.

---

[3] Of course, this means that British linguists have no way of distinguishing between mention qua quotation and mention qua meaning. Silly Brits.
[4] Note the mention qua irony in my selection of *fuck* for this sentence.

To illustrate this phenomenon, consider the following episode from Penn and Teller's HBO series *Bullshit*. In this particular episode, guests were asked to read a list of words into the camera. Before reading the list, one of the guests, Jonathon McWhorter, who is a linguist, explains that there is nothing inherent in the sounds of a word that makes it bad. He points out there's nothing about the individual sounds in *dog,* [d] [a] [g], that make it refer to a furry pet, nor is there anything about [f] [ʌ] [k] that makes *fuck* offensive. McWhorter even goes so far as to say that taboos are based on superstitious beliefs. Then, as if to prove his point, McWhorter, with academic poise, reads through the list of words: *piss, tits, fuck, cocksucker,*

The bracketed letters given here are from the International Phonetic Alphabet (IPA). [a] represents the vowel sound in *hot,* and [ʌ] represents the vowel sound in *hut.* Linguists use this alphabet to unambiguously represent the sounds of a language. See Chapter 5 for more on the IPA.

motherfucker. But then he comes to *cunt,* and all of his pontificating breaks down, as does he. He tries to say the word and then laughs uncontrollably. After five seconds he collects himself and manages to say the word. Another guest on Penn and Teller's show is Mancow, a radio DJ from Chicago known for being shocking; Mancow refuses to say "cunt" because his wife would kill him if he did.

So we now know one of the two words. What's the other? This was a word that Penn and Teller, two white men, avoided even discussing in their show: *nigger.* Even when simply mentioned, this word causes ire, and it has for a long, long time. When, in 1936, the prominent African American magazine *Opportunity* was informed by the Washington D.C. school district that the magazine would not be allowed in the schools unless they stopped printing the word *nigger* in their articles, the editor, Elmer A. Carter, wrote the following in a letter to the school district. Note the use/mention distinction that Carter draws when defending his magazine (although he doesn't call it by that name).

> Even a casual examination of the magazine will reveal that your recommendation has been based on a total misconception of the use of the term *nigger* when it appears in *Opportunity.* That use is limited to quotations from other writers or is the reproduction in poem or story of the speech and conversation of characters who commonly use this term, and in both cases the word or the line in which it occurs is always set off by quotation marks, italics, or other literary and printing insignia.
>
> It should not be necessary for me to direct your attention to the fact that there is a vast and obvious difference in the use of a word or phrase in quotation and its use as a definitive term in the editorial contents of a publication, nor to affirm that *Opportunity* never employs any epithet of opprobrium in its columns except under the limitations mentioned above. (quoted in Mencken 1962, 627)

CONCLUSION

To summarize, we have use and mention. Use is when you use a word normally—that is, with it's normal linguistic purpose. Mention is when you make some comment about the word. For example, you can discuss linguistic characteristics of the word (mention qua word), in which case we put the word in italics. You can also mention the fact that the word was (or might be/have been) said (mention qua quotation), in which case we put the word in quotation marks. Or you can mention the word as a way of indicating its meaning (mention qua meaning)—for example, when discussing a new word or a word from a foreign language—in which case we put the defining word in single quotation marks. There is another possibility that I have hinted at, namely mention qua irony; this type resembles use in that the word fills a normal position in your sentence; however, you place an ironic distance from yourself and the word, making it clear to the hearer that some people might use this word in this way, but you wouldn't. For example, *special* is often used ironically (e.g., *Grant is a "special" person*). The quotes around *special* here are called scare quotes, and in speech we often represent them by holding up the index and middle finger of each hand while saying the word.

Throughout this book, I try to consistently indicate when I am mentioning a word (when I'm using a word no special indication is needed).[5] On assignments, you should make an effort to also indicate the different types of mention using italics (or underline if writing by hand), quotes, and single quotes.

REFERENCES

Hughes, Geoffrey. 1991. *Swearing: A Social History of Foul Language, Oaths, and Profanity in English.* Cambridge, MA: Blackwell.

Mencken, H.L. 1962. *Supplement One: The American Language.* New York: Alfred A. Knopf.

Sperber, Dan, and Dierdre Wilson. 1991. Irony and the Use-Mention Distinction. In *Pragmatics: A Reader,* ed. Steven Davis, 550–563. New York: Oxford University Press.

---

[5] Although I am at times ironic, I do not use any special notation for mention qua irony—you'll just have to figure it out for yourself.

1. Look through various newspapers to see how they deal with taboo words. Do they distinguish between use and mention? What about radio and television? The Internet?

2. In July, 2008 Jesse Jackson was caught on tape making critical remarks about Barack Obama. This is how the *New York Times* reported the subsequent apology: "The Rev. Jesse Jackson apologized on Wednesday for critical and crude comments he made about Senator Barack Obama, remarks in which he accused Mr. Obama of 'talking down to black people.'" Further on, the article says that Jackson's words "included a vulgar reference." Towards the end of the article, the journalist notes that when "The O'Reilly Factor" played the clip, "At least one of the words had to be blocked out." Nowhere in the article does it say what the "vulgar reference" was. From this article, what would you guess it was?

    According to a *Chicago Tribune* op-ed piece on the original incident, a CNN reporter described the omitted term using the following words: "Manhood, er, genitals. Uh, male private parts." Now, what would you guess the "vulgar reference" was?

    In a CBS web article on the apology, the original statements are quoted, though the "vulgar reference" is not fully reproduced. Here's the statement according to this article: "See, Barack been, um, talking down to black people on this faith based . . . I want cut his n**s off . . . Barack . . . he's talking down to black people." Now do you know what the "vulgar reference" was?

Why are the three news sources so coy? Do you think this is "good reporting"? Why or why not? When it comes to taboo words, where should media draw the line? Should the use/mention distinction play a role?

3. In a class discussion, would you ever use a taboo word? If so, which words? Are there some you would use and some you wouldn't? For any words that you would not use in a class, would you feel comfortable mentioning them?

4. One common way of avoiding the word *fuck* is to say "the f-word." In what ways does *the f-word* substitute for *fuck?* Is it equivalent to other euphemisms for *fuck,* such as *freak* or *fudge?*

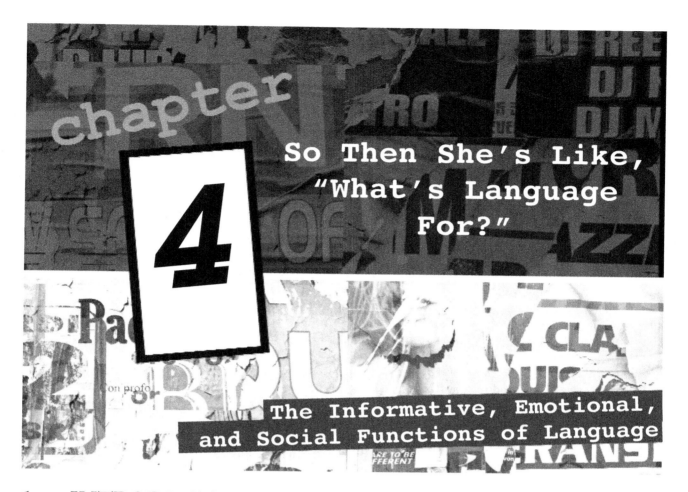

So Then She's Like, "What's Language For?"

The Informative, Emotional, and Social Functions of Language

1. INTRODUCTION

How did language begin? Why did we start using sounds to convey ever more complex thoughts? I'll tell you. It was so we could cuss.

No. I'm kidding. Actually, it was so we could gossip. You think I'm still kidding? Well, I'm not.

When most people think about why we use language, they think of useful things, like buying shoes, informing a friend when his hair's on fire, asking your sister to pass the salt, inquiring of Harvard students where the library's at, telling the taxi driver to follow that car, and learning linguistics. We don't usually include discussions of whether Zac Efron, Zach Braff, or Zach Galifianakis is the dishiest; whether it was hotter for Angelina Jolie to drink Billy Bob Thornton's blood or to kiss her brother; whether Hilary Swank could take Ralph Macchio in a fair fight; or whether Benicio del Toro is related to Guillermo del Toro. Nor do they include conversations about how Gertrude was so wasted Saturday night that she totally hooked up with that one guy with the mole on his cheek, and then Grant got so mad at her that he tried to make it with Abigail, but Abigail was like, "no way," and she told him to screw himself, and then Grant was like, "you're a skank and so's Gertrude," only Abigail's new boyfriend, Carmine, was standing there, and he was like, "you've got to watch yourself, bro," and then Grant totally hurled all over my shoes—it was so gross. Yet, according to Dunbar (1996), two-thirds of our language use is dedicated to these more trivial conversations.

Although I was kidding when I said language began so we could cuss, some scholars have hypothesized that the first words were akin to swearing. Montagu (1967, 5) summarizes the theory as follows: "Before men developed any articulate means of communication with each other, there were already in existence certain emotionally highly charged sounds or expletives."

Dunbar argues that gossip is essential to society. In fact, she believes that language evolved out of our need to gossip. She notes that all non-human primates groom each other. They spend hours a day going through each other's hair, taking out snarls, removing dead skin, snacking on parasites. Grooming may be partly about hygiene, but there is a more important social purpose behind it. Individuals form alliances by grooming. If a male baboon threatens a female, all the females she has groomed and who have groomed her will rush to her defense. These ties that grooming creates are essential to primate society, and they have undoubtedly contributed a competitive advantage to the species: a predator may attack an individual baboon, ape, or monkey but not a group of baboons, apes, or monkeys. The fact that one primate will come to the defense of another makes the individuals that much stronger.

Humans may occasionally groom each other. For example, I've seen women taking pleasure in braiding each other's hair. However, most of the time, we are groomed by strangers (stylists or barbers) whose only social bonds to us are monetary. Nevertheless, we are a remarkably social species. Our social ties are largely formed through language. Our conversations about the three Zac(h)s, Angelina, Hilary and Ralph, the del Toros, and Gertrude, Grant, Abigail, and Carmine may be trivial on the surface, but they create bonds between us. What is the most important factor in a relationship? For most people, it is how much they enjoy talking to each other.

When you walk across campus and you see a friend, what do you say? Typically, something like, "Hey." Maybe you say their name. You might ask a question, "How's it going?" or "What's up?" Do you expect a real answer to the question? Not usually. The most common type of answer would be a variation on "Good, you?" or "Not much, you?"[1] Have you learned anything you didn't already know in the course of such an exchange? No. But that doesn't make the exchange unimportant. You've acknowledged you share a social bond, established you care about this person, and communicated you want to continue being friends (or acquaintances or whatever).

Language is designed to communicate. And when we think of communication, we usually focus on the communication of information. Sure, the previously mentioned conversations communicate information, but that isn't the main point. The speakers make a connection; that's what's important.

Another conversational way to make a connection is commiseration, where we bellyache. We complain about our day, about the student with the post-nasal drip sitting in the front row who kept clearing his throat with a snort, about the 500-word essay on the word *fucking* our Bad Words and Taboo Terms prof assigned, about how our new shoes pinch our pinky toes, about our love-life (or lack thereof), about politics. . . . These gripes also communicate information, but again that's not the point. The point is to express emotions.

In this chapter we focus on these different aspects of linguistic communication: informational, social, and emotional. So far, we've looked at different sorts of conversations. In some conversations, the main emphasis is on the informative side; in some, on the social side; and in some, on the emotional side. Of course, most conversations have a mixture of all three. However, in this chapter, we focus not on conversations, but on words. Words, too, typically have the three aspects. Specifically, we will see that these aspects are part of the linguistic meaning of the words, and thereby part of our lexical knowledge of our language. I should note that we can also communicate emotion and sociability through our tone of voice, gestures, etc., but in that case the communication travels through a different channel from the words themselves. What we're interested in here is how words, especially taboo words, encode these functional aspects of meaning.

2. THE THREE FUNCTIONS OF LANGUAGE

From what I can tell, it was Sadock (1994) who first posited the three "functional aspects" of speech.

1. an informational, representational aspect (INF) in which conversational negotiations are conducted in terms of propositions that can be judged for accuracy against real or possible worlds;

2. an effective, social aspect (EF) by means of which conventional effects on societally determined features of the world are achieved;

3. an affective, emotive aspect (AF) that is used to give vent to and/or display real or apparent feelings of the speaker. (Sadock 1994, 397)

---

[1] Michael Feldman plays on this in his radio show "Whad'ya know?" He begins each broadcast by calling out to the audience, "What do you know?" and the audience answers, "Not much, you?"

In Sadock's conception, these three are independent aspects, though in most utterances all three play a role. Perhaps the best way to examine them is to look at utterances that are deficient in one or more aspects, as in Figure 4.1.[2]

FIGURE 4.1			
Defective speech acts (taken from Sadock 1994, 400)			
	INF	EF	AF
Ouch!	–	–	+
Hi	–	+	–
Huh?	–	+	+
Boy, it's hot	+	–	+
I bet $5	+	+	–

Let's go through each in turn, starting with *Ouch!*, which only has an emotive function. Imagine your friend steps on your thumb while wearing heavy work boots. If you are a polite person (and I'm sure you are), you'll say, "Ouch!" Perhaps sometimes when you utter this word, others will learn that you've hurt yourself, and sometimes uttering the word might cause your hearer to do something (e.g., remove their boot from your thumb). However, Sadock (and I) would argue that the word itself doesn't communicate these aspects. People may infer from your uttering "Ouch!" that you are in pain or that they should step off your thumb, but the main thing that the word itself communicates is an emotion (i.e., pain). We can see that it is not truly informative or social, since we often utter it even when we are alone.

Next, we turn to *Hi*, which only has a social function. When you say "Hi" to a friend, no information or emotion is communicated through the word (though you can convey emotion with your tone of voice). Your utterance primarily establishes a social bond, as discussed previously. Moreover, it triggers a response from your friend, namely, "Hi" or an equivalent greeting.

Our next utterances is *Huh?*, which has both an emotive and social function but no informative function. Imagine you say to a friend, "My teacher is making me write a 500-word essay on *fucking*." Your friend will likely respond with, "Huh?" As with the previous two utterances discussed, the *huh?* does not convey any information. Rather, it communicates an emotion—surprise—and it also creates a social burden on you: you are expected to elaborate. As Sadock (1994: 399) puts it:

> Quite automatically, and conventionally, the target of 'Huh?' is socially burdened. He or she must repeat, clarify, or otherwise do what the situation calls for. It is worse than impolite or inconsiderate not to—it is a breach of the social convention instituted by uttering 'Huh?'

Sadock contrasts this form with another one, *Beg pardon?*, which he argues is similar to 'Huh?' in the informational and social aspects, but the emotional aspect is lacking. With *Beg pardon?*, the speaker is simply asking their collocutor for more information, not expressing surprise.

Certain observational utterances, especially about the weather, lack any real social aspect but are purely emotional and informative. For example, when you say, "Boy, it's hot!" the words don't communicate any social condition (i.e., the hearer is not expected to respond in any particular way). Unlike in the previous examples, the utterance does inform your hearer. Specifically, you are on record as stating that, in your opinion, the temperature is relatively high. But this hardly seems to be the primary communicative purpose. Mainly, you are just venting. Like with *Ouch!*, you may even say this when you're alone.

Sadock's final example, *I bet $5*, demonstrates a situation where emotion is not communicated (indeed, should not be, for it might undermine your purpose), but the informative and social aspects are there. If you and a friend have a disagreement about whether or not Angelina Jolie really drank Billy Bob Thornton's blood, you may say, "I bet $5." In this case, the words do not communicate that you believe Jolie drank Billy Bob's blood; instead, they communicate you are willing to lose $5 if she did not. You can say without contradiction, "I'll bet

---

[2] Sadock calls these "deficient speech acts"; however, he does not intend any judgment with the term, only that the acts do not centrally involve all three functional aspects.

you $5 that Utah will beat BYU, but I'm pretty sure Utah will lose."[3] Compare this to the contradictory statement, "Utah will beat BYU, but I'm pretty sure Utah will lose." The primary aspect of *I bet ____* is social. If, in the original example, your hearer takes the bet, $5 is at stake: If Jolie did not drink Billy Bob's blood, you owe your friend the money, but if she did, then your friend owes you.

3. THE THREE FUNCTIONS AT THE LEVEL OF WORDS

In this section, I argue that we need to expand our understanding of **meaning** to include these three aspects. Many scholars describe informative meaning as **denotative** and group emotional and social as **connotative**. We usually think of denotative meaning as objective and connotative meaning as subjective—denotative as clear and connotative as murky. "Connotation is not specific or well-defined relative to denotation" (Jay 1992, 10). But in my opinion this is a bias. I see no reason that linguists can't rigorously define emotional meaning and social meaning.

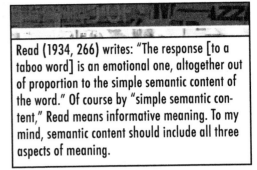

Read (1934, 266) writes: "The response [to a taboo word] is an emotional one, altogether out of proportion to the simple semantic content of the word." Of course by "simple semantic content," Read means informative meaning. To my mind, semantic content should include all three aspects of meaning.

3.1 Informative Meaning

Informative meaning is what most people think of when they think of meaning. It's what dictionaries focus on—though a good dictionary does touch on emotional and social aspects of meaning, as well. In Chapter 3, when we discussed mention qua meaning, we were speaking primarily of informative meaning: for example, when we say that *shit* means 'feces', we're saying that the informative meaning of *shit* is equivalent to the informative meaning of *feces*.[4]

Informative meaning is what we're capturing in our swearing taxonomy in Chapter 1 when we include the category propositional. A proposition is defined by linguists as any statement that can be evaluated according to whether it's true or false.[5] For example, (1) is a true statement, while (2) is a false statement.

1. *The Blues Brothers* is one of the funniest movies ever made.
2. *The Blues Brothers* sucks.

When people swear propositionally, they use taboo words informatively. That is, they use taboo words to add to the larger proposition being expressed, as in (3) and (4).

3. Grant and Gertrude have never fucked.
4. There is piss all over the floor of the men's restroom.

All taboo words have non-taboo counterparts with the same informative meaning (see Chapter 6).

Just as there are "defective" utterances that lack one or more of the functional aspects of communication, there are "defective" words that lack one or more of the three aspects of meaning. We've seen this with *hi* (which lacks any emotional or informative meaning) and *ouch* (which lacks any social or informative meaning), but it's also true of words like *box, plate,* and *crease,* which have little to no social meaning nor emotional meaning.

---

[3] Adapted from an example in Sadock (1994:400).

[4] There are exceptions to this. For example when discussing swear words from foreign languages, sometimes we gloss them according to their informative meaning and sometimes according to their social and emotional meanings. For example, we could say that the Hungarian word *kurva* means 'whore', and that would be true of its informative meaning, but we could also say that *kurva* means 'fucking', and that would be true of its social and emotional meanings.

[5] Although questions and commands cannot be evaluated for truth or falsity, we still say that they're propositional; they have embedded propositions. Thus (i) embeds the proposition (ii) in order to query about its truth value, and (iii) embeds the proposition (iv) in order to request that it be made true.

  i   Do bears crap in the woods?
  ii Bears crap in the woods.
  iii Go crap in the woods.
  iv. You are going to crap in the woods.

3.2 Emotional Meaning

In recent years, more and more researchers have investigated the emotional side of meaning. Potts (2007) has proposed a formal framework for describing the emotional meaning of taboo words (see Chapter 14 for discussion of Potts' theory). Many studies on second language acquisition have looked at the differences between native speakers and non-native speakers with respect to the emotional meaning of words, especially taboo words (see Chapter 11). And many psycholinguistic studies have focused on how we process emotional meaning (see Chapter 12).

We've already established that taboo words carry more emotional meaning than other words. This is largely what makes them special. In Chapter 1, we classified a type of swearing as emotive. We often adapt taboo words solely for the purpose of emoting. In such cases, we bleach the words of their informative meaning and use them purely for the emotional meaning.

Indeed, Jay (2000) argues that the primary function of swear words is to express emotions. When polite people want to express emotion, they might say, "Boy!", as in Sadock's example about the heat in Section 2. Apparently, I don't know many polite people. Most people I know would say something stronger, more taboo, as in (5–8).

When we speak of emotional meaning, we mean the visceral response we have to words. We don't mean words whose informative meanings refer to emotions, such as *happy, sad, elated, discombobulated, surprised, angry,* etc. Of course, we could still say that these words carry emotional meaning, in that we have a positive response to a word like *joy* and a negative response to a word like *furious.*

"The fact is that swearing is an instrument, which like any other can only be effectively played when it is sustained by a sufficient amount of feeling" (Montagu 1967, 68).

5. Jesus, it's hot!

6. Christ, it's hot!

7. Holy shit, it's hot!

8. Fuck, it's hot!

I also have acquaintances who would say (9).

9. Oh my heck, it's hot!

For these acquaintances, *oh my heck* is about as strong a term as they are willing to use, so, I would argue, it fulfills the same need as (5–8) for my other acquaintances.

And yes, swearing is a need. Humans have strong emotions, which sometimes need to be released. Physical violence is one way of releasing emotions. Swearing is another. In fact, as discussed in Chapter 3 (and discussed further in Chapter 12), taboo words are more closely associated with the emotion centers in the brain than any other words.

As we'll see in Chapter 12, swearing may act as a pain regulator. Let's return to an example where your thumb gets hurt, only this time instead of your friend stepping on it, as in Section 2, imagine you hit it with a hammer. What would you say? You could say "Ouch!" as we saw before. But come on, are you so polite that you would only say, "Ouch!"? Seriously? What if it really hurt? Most people would choose something stronger. Here's a list of likely responses, from weak to strong; you can expand it to include your favorites, placing them where you think they fit on the scale.

10. Dang it!

11. Son of a . . . [grunted stifle of what follows]

12. Aw fer . . . [grunted stifle of what follows]

13. Fudge!

14. Damn it!

15. Son of a bitch!

16. Aw fer fuck's sake!

17. Shit!

18. Son of fucking bitch!

19. Fuck!

These can be combined together in any variety of ways, and individual expressions can be repeated.

We swear for all sorts of reasons: discomfort, fear, pain, anger, frustration. We usually associate swearing with negative emotions, but any emotion if it's strong enough can trigger swearing: surprise, joy, pleasure (both physical and mental). Goffman (1978) coined the term **response cry** for any utterance—taboo or not—that is a response to an emotional trigger.

Goffman was interested in response cries because they seem to violate a basic principle of language use: communication requires at least two people. Generally, when somebody is speaking, we expect that i) they are talking to somebody, or ii) they are crazy.

Some years ago, I had an apartment across the street from a homeless shelter. As you can imagine, a lot of strange people walked by my front door. One afternoon, I was preparing a snack in my kitchen when I heard a very loud voice, so loud I thought the person must have a megaphone. I couldn't make out what he was saying, and I wondered if it were a rally or something. I went out to my front porch and saw a man, clearly homeless. He had no megaphone, but

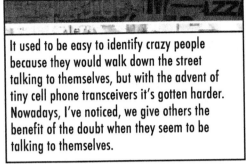

It used to be easy to identify crazy people because they would walk down the street talking to themselves, but with the advent of tiny cell phone transceivers it's gotten harder. Nowadays, I've noticed, we give others the benefit of the doubt when they seem to be talking to themselves.

he did have impressive lung power. Although nothing he said stuck in my memory, I recall that it was as though I were listening to one side of a phone conversation; the man would ask questions and pause for answers, then respond as though he himself had been asked a question. A short while later, the man was still pacing the parking lot in front of my porch carrying on his one-sided conversation, when two bicycle cops showed up. One of the cops tapped his shoulder, startling him. The cop, very sensibly, asked the man who he was talking to. The man responded with what struck me as a very sensible answer: "God." I wondered how the cop could fault him on this answer, but the cop was more clever than me; without missing a beat, he asked, "Why do you have to speak so loudly when talking to God?" The homeless man had no answer, and unfortunately this civil conversation devolved to the point that the police forced the man to the ground and cuffed him.

The point is: it's taboo to talk to ourselves. Nonetheless, there are times when it is perfectly appropriate to speak aloud without addressing anybody, namely with response cries. The exclamations in (5–19) are not addressed to anybody. We don't say things like (20) when we're frustrated, in pain, surprised, angry, happy, etc. In those cases, you say the stripped down form: "Fuck!"

20. Hey somebody, fuck!

Now, you may argue that (14) is actually addressed to God, seeing that we could elaborate on it as in (14').

14'. God damn it.

However, the prosody isn't right for this to be an address to God. Compare a prayer where God is actually addressed, as in (21).

21. God, give me the strength to bear the pain of my throbbing thumb.

Notice that in (21), there is a necessary pause after *God,* just as there would be anytime that you address somebody by name (e.g., "Grant, put your thumb here while I hit it with the hammer"). However, in (14') there is no pause. In fact, we pronounce *god damn* as if it were a compound word; it has the same prosody as *blackboard* ('a board on which teachers write with chalk') not *black board* ('a board which is black in color').[6] In Quang Phuc Dong's (1993) famous piece "English Sentences without Overt Grammatical Subject"[7], he argues that God could not be the addressee of *damn,* since you can say (22) (compare to (23), which is fine if addressed to Grant, but ungrammatical if addressed to Gertrude).

---

[6] A Google search yields 727,000 hits for "God damn it" and 257,000 hits for "Goddamn it."

[7] Quang Phuc Dong was the nom de plume of James McCawley. More on Quang Phuc Dong and McCawley's other pseudonym, Yuck Foo, in Chapter 9.

22. Damn God.

23. Defend Gertrude.

In Goffman's (1978) framework, not all response cries are taboo. Following, I describe the different sorts of response cries he posits:

- **The Transition Display.** Uttered when "[e]ntering or leaving what can be taken as a state of marked natural discomfort—wind, rain, heat, or cold . . ." (p. 801). For example, exiting a warm building on a cold day, one might say, "Brrr." Or entering an air-conditioned building on a hot day, one might say, "Ahh."

- **The Spill Cry.** "Spill cries are emitted to accompany our having, for a moment, lost guiding control of some feature of the world around us, including ourselves" (p. 801). When we trip, drop a glass, spill juice, enter the wrong restroom, etc., we often utter a cry, such as, *Oops!* (Goffman notes that we can also offer a sympathetic spill cry when somebody else loses "guiding control".)

- **The Threat Startle.** "Surprise and fear are stated . . . But the surprise or fear are very much under control—indeed nothing to be really concerned about" (p. 802). Such cries might be uttered when looking over a high cliff, spotting a spider, or considering a gruesome scene. *Yikes!* is a common way of expressing the threat startle. Goffman notes that this is a transformation into verbal form of how we might react to real danger; the threat startle is generally used after we have perceived that danger is not as imminent as we initially thought. As Goffman puts it, "A sort of overplaying occurs that covers any actual concern by extending, with obvious unseriousness, the expressed form which this concern would take" (p. 802).

- **Revulsion Sounds.** "[H]eard from a person who has by necessity or inadvertence come in contact with something contaminating" (p. 803). When you step in dog crap, you might say, "Eew" or "Yuck."

- **The Strain Grunt.** "Lifting or pushing something heavy, or wielding a sledgehammer with all our might, we emit a grunt attesting the presumed peak and consummation of our fully-extended exertion" (p. 803). This often takes the form of a non-linguistic grunt, though I have heard people using a more conventionalized form, such as *hup!*. The non-linguistic grunt, Goffman notes, is exemplified by "the vocal accompaniment we sometimes provide ourselves on passing a hard stool" (p. 804).

- **The Sexual Moan.** Need I describe this? (Watch *When Harry Met Sally* if you need an example.)

- **Floor Cues.** Rather than describe this, Goffman gives the following example: "A worker in a typing pool makes a mistake on a clean copy and emits an imprecation; this leads to, and apparently is designed to lead to, a colleague's query as to what went wrong" (p. 804). Floor cues can take the form of a gasp, a laugh, an "imprecation" (e.g., *Darn!*), or a statement of surprise (e.g., *Wow!*). Goffman casts these as an indirect way to begin a conversation where it might be awkward to do so directly (e.g., with a stranger or with somebody who is otherwise occupied); the floor cue invites the person to inquire about your situation, thereby officially beginning the conversation.

- **Audible Glee.** This is a way of vocally indicating pleasure. For example, saying "yum" when eating a fresh strawberry, saying "yippee" when getting some good news, or saying "ooh" when admiring a good-looking person.

Although, I agree with Goffman that we need to recognize response cries as a unique type of speech act, there are problems with how he describes them and with the list of response cries given. One of the exercises deals with one such problem. We'll come back to response cries in Chapter 14, as well.

All of the response cry types described could be expressed with a taboo word or phrase. In other words, exclamations are a sub-type of response cry. Like all response cries, exclamations are practically automatic. Jay (2000) distinguishes **automatic swearing** and **strategic swearing**. The former covers emotive swearing (especially exclamations, and to a lesser degree emphatics), and the latter covers propositional and invective swearing. Of course, exclamations aren't entirely unconscious since we're able to control to some degree what

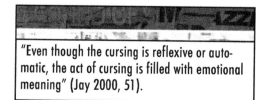

"Even though the cursing is reflexive or automatic, the act of cursing is filled with emotional meaning" (Jay 2000, 51).

comes out. For example, if a child is present when you hurt your thumb, you're more likely to choose one of the weaker of the response cries, while you're likely to choose a more taboo one in other environments.

Strategic swearing is more calculated, and it is usually embedded inside of a larger utterance. For example, consider (24–26).

24. This fucking thing popped up in my browser window and I don't know where it came from.
   (http://www.boingboing.net/2001/03/28/this-fucking-thing-p.html, accessed 7/24/08)

25. Jesus H. Christ on a popsicle stick, that's truly pathetic.
   (http://forums.mtbr.com/archive/index.php/t-86390.html, accessed 7/24/08)

26. Elliot Spitzer: You son of a bitch. Goddamn it, you broke my heart. Resign. And rot in hell. You stupid, hypocritical liar.
   (http://clydefitch.blogspot.com/2008/03/eliot-spitzer-you-son-of-bitch.html, accessed 7/24/08)

I think we can safely conclude that (24–26) are strategic uses of taboo words, seeing that exclamations are not typically typed. Although used strategically, the taboo words are still there to convey the writers' emotions. If we were to recast the sentences without taboo words, as in (24'–26'), we would not get the same sense of the writers' respective annoyance, astonishment, or apoplexy.

24' This thing popped up in my browser window and I don't know where it came from.

25' That's truly pathetic.

26' Elliot Spitzer: You broke my heart. Resign. And rot. You stupid, hypocritical liar.

Potts (2007) argues that pejoratives and name-calling also capitalize on the emotional meaning more than the informative meaning. So in (27–29), the slurs do not add to the informative meaning of the sentences; they point to the negative emotions the speaker has towards the referents (see Chapter 14 for more on this).

27. Out of my way, motherfucker.

28. This piece of shit cost me a hundred bucks.

29. Those whores wouldn't even give me the time of day.

In purely emotive uses of taboo words, they lose their informative meaning. Hughes (1991) sees this as a natural process in the development of swear words; he speaks of two simultaneous processes: **semantic weakening** and **emotive intensifying** (discussed more in Chapter 7). In our terms, semantic weakening is a bleaching of the informative meaning, and emotional strengthening is a capitalization on the emotional force of taboo words. When we use *shit* or *son of a bitch* as an exclamation, and when we use *fucking* or *damned* as an emphatic, we are not invoking their informative meaning. We aren't, at those moments, thinking of feces, Hades, fornication, or religious condemnation. Their non-taboo counterparts don't work as exclamations or emphatics because they lack the emotional meaning:

30. Oh feces!

31. Hades!

32. This is fornicating terrible!

33. That's some condemned good coffee.

3.3 Social Meaning

In Chapter 7, I argue that just as there are the processes of semantic weakening and emotional strengthening, there is the third process of **social stigmatizing**. Social stigmatizing is a process whereby words become taboo. My point is that tabooness is a social aspect of meaning. In Section 1 and 2, we discussed other social aspects of linguistic meaning, but when we focus on taboo words, it is the tabooness that primarily defines the social meaning of the terms.

Tabooness is a part of linguistic meaning, just as much as a word's denotation is. We discussed in Chapter 1 how, for any speech community, we can establish tabooness values for words. Granted, there will be variation. What is taboo in British English differs from what is taboo in American English (e.g., *bloody* and *fanny* are taboo in the UK, but not so much in the U.S.). And what is taboo in one community may differ from what is taboo in another. However, the same differences can be found with informative meaning: in Massachusetts, *milkshake* does not mean 'milkshake'—in Massachusetts English, *milkshake* means 'flavored milk', while *frappé* means 'milkshake'.

Nonetheless, when we look at a given speech community we find remarkable agreement on which words are taboo, as well as on which taboo words have higher tabooness and which have lower tabooness. In fall 2010, my Bad Words and Taboo Terms class conducted an in-class survey where they assigned tabooness values to eighteen taboo words. Here are the words in order from most taboo to least, followed by their average rating on a tabooness scale of 1–7:

1.	nigger	6.4	7.	homo	3.9	13.	shit	2.7
2.	cunt	5.8	8.	cum	3.5	14.	bastard	2.6
3.	spic	5.5	9.	bitch	3.3	15.	damn	2.1
4.	fuck	4.7	10.	cock	3.2	16.	piss	2.0
5.	fag	4.6	11.	honkey	2.9	17.	hell	1.7
6.	dyke	4.0	12.	tits	2.7	18.	crap	1.4

The students' ratings varied greatly; some consistently rating all words relatively high and some rating them all relatively low, but when we look at the list in terms of ranking, rather than raw tabooness ratings, we find a lot of agreement. The top four words and the bottom four words were remarkably consistent among the forty-four native English speakers in the class: only one student had a higher rating for one of the bottom four (*damn, piss, hell, crap*) than for one of the top four (*nigger, cunt, spic, fuck*).[8]

In the previous section, we discussed the role of emotional meaning in automatic swearing, such as exclamations. Social meaning doesn't play a large role in automatic swearing, but there is a large social component to strategic swearing. In (24–26), repeated here, the writers intentionally chose words that would be inappropriate in many social situations.

24. This fucking thing popped up in my browser window and I don't know where it came from.
    (http://www.boingboing.net/2001/03/28/this-fucking-thing-p.html, accessed 7/24/08)

25. Jesus H. Christ on a popsicle stick, that's truly pathetic.
    (http://forums.mtbr.com/archive/index.php/t-86390.html, accessed 7/24/08)

26. Elliot Spitzer: You son of a bitch. Goddamn it, you broke my heart. Resign. And rot in hell. You stupid, hypocritical liar.
    (http://clydefitch.blogspot.com/2008/03/eliot-spitzer-you-son-of-bitch.html, accessed 7/24/08)

This is most obvious with (26), which was Leonard Jacobs' blogged response to New York Governor Elliot Spitzer's sexual dalliances. In a typical political discussion, one is not expected to cuss. Because Jacobs transgressed what is socially appropriate—that is, violated a taboo—he was able to better convey his emotions. A glance at the comments on the blog confirms this; one reader wrote: "Dear Mr Jacobs, please tell me how you really feel." In another comment, we find that at least one reader was not as comfortable as Jacobs in transgressing the social expectations, writing of Spitzer, "What a flippin' tool."

The truth is, we don't always swear in order to communicate emotions. Let's consider a different sort of strategic use, one in which no strong emotions are conveyed.

34. You want to go get some shit to eat?

I heard (34) in 2006 as I was walking through the student union building at the University of Utah. I passed a trio of male undergraduates who were milling around, and one of them uttered the sentence. He said it casually, without any emotion.

---

[8] This particular student assigned a relatively low value of 2 to *cunt*. Otherwise, this student's ratings were similar to the majority.

Pause a moment to fully consider the meaning of *shit*. Under the informational aspect, it denotes 'feces'. Under the emotional aspect, it expresses strong negative emotion, (e.g., anger, surprise, disdain, dismay). And under the social aspect, it is a taboo word, proscribed in many situations, especially formal ones.

Now, I'm guessing that the guy who said (34) in the student union wasn't speaking literally, which is to say (34') is not an appropriate paraphrase of what he said.

34' 'Do you desire to obtain fecal matter for consumption?'

If he'd wanted to be literal, he could have as easily replaced *some shit* with words like *something, some food,* or, seeing that it was a student union cafeteria, *some barely edible calorie dispensers*. So why didn't he speak literally?

We'll return to this example in Chapter 14. For now, we can observe that a taboo word like *shit* is sometimes used purely for its social meaning. In (34), we've already concluded that *shit* was not used for its informative meaning, and the speaker's manner and voice did not suggest strong emotions. This, of course, only leaves social meaning. Swearing is sometimes used to build solidarity; speakers demonstrate how comfortable they feel with their hearers through casual swearing (see Chapter 13). By using *shit,* which is proscribed in formal situations, the guy is establishing (re-establishing) that their friendship is not in any way formal.[9]

Since we're talking about formality, we should bring up another aspect of social meaning: **register.** Register usually refers to the level of formality of an utterance. For example, (35) and (36) make the same request, but the second is more formal.

35. Hey, give me a hand, would you?

36. Excuse me, could you please help me?

But we can also say that register is part of the social meaning of words; some words are more formal and some less. This is easy to see with taboo words, which are on the informal side. Moreover, virtually all taboo words have a clinical, non-taboo synonym[10]: *piss* vs. *urine, cock* vs. *penis, pussy* vs. *vagina, spic* vs. *Latino, asshole* vs. *anus*. Part of our knowledge of these words is that the clinical, non-taboo terms are reserved for formal situations, such as doctor's visits, textbooks, news reports, etc. We return to register in Chapter 6.

4. CONCLUSION

In sum, although we usually think of the informative aspect as the most important function of language, there are two other aspects which play equally important, if less obvious, functions, namely social and emotional. One prominent theory states that language evolved primarily to fulfill a social function. But it's equally clear that emotional language plays a huge role in our lives.

I have argued that we need to recognize three aspects of linguistic meaning: informative, emotional, and social. Some words, such as *hi* or *ouch,* may lack any informative meaning, while many words lack emotional and social meaning (e.g., *table, walk, write*). Taboo words have all three aspects of meaning: they have an informative (propositional) meaning, usually synonymous with a clinical, non-taboo word; they have strong, generally negative, emotions attached to them; and they are socially stigmatized and forbidden (i.e., they are taboo). Because the emotional and social aspects of their meaning are relatively stronger than those of other words, we sometimes use taboo words solely to communicate emotional meaning and/or social meaning.

In this chapter, we have concentrated on the conventional meanings of expressions, examining what they contribute informationally, socially, or emotionally; we look in more detail at how we use these conventional meanings to communicate when we turn to pragmatics in Chapter 15.

---

[9] The guy may have used *shit* for other purposes beyond showing how comfortable he is with his friends. For example, you could argue that he wanted to make light of or diminish his suggestion that the group dine together, or he could have been commenting about the quality of the cafeteria's food. However, these purposes would take us beyond the three aspects of linguistic meaning and into the realm of pragmatics, the study of language use, which we discuss in Chapter 14.

[10] Synonyms are two words that share the same informative meaning (though not necessarily the same social or emotional meaning).

REFERENCES

Dunbar, Robin I.M. 1996. *Grooming, Gossip and the Evolution of Language.* London: Faber and Faber.

Goffman, Erving. 1978. Response Cries. *Language* 54(4): 787–815.

Hughes, Geoffrey. 1991. *Swearing: A Social History of Foul Language, Oaths, and Profanity in English.* Oxford: Blackwell.

Jay, Timothy. 1992. *Cursing in America: A Psycholinguistic Study of Dirty Language in the Courts, in the Movies, in the Schoolyards, and on the Streets.* Philadelphia: John Benjamins.

Jay, Timothy. 2000. *Why We Curse: A Neuro-Psycho-Social Theory of Speech.* Philadelphia: John Benjamins.

Montagu, Ashley. 1967. *The Anatomy of Swearing.* New York: The Macmillan Company.

Potts, Christopher. 2007. The Expressive Dimension. *Theoretical Linguistics,* 33(2):165–198.

Quang Phuc Dong. 1993. English Sentences without overt Grammatical Subject. In *Studies out in Left Field: Defamatory Essays Presented to James D. McCawley,* eds. A.M. Zwicky, P.H. Salus, R.I. Binnick, and A.L. Vanek, 3–10. Philadelphia: John Benjamins.

Read, Allen. 1934. An Obscenity Symbol. *American Speech* 19(4): 264–278.

Sadock, Jerrold. 1994. Toward a Grammatically Realistic Typology of Speech Acts. In *Foundations of Speech Act Theory: Philosophical and Linguistic Perspectives,* eds. S. L. Tsohatzidis, 393–406. London: Routledge.

1. Come up with "defective" speech acts that involve taboo words. In other words, come up with a) an act of swearing that is purely emotional and lacks any informative or social function, b) an act of swearing that is purely social and lacks any informative or emotional function, c) an act of swearing that is purely informative and lacks any social or emotional function, d) an act of swearing that is informative and social but lacks any emotional function, e) an act of swearing that is informative and emotional but lacks any social function, and f) an act of swearing that is social and emotional but lacks any informative function.

2. Goffman (1978: 800) states that response cries are not lexical items: ". . . RESPONSE CRIES, i.e. exclamatory interjections which are not full-fledged words." Given our earlier discussion of the functions of language, as well as our discussion of grammar and phonology, do you agree with him? What arguments could you give that at least certain response cries, such as *Oops!*, are full-fledged words? What about other response cries, such as grunts, moans, and the screams indicated in comic strips with "Aargh!"? And exclamations? When you shout "fuck" because you're frustrated, have you used a "full-fledged word"?

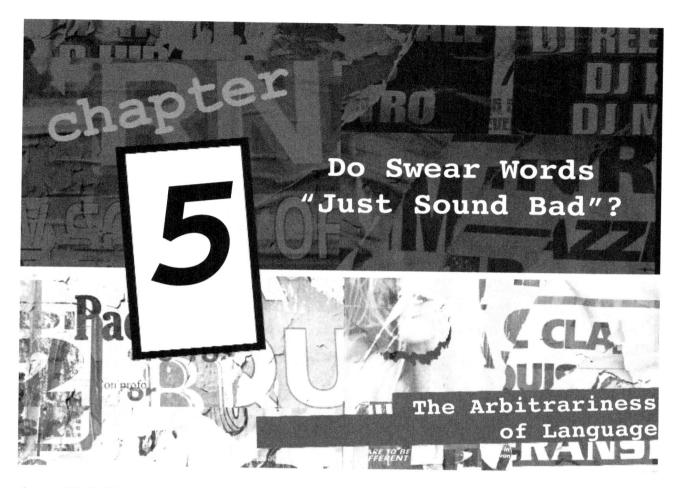

Do Swear Words
"Just Sound Bad"?

The Arbitrariness
of Language

1. INTRODUCTION

In this chapter, we talk about the sounds of language and how those sounds come to have meaning for us. We start by looking at how we make speech sounds, and then we talk about the relationship between sound and meaning.

2. SPEECH PRODUCTION

Say the word *fuck* ([fʌk]). Where do the sounds come from? The mouth, duh! Alright, smartass, where do they begin? To answer this, it might be better to start by thinking about what sound is. Simply put, sound is compressions in the air. Any compression needs a source. In the case of speech, the source is our lungs.

Lungs are like balloons—it takes more effort to put air in than to take air out. When we speak, we let air out of our lungs, but we don't release it all at once; if we did, we'd only get out one or two words per breath (think about trying to talk while running). So we control the flow, like you do with a balloon when you want it to make that farting noise.

Of course when you fart, it doesn't always sound the same. We usually think of a fart as producing a note of sorts, but there are also those hissing farts. If you can, let one go right now. (If you can't fart on command, just let out a sigh.) Hear that? What's it sound like? Not much, right? Just air rushing out. We call this **white noise**. Sound is, as we said a second ago, compressions in the air. These compressions are air waves. We can compare them to waves in water. Throw a rock in a pond, and you get a wave. Throw two rocks, and you get two waves that intersect and affect each other in a complex way. Throw in a whole handful of rocks and you get a random effect—no visible waves, just ripples all over the place. That's what white noise is: a whole bunch of sound waves with no discernible pattern to them.

As the air leaves your rectum there's no regular pattern to the sound waves. If the anal sphincter is open, then you get that sigh-like fart. However, if the sphincter is drawn tight, you get the note. You can do the same thing with air from the lungs; you can buzz your lips in a mouth fart (in polite society this is called a Bronx cheer or a raspberry). Trumpet players can change the pitch of their mouth farts from quite low to quite high. What's happening is the lips are brought close together as the air moves out; the air moving past the tightened lips causes them to flap, and this flapping creates a regular pattern in the air waves (a sound). The faster the lips flap, the higher the sound. This is the same process that happens when the anal sphincter flaps (farts)—talented people can control the pitch on farts, too.

This brings us back to speech. People don't often use mouth farts as speech sounds (never in English), and we never use our anus. Instead, we use a part of our body especially adapted to this purpose, namely the **vocal folds.**[1] The vocal folds are a part of the larynx; they're a mass of muscles that can come together or spread apart (like the lips and the sphincter). You can get a sense of this if you cough. When the cough begins, your vocal folds are fully closed, and when they're released, the air rushes out. If we draw them together, without fully closing them, they flap. See Figure 5.1 for a really lousy drawing of a cross-section of a person's head showing where all the speech organs are.

Put your fingers on your larynx (halfway down the front of your neck). Let out a long sigh. You shouldn't feel anything. Now say *uh* ([ʌ]). Feel that? Your vocal folds are vibrating. Keep your fingers on your lar-

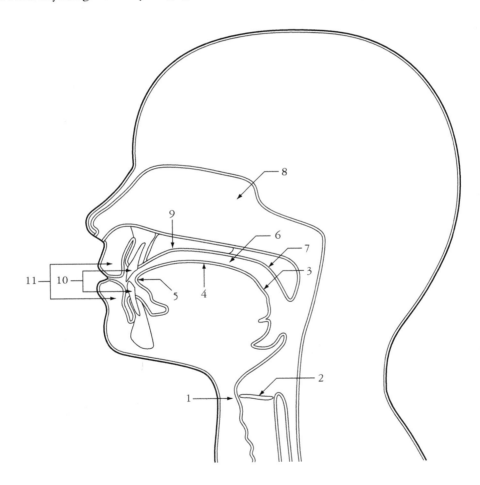

1. Larynx	5. Tip of Tongue	9. Hard Palate
2. Vocal Folds	6. Oral Cavity	10. Teeth
3. Back of Tongue	7. Velum (Soft Palate)	11. Lips
4. Blade of Tongue	8. Nasal Cavity	

FIGURE 5.1 *Speech Organs*

---

[1] These are often referred to as vocal chords; however, folds is more descriptively adequate.

ynx. Now say [fʌk]. Say it slowly; really draw it out. At the beginning, while you're on [f], there's no vibration, but then you hit [ʌ] and it starts vibrating. Now say [fʌk] with a really deep, low voice in your best Barry White imitation. Then say it in a Michael Jackson voice. Feel the difference in vibration?

The vocal folds are used for all vowels and many consonants. If the vocal folds vibrate when a sound is articulated, we call it a **voiced** sound. All other sounds (like [f] and [k], for example) are **voiceless**. But voicing isn't the only way we can manipulate the air leaving the lungs. We can also use our tongues, our lips, and even our velums (see Figure 5.1).

Vowels don't all sound the same, right? But it's not the pitch that makes the difference. It's the quality. Imagine a piano, a trumpet, and a saxophone all playing the same note, say C#. The pitch is identical, but they sound different. The difference is the quality.[2] We change the quality of speech sounds by where we position our tongue and our lips. [ʌ] is a neutral sound in that your lips are relaxed and so is your tongue. Say *nuts* [nʌts]. Take stock of where the tongue is. Now say *knots* [nats]. The tongue has changed position. Now say *gnats* [næts]. Again the tongue has changed position. Now just say the vowel sounds. Start with [æ]; then, without stopping, move your tongue to [ʌ]; and, finally, move to [a]. Feel how the tongue moves progressively further back?

We can also move the tongue higher or lower. Say *skeet* [skit], *skate* [sket], and *scat* [skæt]. Then move from [i] to [e] to [æ]. Feel it?

Finally, consider the lips. What do you say when you have your picture taken? "Cheese," right? That's because your lips are spread when you say the [i] sound, like a smile. Notice you don't say "Choose." If you did, you'd look like you were making a kiss not a smile.

With the consonants, we have all sorts of things we can do. We can momentarily stop the air from moving, as we do with [p,b,t,d,k,g]. Or we can make a tight opening as with [f,v,s,z]. We make these full or partial closures either with our lips or with our tongues. Where we place our tongues (against the teeth, the hard palate, or the velum) determines the sound. Also notice that all of these sounds come in pairs (e.g., [p,b], [s,z]), one voiceless, the other voiced.

The velum can also move up and down. The velum moves down when you breathe out of your nose, and it moves up when you breathe out of your mouth. When the velum is up, the nasal cavity is blocked, so air can't get out that way. Most of our speech sounds are made with a partially closed nasal cavity. If you talk with it fully closed, you'll sound like Sylvester Stallone, and if you talk with it more than slightly open, you'll sound like Woody Allen.

Some speech sounds require a fully open nasal cavity, namely [m,n,ŋ]; we call these **nasals**. When you make these sounds, your tongue is in the same position as the voiced stops [b,d,g], respec-

> My mom was the director of a daycare center for many years. One day during free-play, she found a young boy pointing at the ground, saying, "Shit! Shit! Shit! Shit!" She asked what he was doing, and he told her, "I'm teaching my pet shnake to shit."

tively. The difference is that with [b,d,g] the nasal cavity is closed, while with [m,n,ŋ] it's open. You can see this by saying *come* [kʌm]. Draw out the [m], and while you are saying it, pinch your nostrils closed. The sound stops, right? When you have a bad cold, the word *funk* [fʌŋk] comes out sounding like *fuck* because the nasal cavity is all filled up with snot.

3.   THE ARBITRARINESS OF LANGUAGE

I get it a lot when I mention I'm an expert on swearing: Are some words just made to be swear words?[3] What they mean: *fuck* and *shit* and *piss* and *fag* just sound like they ought to be bad words. Or they might even mean: *cunt* has such an ugly sound, it was just made to be a bad word.

You've probably already guessed how I respond to this—but I'll say it anyway because this is important, really important. Sounds are just sounds. The sounds of a word are arbitrarily related to its meaning. What this means: there's nothing special about the combination of the sounds in *man* ([mæn]), for example, that points us toward an adult human with a penis, nor is there anything about the sounds in *woman* ([wʊmən]) that point us toward an adult human with a vagina. [fʌk] could have been associated with 'gelatinous dessert' and [dʒɛlo] with

---

[2] I imagine there are quality differences with farts, too—that is, with regard to sound, not smell. Different shaped people will presumably produce different sounding farts. I'm no expert on farts, but I think this is correct.

[3] I also get some funny looks.

'sexual intercourse'.[4] It is a convention that the sounds in [kʌnt] are considered naughty in isolation but not when combined with [ri], as in *country*. (I once made the mistake of asking a fraternity member which "frat" he belonged to. He told me, "We never call our fraternity a frat because we would never call our country a cunt.")

Now, some people have a hard time accepting that there's no natural connection between sound and meaning. In fact, there are people who suffer from a mental disorder which makes it impossible for them to accept that sounds are arbitrarily associated with meanings. As mental disorders go, this is a relatively benign one. I've encountered the writings[5] of several people who seem to suffer from the disorder, and most seem functional, if obsessed. In one case I know of, however, the sufferer was clearly insane. This man sent two long manuscripts to the Linguistics Department at the University of Chicago. His mission in life was apparently to uncover the hidden meaning of every human speech sound. That is, he would choose a sound, say [k], and investigate every word that had that sound in order to determine what single meaning the sound contributed to the words. As you can imagine, this would be a daunting task to do for just one language; however, this man was raised in Canada by Estonian parents, so he spoke English and Estonian equally fluently, making his task monumentally more complicated. When I say he was insane, I'm serious: in one of his manuscripts, which was clearly produced on a typewriter, he mentions his computer; a few pages later he describes how he built the computer: he took an old pot, filled it with rusty nails, and urinated in it.

Did this Estonian-Canadian man go insane because he couldn't accept the arbitrariness of words? Who knows? But I wouldn't take any chances if I were you. So please believe me, the sounds of a word are only connected to its meaning through an arbitrary convention. This is a basic tenet of modern linguistics that dates back to early twentieth-century lectures by Ferdinand de Saussure (de Saussure 1966). Saussure argued that this arbitrariness was a defining characteristic of human language and that every word (or sign) of a language had two parts: a signifier and a signified. The signifier is the sound-form and the signified is the meaning (see Figure 5.2[6]).

> A **convention** is a societal agreement or understanding (not necessarily conscious). Conventions are arbitrary because society could have come to a different understanding. Take traffic signs, for example. There's nothing special about red that means stop—it could have been yellow. A triangle could have been used for stop signs, and an octagon for yield signs.

> "*Shit*, and all other words that we may label as bad 'language,' are innocuous in the sense that nothing particularly distinguishes them as words. They are not peculiarly lengthy. They are not peculiarly short. The phonology of the words is unremarkable. While it might be tempting to assume that swear words are linked to 'guttural' or some other set of sounds we may in some way impressionistically label as 'unpleasant,' the fact of the matter is that the sounds in a word such as *shit* seem not more unusual, and combine together in ways no more interesting, than those in *shot, ship* or *sit*."
>
> (McEnery 2006, 1)

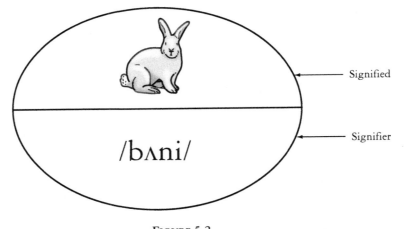

FIGURE 5.2
Signified and signifier of bunny

---

[4] In which case, finger fuck would be a dessert and finger jelloing would be a sex act.

[5] *Rantings* may be a better word.

[6] I considered representing *fuck* but had troubles finding clip art for the signified part.

Both these parts, the signifier and signified, are essential for somebody to know a word. However, language is an arbitrary sign system, meaning the signifier and signified are united purely through a linguistic convention, not through any extra-linguistic connection. This goes for *bunny* as much as it does for *fuck, shit, cunt, nigger, spic, fag, cracker, piss, zounds,* or *bugger.*

4. CONCLUSION

In sum, we've seen how speech sounds are produced in our vocal tract. And we've seen that the sounds themselves have no meaning—meaning comes from a convention that associates a string of sounds (a signifier) with a meaning (a signified).

REFERENCES

de Saussure, Ferdinand. 1966. *Course in General Linguistics.* New York: McGraw-Hill.

McEnery, Anthony. 2006. *Swearing in English: Bad Language, Purity and Power from 1586 to the present.* New York: Routledge.

The Dirty Details

1. INTRODUCTORY JOKE

I remember a party, back when I was a young man, when a group of us fellows and gals were sitting around telling jokes. Some of the jokes were a little dirty, but it was all in the spirit of fun and everyone joined in. Everyone, that is, except for one fellow who'd been silent the whole while. We urged him to participate, but he declined saying the only joke he knew contained words which he was too embarrassed to voice in mixed company. We—including the young women present—requested he overcome his shyness, and contribute to the general merriment. Again he expressed his timidness . . . Finally, he agreed to tell his joke, but only on this condition: when he got to the 'f' word he would say the number 1 instead of the word itself. When he got to the 'c' word he would say the number 2.

"Okay," we agreed.

"Well, it goes like this: there were a couple of French cocksuckers walking down the street . . ."

(Wing 1988, 261–262)

2. X-PHEMISMS

First, let's get something straight: the X in **X-phemism** is not the same X you see associated with certain movies. The X in X-phemism is like a mathematical variable, where X stands in for *eu-, dys-, ortho-,* or *faux-*.[1] Okay, I just wanted to make that clear.

---

[1] Mathematically, X ∈ {*eu-, dys-, ortho-, faux-*}.

The place to start is with some terms. In most of the linguistic literature, the X stands in for either *eu-* or *dys-*, which is to say there are **euphemisms** and **dysphemisms**. Allan and Burridge (2006) add another item to the set, *ortho-*, giving us **orthophemism**. And I've added yet another item, *faux-*, giving us **fauxphemism**. Breaking the terms down into morphemes can be useful here. Let's go from right to left. The first morpheme, *-ism*, I trust you're familiar with; it doesn't have any real meaning, but functions to turn an abstract act or concept into something more concrete (e.g., *terror ~ terrorism; active ~ activism; true ~ truism*). The second morpheme, *-phem*, comes from Greek for 'speech' or 'speak' (e.g., *blaspheme* 'evil speaking', *tachyphemia* 'rapid speech', *aphemia* 'no speech'). The next morpheme, *eu-*, means 'good' (e.g., *euphonic* 'good sounding', *eufunctional* 'good functioning', *eupepsia* 'good digestion', *eudemon* 'good angel'), giving us *euphemism*, literally 'good speech'. The next morpheme, *dys-*, means 'bad' (e.g., *dysphonic*

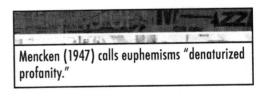

Mencken (1947) calls euphemisms "denaturized profanity."

'bad sounding', *dysfunctional* 'bad functioning', *dyspepsia* 'bad digestion', *dysentery* 'bad bowels'), giving us *dysphemism*, literally 'bad speech'. Our next morpheme, *ortho-*, means 'straight' or 'correct' (e.g., *orthodontics* 'teeth straightening', *orthogonal* 'straight angle', *orthodox* 'correct opinion', *orthography* 'correct spelling'), giving us *orthophemism*, literally 'straight speech'. Our final morpheme, *faux-*, means 'false' (e.g., *faux fur* 'false fur', *faux-pas* 'false step', *fauxnaif* 'false innocence'), giving us *fauxphemism*, literally 'false speech'.

So much for etymologies. What do the terms actually represent? We'll get at some definitions for the first three in Section 3, and we'll save fauxphemisms for Section 6. For now, let's just start with some examples. Allan and Burridge (2006) give us the following table contrasting orthophemisms, euphemisms, and dysphemisms:

TABLE 6.1		
Contrasting X-phemisms (adapted from Allan and Burridge 2006, 32)		
Orthophemism	*Euphemism*	*Dysphemism*
feces	poo	shit
toilet	loo	shithouse
menstruate	have a period	bleed
my vagina	my bits	my cunt
Jesus	Lord	Christ! {profanity}

Intuitively, I think we can see the difference between these terms. The orthophemisms are "official" terms, the euphemisms are "soft" or "gentle" terms, and dysphemisms are "bad" terms.

In the examples given in Table 6.1, the euphemisms exist primarily in order to avoid saying a taboo word. However, euphemism is often applied to any sort of substitution. For example, we see this in politics, where more palatable words replace words that are problematic for one reason or another: *pro-life* vs. *anti-abortion; pro-choice* vs. *pro-abortion; collateral damage* vs. *civilian casualties* vs. *innocent deaths; progressive* vs. *liberal*; etc.

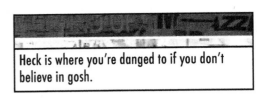

Heck is where you're danged to if you don't believe in gosh.

Another realm where we often speak of euphemisms is with job titles: Mencken (1947) lists some euphemisms that were coined during the first decades of the twentieth century: *mortician* for *undertaker*, *realtor* for *real estate agent*, *electrologist* for *electrical contractor*, *aisle manager* for *floor-walker*, *beautician* for *hair-dresser*, *exterminating engineer* for *rat-catcher*. Some of these, as you can observe for yourself, took, and some didn't. Mencken (1947, 287) was particularly amused by the euphemisms surrounding the business of funerals:

> *Mortician*, of course, was suggested by *physician*, for undertakers naturally admire and like to pal with the resurrection men, and there was a time when some of them called themselves *embalming surgeons*. A *mortician* never handles a *corpse*; he *prepares* a *body* or a *patient*. This business is carried on in a *preparation room* or *operating-room*, and when it is achieved the patient is put into a *casket* and stored in a *reposing-room* or *slumber-room* of a *funeral-home*.

We should be interested in euphemisms that exist in the absence of a truly taboo term and substitute instead for an orthophemism because they tell us what concepts and topics are taboo in our society, even when there are no taboo words for the concepts. Death, as we've already observed, is a taboo topic. Politics is too. And, as we see from Mencken's discussion, even jobs have taboos around them, probably because of associated taboos (sex, death, dirt, or money). We can often identify where taboos exist in a culture by where euphemisms exist.

Nonetheless, in this chapter, we will limit our scope to how X-phemisms and taboo words interact, mostly ignoring those areas where there are euphemisms and orthophemisms in the absence of taboo words. In Section 3, we compare two approaches to defining X-phemisms, ultimately settling on an approach that captures the advantages of both. In Section 4, we look at the strategies used to create euphemisms. In Section 5, we explore why people use euphemistic language. And, in Section 6, we look at an odd sort of construction, fauxphemisms, that hints at taboo words without technically producing them.

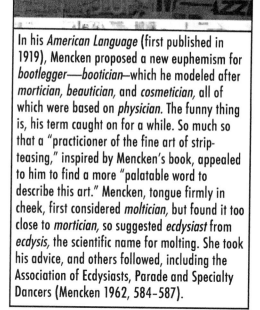

In his *American Language* (first published in 1919), Mencken proposed a new euphemism for *bootlegger—bootician*—which he modeled after *mortician, beautician,* and *cosmetician,* all of which were based on *physician*. The funny thing is, his term caught on for a while. So much so that a "practicioner of the fine art of strip-teasing," inspired by Mencken's book, appealed to him to find a more "palatable word to describe this art." Mencken, tongue firmly in cheek, first considered *moltician,* but found it too close to *mortician,* so suggested *ecdysiast* from *ecdysis,* the scientific name for molting. She took his advice, and others followed, including the Association of Ecdysiasts, Parade and Specialty Dancers (Mencken 1962, 584-587).

3. PROPOSED DEFINITIONS

Many definitions have been proposed for euphemisms. Casas Gómez (2009) divides the definitions into two main types: linguistic definitions and extralinguistic definitions (which mostly look at the psychological motivation for euphemisms). Given my bent, it's not surprising that we focus in this book on linguistic definitions. Casas Gómez goes on to argue that there are two types of linguistic definitions: **semantic** (see Chapter 2) and **pragmatic** (see Chapter 14). The semantic definitions focus on the meaning of euphemisms as lexical items absent any context, while the pragmatic definitions focus on the use of euphemisms in a particular context. Both of these approaches have merits, but we need to distinguish between them. Just as in Chapter 1, where we distinguished between types of taboo words (lexical items) and types of swearing (use of taboo words), we need to distinguish between euphemisms, dysphemisms, and orthophemisms as classes of lexical items and **euphemistic** and **dysphemistic utterances** as classes of language use.

3.1 *Semantic Definitions*

Semantic definitions focus on the qualities of euphemisms as words, specifically on the informative, social, and emotional meaning. However, as if there weren't already enough confusion, we find that even within the semantic definitions there is conflict between whether we should think of euphemism and dysphemism as classes of words or as processes. Casas Gómez prefers to use *euphemism* to refer to a process and *euphemistic substitutes* to refer to the words. We can see the process vs. word debate as a question of whether we look at the phenomenon from the point of view of grammar or lexicon (see Chapter 2). If it's a process, then it's a set of rules, and rules belong to the grammar. If it's a word, then it belongs to the lexicon. In the end, we will define euphemism as a term for a word, not for a process (cf. section 3.3.2).

Let's begin with process-based definitions. Casas Gómez (2009, 732) summarizes this approach as follows: "euphemism is defined, in principle, as the linguistic process which, by means of associative formal or semantic resources, achieves the lexical neutralization of the prohibited word." In other words, we have certain linguistic rules that allow us to associate a non-taboo form with a taboo word, and these rules make up a process which we call "euphemism."

Similarly, Crespo Fernández (2006, 96) describes euphemism as "the semantic or formal process by which the taboo is stripped of its most explicit or obscene overtones" and dysphemism as "the process whereby the most pejorative traits of the taboo are highlighted with an offensive aim to the addressee or to the concept itself." Again, euphemism is seen as the process that allows us to substitute a non-taboo form for an alternative taboo form.

Dysphemism, on the other hand, is seen as the opposite sort of process where a taboo form is willfully substituted for an alternative that is less taboo.

When people talk about euphemisms in common parlance, they're talking about words, not rules. For that reason alone, a lexicon-based approach seems better to me. Jay (2000, 128) gives a straightforward definition along these lines: "Euphemisms are expressions that are substituted for offensive or taboo expressions." This is similar to the definition I propose in Section 3.3.2. Of course, defining the term lexically does not preclude us from looking at the processes that create euphemisms; in Section 4 we look at such processes.

3.2 *Pragmatic Definitions*

Pragmatic definitions of euphemism, dysphemism, and orthophemism see the terms as contextual. That is, words themselves are not euphemisms, dysphemisms, or orthophemisms, only uses of the words. As Allan and Burridge (1991, 28) put it, being a euphemism or a dysphemism "is not necessarily a property of the word itself, but of the way it is used." According to pragmatic approaches, we can only determine if an utterance of a term makes it a euphemism once we know who it was said by, who it was said to, where it was said, when it was said, how it was said, why it was said, etc. Many pragmatic definitions appeal to whether the use of the term is considered polite or offensive.

It turns out the process vs. word debate also exists for pragmatic definitions. Ayto (1993, 1) defines a euphemism as a "set of communicative strategies we have evolved to refer to a topic under a taboo. . . ." And Read (1977, 14) refers to a dysphemism as a "rhetorical device of speaking ill of a thing . . ." Both "communicative strategies" and "rhetorical device" refer to processes not words. However, when we're in the realm of language use (pragmatics) we don't usually speak of linguistic rules, which we reserve for discussions of grammar.

Most pragmatic definitions look at the words themselves, not the processes.[2] For example, Lechado García (2000, 14) defines euphemism as, "Any word or expression that replaces another, which, for a number of reasons, appears inappropriate to the speaker and to the hearer in a given context" (quoted in Casas Gómez 2009, 732). Warren (1992, 135) says that a term is a euphemism "if the interpreter perceives the use of [the] word or expression as evidence of a wish on the part of the speaker to denote some sensitive phenomenon in a tactful and/or veiled manner."

Of the scholars who have given pragmatic definitions for euphemism, dysphemism, and orthophemism, the most prominent are Keith Allan and Kate Burridge. Following, I'll list the various definitions they've given for the terms, and then we will discuss their approach in some depth.

- [W]e can . . . describe euphemism as 'expression that seeks to avoid being offensive.' (Allan & Burridge 1991, 3)
- A **euphemism** is used as an alternative to a dispreferred expression, in order to avoid possible loss of face: either one's own face or, through giving offense, that of the audience, or of some third party. (Allan & Burridge 1991, 11)
- Euphemisms are alternatives to expressions that, for one reason or another, have too many negative connotations to felicitously execute Speakers' particular communicative intention in a given context. (Allan & Burridge 1991, 26)
- Dysphemism is, roughly speaking, the contrary of euphemism. (Allan & Burridge 1991, 3)
- A **dysphemism** is an expression with connotations that are offensive either about the denotatum or to the audience, or both, and it is substituted for a neutral or euphemistic expression for just that reason. (Allan & Burridge 1991, 26)
- [A] **dysphemism** is a word or phrase with connotations that are offensive either about the denotatum and/or to people addressed or overhearing the utterance. (Allan and Burridge 2006, 31)
- The dysphemism is tabooed as the impolite choice . . . ; it is the expression most likely to be deemed offensive. (Allan and Burridge 2006, 31)

---

[2] Exceptions to this are the approaches taken by Casas Gómez (2009) and Crespo Fernández (2007, cited in Casas Gómez 2009, 733).

- *Orthophemism* . . . is a term we have coined in order to account for direct or neutral expressions that are not sweet-sounding, evasive or overly polite (euphemistic), nor harsh, blunt or offensive (dysphemistic). (Allan and Burridge 2006, 29)
- **Orthophemisms** and **euphemisms** are words or phrases used as an alternative to a dispreferred expression. (Allan and Burridge 2006, 32)

In these definitions, there's terminology that is important to clarify. Terms that keep popping up: **dispreferred expression, denotatum, polite, offensive,** and **face.** Dispreferred expression is easy—we can just think of that, for our purposes at least, as a taboo word: "Dispreferred expressions might alternatively be dubbed tabooed expressions" (Allan & Burridge 2006, 32). The denotatum of a word is whatever the word is used to refer to (i.e., denote); in other words, when you use *shit* to mean 'feces', its denotatum is the actual yucky stuff that comes out of animals' rectums. For the final three terms of art—polite, offensive, and face—we need to get into theory a bit.

We use the words *polite, offensive,* and *face* frequently in conversation, but not in the same way Allan and Burridge use them in their definitions. For linguists, they belong to the technical terminology of a particular pragmatic theory called **Politeness Theory** (cf. Brown & Levinson 1987).

In our everyday speech, we sometimes use *polite* and *formal* interchangeably. But linguistically we should keep the concepts of **politeness** and **formality** separate. After all, while formal language is polite in formal situations, it can be impolite in informal situations—think about "yes, sir" and "yes ma'am," which sound courteous when said to some people, but rude and sarcastic when said to others. In Chapter 4, we introduced the term *register* to refer to levels of formality: a high register is formal, and a low register is informal.

Politeness is independent of register. Brown and Levinson (1987) describe politeness in terms of face, a person's public self-image. Under this account, a speaker's utterance is polite insofar as it preserves or increases the hearer's face. A person's face can be threatened in two ways: i) the person's independence is restricted; ii) the person perceives that people dislike him/her or things associated with him/her. Similarly, a person's face can be increased in two ways: i) the person's independence is increased; ii) the person perceives that people like him/her or things associated with him/her. An invitation or a compliment is inherently polite by this definition (cf. 1–2).

1. Have another piece of haggis.
2. Your haggis is divine.

In contrast, a request or an insult is inherently impolite (cf. 3–4).

3. Cook me a haggis.
4. This haggis is too salty.

Although a request or insult is inherently face-threatening, we have tactics to make the utterance itself polite. One strategy is based on the principle of an accountant's ledger; you can balance the face you've cost your hearer by adding to their face at the same time, leading to a wash. For this reason, we often kiss up to our hearer when making a request, or we compliment them before insulting them (see 5–6).

5. Cook me a haggis. You know how much I love it when you do.
6. Your cooking is virtually always divine, but this haggis is too salty.

A similar tactic is for the speaker to reduce their own face, which somehow balances out the threat to the hearer's face.

7. Cook me a haggis, and I'll do the washing up.
8. I wish I knew how to cook. I'm a nightmare in the kitchen compared to you. This haggis is too salty, though.

Another strategy, common in English, is to use extra words. It seems that the more words the speaker uses, the more the threat to the hearer's face is reduced.[3]

---

[3] This also applies to euphemisms and taboo words: Mencken (1962, 659) quotes Rupert Hughes as writing, "A long word is considered nice and a short word nasty."

9. Would you please, please, please cook me a haggis?

10. Don't take this the wrong way because it's only meant as constructive feedback, but I kind of think that maybe you used just a little more salt than was necessary when cooking this haggis.

Finally, we can say things indirectly to hide the threat to the hearer's face (cf. 11–15).

11. Boy, a haggis would really hit the spot.

12. If you're not too busy, it would be absolutely marvelous if you cooked a haggis.

13. It must be hard to get the seasoning right on a haggis, huh?

14. This haggis really makes me thirsty.

15. This haggis is fantastic, but, you know, I have hypertension.

This way we're not on the record with having threatened the hearer's face. If, when you say (11) or (12), the hearer makes a haggis, well, that's not your fault, right? You never asked him to. Or if your host understands (4) from (13), (14), or (15), you never actually said that her haggis was too salty, so you never actually said anything impolite.

What were we talking about? Oh yeah. All this about politeness is necessary to understand what Allan and Burridge mean by polite, offensive, and face. Face refers to a person's desire to be liked and to be independent; a polite utterance is one where the hearer's face is preserved; an offensive utterance is one where the hearer's face is threatened.

We can all agree that (16–20) are offensive.

16. You're a piece of shit.

17. You motherfucker.

18. Quit being a bitch.

19. Sometimes you can be such an asshole.

20. Numb nuts!

It's not hard to see how these utterances threaten a hearer's face—a slur is a direct attack on a person's desire to be liked, so (16–20) are offensive. Other invectives might simultaneously attack a person's desire to be liked and their desire not to be told what to do.

21. Go fuck yourself.

22. Bite me.

23. Suck my cock.

24. Eat shit and die.

With such invectives, the speaker has no intention to be polite and intends to offend the addressee.

Allan and Burridge would argue that exclamations—utterances not addressed to anybody (cf. Chapter 4)—can also threaten a hearer's face (e.g., 25–32).

25. Damn!

26. Fuck!

27. Shit!

28. Son of a bitch!

29. Shit-o-dearsky!

30. This fucking computer is a piece of shit!

31. Hell's bells!

32. Jesus H.[4] Christ on a popsicle stick!

---

[4] According to the film *Jesus Christ Vampire Hunter* the H. stands for Hector.

But how do these threaten a hearer's face when they're not even directed at anybody? In (25–32), the speakers probably did not intend to offend, yet the utterances may still do so. How? If we define offensive in terms of Politeness Theory, then it would seem that the utterances have to affect a hearer's face. It's hard to see how these exclamations could affect a person's desire to be liked, so that only leaves their desire for independence.

How does the utterance of a dysphemism restrict a hearer's freedom, as would be necessary for their face to be diminished? The obvious answer seems to be that they are unwillingly exposed to taboo words. This only makes sense if taboo words can somehow harm people. And this is precisely what people seem to think. Parents clamp their hands over their children's ears when bad words are in the vicinity in order to protect them. The Parents' Television Council's president, Tim Winter, complaining of an interview on the *Today* Show, said, "We condemn NBC for its arrogance in choosing not to bleep this profanity [*shit*], and for its arrogance in choosing not to apologize to its viewers, many of whom included children."[5] An actor in a Salt Lake production of *Sylvia* asked to have some of the taboo words removed from the script because she was uncomfortable speaking or hearing them (Brooke Bartlett pers. comm.). Parents might wash a child's mouth out for uttering a bad word. We seem to think the words can contaminate people; we even call the words "dirty." It's as though the words are so closely associated with their taboo denotata that they have become contaminated and can thereby contaminate anybody they "touch" (whether through the vocal or aural tracts).

Because the words are contaminated, it is an imposition to make people come in contact with them unwillingly. In the same way, it is considered offensive to have body odor, to fart, or to show people a stool sample—we're not supposed to subject people to things they don't want to be subjected to, and that includes words.

To come back to Allan and Burridge's definitions, we now see that the utterance of a word is a dysphemism if a hearer is offended by it, that is, if their face is threatened by the speaker's utterance of the word. Typically, then, dysphemisms are acts of swearing, as taboo words are the ones most likely to offend. On the other hand, when a speaker goes out of their way to avoid a dysphemism and choose an alternative word in order not to offend (i.e., to be polite or to preserve the hearer's face), then the utterance of the word is a euphemism or an orthophemism (we'll get into the difference between euphemisms and orthophemisms in Section 3.3.2). In all of these cases, the emphasis is on choice: in every context, the speaker chooses among several alternatives, and the polite alternatives (for that context) are euphemisms and the offensive alternatives (for that context) are dysphemisms. Putting this into practice, we can imagine scenarios and alternative utterances:

- Scenario A: Speaker drops a brick on her foot and says: a) "Damn!" b) "Dang!" c) "Ouch!"

- Scenario B: Speaker is eating dinner with friends and excuses himself saying: a) "I have to go take a piss." b) "I have to go see a man about a horse." c) "I have to go urinate."

- Scenario C. During an interview, the wife of the vice president describes the opposition's vice presidential candidate as: a) "that four million dollar bitch." b) "that four million dollar—I can't say it, but it rhymes with *rich*."[6] c) "that four million dollar witch."

- Scenario D. A journalist is reporting what Mel Gibson said and writes: a) "At one point during the phone call he used the word *nigger*." b) "At one point during the phone call he used the n-word." c) "At one point during the phone call he used a racial slur for African Americans."

- Scenario E. Speaker is complaining about the state of the apartment she shares with a roommate and says: a) "This place looks like shit!" b) "This place looks like crap!" c) "This place looks horrible!"

In principle, for each scenario the (a) utterance contains a dysphemism, the (b) utterance contains a euphemism, and the (c) utterance contains an orthophemism. However, since Allan and Burridge's definitions hinge on context, we need to know if the dysphemistic utterances are offensive and if the euphemistic and orthophemistic utterances are polite. And determining if they're offensive or polite depends largely on the hearer. In this day and age, few people would be offended by *damn* as uttered in Scenario A; therefore, unless the hearer happens to be, say, a fundamentalist Christian, this utterance of *damn* is not a dysphemism. Scenario B depends on the type of dinner, the type of friends, and the type of place where the dinner is being eaten; in some contexts (a) would be

---

[5] http://www.parentstv.org/PTC/news/release/2008/0911.asp (accessed 9/24/08).
[6] This is how Barbara Bush actually described Geraldine Ferraro during an interview in 1984—in her defense, she thought it was off the record. She also claimed that she'd meant *witch*.

preferred and (c) would be dispreferred because it's too stuffy, meaning that *piss* would be considered the euphemism and *urinate* the dysphemism.

I know. It seems odd to me, too. Intuitively, *piss* should always be the dysphemism and *urinate* the orthophemism. Yet, by the politeness-based definitions, we have to conclude that for some contexts things go topsy-turvy—what would ordinarily be a dysphemism becomes a euphemism and what is ordinarily a euphemism or an orthophemism becomes a dysphemism. This can even happen with slurs; for example, in the right context, with the right intonation, "you dipshit" could be a compliment[7], thus, by Allan and Burridge's account, not offensive, and therefore not dysphemistic.

In sum, if we follow Allan and Burridge's definitions of dysphemisms, euphemisms, and orthophemisms, we must conclude that the terms do not apply to words—only tokens of words. And Table 6.1, which lays out some examples of each and which I adapted from a table of theirs, is meaningless. Now, I don't want to make Allan and Burridge out to be stupid. They're clearly not. They've thought this through and are as aware of this conclusion as we are. In Section 3.3 we will look at their way out of this conundrum, and I will propose my own approach to X-phemisms.

3.3 Having Our Cake and Eating It Too: Separating the Semantic From the Pragmatic

One big advantage of the semantic definitions for X-phemisms is that they match our intuitions well. Intuitively, we sense that there's a difference between *feces, poo,* and *shit.* Allan and Burridge (2006, 34) provide the following tree diagram[8] (Figure 6.1) to show the differences.

The trouble is that lexical definitions tacitly imply use; a euphemism is understood relative to a dysphemism that a speaker chooses not to use. Choice is at the heart of the distinction between euphemism, dysphemism, and orthophemism—these represent words with the same denotatum but affect people differently depending on which we choose to use. Choice, of course, brings us into the realm of language use (pragmatics), and outside of grammar, where semantics resides. Furthermore, a lexical approach cannot account for novel examples of euphemisms—that is, when somebody creates a euphemistic substitute for a taboo word on the fly, it's brand new, so the expression can't be listed as a euphemism in the lexicon.

On the other hand, a purely pragmatic approach makes it impossible for us to apply the terminology to words. Figure 6.1 is unsustainable in a purely pragmatic approach. To my mind, it doesn't really make sense to

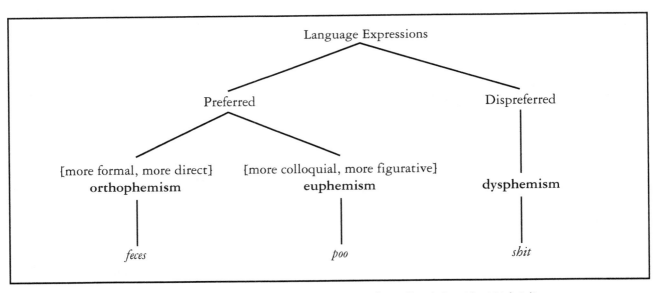

FIGURE 6.1   *Distinguishing X-phemisms (adapted from Allan & Burridge 2006, 34)*

---

[7] See Chapter 14 for more discussion of affectionate uses of slurs.
[8] Linguists like trees.

use the noun-forms at all under a pragmatic approach: under such an approach, there are no euphemisms, dysphemisms, or orthophemisms—only euphemistic, dysphemistic, and orthophemistic utterances.

What we need is an approach that captures the usage-based facts, while still allowing us to use the terms in a straightforward, intuitive fashion and still capturing the idea that euphemisms are a special category in the lexicon.

3.3.1 How Allan and Burridge Slice the Cake

Allan and Burridge recognize that by their approach we can't talk about euphemisms, dysphemisms, or orthophemisms in any abstract, context-independent way. And they recognize that this is counterintuitive. They are committed to their pragmatic approach to X-phemisms, but they also see the utility in being able to classify words according to which type of X-phemism they are. So they've devised an out, which they call **the middle-class politeness criterion** (MCPC).

Essentially, the MCPC sets up a default context by which to judge lexical items. This is the criterion by which words are judged in the abstract to determine how they should be classified:

> In order to be polite to a casual acquaintance of the opposite sex, in a formal situation, in a middle-class environment, one would normally be expected to use the euphemism or orthophemism rather than the dispreferred counterpart. The dispreferred counterpart would be a dysphemism. (Allan and Burridge 2006, 35)

If, in this context, a term is judged offensive in comparison to other terms, then the term is a dysphemism. Note what goes into this default context: it is formal, the speaker and hearer are not friends, they are of opposite sexes, and they are "in a middle-class environment." The first three aspects of the context ensure that speakers will be using a relatively high register and be relatively conscious of politeness. The last aspect establishes a cross-societal norm, ensuring that we can judge a language according to the standard dialect, not the numerous non-standard dialects. Note, too, that by saying "middle-class environment," they have left open the possibility that different communities will have different standards. What is a dysphemism according to England's middle-class may not be according to America's or Australia's. Moreover, what is a dysphemism in Utah, may not be in New York.

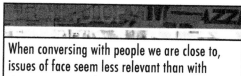

When conversing with people we are close to, issues of face seem less relevant than with strangers or casual acquaintances. For example, you can impose on close friends by asking them to help you move, but you wouldn't ask this of your new neighbors. And you can make fun of the zit on your significant other's nose, but you shouldn't do that on a blind date.

With the MCPC, Allan and Burridge can preserve their politeness approach to defining dysphemism, while still being able to use the noun form. An utterance is dysphemistic depending on the actual context in which it is used, independent of whether it contains a dysphemism or not. Likewise, an utterance is euphemistic depending on the actual context in which it is used, independent of whether it contains a euphemism or not. An utterance is dysphemistic to the extent that it is more offensive than an alternative utterance with the same denotata, or it is euphemistic to the extent that it is more polite than an alternative utterance with the same denotata. A word is a dysphemism insofar as it is considered an offensive option according to the MCPC, or it is a euphemism insofar as it is considered a polite option according to the MCPC.

In this way, we can have what Allan and Burridge (2006, 39) term "dysphemistic euphemisms."[9] Examples would be cases where people use dysphemisms in a joking manner, as in (33–34).

33. Mario I don't say this often, but you are one crazy son of a bitch. In other words, "I love you."

 (http://profile.myspace.com/index.cfm?fuseaction=user.viewprofile&friendid=78999540, accessed 9/24/08)

34. i love you, motherfucker!

 (http://bekahlikewhoa.blogspot.com/2008/04/talking-like-turnstiles.html, accessed 9/24/08)

---

[9] To me, it would make more sense to call these "euphemistic dysphemisms" in that the terms are dysphemisms, but they are being used euphemistically.

Other examples that Allan and Burridge give of "dysphemistic euphemisms" are cases when we make light of a topic by using a flippant expression (the following examples are mine): *become worm food* for 'die', *taking Carrie to the prom* for 'menstruating', *spank the monkey* for 'masturbate', *bumping uglies* for 'fornicating'.

Symmetrically, Allan and Burridge (2006) also introduce the term *euphemistic dysphemisms*. Their examples mostly involve response cries where a speaker substitutes a similar-sounding word for a taboo exclamation (e.g., *heck* for *hell*, *gaw* for *god*, *fudge* for *fuck*, *cheese and rice* for *Jesus Christ*).[10]

In my opinion, the MCPC is a laudable attempt to patch some of the flaws in a purely pragmatic approach. However, I still find it wanting—for starters, it's hard for me to see how we could implement the MCPC in a reliable, empirically valid way. Nor will it get the results we want. Applying the MCPC, I can't see that *feces* and *poo* in (35) and (36) are any more preferable to *shit* in (37). I doubt I could politely utter any of these sentences to a stranger of the opposite sex in a formal situation and middle-class environment.

35. Pardon me, I need to go squeeze some feces out of my colon.

36. Pardon me, I need to go make poo.

37. Pardon me, I need to go take a shit.

Furthermore, by positing a default context, Allan and Burridge are attempting to account for conventional characteristics of words, while retaining a usage-based definition of those characteristics. But if these truly are conventional characteristics, then they belong to our lexical knowledge of the words—they are part of a speaker's mental grammar (see Chapter 2). In the following section, I propose a semantic definition for X-phemisms, while allowing for a pragmatic definition of the adjectival forms: euphemistic, dysphemistic, orthophemistic.

3.3.2 How I Slice the Cake

To define the different X-phemisms, we begin with the concept of taboo word. We have empirical ways (discussed in Chapters 1, 3, 11, and 12) to test the relative tabooness of a word, so it seems to me that a good place to begin would be to say that dysphemisms are taboo words. As I argue in Chapter 4, tabooness is part of the linguistic meaning of a word, belonging to the social aspect of semantics; therefore, dysphemism is a linguistic category. Of course, our account raises the question why we need the term *dysphemism* if it is synonymous with *taboo word*.

Good question: Why do we need the term *dysphemism?* Dysphemism highlights the existence of an alternative. When we speak of dysphemisms, we imply there are alternative, non-taboo expressions with the same informative meaning. Thus, speaking of a dysphemism implies a corresponding orthophemism and/or euphemism.

Let's take a stab at formally defining our terms.

- **Dysphemism:** a taboo linguistic expression.
- **Orthophemism:** a non-taboo linguistic expression with the same informative meaning as some dysphemism.
- **Euphemism:** a non-taboo linguistic expression with the same informative meaning as some dysphemism which acts as a substitute for the dysphemism.

Note that the difference between orthophemism and euphemism is that a euphemism is designed as a substitute, while an orthophemism is an already existing word or phrase with that informative meaning. Chamizo Domínguez (2005, 11) distinguishes between "three stages in the life of a euphemism": novel euphemisms, semi-lexicalized euphemisms, and lexicalized (or "dead") euphemisms. The idea is that, at some point, some speaker chooses to avoid a dysphemism and invents a brand new way to do so (a novel euphemism); for example, in avoiding saying *fuck,* the speaker says, "They . . . um . . . fused!" Other people begin picking up on this new euphemism and begin using *fuse* in place of *fuck,* but it is just vague and ambiguous enough to not be taboo, so it's semi-lexicalized. Over time, if enough people use *fuse* to mean 'fornicate', then it will become fully lexicalized.

According to Chamizo Domínguez, "When a euphemism is lexicalized it usually becomes a taboo term" (11). What he is getting at is the **euphemism treadmill:** if a euphemism becomes too associated with a taboo

---

[10] Again, the terminology seems backwards to me. In Section 3.3.2, I propose a different approach to such examples.

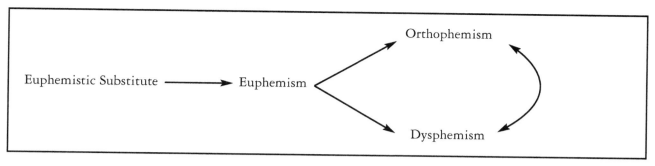

FIGURE 6.2 *The lexicalization process for euphemisms.*

denotatum, it will become a taboo word (see Chapter 7 for more on the euphemism treadmill). In truth, Chamizo Domínguez isn't entirely accurate. Many of our orthophemisms began as euphemisms (e.g., *bowel movement, sexual intercourse, anus, vagina*[11]). Furthermore, it's hard to deny that *heck, dang, freaking, poo, go to the bathroom, sleep together,* etc. are lexicalized, but they are not taboo, and I would argue that most native speakers would still classify these as euphemisms. But there is a tendency for euphemisms to follow a pattern illustrated in Figure 6.2.

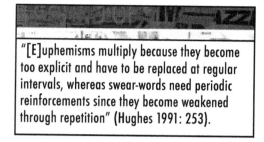

"[E]uphemisms multiply because they become too explicit and have to be replaced at regular intervals, whereas swear-words need periodic reinforcements since they become weakened through repetition" (Hughes 1991: 253).

At some point, somebody invents a brand new euphemistic substitute for a dysphemism; this is the first stage in Figure 6.2. Once enough people adopt the substitute, it becomes part of a speech community's lexicon (it becomes lexicalized) and thus becomes a euphemism. At this point, there are two likely directions a euphemism can take: it may become the accepted non-taboo term, an orthophemism, or it may become taboo, a dysphemism. Also, we should recognize that sometimes dysphemisms lose their tabooness and become orthophemisms (*gay* meaning 'homosexual' is an example).

Chamizo Domínguez also argues that "[A] word can only function as a euphemism if its interpretation remains ambiguous, that is, when the hearer can understand the utterance both in a literal and in a euphemistic way. Ambiguity is unavoidable when we speak euphemistically . . ." (Chamizo Domínguez 2005, 10). Again, he is thinking of novel and semi-lexicalized euphemisms. And again, I would disagree with him insofar as some euphemisms are fully lexicalized and unambiguous—*heck, dang,* and *poo* are not ambiguous in English.

My definition of euphemism does not apply well to novel euphemisms. My semantic approach to the terms assumes that being a euphemism is a linguistic attribute of a word. So when a new euphemistic substitute is invented, it does not yet have the characteristic of being a euphemism. This is exactly why usage-based definitions are favored by some scholars. I'll shortly come back to this problem and offer a solution.

But, first, let's work on the difference between euphemisms and orthophemisms. As I've already said, euphemisms can become orthophemisms over time. In that sense, I think Chamizo Domínguez is correct; once a euphemism becomes fully lexicalized it is likely to become either an orthophemism or a dysphemism (a taboo word). In that sense, orthophemisms and dysphemisms are more established parts of the language than are euphemisms.

Allan and Burridge (2006) give the following descriptions of how orthophemisms and euphemisms differ:

- An **orthophemism** is typically more formal and more direct (or literal) than the corresponding euphemism.

- A **euphemism** is typically more colloquial and figurative (or indirect) than the corresponding orthophemism.

(Allan & Burridge 2006, 33)

---

[11] See Chapter 7 for the etymology of *vagina.*

Their first distinction between orthophemisms and euphemisms (i.e., formality) does not apply to all cases. For example, *die* is an orthophemism meaning 'to cease to live', but I would not categorize it as more (or less) formal than certain euphemisms we have for the same meaning (e.g., *to pass (away)* or *go to heaven*).[12] Nonetheless, they're probably right for the majority of cases (e.g., *feces* and *poo*), so if we take the formality rubric as a rule of thumb, but not a rule, we're safe.

Their second distinction is interesting—though not necessarily more accurate. Essentially, they're saying that orthophemisms are more literal, while euphemisms are more figurative. This is certainly true for many euphemisms, as with the (a) and (b) versions in the following examples:

38. a. I've got to go urinate.

    b. I've got to go powder my nose.

39. a. Did you masturbate?

    b. You're still master of your domain?

    (*Seinfeld,* The Contest)

40. a. Have Grant and Gertrude fornicated?

    b. Do Grant and Gertrude have carnal knowledge of one another?

Again, this is a rule of thumb. I can't see how *poo* is any more indirect than *feces;* neither are other euphemisms, such as *darn, frick, wussy,* etc.

We think of euphemisms as being less formal and less direct than orthophemisms because of the different reasons we use them. We typically use orthophemisms, such as *feces, fornicate, urinate, penis, vulva,* in situations like doctor's visits and biology lessons. These are formal situations where directness is valued. On the other hand, we commonly use euphemisms when children are present and we want to protect them from the dysphemisms. Such situations tend to be informal, and we value indirectness because it allows us the comfort of thinking that the children don't know what we're talking about.

One last potential problem remains with our definition of dysphemism, where we define them as taboo words. As Chamizo Domínguez (2005, 11) points out, "Sometimes a word is not taboo at all, but it can become a dysphemism in a given context." For example, according to the pragmatic definitions, *feces* in (35), repeated below, is a dysphemism:

35. Pardon me, I need to go squeeze some feces out of my colon.

I would argue, however, that it is an orthophemism that is used dysphemistically.

Under our account, in contrast to that of Allan and Burridge, a term like *fucking* is always a dysphemism, whether or not it is meant to be offensive and whether or not it is taken as offensive. That is not to say, however, that the utterance of "fucking" is always dysphemistic. For example, when said between friends, (41) probably isn't.

41. I'm so fucking stoked.

Where I'm leading is to say that we can preserve Allan and Burridge's account of the terms *dysphemistic* and *euphemistic* when describing utterances. By definition, utterances belong to pragmatics, so it makes sense that when the adjective *dysphemistic* is applied to an utterance, it describes a pragmatic attribute of the utterance. We can call that attribute "offensive."

We choose which word we want to use to fit the context. If we wish to offend, we typically choose a dysphemism. If we wish to be polite, depending on the context, we will choose a euphemism or a dysphemism. As Jay (2000, 128) puts it, "Speakers choose euphemisms as they select a level of formality in speaking, depending on the speaker-listener relationship, the setting, and the topic at hand."

But language is adaptable. When we use the conventional (i.e., grammatical) tools of a language, we can negotiate their informative, social, and emotional function. Just as words have these different aspects of their meaning, utterances can communicate these three aspects. Although a dysphemism may have as part of its semantics a high level of tabooness, it won't always offend. And although a euphemism or orthophemism is not taboo, it can still offend.

---

[12] Though it is more formal than *kick the bucket* or *buy the farm.*

Also, taboo words have as part of their semantics a high emotional content, but they're not always used emotionally, as in the following example introduced in Chapter 4:

42. Do you guys want to go get some shit to eat?

In contrast, orthophemisms lack much of an emotional meaning. Euphemisms are probably in between, especially euphemisms that stand in for emotive swearing. Montagu (1967, 105) introduces the term **euphemistic swearing** to describe "a form of swearing in which mild, vague, or corrupted expressions are substituted for the original strong ones." This would describe exclamations in which we substitute *fudge* for *fuck* or *dang* for *damn* or *shoot* for *shit*. And it would describe emphatics in which we substitute *freaking* for *fucking* or *darned* for *damned*. There is still some emotional content stored in these euphemisms, but it's certainly not as high as that found in the taboo words. Jay (2000, 52) writes that "Touretters report more relief from uttering obscenities than from uttering euphemisms." We discuss Tourette Syndrome in more depth in Chapter 12.

As we'll see in the next section, not all euphemistic utterances make use of euphemisms. This brings us back to Chamizo Domínguez's "novel euphemisms." Often, when we wish to avoid saying a taboo word, we find a new substitute on the fly, creating a new euphemistic expression (or sometimes, as we'll see, we avoid saying any word). Under our definition for euphemism, these novel euphemistic expressions don't qualify because they are not lexicalized—they're not yet part of our mental grammar as a substitute for a dysphemism. That doesn't make them any less euphemistic, though.

We can offer clear definitions for **euphemistic dysphemisms** and **dysphemistic euphemisms**. A euphemistic dysphemism is a dysphemism that, in a particular context, would be considered more polite than a corresponding euphemism or orthophemism; for example, in some contexts it would be considered "prissy" to say *pee* or *urinate* instead of *piss*. A dysphemistic euphemism is a euphemism that, in a particular context, would be considered more offensive than a corresponding dysphemism or orthophemism; for example, *gash* is for many people more offensive as a term for 'vagina' than either *vagina* or *pussy* (or perhaps even *cunt*).

In sum, we have the following three definitions for X-phemisms:

- **Dysphemism:** a taboo linguistic expression.
- **Orthophemism:** a non-taboo linguistic expression with the same informative meaning as some dysphemism.
- **Euphemism:** a non-taboo linguistic expression with the same informative meaning as some dysphemism which acts as a substitute for the dysphemism.

And we have the following definitions for the adjectival forms *dysphemistic* and *euphemistic:*

- **Dysphemistic:** a description of an utterance that is offensive in comparison to an alternative expression with the same denotatum.
- **Euphemistic:** a description of an utterance that is polite in comparison to an alternative expression with the same denotatum.

By separating the definitions of the noun forms, which are semantically based, from the definitions of the adjectival forms, which are pragmatically based, I believe we can have our cake and eat it too.

4. CREATING EUPHEMISMS AND EUPHEMISTIC UTTERANCES

There are established techniques for finding substitutes for dysphemisms. In this section we go over the most prominent of these techniques.

In an early translation of François Rabelais' seventeenth-century masterpiece of vulgarity, *Gargantua and Pantagruel*, the following euphemisms for *penis* can be found in three successive sentences: *little dille, staff of love, quillety, faucetin, dandilolly, peen, jolly kyle, bableret, mebretoon, quickset imp, branch of coral, female adamant, placket-racket, Cyprian scepter, jewel for ladies, bunguetee, stopple too, bush-rusher, gallant wimble, pretty borer, coney-burrow-ferret, little piercer, augretine, dangling hangers, down right to it, stiff and stout, in and to, pusher, dresser, pouting stick, honey pipe, pretty pillicock, linky pinky, futilletie, lusty andouille, crimson chitterling, little coquille bredouille, pretty rogue* (cited in Hughes 1991, 141).

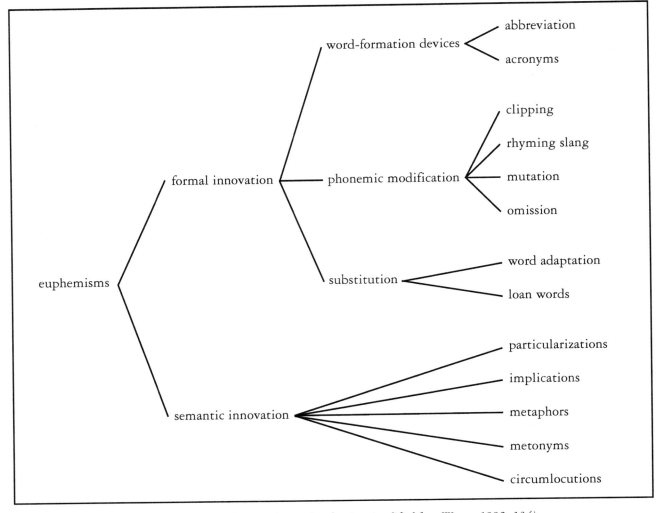

FIGURE 6.3   *Classification of types of euphemisms (modified from Warren 1992, 134).*

Warren (1992) has given one of the clearest taxonomies of these techniques. She first distinguishes between euphemisms that are created based on the form of the expression or based on the meaning of the expression: **formal innovation** vs. **semantic innovation**. She then divides formal innovation into three subtypes: **word-formation devices, phonemic modification,** and **loan words.** Word-formation devices, phonemic modification, and semantic innovation can also be divided further. I have modified her taxonomy slightly, preserving her major divisions (with the exception of "loan words," which I see as a subtype of **substitution**) but not all of her subtypes. Figure 6.3 is an adapted version of a tree diagram that she provides (linguists really like trees).

We begin by looking at the types of formal modification in Section 4.1, and then we look at types of semantic modification in Section 4.2.

4.1   Formal Modification

As we discussed in Chapter 1 and Chapter 5, tabooness is simply a characteristic of words. A word consists of two parts: the signifier and the signified. Or in more common terms: the form and the meaning. So if we change the sounds of a taboo word or if we find a new string of sounds for the existing informative meaning, this new form will not have the same tabooness as the old one.

The first type of formal modification is word-formation devices. This strategy uses the morphological resources of the language to create new words. This one can be subdivided into two subcategories: **abbreviation** and **acronyms.** Abbreviations are where we take the initial letters of the taboo expression and create a new form by pronouncing the letters. Some abbreviations name the word according to its first letter: *the f-word* for *fuck, the* *c-word*, for *cunt*, the *n-word* for *nigger*. Another example is simply using the first letter in place of the word: *f* (sometimes spelled <u>ef</u>) for *fuck*. The most common type of abbreviation is for longer expressions that include a taboo word; examples include: *SOB* (from *son of a bitch*), *WTF* (from *what the fuck*), *OMG* (from *oh my god*), *BS* (from *bullshit*). Acronyms are similar to abbreviations except that the letters are spelled out but pronounced as a new word: *milf* (from *mother I'd like to fuck*), *snafu* (from *situation normal all fucked up*), *fubar* (from *fucked up beyond all repair*).

The next type of formal modification is phonemic modification. This involves changing or omitting one or more sounds in the taboo word to produce a new form. This type can be divided into four subtypes: **clipping, rhyming slang, mutation,** and **omission.**

Clipping is where we chop off part of the word (generally, the end part), for example, *Geez* for *Jesus, gaw* for *god, fuh* for *fuck, bull* for *bullshit*. One of my favorite examples comes from a Flight of the Conchords song "Mother Uckers," whose chorus includes the line, "Too many mother uckers ucking with my shi."

Rhyming slang is probably best known from Cockney, a working-class dialect spoken in London. Cockney rhyming slang is a particularly innovative way of creating euphemisms. Examples abound: *ginger* means 'homosexual' (*ginger beer* rhymes with *queer*); *trolley* means 'copulate' (*trolley and truck* rhymes with *fuck*); *bottle, North Pole* and *Khyber* each mean 'bottom' (*bottle and glass* rhymes with *ass, North Pole* rhymes with *hole,* and *Khyber Pass* rhymes with *ass*); *Niagara* means 'rubbish' (*Niagara Falls* rhymes with *balls* = 'bullshit'); *cobblers* means 'rubbish' or 'testicles' (*cobbler's awls* rhymes with *balls*); *Friar Tuck* means 'fuck'; *Berkeley Hunt* (or *Berk*) means 'cunt' (in the sense of a slur, not 'vagina'); *Rory O'More* means 'whore'. (All examples taken from Ashley 1987.)

Mutation is where we create a new word by changing one or more sounds in the original word, for example, *shucks* for *shit, dang* for *damn, gosh* for *god, fugging* for *fucking, cripes* for *Christ*.

Omissions are where we simply leave the taboo word out altogether. Sometimes we leave a pause, or sometimes we put in nonsense syllables to replace the word (e.g., *ahem*). In a performance on *The Dennis Miller Show*, Jack Black asks the women in the audience to "drop trou and show us a little . . ." and then whistles to stand in for, presumably, *cunt* or *pussy*. I should point out that omissions do not lead to actual euphemisms since the substituted form is not a lexical item. Instead, we can say these are euphemistic utterances.

Our final type of formal innovation is substitutions, where we substitute one word for another: we can adapt a word already in the language (**word adaptation**) or borrow a word from another language (**loan words**).

After Lenny Bruce was arrested for saying *cocksucker* in his standup comedy routine, his subsequent routines included discussions of the trial, where witnesses had to say the exact word that Bruce was arrested for saying. However, Bruce went out of his way in these routines not to actually say the word, so when he quotes the bailiff reporting what a witness had reported Bruce as saying he substitutes nonsense syllables for *cocksucker*: "Yeah he said it . . . He said, 'dadadada.'" (Lenny Bruce, *Live at the Curran Theater*, 1961)

When we adapt a word already in the language, it's generally because of a similarity in sound or meaning. For example, when my nephew, Jakob, was about three, his parents were concerned that he was too violent when playing with his action figures, always talking about one killing the other, so his parents told him that he shouldn't say *kill*, that it was a "bad word." I visited him about this time and found him in the backyard stamping the sidewalk. I asked him what he was doing, and he said he was "dieing ants." Other examples of word adaptation are *poo* for *shit; coochie* for *cunt* or *pussy; willie* or *johnson* for *prick, dick* or *cock*. Many adaptations are based on sound similarity: *peter* for *penis, fudge* for *fuck, cheese and rice* for *Jesus Christ, freaking* for *fucking*.

Borrowings are a rich source of euphemisms. Latinized words were used abundantly as euphemisms during the eighteenth century (Hughes 1991, 145). Many of today's orthophemisms began life as euphemistic borrowings from Latin, for example, *fornicate, defecate, urinate, anus*. An interesting example of borrowing is *enceinte,* which from the early 1600s to the mid-1800s was a euphemism for 'pregnant'. Historically, English speakers have been squeamish about pregnancy (not surprising, given how a woman contracts that particular parasitic infection), so we borrowed the French word for 'pregnant'

Frig as a euphemism for *fuck* has a long and complex history. It originally meant 'to move restlessly', but by the sixteenth century it was already being used as a euphemism for *fuck*. During the seventeenth and eighteenth centuries it was probably just about as taboo as *fuck*. Today, it's gone back to being a euphemism and has no real independent status in the language (i.e., it's no longer used for any other purpose but as a substitute for *fuck*).

enceinte, which itself was originally a euphemism in French literally meaning 'girdled'. (Of course, *pregnant* was also a borrowing from French, so here we see the cyclic nature of euphemisms—see more on the euphemism treadmill in Chapter 7).

All of these techniques are primarily speech-based. We also have specifically written euphemisms. For example, the convention in comic strips is to substitute symbols, such as #$@*!, for any taboo word. Newspapers will often list the first letter of a taboo word and replace the remaining letters with dashes or asterisks, for example, *f*—- or *n*****. Mencken (1947, 316) cites the following written euphemisms that change the spellings but would be pronounced the same as the taboo words: *damphool, damfino, helluva.* Similar examples are now found on the Internet where users attempt to avoid the filters on chatrooms and comment boards: *phuck, b!tch, k(_)nt, kok.*

4.2 *Semantic Modification*

Semantic modification is where existing words are used to point at the same denotatum as some dysphemism. There are five strategies used in this approach: **particularizations, implications, metaphors, metonyms, circumlocutions.**

Particularizations are where a general term is used with a specific meaning. Examples include *thing* for *dick, cock,* or *prick; nether regions* for *pussy, cunt, dick, cock,* or *prick;* and *relieve oneself* for *shit* or *piss.* Mencken (1947 & 1962) collected particularized euphemisms for various sex-related terms from London newspapers in the early twentieth century. See the list in Table 6.2.

Implications are along the lines of an *if . . . then* statement, and generally the euphemism is the *if* clause. For example, if someone goes to the bathroom, then they presumably defecate or urinate; thus *go to the bathroom* is a euphemism for *shit* or *piss.* Note that this particular euphemism is fully lexicalized in that we can now say sentences like (43).

43. My dog went to the bathroom in my living room.

Other examples of implicational euphemisms include *go to bed with* for *fuck* and *likes men* for *slut* or *homosexual.* Although most of the euphemisms represent the *if* clause, the euphemism can represent the *then* clause in some cases—for example, *sleep together,* where the implication is that if two people have fornicated, then they fall asleep together afterwards.

Metaphors are where, due to a perceived similarity, an expression that refers to one thing is used to refer to another. For example, *make the beast with two backs* for *fuck; trouser trout* for *cock, dick,* or *prick; garage* for *pussy* or *cunt.* Of course *pussy* and *cock,* before they were taboo words, were metaphoric euphemisms (see Chapter 7 for more on such derivations). Warren (1992, 147) mentions *dumplings* as a metaphoric euphemism meaning 'breasts'. An early example of a metaphoric euphemism is *to box the Jesuit* meaning 'to masturbate', which comes from a text written in 1640 (cited in Hughes 1991, 130). For some reason, masturbation euphemisms tend to be metaphoric.

Metonymy is when one term or concept is used to substitute for a related word or concept. The relation between the two words may be cause-effect, locational, or whole-part. For example, we can substitute *fucking* with

TABLE 6.2	
Euphemisms Used by London Newspapers, First Half of the Twentieth Century **(collected by Mencken 1947, 311 & 1962, 646)**	
Meaning	*Euphemism*
'prostitute'	*woman of a certain class*
'prostitution'	*mode of living*
'pregnant'	*in a certain condition*
'performing an abortion'	*producing a certain state* or *a certain result*
'pandering'	*having for purposes of gain, exercised influence over the movements of* the girl victim
'homosexuality'	*improper assault*
'rape'	*improper assault* or *to interfere with*
'syphilis'	*a certain illness*

its potential result: *making babies.* We often substitute the location for the thing, as in *bathroom* for *toilet* and *groin* for *balls.* For sex and evacuation organs, it's common for us to describe them according to some larger whole that includes them as a part; for example, *hind-end* for *butt* or *chest* for *boobs* or *tits. Tits* as a dysphemism for *breasts* is the opposite process, where the part stands in for the whole (*tits* originally meant 'nipples'); we often find that the same processes that lead to euphemisms can also lead to dysphemisms.

Circumlocutions are where we expend extra words to describe a concept without actually saying the word for it—for example, *use the toilet* for *shit* or *piss; the area between my legs* for *cunt* or *pussy; join together in sexual union* for *fuck.* This is often seen as a roundabout way of explaining something.

5.   WHY SPEAK EUPHEMISTICALLY?

Many people dislike euphemisms and euphemistic speech. Read (1977, 16) states his distaste rather vigorously: "That any one should pass up the well-established colloquial words of the language and have recourse to the Latin *defecate, urinate,* and *have sexual intercourse,* is indicative of grave mental unhealth." Walt Whitman wrote in *An American Primer:* "The blank left by words wanted, but unsupplied, has sometimes an unnamably putrid cadaverous meaning." Even some of those who are opposed to swearing complain about euphemistic speech; in 1647, Robert Boyle published *A Free DISCOURSE AGAINST Customary Swearing AND A DISSUASIVE FROM CURSING,* in which he writes of euphemisms: "Well may this childish Evasion cheat our own souls, but never him, who judgeth as well as he discerns Intents . . ." (quoted in Hughes 1991, 118). According to Jay's (1992) research, some dysphemisms are more frequently used than their counterpart euphemisms or orthophemisms.

So why do we speak euphemistically? We've touched on some reasons throughout this chapter. The most commonly referenced reason has to do with children. We should choose alternatives because we don't want to expose children to "harmful" words. I, myself, feel this way; I try not to swear in front of children, and I don't particularly like when other people do. Rationally, however, I know that this is a rather strange feeling. It's as if adults think that children have not been exposed to the dysphemisms before and that, by substituting euphemisms, we are speaking a kind of code, similar to how parents may spell words out in front of pre-literate children to keep them from knowing what's being discussed. But Jay (1992) has demonstrated that children from a remarkably young age are familiar with taboo words. This fact is illustrated well in the following letter:

> When I was a very small child (I read a lot in those days) and came across abbreviations like h—, or d—, etc., I had the idea that they were printed in this way to protect small children like myself from learning these wicked words, and I felt very cute and discerning because I knew the words that were indicated; and so felt, also, that the trouble to disguise them had been wasted, so far as I was concerned. And as I grew older I became more and more puzzled at the initial letter and stroke, seeing that everybody knew what was intended. If it wasn't liked, why was it used at all? and if it was, why disguise it? (Letter quoted in *English,* II, November, 1920, 413, and quoted again in Read 1934, 265)

Allan and Burridge (2006) make a useful distinction between **censorship** and **censoring** (see Chapter 15 for more on this distinction). Censorship "is typically an institutionalized practice" that is carried out "by powerful governing classes, supposedly acting for the common good by preserving stability and/or the moral fibre in the nation" (24). Censoring "encompasses both the institutionalized acts of the powerful and those of ordinary individuals: everyone *censors* his/her own or another's behaviour from time to time . . ."; they go on to say, "All kinds of tabooed behaviour are subject to *censoring,* but only certain kinds are subject to *censorship* . . ." (24). I will use censorship to refer to censoring done by any authority, whether governmental or not (e.g., employers can censor employees in the workplace and teachers can censor students in the classroom).

Much euphemistic speech is due to censorship. Some authority has determined that certain dysphemisms should not be used in certain places, and so speakers are forced to use euphemisms. In some cases, individuals use these euphemisms only reluctantly; for example, Holly Mullen (pers. comm.) has indicated that some journalists for the *Salt Lake City Weekly,* an alternative weekly newspaper, chafed at an editorial policy not to print the terms *shit* and *fuck;* she also explained that the editorial policy was made for financial reasons, namely, some advertisers threatened to pull their ads if the newspaper continued to print the words. In other cases, employees might have self-censored anyways; for example, Bill Allred, the co-host of "Radio from Hell," a talk radio show in Salt Lake

City, has indicated that, although he likes to push boundaries, he has no desire to offend his listeners with words they don't want to hear (Allred pers. comm). Mike Place (pers. comm.) explained that when he and the other founders began an Internet radio station called UtahFM, they had to wrestle with the question of what would be appropriate to broadcast; even though the FCC had no governance over them (unlike Allred's show), they decided that they would avoid the most taboo words because listeners had indicated that they wouldn't be able to play the station at work otherwise.

Just as we saw with the pragmatic approaches to euphemistic speech, the issue typically comes down to politeness. In general, we don't want to offend others. Even if we ourselves are not offended by the dysphemisms and even if we know that our friends are not offended by them, when we are in public we censor ourselves so as not to offend overhearers. In other contexts, though, where we don't think anybody will be offended—or we don't care if they are offended—we will choose to use the dysphemisms over the euphemisms or orthophemisms.

Of course, we also have to recognize that we avoid some dysphemisms not because we fear offending others, but because we believe the words reflect badly on ourselves. For example, as a white, heterosexual, male I choose not to use dysphemisms for other races, homosexuals, or females—I do not want to appear racist, homophobic, or misogynistic. Others will not utter profanity because it goes against their religious beliefs.

There's still a lingering question, though. Why euphemisms? That is, why a substitution? Especially substitutions for emotive uses of taboo words? For example, when in pain, why would anybody choose (44–48) over (49)?

44. Fudge!

45. Son of a gun!

46. Crippled crutches!

47. Shoot!

48. Aw for crying out loud!

49. Ouch!

And when surprised, why would anybody choose (50–52) over (53)?

50. Holy cow!

51. Oh my gosh!

52. Good golly!

53. Wow!

And when emphasizing, why would anybody choose (54–56) over (57)?

54. I'm gosh-darned tired.

55. I'm freaking tired.

56. I'm frigging tired.

57. I'm really tired.

All right, here's my attempt to answer these questions. As we've discussed before, much of the reason we use taboo words is because of the emotional force they hold. I've argued that this emotional force is part of their meaning. Dysphemisms are taboo words that share the same informative meaning with non-taboo terms (euphemisms and orthophemisms). Dysphemisms differ from their euphemisms and orthophemisms mostly with respect to their social meaning; dysphemisms have high tabooness, while euphemisms and orthophemisms have low tabooness. But dysphemisms also differ from their euphemisms and orthophemisms with respect to their emotional meaning; dysphemisms have more emotional force than their non-taboo counterparts. However, some euphemisms acquire emotional meaning by their association with the dysphemisms they replace; this seems to be especially the case with euphemisms derived through phonemic modification. Granted, *fudge* is not as emotional as *fuck*, it is certainly more powerful to shout, "Fudge!" than it is to shout, "Fornicate!" Orthophemisms, of course, lack any real emotional force, so they aren't used emotively. They also tend to be formal, so when the situation calls for a low-register, non-taboo term, we opt for a euphemism.

No matter what the motivations, we can succinctly explain why euphemisms work as substitutes for taboo words. Tabooness is an arbitrary, conventional, semantic property of words. Words are composed of two arbitrarily connected parts: the form and the meaning (see Chapter 5). The social meaning of taboo words includes their tabooness. Because the tabooness is associated with a particular form, if we substitute a different form (even one that sounds very similar) we get a new linguistic expression, one that is not (for the time being, at least) taboo. Of course, over time, what began as euphemisms can become dysphemisms (see Chapter 7); that is to say, the social meaning of euphemisms may change over time, their tabooness increasing until they become taboo words in their own right.

6. FAUXPHEMISMS

A related, but inverse, phenomenon to euphemisms is where innocent constructions are assembled in such a way as to bring dysphemisms to mind. Pinker (2007, 333) gives the following examples: "the restaurant chain Fuddruckers, the clothing brand called FCUK (French Connection UK), and the movie called *Meet the Fokkers*." I've seen examples on t-shirts: "Give me Rossignol or give me Head," "Ski with a Hart on," and "SL,UT" (for Salt Lake, Utah). Let's call these **fauxphemisms**. Even against one's will, fauxphemisms, because of a phonetic or visual similarity, bring to mind a taboo expression. The fact is, we can't avoid processing language, as is proven by the Stroop effect. When we hear a taboo word, or even when we think we hear a taboo word, we have an automatic emotional response to it. As Pinker (2007, 333) writes: "The upshot is that a speaker or writer can use a taboo word to evoke an emotional response in an audience quite against their wishes." A lot of childish humor is related to fauxphemisms. For example:

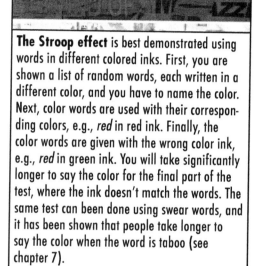

The Stroop effect is best demonstrated using words in different colored inks. First, you are shown a list of random words, each written in a different color, and you have to name the color. Next, color words are used with their corresponding colors, e.g., *red* in red ink. Finally, the color words are given with the wrong color ink, e.g., *red* in green ink. You will take significantly longer to say the color for the final part of the test, where the ink doesn't match the words. The same test can been done using swear words, and it has been shown that people take longer to say the color when the word is taboo (see chapter 7).

Child: How do you spell *cup?*

Adult: C-U-P

Child: Gross!

But it's not just children who enjoy fauxphemisms. Shakespeare used one in the title of a famous play: *Much ado about Nothing* = "Much ado about an O thing," where *O thing* was an expression meaning 'vagina' (Hughes 1991, 108).

7. CONCLUSION

Most, if not all, taboo words have non-taboo counterparts with the same informative meaning. The taboo words, we call dysphemisms. Non-taboo words with the same informative meaning as dysphemisms are called either orthophemisms or euphemisms. Orthophemisms are words that exist independently of the dysphemisms; they are typically formal and often clinical. Euphemisms are words that were created in order to avoid a dysphemism (or sometimes an orthophemism); some euphemisms are existing words that are given a new "twist" (e.g., *Johnson*), while others are invented explicitly as euphemisms (e.g., *heck*); euphemisms often involve figurative language, such as metaphor or metonymy.

We discussed two approaches to defining euphemisms, dysphemisms, and orthophemisms: semantic (lexically based) and pragmatic (usage based). We saw that both approaches have advantages. The semantic approach captures our intuitions that some words, absent any context, have the property of being dysphemisms, euphemisms, or orthophemisms. The pragmatic approach captures how euphemisms and dysphemisms are used to be polite or to offend, and it also captures how novel euphemistic substitutes can be created on the fly. In the end, we concluded that there was only one reasonable way to define our terms: mine.

Under the approach described here, the noun forms, dysphemism, euphemism, and orthophemism, are defined according to semantic properties that are part of our linguistic knowledge of the lexicon of our native language, while the adjectival forms, dysphemistic and euphemistic, describe properties of utterances that are used in a particular context, specifically the properties of being polite or being offensive. The formal definitions we will use are as follows:

- **Dysphemism:** a taboo linguistic expression.
- **Orthophemism:** a non-taboo linguistic expression with the same informative meaning as some dysphemism.
- **Euphemism:** a non-taboo linguistic expression with the same informative meaning as some dysphemism which acts as a substitute for the dysphemism.
- **Dysphemistic:** a description of an utterance that is offensive in comparison to an alternative expression with the same denotatum.
- **Euphemistic:** a description of an utterance that is polite in comparison to an alternative expression with the same denotatum.

We also saw that there are established strategies for creating euphemisms or for speaking euphemistically. We can divide the strategies into those that target the form and those that target the meaning. Formal innovation creates a euphemism (or euphemistic substitute) by using word-formation rules, modifying the sounds of the dysphemism, or substituting an existing word (either from the same language or from another language). Semantic innovation creates a euphemism by figuratively or indirectly indicating the same meaning as some dysphemism.

We briefly explored why people speak euphemistically. Euphemisms work because the sounds of a taboo word are arbitrarily associated with tabooness (see Chapter 5); thus by substituting a different sound in place of the dysphemism, we get a non-taboo expression. People speak euphemistically both because of censorship and because of self-censoring. In some cases an authority forbids us from using taboo words (censorship); in other cases we avoid taboo words either because we don't want to damage others' face or we don't want to damage our own face. Finally, we opt for euphemisms over orthophemisms because of issues of register (part of the social meaning of the words) and emotion (the emotional meaning of the words); euphemisms are usually less formal and so are more common in low register situations, and euphemisms acquire some emotional meaning from their association with the respective dysphemisms.

Finally, we looked at a playful type of language: fauxphemisms. With fauxphemisms, people create expressions that remind people of dysphemisms while being different enough that they don't qualify as taboo expressions (though they may be dysphemistic in that people are offended by them).

REFERENCES

Allan, Keith, and Kate Burridge. 1991. *Euphemism and Dysphemism: Language Used as Shield and Weapon.* New York: University Press.

Allan, Keith, and Kate Burridge. 2006. *Forbidden Words: Taboo and the Censoring of Language.* Cambridge: Cambridge University Press.

Ashley, Leonard R.N. 1987. The Cockney's Horn Book: The Sexual Side of Rhyming Slang. In *The Best of Maledicta,* ed. Reinhold Aman. Philadelphia: Running Press.

Ayto, John. 1993. *Euphemisms: Over 3,000 Ways to Avoid Being Rude or Giving Offence.* London: Bloomsbury.

Brown, Penelope, and Stephen Levinson. 1987. *Politeness: Some Universals in Language Usage.* Cambridge: Cambridge University Press.

Casas Gómez, Miguel. 2009. Towards a New Approach to the Linguistic Definition of Euphemism. *Language Sciences,* 31: 725–739.

Chamizo Domínguez, Pedro J. 2005. Some Theses on Euphemisms and Dysphemisms. *Seria Filologiczna, Studia Anglica Resoviensia* 3: 9–16.

Crespo Fernández, Eliecer. 2006. Sex-Related Euphemism and Dysphemism: An Analysis in Terms of Conceptual Metaphor Theory. *Atlantis. Journal of the Spanish Association of Anglo-American Studies,* 30(2): 95–110.

Crespo Fernández, Eliecer. 2007. *El Eufemismo y el disfemismo. Procesos de manipulación del tabú en el language literario ingles.* Alicante: Universidad de Alicante.

Hughes, Geoffrey. 1991. *Swearing: A Social History of Foul Language, Oaths, and Profanity in English.* Cambridge, MA: Blackwell.

Jay, Timothy. 1992. *Cursing in America: A Psycholinguistic Study of Dirty Language in the Courts, in the Movies, in the Schoolyards, and on the Streets.* Philadelphia: John Benjamins.

Jay, Timothy. 2000. *Why We Curse: A Neuro-Psycho-Social Theory of Speech.* Philadelphia: John Benjamins.

Lechado García, J.M. 2000. *Diccionario de Eufemismos.* Madrid: Verbum.

Mencken, H.L. 1947. *The American Language: An Inquiry into the Development of English in the United States.* New York: Alfred A. Knopf.

Mencken, H.L. 1962. *Supplement One: The American Language.* New York: Alfred A. Knopf.

Montagu, Ashley. 1967. *The Anatomy of Swearing.* New York: The Macmillan Company.

Pinker, Stephen. 2007. *The Stuff of Thought.* New York: Viking.

Read, Allen. 1934. An Obscenity Symbol. *American Speech* 19(4): 264–278.

Read, Allen. 1977. *Classic American Graffiti: Lexical Evidence from Folk Epigraphy in Western North America.* Waukesha, WI: Maledicta Press.

Warren, Beatrice. 1992. What Euphemisms Tell us about the Interpretation of Words. *Sudia Linguistica,* 46(2): 128–173.

Wing, Fing F. 1988. *Fuck, Yes! A Guide to the Happy Acceptance of Everything.* Redmond, WA: Shepherd Books.

1. Let's assume that there are individuals who never use any dysphemisms but engage in "euphemistic swearing"—for example, exclamations like *Fudge!*, *Shoot!*, *Dog vomit!*, *That bastage!*. For such an individual, do these exclamations count as swearing? In other words, in this individual's mental grammar are these expressions considered taboo? Explain your answer.

2. List as many fauxphemisms as you can find.

3. Are there other motivations for speaking euphemistically besides those discussed in Section 5?

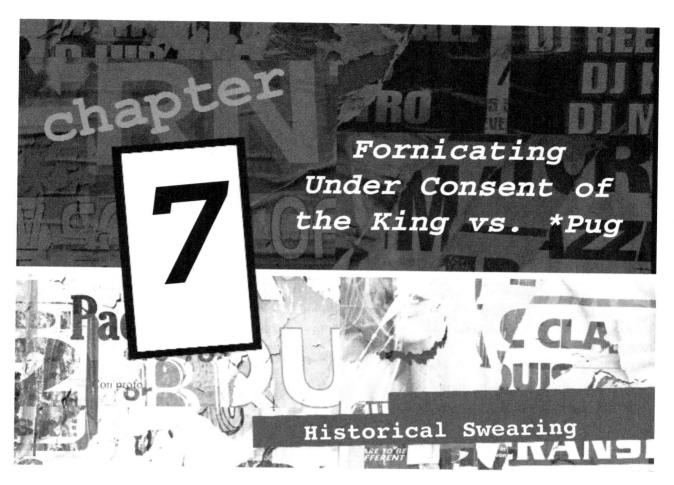

chapter 7

Fornicating Under Consent of the King vs. *Pug

Historical Swearing

1. INTRODUCTION

I find many people take perverse pride in the ingenuity of present-day swearing. Especially young people believe we've somehow reached the apex of what is possible with bad words. It's humbling, then, to look back and see some of the lyrical and graphic insults that were exchanged way-back-when. Hughes (1991, 121–124) quotes some examples of ritual insulting (flyting) from the fourteenth through early sixteenth centuries (before Shakespeare's time):

"cuntbitten crawdon"[1] ('pox-smitten, coward')

"a schit but wit" ('a shit without wit')

". . . like to throw shit by the cartload"

"fals tratour, feyndis get" ('false traitor, fiend's bastard')

"kis Þe cunt of ane kow" ('kiss the cunt of a cow')

"thou shitten knave" ('you shitty knave')

"thou jakes" ('you shithouse')

Nevertheless, we often find past swearing quaint or even silly. The reason for this is simple: what was taboo is no longer taboo. Over time, the strength of taboo words weakens. In an enviable turn

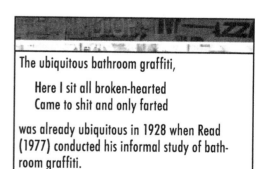

The ubiquitous bathroom graffiti,

> Here I sit all broken-hearted
> Came to shit and only farted

was already ubiquitous in 1928 when Read (1977) conducted his informal study of bathroom graffiti.

---

[1] *Cuntbitten* plays on the literal image, as well as meaning 'pox-smitten', that is, 'syphilitic' and 'impotent' (because of syphilis). And *crawdon* refers literally to a 'cock who can't fight any longer', hence a coward or "chicken", but it also probably plays on the sexual connotations of *cock*.

of phrase, Mencken (1947, 315) puts it: "All expletives tend to be similarly dephlogisticated by over-use."[2] Once that happens, we have to find new ones.

In Section 2, we follow some highlights of the history of swearing in English, from inception to modern day. In Section 3, we look at some processes that create and change taboo words. In Section 4, we debunk some popular, but false, etymologies for taboo words. In Section 5, we explore some true etymologies. And, in Section 6, we consider a detailed etymology for *fuck*.

2. THE HISTORY OF ENGLISH SWEARING

At the dawn of English, swearing was mostly a matter of oath-making, what Hughes calls "swearing by." Swearing was a way of establishing the credibility of what you were saying. We have vestiges of this today in certain rituals; for example, in the Oath of Office, the Presidents of the United States "do solemnly swear" to "faithfully execute the office of President of the United States, and . . . preserve, protect and defend the Constitution of the United States;" in court, witnesses "swear to tell the truth, the whole truth, and nothing but the truth;" and on the playground, school children guarantee their word by saying "cross my heart, hope to die, stick a needle in my eye."

In medieval times, most oath-making relied on Christian beliefs, so the oaths often invoked faith, God, or Jesus, giving us expressions like *by my faith, God blind me,* and *by God that sits above.* Of course, oath-making itself was not taboo—what was taboo was "loose swearing," taking an oath without the proper reverence behind it.[3] For example, (1) and (2) would have been acceptable uses of *by God,* but (3) is too flippant and banal, and (4), where it's just an exclamation (response cry, see Chapter 4), is even worse.

1. By God, I will catch my father's killer.
2. By God, I am no liar.
3. By God, I am hungry.
4. By God!

We can see why loose swearing would be taboo: if your compatriots throw around expressions like *by God* too loosely, then it weakens its power, and when you go to make a real oath, it lacks punch.

As expressions were overused, a whole lot of new expressions, more and more elaborate, were invented to replace those that lost their power: *by Goddes precious herte* ('by God's precious heart'), *by Goddes corpus, Christes passioun, by the blood of Christ, by his nayles* (a reference to the nails used to crucify Christ), *by Goddes armes, by his death, by his life.* For Chaucer, writing in the late fourteenth century, strong swearing would have included *by nayles, by blood* (cited in Hughes 1991, 82). Eventually, creativity became an end in itself, and swearers competed to come up with the most imaginative oaths: *his lid* (referring to God's eyelid), *his light, his wounds, his body, his foot.* Taking this even further, a diminuative suffix *–ikins* begins being used: *God's bodikins* ('God's little body'), *his lidikins* ('his little eyelids'). By this point, the terms were used more for their emotional strength than their spiritual strength.

Similarly, *Mary* was originally used as an oath drawing upon the power of the Virgin Mary to verify one's words. But by the fourteenth century, the religious meaning of the word began to be lost, and the word, often spelled with two rs (*marry*), began to be used purely as a marker of emotional strength. By the sixteenth century, the word had lost all of its original meaning, was no longer taboo, and had come to mean simply 'to be sure' (Hughes 1991, 95).

Chaucer's writing in the fourteenth century includes plenty of swearing (indeed, in the prologue to *The Canterbury Tales* he apologizes to his readers and warns them about the language used). In his works, the most common expression for annoyance is *Benedicitee!* (cited in Hughes 1991, 75), which originally meant 'bless you'.

---

[2] If you're not familiar with phlogiston chemistry—and I don't expect you are—*dephlogisticate* refers to the process of removing the combustible element from organic material. Early chemists believed there was an atomic element, phlogiston, common to all things that burned, and it was this element that was released by flames. I'm rather fond of this image as applied to cussing—imagine some as yet undiscovered linguistic atom that makes words taboo.

[3] My friend, Kathleen Koprowski, asked when the word *swear* came to have its present meaning of 'using taboo words' instead of the original meaning of 'to make an oath'. I had to confess ignorance, so I looked it up in the OED. Their first entry for the former meaning comes from 1430, so we can guess that it started being used that way somewhere in the late 1300s.

For him, the taboo is mostly on profanity, but we also find secular terms of abuse, which Hughes (1991, 65) observes, "To us . . . have lost their 'bite' and wounding sharpness in the intervening centuries." But in Chaucer's time the terms were "fire-new, fresh-minted and well able to burn the ears of a contemporary audience" (64–65). What were these "hot" terms? Here they are: *foul, lousy, old, shrew, swine, idiot.*

Among the slurs that were common in the middle ages were especially terms for people of other races and creeds (see Section 3.3). We also find slurs on a person's heritage, especially *horson* 'son of a whore', which according to Hughes (1991, 89) was "the most wounding insult in English" in the fourteenth century. In a similar vein, Shakespeare introduced us to *son of a bitch,* which Hughes (112) claims was first used in *King Lear* (written around 1605). Hughes (28–29) gives us this nice list of slurs along with the dates they were first used as slurs:

fart[4]	c. 1450
shit	c. 1508
shitfire	c. 1598
shitabed[5]	c. 1690
bugger	1719
shitsack	c. 1769
bastard	1830
fucker	1893
prick	1928
cunt	1929
twat	1929
tit	1947

During the English Renaissance, profanity was where the strongest taboos lay. It was more acceptable to use obscenity than profanity. For example, in the 1600s, Rochester's poetry was extremely sexual—as Hughes (1991, 140) puts it, "Rochester's is a world seen from crotch level . . .", but his emotional exclamations were religious: "Gods!" Never-theless, obscenity was certainly considered taboo, enough so that we find Shakespeare avoiding *fuck,* instead resorting to French *foutre* ('fuck') or the euphemism *fig,* as well as using double entendres to slip past the censors.

Among the euphemisms for profane utterances, we find expressions that simply squished the words of the earlier oaths together: *'sblood, 'slid, 'slight, 'snails, zounds* (from *his wounds*), *'sbody, 'sdeath, gadzooks* (from *God's hooks*), *'slife, 'slidikins, odsbodkins* (from *God's bodikins* 'God's little body'). In Shakespeare's time, these were euphemisms to avoid the taboo expressions, but as they were used more and more, they became taboo themselves (see Section 3.2 on the euphemism treadmill). Their connection to religious oaths began to be lost to the extent that speakers no longer understood the ori-gins of the expressions. For example *'struth,* which was a clipped ver-sion of *his truth,* was often spelled *'strewth;* and *zounds,* which originally rhymed with *wounds,* was reinterpreted to rhyme with *hounds.* As the terms lost their connection to the

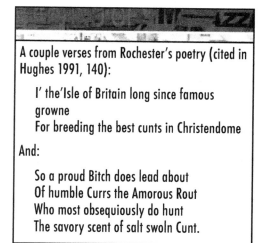

A couple verses from Rochester's poetry (cited in Hughes 1991, 140):

I' the 'Isle of Britain long since famous growne
For breeding the best cunts in Christendome

And:

So a proud Bitch does lead about
Of humble Currs the Amorous Rout
Who most obsequiously do hunt
The savory scent of salt swoln Cunt.

terms they substituted for, their emotional meaning strengthened and their tabooness strengthened (see Section 3.1 on emotive strengthening, semantic weakening, and social stigmatizing), so much so that the satirist Jonathon Swift used dashes for *zounds* in his 1732 piece "In the Lady's Dressing Room" (cited in Hughes 1991, 162). Notably, there must have been a taboo on scatological terms, too, since Swift also used dashes for *piss* and *shit.*

---

[4] Also, *fartcatcher* 'footman', *fartsucker* 'toadie'.

[5] Although *shitabed* was a slur, about the same time there was the word *pissabed,* which was a slang term for dandelion (because dandelions, apparently, have diuretic properties).

By the beginning of the nineteenth century, terms like *zounds, gadzooks,* and *odsbodikins* died out, leaving *bloody*[6], *hell,* and *damn* as the taboo terms with the strongest emotional meaning (Hughes 1991, 151). Towards the end of the nineteenth century came the Victorian Age with its sexual prudery. During that time, we find taboos on what today are some of the most neutral terms. For example, *trousers* was a taboo word. Consider this passage from Charles Dickens' *Oliver Twist* (cited in Hughes 1991, 153):

> "I tossed off the [bed] clothes," said Giles . . . looking very hard at the cook and the housemaid, "got softly out of bed; drew on a pair of —"
>
> "Ladies present, Mr. Giles," murmured the tinker.
>
> "— of *shoes* sir," said Giles, turning on him and laying great emphasis on the word.

Read (2003) discusses several nineteenth century euphemisms for *trousers: unmentionables, unwhisperables, don't speak of 'ems.*

Read (2003) suggests that Victorian prudishness began well before Queen Victoria ascended to the throne in 1837, the apex was around 1830, and it was stronger in the States than in England. He quotes Samual Peters' *General History of Connecticut,* written in 1781: "It would be accounted the greatest rudeness for a gentleman to speak before a lady of a garter or a leg" (10). Euphemisms for *leg* included *limb, benders,* and *wire.* In 1833, Noah Webster censored his version of the Bible, substituting "*breast* for *teat, in embryo* for *in the belly, peculiar members* for *stones* (Leviticus XXI, 20), *smell* for *stink, to nurse* or *to nourish* for *to give suck, lewdness* for *fornication, lewd woman* or *prostitute* for *whore, to go astray* for *to go a-whoring,* and *impurities, idolatries* and *carnal connection* for *whoredom*" (Mencken 1942, 303). Mencken notes that when Webster couldn't find an inoffensive replacement for something, he got rid of the whole verse.

Brits were amused by Americans' sensitivity to the word *leg,* but they had their own idiosyncrasies. For example, *stomach* was used in England instead of *breasts,* which lead to some amusement for Americans. Read (2003, 12) quotes a letter from Helen Hunt Jackson in 1869: "An Englishwoman ties on a compress over the upper stomach . . . did you know that we had more than one?" But then, of course, *stomach* itself quickly became taboo in England because of its association with breasts.

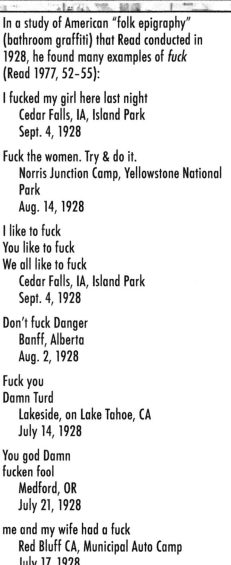

In a study of American "folk epigraphy" (bathroom graffiti) that Read conducted in 1928, he found many examples of *fuck* (Read 1977, 52-55):

I fucked my girl here last night
    Cedar Falls, IA, Island Park
    Sept. 4, 1928

Fuck the women. Try & do it.
    Norris Junction Camp, Yellowstone National Park
    Aug. 14, 1928

I like to fuck
You like to fuck
We all like to fuck
    Cedar Falls, IA, Island Park
    Sept. 4, 1928

Don't fuck Danger
    Banff, Alberta
    Aug. 2, 1928

Fuck you
Damn Turd
    Lakeside, on Lake Tahoe, CA
    July 14, 1928

You god Damn
fucken fool
    Medford, OR
    July 21, 1928

me and my wife had a fuck
    Red Bluff CA, Municipal Auto Camp
    July 17, 1928

This is a fuck of a rain
    Tejon Camp, near Tejon Pass, CA
    July 3, 1928

Although Victorian society was discrete and inhibited, not all Victorians were. There were certainly subcultures within England and America that were anything but inhibited. It's interesting that Frank Harris, writing towards the end of the nineteenth century, discussed sex frankly, yet still used a dash for *damn:* "a d— bad temper" (cited in Hughes 1991, 154). At about this time, we first find *fucking* being used non-literally, purely as an emphatic; Hughes (1991, 161) cites a nineteenth century slang dictionary that describes *fucking* as a synonym for *bloody,* but more violent.

Although *fuck* and its variants were clearly being used regularly in certain speech communities during the late nineteenth century, it probably didn't reach the mainstream society until the twentieth century. For example,

---

[6] *Bloody* never took off in America as a taboo word, but it had quite some power in England and in Australia and is still somewhat taboo in those countries today. Some have speculated that *bloody* was originally a euphemistic clipping of *by our lady,* but that is almost certainly a folk etymology (see Section 4). Another possible explanation is that it refers to Christ's blood, but the most likely explanation is that it is simply a scatological term (Lyle Campbell pers. comm.). As Eric Partridge puts it "There is no need of ingenious etymologies; the idea of blood suffices" (quoted in Mencken 1962, 680). Blood is gross to most people, and it might especially have referred to menstrual blood, which a lot of people (especially men, in my experience) consider super gross.

Hughes (1991, 169) notes that Mencken, writing in 1936, hardly mentions *fuck* in his discussion of American swearing, remarking only on its existence in coded terms. On the other hand, Mencken (1947 & 1962)[7] generally mocks others' squeamishness to print taboo words, so the fact that he censors himself from writing the word, or even discussing it, suggests how taboo it was at the time. The two most common American swear words according to Mencken were *son of a bitch* and *hell*. On the other hand, Read (1934) devotes an entire article to *fuck* (though, due to censors, he never actually prints the word in the piece), calling it "the word that has the deepest stigma of any in the language" (264) and "the most disreputable of all English words" (267), but he also notes that it is "universally known by speakers of English" (267). A year later, Read says of *fuck*, "Of the low words in the English vocabulary this is probably the most widespread and ever-present" (Read 1977: 51).[8]

By the end of World War II, attitudes began shifting. As Hughes (1991, 197) puts it, "from 1950 to 1970, a radical shift in attitudes occurred [in America], marked by spectacular and often scandalous instances of public profanity." However, although swearing became more common in movies and TV during the 1960s, Hughes believes that regular people did not swear any more than previously (195). We discuss this development in more detail in Chapter 15.

Before the twentieth century, our strongest taboos (in English) were on profanity. Following the Victorian age, obscenity became a stronger taboo. By the end of the twentieth century, racial, sexual, and sexually oriented slurs became our strongest taboos. For example, Hughes (1991, 239) observes that the first *Supplement* to the *Oxford English Dictionary* (1933) omitted sexual terms, while the second *Supplement* (1972–1986) was pressured to (but didn't) avoid negative racial terms[9]. This is where we find ourselves today: aside from some especially religious communities, profanity is only weakly taboo in contemporary English; obscenity is moderately to highly taboo (again, depending on the community); and slurs are highly taboo.

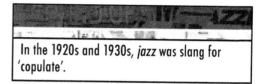

In the 1920s and 1930s, *jazz* was slang for 'copulate'.

According to Hughes (1991, 201), *motherfucker* began among African Americans, spread to whites in Vietnam among integrated troops, and then made it back to the States and into the population as a whole during the 1970s. Norman (1956, 111) gives a similar progression from African Americans to whites through the integrated army, but Norman puts the time-frame back twenty years to the early 1950s. A search of the OED shows Norman Mailer using the corrupted form (because of censors) *motherfugger* in his World War II novel *The Naked and the Dead* published in 1948.

3. TABOO PROCESSES

Now that we've got a sketch of how swearing evolved over the history of English, we'll look at some of the processes of change, how non-taboo words become taboo, and how taboo words become non-taboo.

In Section 3.1, we discuss how words may lose informative meaning and at the same time gain emotional and social meaning. In Section 3.2, we discuss how euphemisms can lead to a vicious circle of taboo words. In Section 3.3, we discuss how neutral words are turned into slurs. And in Section 3.4, we discuss how taboo words can taint non-taboo words.

3.1 *Emotive Intensifying, Semantic Weakening, and Social Stigmatizing*

Hughes (1991, 57) refers to the "twin processes" of **emotive intensifying** and **semantic weakening** as being essential to understanding swearing. Emotive intensifying is where words take on more emotional meaning. And semantic weakening is where the informative meaning becomes vague or even non-existent. These twins are very old. For example, back around 1300 we find *Devil* being used as an intensifier to mean 'very'—similar to how *fucking* is used today (Hughes 1991, 79).

In addition to the twins, emotive intensifying and semantic weakening, we should include a third sibling, the younger brother who follows the twins around: **social stigmatizing.** Social stigmatizing, of course, affects the third aspect of meaning, the social aspect, marginalizing the word and making it taboo. We see this with the

---

[7] The first was written in 1936 and the latter in 1945.
[8] Read originally published the book privately, in Paris, in 1935. See Chapter 15 for more on the book's publication.
[9] We discuss this further in Chapter 15.

British (and Australian) taboo word *bloody,* the Hungarian word *kurva* 'whore', and the French word *putain* 'whore', as in (5–7).

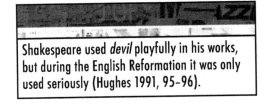

Shakespeare used *devil* playfully in his works, but during the English Reformation it was only used seriously (Hughes 1991, 95-96).

5. Get ALL cars off the pavement. It's for walking on not for parking your **bloody** car on!

   (http://www.weeklygripe.co.uk/a278.asp, accessed 7/6/2010)

6. La **putain** de voiture est toute rouillée . . .

   'the **whore** of a car is totally rusty'

   (http://fr.answers.yahoo.com/question/index?qid=20100629163023AAiXRYS, accessed 7/6/2010)

7. Hol van már az a kibaszott **kurva** kocsi

   'where is that fucked up **whore** car?'

   (http://kutyascsajj.blogol.hu/read/?d=2008-7, accessed 7/6/2010)

The twins don't let their brother follow them everywhere. There are words that show emotive intensifying and semantic weakening without becoming taboo. For example, American English *wicked,* French *vache(ment)* 'cow(ly)', and Hungarian *tök* 'pumpkin', as in (8–10).

8. It [the quilt] may be wicked easy but it's also wicked beautiful.

   (http://silverthimblequilting.blogspot.com/2007/02/wicked-easy-quilt-flimsy.html, accessed 7/6/2010)

9. Je trouve que la vie est quand même **vachement** belle . . .

   'I find that life is still **cowly** beautiful'

   (http://www.atlantyd.org/messagep20216.html, accessed 7/6/2010)

10. Találtam magamnak egy **tök** szép ruhát

    'I found myself a pumpkin beautiful dress'

    (http://angliabol.blogspot.com/2009/08/london-winchester-laza-het.html, accessed 7/6/2010)

Although *wicked, vache(ment),* and *tök* are not taboo in any sense, they are considered slang and would not be used in formal situations.

It's worth noting that social stigmatizing applies when the emotional strengthening leads to a negative emotion, while it doesn't apply when the emotional strengthening leads to a positive emotion, as is generally the case for *wicked, vache(ment),* and *tök.* As we discuss in Chapter 14, most taboo words are negative but can be used positively. We could speculate that as a taboo term is more and more associated with positive emotions, it may become less and less taboo.

A final example shows a case where semantic weakening is accompanied by taboo weakening (the opposite of social stigmatizing). In this case, we have another adverb, *hella* ('very' or 'a lot of'), derived from the weakly taboo word *hell,* probably from *hell of a* (the OED posits that *hella* came from *hellacious* or *helluva*). The word started in the late 1970s or early 1980s in the Bay Area of California. Today it is mostly restricted geographically to northern California. To get a sense of its present usage, I interviewed my two nieces, Sukie, age 14, and Becca, age 11, both living and going to school in Alameda, CA. Sukie says she uses it occasionally, as do her friends (but it would be unusual), while some of her classmates use it regularly; Becca claims she never uses *hella* (though I swear I've heard her use it), but one of her friends, one of her teachers, and some of her classmates use it. Although the OED (as well as other sites) mentions that *hella* can be used to modify nouns, as in *hella people* 'lots of people', my interviews with each girl (conducted separately) elicited only examples where *hella* modifies adjectives (11–16).

11. That's hella awesome.

12. That's hella cool.

13. You're hella stupid.

14. He's hella annoying.

15. Our science teacher is hella hard.

16. You're hella tall.

Both girls were unequivocal that *hell* is a worse word than *hella,* and both said that a student could use *hella* in class and not get in trouble for it. In contrast, they both felt that *hell* would be less likely to be used in class, and Becca said at least some teachers would get angry if a student used *hell.* Thus, it seems that *hell of a,* as in "a hell of a hard test," got reinterpreted as a single word meaning 'very', and at the same time lost its social stigma as a taboo word (though it is, like *wicked,* still considered slang).

3.2   The Euphemism Treadmill

The **euphemism treadmill** goes like this: a euphemism is invented to substitute for a term that has become too taboo, it is used so extensively that it becomes fully (conventionally) associated with what it denotes, it becomes taboo, a new euphemism has to be invented. As Bloomfield (1933, 401) puts it: "The substitutes [for taboo words] may in time become too closely associated with the meaning and in turn become tabu." Our terms for the room where one "does one's business" offer a good example: Originally the term was *water closet,* which became too indelicate, so it was abbreviated to *WC,* soon to be replaced by *toilet* (a French borrowing, which originally meant 'small towel' but came to be associated with the room where one used a small towel and ultimately with the commode itself) and then by *bathroom* (Campbell 2006–2009). *Go to the bathroom,* originally a circumlocution for elimination (not for, say, bathing or tooth-brushing), is now so conventionally associated with elimination that it's often heard in constructions that, if taken literally, would sound bizarre: "My dog went to the bathroom in my living room" (see Chapter 6). Today, *bathroom* is often seen as too indelicate, so we have other terms, like *ladies' room, little boys' room,* and *restroom,* and circumlocutions, like *I need to relieve myself* or, as my graduate advisor, Jerry Sadock, used to say, "let's take an uncoffee break."

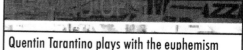

Quentin Tarantino plays with the euphemism *powder my nose* in his movie *Pulp Fiction.* Uma Thurman's character excuses herself from the table by saying, "I have to go powder my nose," and in the next scene we see her in the restroom snorting cocaine.

We saw the euphemism treadmill in action in Section 1 with euphemisms for oaths, such as *gadzooks, odsbodkins,* and *zounds.* Originally, these clipped versions of taboo expressions were a way of avoiding saying something bad (like saying "fuh" today, or, as the musical duo Flight of the Conchords sing, "All those mother-uckers ucking with my shi"). But over time, the euphemisms became taboo, even as people lost sight of their religious origins, so that in writing they were often represented with dashes after the first letters, just as today we substitute *f—, s—,* and *n—er* for *fuck, shit,* and *nigger.*

Mencken (1962, 639-640) traces how public restrooms came to be labeled "Women" and "Men": Originally the signs on the doors said "For Ladies Only" and "For Gents Only"; subsequently they were shortened to "Ladies Only" and "Gents Only" then to "Ladies" and "Gentleman," which were then changed to "Women" and "Men."

One of the best places to understand the euphemism treadmill is with PC terms (Campbell 2006–2009).[10] As a society, we gradually become uncomfortable with terms for mental and physical conditions and with terms for minorities. As the terms become more and more familiar, they become stigmatized and replaced.

- *lame → crippled → handicapped → disabled → differently-abled*

- *retarded → mentally handicapped → mentally challenged → special*

- *colored → negro → Black → African American → People of Color*

- *shell shock (World War I) → battle fatigue (World War II) → operational exhaustion (Korean War) → post-traumatic stress disorder (Vietnam War) → PTSD (present).*

What, to us, is an innocuous word, *occupy,* used to be taboo, so much so that, according to Read (1977, 276), it was practically absent from the language from the second half of the seventeenth century to the first half of the eighteenth century. What happened is it was a euphemism for 'fornication', which led to it becoming taboo. Sometime in the eighteenth century the word was revived with its original meaning and today we have no vestiges of its sexual meaning.

---

[10] See Chapter 15 for more on PC-ness.

3.3 Degeneration

Degeneration (or pejoration) is a process where a neutral word becomes a slur that is used in name-calling or pejoratives. For example, the following negative words were originally neutral words with more specific (or at least different) informative meanings: *wretch, churl, knave, villain* (Hughes 1991, 57). A wretch was originally simply an exile, a churl a man, a knave a male child, and a villain a servant in a villa. Through degeneration, these became common slurs. For example, Shakespeare was fond of putting "villain" in his characters' mouths: Hamlet says of his uncle[11], "O villain, villain, smiling, damned villain!" (*Hamlet* Act I, v, 112). By extension to its meaning 'the deeds of a villain', *villainy,* came to mean 'swearing', so Chaucer can praise a character by writing "He nevere yet no vileynye ne sayde/ In al his lyf unto no maner wight"—'he never said any villainy in all his life to any sort of person' (cited in Hughes 1991, 64, translation mine).

Religious terms are especially susceptible to this practice. Hughes (1991) gives the following examples. Until the crusades, *Saracen* was a neutral word for 'Arab', but during and after the crusades, when hatred for Arabs was at a peak among English speakers, *Saracen* was used strictly as a slur. Around the same period, *Mahounde,* a corruption of the name Muhammad, came to mean 'devil', 'false god', or 'false prophet' and was used in name-calling and pejoratives. The following anti-catholic terms, playing on the word *pope*, were used in invectives during the sixteenth century: *Papist, popish, popery, papistical, papistic, papish, papism, popestant,* and *popeling.* Even some common sect names that we use today were used as pejoratives by those opposed to them during the Reformation: *Quakers, Presbyterian, Methodist.*

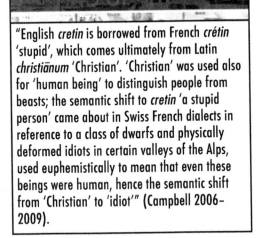

"English *cretin* is borrowed from French *crétin* 'stupid', which comes ultimately from Latin *christiānum* 'Christian'. 'Christian' was used also for 'human being' to distinguish people from beasts; the semantic shift to *cretin* 'a stupid person' came about in Swiss French dialects in reference to a class of dwarfs and physically deformed idiots in certain valleys of the Alps, used euphemistically to mean that even these beings were human, hence the semantic shift from 'Christian' to 'idiot'" (Campbell 2006-2009).

Hughes (1991, 56) notes that during the Middle Ages (beginning around the eleventh or twelfth century) English speakers shifted from "swearing by" to "swearing at" leading to certain adjectives being used emotively rather than literally: *old* ("olde barel-ful of lyes" from Chaucer, cited in Hughes 1991, 74), *precious* ("precious villain" from Shakespeare, cited in Hughes 1991, 57), *lousy* (literally, 'full of lice'). Of these, we find that only *lousy* is used emotively today, aside from a few idioms like *old fool* and *precious little.*

Degeneration is not always permanent. For example, Hughes (1991, 130) reports that *Jew* was a slur from 1600 to 1850 (see also Mencken 1947, 297–299). Some negative connotations may linger with the word—some people avoid it, preferring alternatives such as *Jewish person*—however, it now seems largely accepted as neutral (Hughes, himself, uses it orthophemistically). Similarly, *gay,* meaning 'homosexual', does not have the negative meaning today that it once did.

Oddly, though, *gay* seems to be diverging into two separate words, a neutral one meaning 'homosexual' and a negative one meaning 'uncool'. For example, in a comic strip from the mid 2000s (*Zits* by Jerry Scott and Jim Borgman), the following dialogue is found:

Jeremy: Ha! Ha! Billy, your shoes look so gay!

Billy: I am gay, Jeremy.

Jeremy: I know. I didn't mean "gay" as in homosexual. I meant "gay" as in lame.

In class discussions with my Bad Words and Taboo Terms class, I find that many college students today see these as separate words. Some students have remarked that in high school they didn't even realize the two words were related, and they stopped using *gay* to mean 'uncool' once somebody pointed out that it was derogatory to homosexuals. This strikes me as a change from my generation (late 1980s) when both uses were current, but the latter one more clearly meant 'uncool' because of a purported association with homosexuality ("gay shoes" would have meant 'shoes that a homosexual would wear'). It's interesting to note that the word Jeremy uses to gloss his intended

---

[11] Who is simultaneously Hamlet's step-father and the murderer of Hamlet's father.

meaning, *lame,* went through a similar degeneration process from 'disabled' to 'uncool'. In that case, though, the original meaning seems antiquated.

Degeneration is especially common with terms for women. *Whore* was probably a euphemism way-back-when; according to Bloomfield (1933, 401), it derived from the same original word as Latin *cärus* 'dear'. Before *mistress* came to mean 'a female paramour', it was simply the feminine counterpart to *master*. *Madam,* before being associated with brothels, was a polite way to address a woman (modern day *ma'am* is derived from it). *Spinster* originally meant 'one who spins' (the *-ster* suffix serves the same purpose as *-er*) but degenerated to be a pejorative for 'unwed woman'.[12] *Slut* originally was used for 'untidy woman' and attained its sexual connotations later. We discuss English slurs for women in more detail in Chapter 13.

The degeneration of terms for women is not unique to English. Campbell (2006–2009) lists the following examples:

Spanish: *ramera* 'prostitute' originally meant 'inn-keeper's wife'; *puta* 'whore' originally meant 'girl'

Italian: *putta* 'whore' also originally meant 'girl'

German: *Weib* 'ill-tempered woman' originally meant 'woman' (English *wife* derived from the same Germanic word as *Weib*)

3.4   Taboo Tainting

Neutral words can be tainted by perceived similarities to taboo words. I call this process **taboo tainting.** Sometimes it happens because a neutral word is used as a euphemism and, over time, becomes too associated with this new usage, at which point any use, even with its original meaning, is taboo. For example, *bitch,* except among dog breeders, is no longer used to refer to a female dog[13]; and, in my experience, most people are uncomfortable calling a cat "a pussy." Taboo tainting can also happen to unrelated words if they sound too similar to a taboo word. For example, even though *niggardly* is in no way related to *nigger,* it has fallen out of popular use. Indeed, in 1999, after a co-worker complained that David Howard had used *niggardly* in a discussion, Howard resigned from his job as aide to Washington D.C. Mayor Anthony A. Williams (Woodlee 1999).[14]

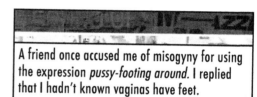

A friend once accused me of misogyny for using the expression *pussy-footing around.* I replied that I hadn't known vaginas have feet.

In British English, where *bloody* is a bad word, you don't hear people talking about "bloody noses"; instead, they use *blood nose* or *bleeding nose* (Campbell 2006–2009).

Although it is perfectly proper to pronounce *Uranus* with stress on the second syllable ([jərénəs]), most people prefer to pronounce it with the stress on the first syllable ([júrənəs]) because otherwise it sounds too much like *your anus.* On the other hand, *Dictionary.com* indicates that if you stress the first syllable, it sounds like *urinous.*

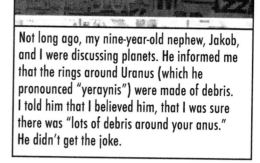

Not long ago, my nine-year-old nephew, Jakob, and I were discussing planets. He informed me that the rings around Uranus (which he pronounced "yeraynis") were made of debris. I told him that I believed him, that I was sure there was "lots of debris around your anus." He didn't get the joke.

Because *cock* became too associated with 'penis', Americans coined a new word for 'male chicken', *rooster,* literally 'one who roosts'. In fact, Read (2003, 11) notes that some people preferred *roosterswain* to *coxswain* during the nineteenth century. You may wonder (I know I have) how 'male chicken' came to be associated with 'penis'. Here it is: certain short pipes or spouts, especially with a valve to stop the

---

[12] Note that *bachelor* does not have the same negative emotions associated with it—historically it was more acceptable for a man to remain unwed than a woman. On the other hand, the term *confirmed bachelor* used to be a euphemism for 'homosexual man'; today, however, it is more commonly used to refer to a heterosexual man who never intends on marrying. As our society has changed, *spinster* has become somewhat archaic, as it is no longer considered so horrible for a woman not to wed. Notice that when ABC introduced a female version of their show *The Bachelor,* they chose to call it *The Bachelorette,* not *The Spinster.*

[13] For a short while during the Victorian age, the word for a female dog was *slut,* not *bitch* (Read 2003: 11).

[14] Williams later admitted that he had accepted Howard's resignation too hastily and rehired him in a different position in his administration.

flow, were called cocks (cf. *stopcock*[15]) beginning in the fifteenth century, probably because of a perceived resemblance to roosters (nobody's quite sure what the pipes looked like), so the 'penis' meaning was based on the 'pipe' meaning, which was based on the 'rooster' meaning (OED).

When I discuss *ass* with my Bad Words and Taboo Terms class, I find that students are baffled as to how the word for the animal came to refer to a person's back end. Furthermore, when I ask them about the related word *arse,* most believe that it is a euphemism for *ass.* Well, here's the real story. *Arse* was originally the word for 'bottom', and *ass* was the euphemism. Because of its similarity in pronunciation (especially in dialects where /r/ is dropped after a vowel), *ass* was a good candidate, in the same way as someone today might say "ash-hole" instead of *asshole.*[16] In England, *arse* is still used, but in the U.S., the taboo word fell out of existence, and its euphemistic counterpart took over, which then became taboo itself. At that point, we Americans could no longer refer to the animal as an "ass," so we needed a new word; we coined the word *donkey,* which started as a joke—a squishing together of *dun*[17] *monkey* (for some reason people thought it was funny to think of a donkey as being a type of monkey)—but nevertheless took off.

In the Ozarks at the beginning of the twentieth century, "[t]he sex organs in general are known as the *prides,* and the word *pride* has thus acquired an obscene significance" (Randolph 1928, quoted in Mencken 1962, 655).

Bunny is an interesting example of taboo tainting (Campbell 2006–2009). Originally the word was *coney,* as in Coney Island in New York, which got its name from all the rabbits on it. The word rhymed with *money* (our present pronunciation of Coney Island is reinterpretation based on spelling). The problem was that there was another English word that was pronounced just like *coney* (though spelled differently). Can you guess what it was? Wait for it . . . Wait for it . . . *Cunt.* Yes, *cunt* was, in some dialects, pronounced [kʌni]. Something had to give, so folks changed the first sound of *coney* to /b/, giving us *bunny.*[18]

Taboo tainting is certainly not unique to English. Campbell (2006–2009) gives the following examples from Latin America:

- Spanish *huevo* means 'egg' but also 'testicle'; thus in colloquial Mexican Spanish *huevo* as 'egg' is avoided and replaced by *blanquillo* 'small white thing' (*blanco* 'white' + *-illo* 'diminutive').
- In Latin American Spanish *pájaro* 'bird' is associated with 'penis'; *pajarito* is usually substituted for 'bird' (*pájaro* 'bird' + *-ito* 'diminutive'). This avoidance is carried to Kaqchikel and K'iche' (Mayan languages of Guatemala), where native *ts'ikin* 'bird' has come to mean 'penis' due to Spanish influence, and *čikop* '(small) animal' has been extended to include both '(small) animal' and 'bird'.
- Spanish *coger* 'to take, pick up', means 'fuck' in Mexico, leading to other words for 'take' and 'grab': *agarrar* 'to grab', *tomar* 'to take'.
- Spanish *concha* 'shell' is obscene in parts of Latin America (female genital associations), which has led to native words for 'shell' being replaced in some Mesoamerican Indian languages.
- The word for 'rabbit' in Chulupí (a native language in Paraguay and Argentina) is *puta,* but is being replaced due to its similarity to Spanish *puta* 'whore' by *nanxatetax* (*nanxate* 'hare' + *-tax* 'similar to').

Sometimes instead of the neutral word being lost, the taboo word is lost. There used to be a word *quean* which meant 'low woman'. Originally it was pronounced with [ɛ] as the vowel, so it rhymed with modern-day *when,* and *queen* was pronounced with [e] as the vowel, so it rhymed with modern-day *wane.* However, due to a sound change, the two words merged in their pronunciation. Obviously, we couldn't have the Queen associated with a low woman, so the word *quean* fell out of usage in all but those dialects in southwest England where the two vowels remained distinct (Campbell 2006–2009).

---

[15] Not to be confused with *cock-block.*

[16] To confuse things, though, *ass* was used as faunality to refer to silly people for centuries before it began being used in place of *arse.* Read (1977, 30), writing in 1935, reports that many people at that time pronounced *ass* meaning 'dolt' so that it rhymed with *loss* not *lass.*

[17] *Dun* means 'grey'.

[18] I have to wonder whether Hugh Hefner was aware of this history when he began calling the women in his magazine "bunnies."

4.   FOLK ETYMOLOGIES

When I was in college, I knew a fellow undergraduate, a radical feminist, who argued that women should reclaim the word *cunt* for 'vagina' because (I'm paraphrasing here) what should be a beautiful word was transformed by patriarchal society into a bad word. To support her argument, she offered this interesting historical tidbit: *cunt* is related to the German word *kunst* meaning 'art'. Others have argued for reclaiming or co-opting *cunt* (cf. especially Muscio 2002); however, she's the only one I've ever known to bring up the etymological connection between *cunt* and *kunst*. Why is that? Well, because it's wrong.

Folks love to speculate about where words come from, and these speculations are called **folk etymologies.** For example, there's a story floating around that sexism is endemic to golf, even down to its name, which derives from "gentlemen only, ladies forbidden." A golf-illiterate linguist, like myself, has no expertise in speaking to the purported sexist nature of golf; however, I can say with confidence that the word *golf* did not derive from an acronym. According to the *Oxford English Dictionary* (OED), the word's origins are not certain, but it dates back at least to the fifteenth century; some experts speculate that it came from a Dutch word for 'club' and others that it came from a Scottish dialectal word for 'a blow with the open hand'.

Similarly, there are a whole bunch of folk etymologies on the web claiming that *fuck* is actually an acronym. Posited examples include:

- For Unlawful Carnal Knowledge
- Fornication Under Consent of the King
- Fornication Under Charles the King
- Fornication Under Crown of the King
- Fornication Under Christ, King
- Forbidden Under Charter of the King
- Forced Unlawful Carnal Knowledge
- File Under Carnal Knowledge

These etymologies are usually accompanied by entertaining stories about how England's king used to regulate who could and could not have sex. Need I say that these stories are all utter nonsense? Some of them are ridiculous in that they contain words, such as *fornication,* which came into English after *fuck* did. In fact, it is probable that *fuck* predates English; most linguists accept that it is at least of Proto-Germanic heritage (c. 1000 BC—see Figure 7.1). It's doubtful our predecessors were using acronyms before they had a spelling system.

The same goes for folk etymologies that claim *shit* came from an acronym for "ship high in transit" or "store high in transit." These etymologies usually go on to explain that when manure was transported in ships it had to be stored high enough that it wouldn't get wet, so it was stamped with "S.H.I.T." So what can we say about this etymology? It's B.S.

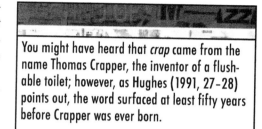

You might have heard that *crap* came from the name Thomas Crapper, the inventor of a flushable toilet; however, as Hughes (1991, 27-28) points out, the word surfaced at least fifty years before Crapper was ever born.

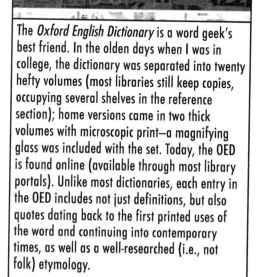

The *Oxford English Dictionary* is a word geek's best friend. In the olden days when I was in college, the dictionary was separated into twenty hefty volumes (most libraries still keep copies, occupying several shelves in the reference section); home versions came in two thick volumes with microscopic print—a magnifying glass was included with the set. Today, the OED is found online (available through most library portals). Unlike most dictionaries, each entry in the OED includes not just definitions, but also quotes dating back to the first printed uses of the word and continuing into contemporary times, as well as a well-researched (i.e., not folk) etymology.

Although etymologies that explain taboo words through acronyms are generally false, we certainly have words that began as acronyms whose full form include taboo words: *fubar* "fucked up beyond all repair," *snafu* "situation normal, all fucked up." There are also euphemistic abbreviations: *B.S.* "bullshit," *SOB* "son of a bitch," *WTF?* "what the fuck?", *OMG* "oh my god," *FMB* "fuck me boots," as well as one coined by sex advice columnist Dan Savage *DTMFA* "dump the motherfucker already."

5. TRUE ETYMOLOGIES

Back to *cunt*. This is a very old word in English. The first written examples of the word date back to the thirteenth century, when there was a London street named *Gropecuntelane*. Surprisingly, this name means exactly what you'd think it should—'grope cunt lane'—and it was presumably a street where prostitutes could be found.

The OED gives this etymology for *cunt*: "ME. *cunte, count(e)*, corresponding to ON. *kunta* (Norw., Sw. dial. *kunta,* Da. dial. *kunte*), OFris., MLG., MDu. *kunte*: Gmc. **kunt n* wk. fem.; ulterior relations uncertain." What this means: In Middle English, the word was spelled <u>cunte</u> or <u>count</u> or <u>counte</u>; there are similar words in Norwegian, dialects of Swedish, and dialects of Danish, and there was an Old Norse word *kunta* with the same meaning; Old Frisian, Modern Low German, and Modern Dutch have *kunte*; all this leads one to speculate that it came from a Proto-Germanic "weak" noun **kunt*[19], which was feminine; "ulterior relations uncertain" means the OED deems inconclusive any etymologies that date the word any further back than that.

We can be fairly certain that *cunt* is not related to French *con* ('cunt') or Spanish *coño* ('cunt'), as many folk etymologies would have it. On the surface, you might think these words are related, especially given that *con* and *coño* come from the Latin word *cunnus* ('female pudenda', cf. *cunnilingus* 'vagina-tongue'); and they look even closer when you realize that *–us* is a suffix, so the Latin root is *cunn-*. It would seem that all we'd need to do is to figure out how the /t/ got on the end. Unfortunately, things aren't so simple in the world of etymologies. The fact is you can't just look at words from two different languages, see a form and meaning similarity, and assume they're related. I'll try to explain why as briefly as I can.

Languages change. That's what they do. Sometimes slowly, sometimes quickly, but always change. Languages add new words and slough off old words. They lose and gain prefixes, suffixes, and infixes (see Chapter 2 and Chapter 8 for more on affixes). They change their syntax, semantics, morphology, and, most importantly for our discussion, phonology. Often, we keep words, but change their sounds. For example, *knife* used to have a /k/ at the beginning, hence the spelling. We see this with *cunt*, which was earlier pronounced with /u/ (as in *boot*) in the middle instead of /ʌ/ (as in *butt*). Sounds change systematically and regularly: it's rare for a sound in one word to change and for the sound not to change in other words; typically, all the words containing a particular sound change. Thus, words in an earlier form of English that were pronounced with /u/ are now pronounced with /ʌ/.

Now, let's think about where Latin fits in. Latin and English are related, but only distantly. All those Latin based words that we've got in English are borrowings (mostly via French[20]). Somewhere around 4000 BC (give or take a few millennia), there was a language, Proto-Indo-European, probably spoken in west-central Asia. As the speakers dispersed, the language broke into different dialects and eventually languages. The language families descending from Proto-Indo-European are Hellenic, Celtic, Indo-Iranian, Slavic, Italic, and Germanic, along with a few others (see Table 7.1). Italic includes Latin and the languages descended from it (French, Italian, Portuguese, Spanish, Romanian, etc.). And Proto-Germanic led to the Germanic languages, including German, Dutch, Norwegian, Swedish, Danish, English, etc. (see Figure 7.1).

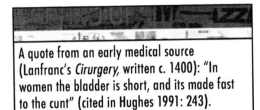

A quote from an early medical source (Lanfranc's *Cirurgery,* written c. 1400): "In women the bladder is short, and its made fast to the cunt" (cited in Hughes 1991: 243).

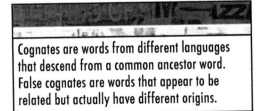

Cognates are words from different languages that descend from a common ancestor word. False cognates are words that appear to be related but actually have different origins.

Here's a fun (and true) etymology for *vagina*: believe it or not, *vagina* and *vanilla* derive from the same word (Campbell 2006-2009). They were both borrowed into English, and both come from a Latin word meaning 'sheath'. It shouldn't be hard for you to see how sheaths would make a good metaphoric euphemism (see Chapter 6) for the female pudenda, but it might not be as obvious how vanilla fits in—well, the pod of the vanilla bean is shaped like a sheath. Next time you're at a party, you can break the ice with this factoid.

---

[19] Note this is a different use of the asterisk than what we've seen in other chapters, where it indicates an ungrammatical form; in historical linguistics, the asterisk before a word indicates that it is "reconstructed." When you trace words back far enough in time, you get to a point when the language was not written and, therefore, we have no records of what words existed. Nevertheless, we can make educated guesses, which we call reconstructions and which we indicate with an asterisk. Proto-Germanic was an early predecessor of Norwegian, Swedish, Danish, German, Dutch, and English (among other languages).

[20] On a family tree, English and French would be, like, third or fourth cousins—it would be legal for them to marry in every part of the United States. In fact, some might argue they mated during the eleventh century following the Norman Conquest, and the present form of English is the bastard child of English and French.

TABLE 7.1
Major Proto-Indo-European Families with Representative Languages

Indo-Iranian	Celtic	Slavic	Hellenic	Italic	Germanic
Persian, Farsi, Pashto, Kurdish, Hindi, Urdu	Irish Gaelic, Scots Gaelic, Breton, Cornish, Welsh	Russian, Ukranian, Polish, Slovak, Czech, Slovak, Serbo-Croat, Bulgarian	Greek, Macedonian	Latin, Italian, French, Spanish, Portuguese, Romanian	German, Norwegian, Swedish, Danish, Dutch, English

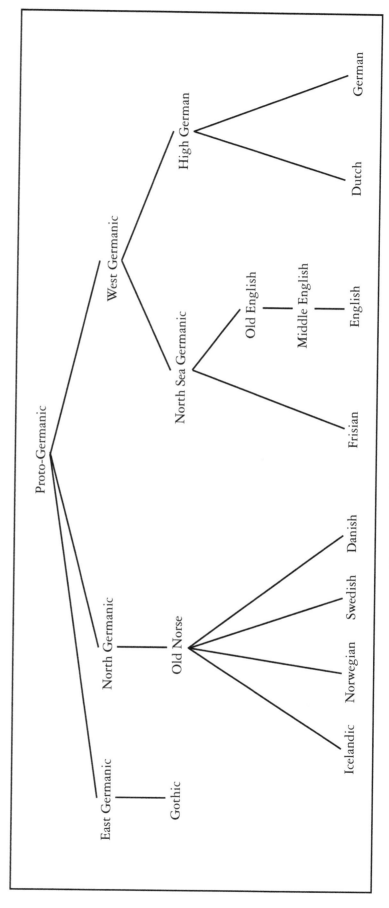

FIGURE 7.1   *The germanic languages' family tree*

TABLE 7.2

English-Latin Cognates		
English	*Latin*	*Latinate Borrowings in English*
father	*pater*	*paternity*
ford	*portus*	*port or portage*
thirst	*torrēre*	*torrefaction*
thunder	*tonāre*	*tonant*
horn	*corn*	*cornucopia*
heart	*cord*	*cardiac*

Because Latin is related to English (they're both descendants of Proto-Indo-European), we can find Germanic words in English with Latin cognates (i.e., Latin words that derive from the same ancestor word, or proto-word). See the examples in Table 7.2.

Notice a pattern? The English words begin with a fricative, a sound created by partially closing the vocal tract, and the Latin words begin with a stop, a sound created by fully closing the vocal tract (see Chapter 5 for more on speech production). This pattern is part of what's called Grimm's Law, which observes that Proto-Indo-European voiceless stops became fricatives in Germanic languages.

All this leads us to why French *con* and Spanish *coño* are not related to English *cunt.* The Latin ancestor of the French and Spanish words began with /k/, which means that the Proto-Indo-European word began with **/k/*, which means that any English word derived from the original word would begin with /h/. *Cunt* begins with /k/; therefore, it cannot be related to Latin *cunnus,* unless it was borrowed, which seems unlikely given how far we can trace it back in Germanic languages.

A similar argument can be made for why *fuck* can't be related to French *foutre* 'to fuck', Italian *fottere* 'to fuck', and Latin *future* 'to fuck'. All of these are ruled out because, if it is related to Latin, the Latin word should begin with /p/ not /f/.[21] On the other hand, there are two Latin words that it is plausibly related to: *pungere* and *pungo,* both meaning 'to sting'. We'll see how this works in Section 5.

Here's the etymology, the OED gives for *fuck:*

> Probably cognate with Dutch *fokken* to mock (15th cent.), to strike (1591), to fool, gull (1623), to beget children (1637), to have sexual intercourse with (1657), to grow, cultivate (1772), Norwegian regional *fukka* to copulate, Swedish regional *fokka* to copulate (compare Swedish regional *fock* penis), further etymology uncertain . . .

The OED goes on to give an etymology posited by Lass (1995) that traces the word back to Proto-Indo-European. We'll look in some depth at Lass' etymology in the next section.

6.   LASS' (1995) ETYMOLOGY FOR *FUCK*[22]

In the course of his research, Lass found that scholars have proposed quite a few foreign words as being potential cognates for *fuck.* Table 7.3 gives a list of such possible cognates ordered alphabetically by language. If we filter the list down to just those words that mean 'fuck', then the best candidates are given in Table 7.4.

Of these languages, Dutch, Norwegian, Swedish, and German are the closest relatives to English. Admittedly, *fokken* in Dutch is used primarily for cattle, but the sense of 'copulation' is still there, and, moreover, its form is close to *fuck,* especially when we consider that the *—en* at the end is a suffix, and the base form of the verb is *fokk-.* In all of the Germanic languages (see Figure 7.1), we have the 'copulation' meaning and the /f/ and /k/

---

[21] Latin /f/ originated as Indo-European **/bʰ/*, leading to Germanic /b/.

[22] It's interesting to note that Lass' etymology was first posited sixty years earlier by Read (1934). Apparently Read's work escaped Lass' notice, since he does not cite it.

	TABLE 7.3	
	Possible Cognates for *Fuck*	
Language	*Word*	*English Gloss*
Dutch	*fokhengst*	'stallion'
	fokken	'to strike, to copulate, to breed (cattle)'
	fokker	'cattle-breeder'
	fokkerij	'cattle-breeding, stud-farm'
	fokvee	'breeding-cattle'
French	*foutre*	'to fuck'
German	*fichte*	'spruce tree'
	ficken	'to fuck'
Greek	*pyg-*	'buttocks'
Icelandic	*fjúka*	'be tossed by wind'
Italian	*fottere*	'to fuck'
Latin	*frango*	'to break'
	frico	'to rub'
	future	'to fuck'
	pungere	'to prick, to sting'
	pungo	'to sting'
Lithuanian	*pušis*	'spruce tree'
dialectal Norwegian	*fukka*	'to copulate'
dialectal Swedish	*fock*	'penis'
	focka	'to copulate'

	TABLE 7.4	
	Possible Cognates for *Fuck* Based on Meaning	
Language	*Word*	*English Gloss*
Dutch	*fokken*	'to strike, to copulate, to breed (cattle)'
French	*foutre*	'to fuck'
German	*ficken*	'to fuck'
Italian	*fottere*	'to fuck'
Latin	*future*	'to fuck'
dialectal Norwegian	*fukka*	'to copulate'
dialectal Swedish	*focka*	'to copulate'

sounds. However, the vowels are different from the English vowel /ʌ/: /o/ in Dutch and Swedish, /u/ in Norwegian, and /i/ in German. No big deal (mostly). Even in English, *fuck* wouldn't have always been pronounced with /ʌ/—earlier it would have been pronounced /u/ (as in *boot*), like the Norwegian. Over the course of several centuries, mostly from the fifteenth to sixteenth centuries, English /u/ changed to /ʌ/ as a result of the Great Vowel Shift.[23] We saw this happening with *cunt,* as well.

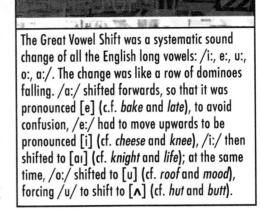

The Great Vowel Shift was a systematic sound change of all the English long vowels: /iː, eː, uː, oː, aː/. The change was like a row of dominoes falling. /aː/ shifted forwards, so that it was pronounced [e] (c.f. *bake* and *late*), to avoid confusion, /eː/ had to move upwards to be pronounced [i] (cf. *cheese* and *knee*), /iː/ then shifted to [aɪ] (cf. *knight* and *life*); at the same time, /oː/ shifted to [u] (cf. *roof* and *mood*), forcing /u/ to shift to [ʌ] (cf. *hut* and *butt*).

In all likelihood, the Proto-Germanic word would have been **fuk,* pronounced with an /u/. Swedish and Norwegian preserved the same vowel, but it changed somewhat in English, Dutch, and German. The change from */u/ to present-day /o/ in Dutch is found in other words, so it's not surprising it happened with *fokken.* But */u/ becoming /i/ in German is a little surprising. Lass spends some time trying to show that it's possible. We don't need to go into the details—but the point is that there are some sound changes that are more likely than others; for example, an /u/ becoming /o/ is not surprising because it just involves a slight lowering of the tongue, but /u/ becoming /i/ is less common because it involves the tongue moving forward and the lips un-rounding. In order to make sense of this alleged German change of */u/ to modern /i/ in *ficken,* Lass suggests that there was an intermediate stage where the word had /ü/ in it. The /ü/ sound in German is a high front rounded vowel. It's similar to /i/ in that it's high and front—but the difference is in the lips. Try saying /i/, as in *cheese,* hold it, and then purse your lips as you make the vowel: the sound you get is /ü/. Getting /i/ from /ü/ is just a matter of unrounding the lips, so that's easy. Lass points out that this chain of changes in German from */u/ through /ü/ to /i/ is unusual, but is found in other words.

We can be pretty confident of this Proto-Germanic etymology for *fuck.* We can speculate that for our distant ancestors **fuk-* might have been an orthophemism, akin to *mate* or *procreate* for us today. Orthophemisms, however, often become dysphemistic over time, which is what happened in German and English, where the two cognates, *fuck* and *ficken,* are taboo today (though note that in Dutch *fokken* is not so taboo).

Now, Lass' question is: can we push the etymology any further back? As we discussed, the supposed cognates from Romance languages (French *foutre,* Italian *fottere,* and Latin *future*) are false cognates with *fuck.* They could not have evolved from a common ancestor word because, if there is such a word, it must have begun with /p/, not /f/, given Grimm's Law (cf. English *father,* Spanish *padre,* and Latin *pater*). This brings us to some rather odd potential cognates, as seen in Table 7.5.

'So, you ask, why would anyone think that words for 'buttocks', 'sting', and 'spruce tree' are related to *fuck?* What? Don't you see it?

All right, it goes like this. The original Proto-Indo-European word was probably **pug* pronounced /pug/. Originally, it wouldn't have had anything to do with sex, not until Proto-Indo-European dissolved into its various branches. The sex part came from Proto-Germanic. Previously, I suggested that the Proto-Germanic word was probably an orthopemism, but before it was an orthopemism, it was probably a euphemism. In fact, we can even

TABLE 7.5		
Odd Potential Cognates for *Fuck*		
Language	*Word*	*English Gloss*
German	*fichte*	'spruce tree'
Greek	*pyg-*	'buttocks'
Latin	*pungere*	'to prick, to sting'
	pungo	'to sting'
Lithuanian	*pušis*	'spruce tree'

---

[23] I'm serious, that's what it's called. See sidebar for more information.

suggest what type of euphemism: a metaphor. The word *pug, according to Lass, originally meant 'to prick', as in what a sharp object can do. Imagine a needle penetrating leather—if you have a dirty mind, this image conjures up an obscene analogy. We can imagine, then, our Proto-Germanic ancestors censoring their speech in front of the children; instead of saying the taboo word for intercourse (whatever that was) they used a metaphoric euphemism that the adults would get but the children wouldn't.

In Latin, *pug preserved its original meaning in *pungere* and *pungo* (the extra /n/ was probably added at some point because of confusion with the words *pugno* 'fight' and *pugnus* 'fist'). The Greek *pyg-* meaning 'buttocks' might have resulted from the verb being interpreted from the receiving side (what is penetrated) rather than the sending side (what penetrates—see Swedish *fock* 'penis').

The Latin and Greek you get, right? But you're still wondering how spruce trees fit into this. It's simpler than you might think. When I was fifteen, a friend of my father's taught me how to distinguish a fir tree from a spruce tree. When you press your finger tips against a fir tree's needles, it feels soft, but when you do the same with a spruce tree, it hurts. Get it? A spruce tree is a tree whose needles prick. Thus, in Lithuanian, the Proto-Indo-European word *pug became *pušis* meaning 'spruce'. A similar thing happened, apparently, in German, where *fichte* is the word for 'spruce'.

To summarize, *fuck* is a word with a long history. We can plausibly trace it back to our earliest known ancestor language, Proto-Indo-European, where it was simply a verb, meaning 'to prick' and was pronounced /pug/. Our more recent ancestor language, Proto-Germanic, transformed the pronunciation to /fuk/ and used it metaphorically as a euphemism for sex. Over time, the euphemism lost its metaphoric value, which is to say that people stopped seeing it as an indirect way to refer to sex, but rather as a direct way. By the time that Old English came onto the scene, *fuck* was probably an orthophemism. Over time, it came to be seen as vulgar, so that by Modern English times it was taboo, and we had to come up with new, polite terms. For example, we borrowed *copulation* and *fornication* from Latin, and we invented circumlocutions like *sexual intercourse*.

7. CONCLUSION

Speakers have always sworn. Speakers always will swear. Although commonly believed, it makes no sense to say that people today use more and stronger taboo words than they did in the past. The problem is that it feels like people swear more and worse today because when we hear past swearing it doesn't sound like swearing to our ears. Languages change. Swearing changes. In this chapter we traced the changes in English swearing from early oath-making to middle ages profanity, from Victorian prudishness to twentieth century obscenity, and finally to modern-day slurs. We also looked at the process involved in shaping how taboo words change: emotional strengthening, semantic weakening, and social stigmatizing; the euphemism treadmill; degeneration; and taboo tainting. We explored folk etymologies and looked in depth at a possible etymology for *fuck*.

REFERENCES

Bloomfield, Leonard. 1933. *Language.* New York: Henry Holt.

Campbell, Lyle. 2006–2009. Taboo, Obscenity, and Lexical and Semantic Change. Lecture given for Bad Words and Taboo Terms, University of Utah, Salt Lake City, UT.

Hughes 1991. *Swearing: A Social History of Foul Language, Oaths, and Profanity in English.* Cambridge, MA: Blackwell.

Lass, Roger. 1995. Four Letters in Search of an Etymology. *Diachronica* XII: 1, 99–111.

Mencken, H.L. 1947. *The American Language: An Inquiry into the Development of English in the United States.* New York: Alfred A. Knopf.

Mencken, H.L. 1962. *Supplement One: The American Language.* New York: Alfred A. Knopf.

Muscio, Inga. 2002. *Cunt: A Declaration of Independence* (2nd ed.). New York: Seal Press.

Norman, Arthur N.Z. 1956. Army Speech and the Future of American English. *American Speech* 31(2): 107–112.

OED. *Oxford English Dictionary.* Online Edition.

Randolph, Vance. 1928. Verbal Modesty in the Ozarks. *Dialect Notes,* VI, Part I: 57–64.

Read, Allen. 1934. An Obscenity Symbol. *American Speech* 19(4): 264–278.

Read, Allen. 1977. *Classic American Graffiti: Lexical Evidence from Folk Epigraphy in Western North America.* Waukesha, WI: Maledicta Press.

Read, Allen. 2003. The Geolinguistics of Verbal Taboo. *Geolinguistics* 29:7–21.

Woodlee, Yolanda. 1999. D.C. "Mayor Acted 'Hastily,' will Rehire Aide." *Washington Post,* Feb. 4, 1999, A1.

1.   Look up the etymologies of your favorite taboo words in the *Oxford English Dictionary.*

2.   It's been suggested that *suck* is less taboo today than it was two or three generations ago. If so, we should expect that younger people will find it less taboo than older people. Interview as many people as you can from different generations (under 18, 18–30, 31–50, 51–70, over 70), and ask them what they think of the word *suck,* as in "This sucks!", and whether they consider the word to be obscene. Is there any trend? Do you find, as we hypothesized, that older people find it more obscene than younger people?

3.   Can you think of other words that you would predict are taboo for older generations and not for younger generations? If so, try the same experiment with those words.

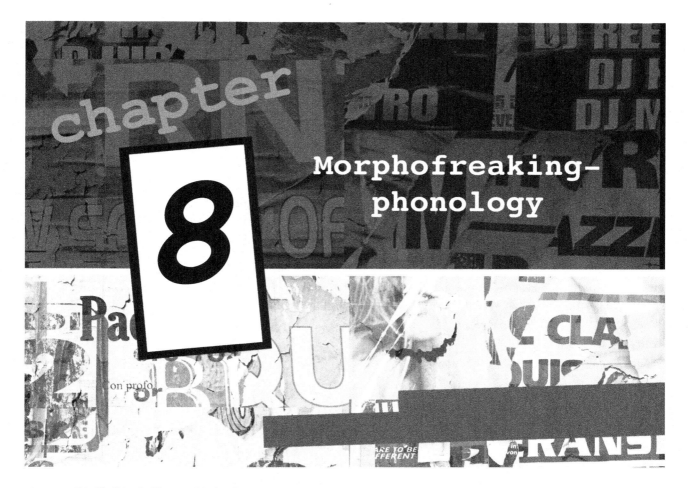

1. INTRODUCTION

In this chapter, we're going to look at the nexus between phonology and morphology (see Chapter 2). Phonology is about the sound structure of words, and morphology is about the meaning structure of words. Words are, of course, composed of sounds, but before the sounds form words, they're grouped into syllables; moreover, as we discuss in this chapter, those syllables combine together to form feet (typically thought of as pairs of syllables). Words are also composed of morphemes, the smallest meaningful elements of a language; these morphemes also combine together in a structured manner.

So what's this got to do with cussing? Good question. Read on.

2. INFIXATION[1]

As we discussed in Chapter 2, there are two types of morphemes: **free** and **bound**. Free morphemes, like *shit, fuck, damn,* and *felch,* are full words all by themselves. They are simple words that can't be morphologically deconstructed any further. Bound morphemes are like parasites—they can't survive on their own. They need a host (usually an existing word) to attach to. Examples are *-y* and *-less,* as in *shitty* and *shitless; -ing, re-* and *-er,* as in *fucking, refuck,* and *fucker; -ed* and *-ation,* as in *damned* and *damnation; un-* and *-able,* as in *unfelchable.* The vast majority of bound morphemes in English are **prefixes** (*re-, un-, in-, mis-,* etc.) or **suffixes** (*-ing, -er, -ed, -ation,* etc.); that is, they come before or after a free morpheme.

Another possibility, one less common around the world, is for a bound morpheme to be inserted inside a word. It's important to note that it's not enough for a morpheme to be in the middle of a word; it has to be injected

---

[1] The ideas, theory, and analysis presented in the rest of this chapter borrow heavily from John McCarthy's (1982) landmark paper, "Prosodic Structure and Expletive Infixation."

there. For example, -y in *sluttier* (from *slut* + *-y* + *-er*) and *-able* in *damnability* (from *damn* + *-able* + *-ity*) are not infixes; they simply attach to a free morpheme to form a word (*slutty, damnable*) and then a second suffix is added (*-er, -ity*). An infix would be the equivalent of creating something like *slyut* or *dableamn*. Infixes are common in some languages, but most people don't think of them existing in English—I doubt your high school English teacher ever mentioned the term. Nonetheless, there are several productive infixes in English. Consider the following words:

1. Infreakingcredible
2. Absobloodylutely
3. Polifuckingticians
4. Alagoddamnbama

For some reason, English infixes tend to be derived from taboo words (or euphemisms transformed from taboo words). Mencken (1947, 315–316) notes *goddam* as an infix, citing either Joseph Pulitzer as having the first usage with "The trouble with you Coates, is that you are too indegoddampendant!" or Foster Coates with "Tell Mr. Pulitzer that I'm under no obligoddamnation to do that, and I won't." Moreover, Mencken, with no small amount of national pride, claims that Australians adopted *bloody*-infixation from Americans' *goddam*-infixation. However, Hughes (1991, 173) argues infixation was more likely innovated by Australians than by Americans. In "The Australaise," an Australian marching song written in 1908, *bloody* (euphemized with dashes) is found in nearly every line. Here's the chorus:

Get a --- move on,

Have some --- sense.

Learn the --- art of

Self de- ---- -fence.

Other infixed words from "The Australiaise": *Australibloodyar, enthusibloodyasm, posterbloodyity, adbloodyvance, Spiflerbloodycate.*[2]

In the United States today, the infix *-fucking-* is the most common, and it clearly has a functional and etymological kinship with the free morpheme *fucking*, a modifier that can add stress to just about any noun, verb, or adjective:

5. My fucking idiotic fucking professor is fucking making me fucking read this fucking lousy fucking book.[3]

Unlike *fucking,* the free morpheme, *-fucking-*, the infix, is fairly selective in which words it can combine with (see Chapter 9 for a discussion of the free morpheme *fucking*). For example, compare the (a) versions to the (b) versions of the following sentences:[4]

6. a. Who are you calling ordifuckingnary?
    b. Who are you calling *regufuckinglar?
7. a. You better learn to recogfuckingnize good shit when you see it.
    b. You better learn to *disfuckingtinguish/*distingfuckinguish good shit from bad shit.
8. a. Microfuckingsoft gives me a headache.
    b. *Linfuckingux/*Lifuckingnux gives me a headache.
9. a. You've got some mofuckingjo.
    b. You've got some *mafuckinggic/*magfuckingic.
10. a. Fanfuckingtastic!
    b. *Fabufuckinglous/*fabfuckingulous/*fafuckingbulous!

---

[2] Of course, in the published version, each *bloody* was represented with dashes.

[3] This *fucking* example nearly reaches my *fucking* threshold—I don't know that I could handle another *fucking* modifier.

[4] I imagine some people will find some of the (b) examples at least marginally acceptable, but I think everybody will agree that the (a) versions are much better than the (b) versions.

This infixation follows a pattern dictated by the phonological shape of the words it attaches in. In the Exercises at the end of this chapter, there's a task: try inserting *-fucking-* inside each of the fifty states of the United States. I recommend doing that now. I'll wait while you work on it.

Okay, done? Good. You probably noticed straight off that the only monosyllabic state, Maine, does not allow for *fucking* insertion. That is, **Mfuckingaine* or **Maifuckingne* just doesn't work. So, observation #1: the target for *fucking* insertion must have at least two syllables. Why can't we insert *-fucking*—within a monosyllabic word? Well, probably because *-fucking-* can't break up syllables. Let's turn this into a hypothesis.

Hypothesis 1: *-fucking-* can only come between syllables (not within syllables)

Let's consider *fantastic* in light of Hypothesis 1. The syllable breaks for this word are as follows: *fan.ta.stic.* We predict—rightly—that *-fucking*—can come between the first two syllables: *fanfuckingtastic.* But it should not come within any of the syllables: **fafuckingntastic, *fantfuckingastic, *fantasfuckingtic, *fantastfuckingic.* Unfortunately, we would predict the following form with *-fucking-* between the final two syllables: **fantafuckingstic.* But that's awful.

Let's return to the states, concentrating on the disyllabic ones. What we find is that two syllables may be a necessary condition, but it's clearly not sufficient. For example, *Ufuckingtah* is pretty good, but **Texfuckingas* is terrible. *Vermont,* on the other hand, is marginal. It's pretty good as long as you stress the first syllable. That is to say, with the normal pattern, where the first syllable has no stress, **vĕrfuckingmónt* (the rounded accent above the *e* indicates an unstressed syllable), it's not so good, but if you say it *Vérfuckingmónt* it sounds all right. This is an interesting observation. Note that *Útáh* is stressed on both syllables, but *Téxăs* is unstressed on the second syllable, as are *Kánsăs* and *Géorgĭa.* The only other disyllabic state, *Néw Yórk,* has two stressed syllables, and, as we would predict, *fucking* insertion is fine: *New fucking York.* This isn't perfect evidence, seeing that this word consists of two free morphemes, so let's consider some other words. Compound words typically have two stressed syllables (e.g., *baseball, whiteboard, hotdog, ice cream*). And all of these are fine with *-fucking-* insertion:

11. Americans love their basefuckingball.
12. This room has a blackfuckingboard instead of a whitefuckingboard.
13. What's for supper? Hotfuckingdogs and ice fucking cream.

It's a little more challenging to find mono-morphemic words with two stressed syllables; here are a few examples: *polo, ugly, latex.* These seem to work all right:

14. He doesn't play baseball; he plays pofuckinglo.
15. That shirt is ugfuckingly.
16. I told you to get oil-based paint and you got lafuckingtex.

Windy is an interesting example because even though it has two morphemes, *wind* and *-y*, *-fucking-* doesn't come between the morphemes, but between the syllables: *winfuckingdy* (not *windfuckingy*).

So here's our second hypothesis:

Hypothesis 2: *-fucking-* must come between two stressed syllables.

Note that this hypothesis predicts Hypothesis 1, so all the data we got right with Hypothesis 1, we also get with Hypothesis 2. Unfortunately, Hypothesis 2 also predicts that many of the words that allow *-fucking-* insertion should not, for example, *Alafuckingbama.* The stress falls on the first and third syllables of this word: *Álăbámă.* In fact, the states that work the very best with -*fucking*-insertion have exactly this pattern of strong, weak, strong, weak syllables:

Álăbámă	Mássăchúsetts	Óklăhómă
Árĭzónă	Mínnĕsótă	Pénnšylvánĭă
Cálĭfórnĭă	Míssĭssíppĭ	Sóuth Dăkótă
Cólŏrádŏ	Nórth Dăkóta	

In all of these cases, -*fucking*- can comfortably come between the second and third syllables.

Álăfuckingbámă	Mássăfuckingchúsetts	Óklăfuckinghómă
Árĭfuckingzónă	Mínnĕfuckingsótă	Pénnšylfuckingvánĭă
Cálĭfuckingfórnĭă	Míssĭfuckingssíppĭ	Sóuth Dăfuckingkótă
Cólŏfuckingrádŏ	Nórth Dăfuckingkóta	

We need to revise Hypothesis 2. What we should ask is: what does the pattern in these quadrisyllabic states have in common with the strong, strong pattern we see with *Utah, New York,* and *latex?* To understand this, we'll have to draw on something you might have learned in a literature class.

What kind of meter did Shakespeare write in? Iambic pentameter, duh! Well, the pentameter side isn't interesting to us—that has to do with how long he made each line of verse. What we're interested in is the iambic part. An iamb is a pair of syllables where the first syllable is weak and the second is strong; *Vĕrmónt* is an example, as are *cŏnnĭve, bĕlíef,* and *sŭbmít.* But you've got to hunt for iambic words in English. The majority of English words show the pattern in *Álăbámă,* where the pairs go strong, weak. This more common pattern is called **trochaic,** and the pair we call a **trochee.** In literature, they use the term **foot** for a pair of syllables, either iambic or trochaic. We linguists use the same word (though slightly differently, as you'll see in the next paragraph).

Unlike poets, who only think of feet in terms of two syllables—one stressed, one unstressed—linguists allow for physically challenged feet, where there's only one syllable in the foot—since there's only one syllable, that syllable has to be strong. So we define a foot as minimally having one stressed syllable. For example, the single syllable in *Maine* is a foot.

Here's where we get into theory: Everybody knows words are composed of syllables and syllables are composed of sounds. But linguists, for some time now, have argued there's a level between syllable and word, which is to say words aren't directly composed of syllables. Instead, they are composed of feet and feet are composed of syllables. Every word minimally has one foot, and every foot minimally has one stressed syllable.

Let's make some trees (linguists really like trees) with W representing a word, Σ a foot, and σ a syllable. Monosyllabic words would look like the tree in Figure 8.1.

FIGURE 8.1 *Monosyllabic word trees*

These trees are boring because they represent the minimal case. More interesting words have more syllables.

With trees for multisyllabic words, we need to distinguish between stressed syllables, which we call **strong,** and unstressed syllables, which we call **weak;** we indicate strong syllables with (s) below the σ, and weak syllables with (w) below the σ. There are three common types of feet in English: i) a single strong syllable, ii) a strong syllable followed by a weak syllable (trochee), iii) a weak syllable followed by a strong syllable (iamb). Trees for these can be seen in Figures 8.2–8.4, respectively.

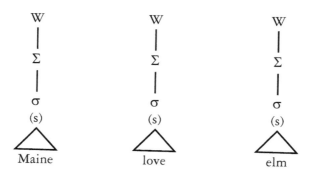

FIGURE 8.2   *Monosyllabic word trees revised*

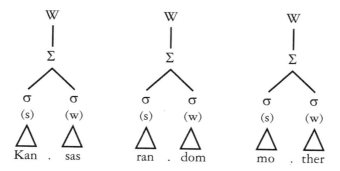

FIGURE 8.3   *Disyllabic trochaic word trees*

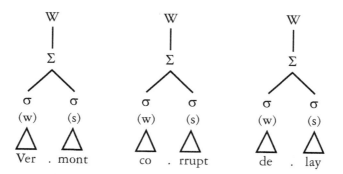

FIGURE 8.4   *Disyllabic iambic word trees*

Notice that none of the words in Figures 8.2–8.4 allow for *fucking* insertion (with the possible exception of *Vermont,* which was discussed previously and will be returned to later). Hypothesis 2 predicts this; however, as we saw, it fails to predict that words like those in Figure 8.5 allow -*fucking*- insertion (cf. (17)).

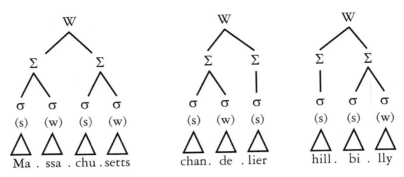

FIGURE 8.5 *Polysyllabic trochaic word trees*

17. Massafuckingchusetts, chandefuckinglier, hillfuckingbilly

Each of the words in Figure 8.5 take insertion between their two feet, but not anywhere else:

18. *Massfuckingachusetts, *Massachufuckingsetts, *chanfuckingdelier, *hillbifuckinglly

Looking back at Hypothesis 2, we can see that the relevant break isn't between stressed syllables but between feet. Since a foot can consist of a single syllable as long as that syllable is stressed, disyllabic words with two stressed syllables have two feet, giving us the trees in Figure 8.6.

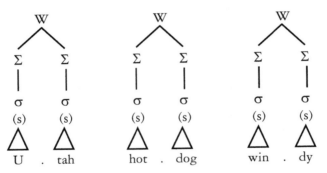

FIGURE 8.6 *Disyllabic strong, strong word trees*

This leads us to Hypothesis 3.

Hypothesis 3: *-fucking-* must come between feet.

This is the hypothesis we'll keep. It captures all the data we've observed so far—even for *Vermont*.

Typically, *Vermont* has the foot structure we see in Figure 8.4. However, there is a less common pronunciation where both syllables are stressed (*Vérmónt*), and this gives us a structure like that in Figure 8.6. So as long as the first syllable in *Vermont* is stressed, giving us two feet, we can get *-fucking-* insertion.

It's time to look for more data—now with an eye to problems for Hypothesis 3. Perhaps the best way to approach this is to list the states that work well with *-fucking-* insertion, those that don't work well, and those that are marginal (see Table 8.1).

TABLE 8.1		
Infixation Judgments for States		
Good	*Marginal*	*Bad*
Ála-báma	Aláska	Connécticut
Ári-zóna	Árkan-sás	Géorgia
Cáli-fórnia	Flórida	Kánsas
Cólo-rádo	Hawáii	Máine
Déla-wáre	Íowa	Míchigan
Ída-hó	Kentúcky	Missóuri
Ílli-nóis	Máryland	Óregon
Índi-ána	Nebráska	Téxas
Louísi-ána	Neváda	
Mássa-chúsetts	Vermónt	
Mínne-sóta	Virgínia	
Míssi-ssíppi	Wáshington	
Món-tána	Wiscónsin	
Néw - Hámpshire		
Néw - Jérsey		
Nórth - Cáro-lina		
Nórth Da-kóta		
Ó-hío		
Ókla-hóma		
Pénnsyl-vánia		
Rhóde - Ísland		
Sóuth — Cáro-lína		
Sóuth Da-kóta		
Ténne-ssée		
Ú-táh		
Wést Vir-gínia		
Wý-óming		

I've indicated the stressed syllables and the foot boundaries (marked with a hyphen) on each state. Note that the good column contains states with at least two feet (you can confirm for yourself that *-fucking-* fits comfortably where I put the hyphen). The two states with more than two feet are *North Carolina* and *South Carolina*. With these two states, there are two equally good options for insertion: *North fucking Carolina, North Carofuckinglina, South fucking Carolina,* and *South Carofuckinglina.*

North Dakota and South Dakota also allow more than one slot for insertion, but to my ear it sounds better when the foot boundary is respected (i.e., *North Dafuckingkota* and *South Dafuckingkota* are better than *North fucking Dakota* and *South fucking Dakota*). The reason it can come after *North* or *South* in these two states has to do with morpheme boundaries: morpheme boundaries can trump foot boundaries. Thus, we get both *unfuckingbelievable* and *unbefuckinglievable,* though the former may be slightly preferred over the latter—even though, by Hypothesis 3, the latter should be the one. So we have an exception to Hypothesis 3: *-fucking-* can break up a foot as long as it respects morpheme boundaries.

Hypothesis 3 explains the good and bad columns. From the marginal column we can explain the following states by noting that when *-fucking-* is inserted, the stress is changed, thereby creating two feet: *Á-láska* (pronounced *Aylaska*), *Kén-túcky*, *Máry-lánd*, *Vér-mónt*, *Vír-gínia*, and *Wís-cónsin*. This leaves only these states to explain: *Árkan-sás*, *Flórida*, *Hawáii*, *Íowa*, *Nebráska*, *Neváda*, and *Wáshington*.

Honestly, I can't explain why *Arkanfuckingsas* doesn't sound better than it does. *Árkansás* has two feet, so it should work fine, but personally I think *Arkanfuckingsas* sounds lousy. So there we go, a mystery.

The others, I think I can explain. These ones, in contrast to *Arkansas*, sound better than they should: *Florifuckingda*, *Hafuckingwaii*, *Iofuckingwa*, *Nefuckingbraska*, *Nefuckingvada*, and *Washingfuckington*. That's not to say these sound all that great—at least not to my ear—but they sound a heck of a lot better than *Kanfuckingsas*.

To understand these marginal ones, let's turn from states to a city, a village, and a lake: *Kálamazóo*, *Tátamagóuche* (pronounced [tætəməguʃ]), and *Wínnipesáukee*. These are interesting because they comfortably allow *-fucking-* in more than one location: *Kalafuckingmazoo*, *Kalamafuckingzoo*, *Tatafuckingmagouche*, *Tatamafuckinggouche*, *Winnifuckingpesaukee*, *Winnipefuckingsaukee*. According to the templates in Figures 8.3–8.4, we should get the structures shown in Figure 8.7 for *Kalamazoo* and *Tatamagouche*.

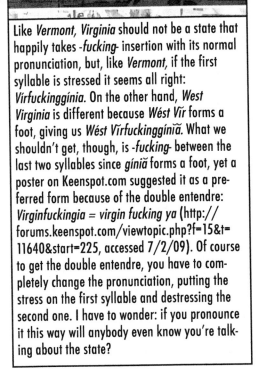

Like *Vermont*, *Virginia* should not be a state that happily takes *-fucking-* insertion with its normal pronunciation, but, like *Vermont*, if the first syllable is stressed it seems all right: *Virfuckinggínia*. On the other hand, *West Virginia* is different because *Wést Vír* forms a foot, giving us *Wést Vírfuckinggínia*. What we shouldn't get, though, is *-fucking-* between the last two syllables since *gíniã* forms a foot, yet a poster on Keenspot.com suggested it as a preferred form because of the double entendre: *Virginfuckingia* = virgin fucking ya (http://forums.keenspot.com/viewtopic.php?f=15&t=11640&start=225, accessed 7/2/09). Of course to get the double entendre, you have to completely change the pronunciation, putting the stress on the first syllable and destressing the second one. I have to wonder: if you pronounce it this way will anybody even know you're talking about the state?

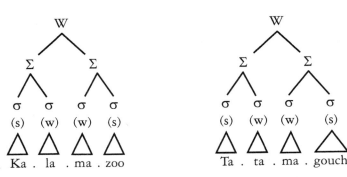

FIGURE 8.7 *Word trees for* Kalamazoo *and* Tatamagouche

But if these are the structures, then according to Hypothesis 3 *Kalamafuckingzoo* and *Tatamafuckinggouche* should be bad because they break up feet. So . . . either Hypothesis 3 is wrong, or our assumption is wrong that Figure 8.7 represents the only structures for these words.

In order to see what's going on, let's look at *Winnipesaukee*. Here we've got two nice trochaic feet: *Wínnĭ* and *sáukĕe*. But we've got this extra syllable: *pĕ*. What to do? Well, the best idea linguists have got is that when there's an extra unstressed syllable, it simply grabs hold of the nearest foot and latches on. In the case of *Winnepesaukee*, though, there's two equally near feet, so it can latch on in either place (the "latching on" is represented with dotted lines) as in Figure 8.8.

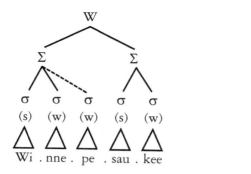
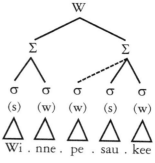

FIGURE 8.8   *Two word trees for* Winnepesaukee

With this latching-on assumption in place, at least this word makes sense: If the word divides according to the initial tree, then infixation gives *winnepefuckingsaukee,* and if the word divides according to the second tree, then infixation gives *winnefuckungpesaukee.*

Now back to *Kalamazoo* and *Tatamagouche.* What if the process is the same here? That is, what if the middle syllable *ma* isn't initially attached to a foot and it just latches on to the closest one? If so, we can get either of the structures in Figure 8.9 for *Kalamazoo.*

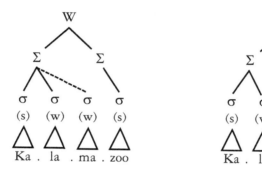

FIGURE 8.9   *Two word trees for* Kalamazoo

Of course, this forces us to reconsider an earlier assumption. We assumed that there were three basic types of feet in English: i) a single strong syllable (Figure 8.2), ii) a trochee (Figure 8.3), and iii) an iamb (Figure 8.4). But now, we see evidence that there are only two basic feet: a single strong syllable and a trochee. All other feet, such as iambs and those three-syllable feet seen in Figures 8.8 and 8.9, result from a process of latching on.

I can now explain that final set of states: *Flórida, Hawáii, Íowa, Nebráska, Neváda,* and *Wáshington.* Here it goes. Each of these states has a basic (trochaic) foot: *Flóri, wáii, Ío, bráska, váda,* and *Wáshing.* The remaining syllables, all unstressed, have to latch on to these basic feet. The latched-on syllables don't have as tight of a bond to the foot; they're like hitchhikers in that they'll ride with anybody and they'll climb on and get out anywhere. So when a new foot comes along, namely *-fúckĭng-,* they'll as happily ride in that car as any other. Let's look at *Florida* and *Nebraska* in Figures 8.10 and 8.11 to see how this works.

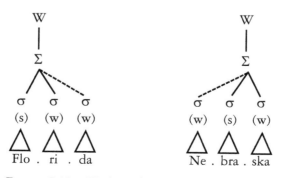

FIGURE 8.10   *Word trees for* Florida *and* Nebraska

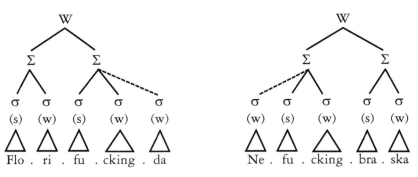

FIGURE 8.11 *Word trees for* Florifuckingda *and* Nefuckingbraska

There. Done.[5]

3. CONCLUSION

There are all sorts of other things that can be said about the phonology of swearing. For example, Cockney rhyming slang requires an even deeper analysis of syllable structure than we've done here, and Aniko Csirmaz (pers. comm.) has found some interesting assimilation patterns in Hungarian swearing. But I'll forbear going into that. Instead, I'm just going to summarize what we've seen in this chapter and consider its significance.

What we've seen is *-fucking-* insertion is a common and productive morphophonological phenomenon in English. But, like with all of grammar, there are rules for how it applies, rules few speakers are ever conscious of, yet follow faithfully. The rules for *-fucking-* insertion require us to not only dissect a word into syllables but also feet (and occasionally morphemes; see *unfuckingbelievable*). At one point in phonological theory, most linguists did not see the need for the foot level in word structure; everybody accepted that there were phones (individual sounds) and syllables, but foot structure seemed superfluous. In the 1980s, however, research began showing the need for feet, and McCarthy's (1982) paper, where he presented the analysis of *-fucking-* discussed here, was one of the most articulate arguments for feet.

REFERENCES

Hughes, Geoffrey. 1991. *Swearing: A Social History of Foul Language, Oaths, and Profanity in English.* Cambridge, MA: Blackwell.

McCarthy, John J. 1982. Prosodic Structure and Expletive Infixation. *Language,* 58(3): 574–590.

Mencken, H.L. 1947. *The American Language: An Inquiry into the Development of English in the United States.* New York: Alfred A. Knopf.

---

[5] For most people, *Connecticut* doesn't take *-fucking-* insertion. I can't explain why, though. It looks like a combination of *Florida,* (s)(w)(w), and *Nebraska,* (w)(s)(w), giving us (w)(s)(w)(w). In that case, we should get both *Cofuckingnnecticut* and *Connectifuckingcut,* but both of these are horrible for me. The only one that is even remotely OK for me is *Connfuckingecticut,* where *Conn* is reanalyzed as a strong syllable á la *Vermont;* however, this reanalysis doesn't work as well for *Connecticut* because *Conn* isn't originally even a syllable—the /n/ belongs with the second syllable.

1. For each of the fifty states of the United States, determine if it is possible to insert the infix *-fucking-*. Write the state name with what seems like the best point of infixation. If the infixation sounds grammatical, put a check mark in front; if it sounds ungrammatical, put an asterisk; and if it is only marginally grammatical, put a question mark. A few have been done for you. Can you notice any pattern that would explain the distribution?

1. Alabama	✓ Alafuckingbama	28. Nevada	
2. Alaska		29. New Hampshire	
3. Arizona		30. New Jersey	
4. Arkansas	?Arkanfuckingsas	31. New Mexico	
5. California		32. New York	
6. Colorado		33. North Carolina	
7. Connecticut		34. North Dakota	
8. Delaware		35. Ohio	
9. Florida		36. Oklahoma	
10. Georgia		37. Oregon	
11. Hawaii		38. Pennsylvania	
12. Idaho		39. Rhode Island	
13. Illinois		40. South Carolina	
14. Indiana		41. South Dakota	
15. Iowa		42. Tennessee	
16. Kansas	*Kanfuckingsas	43. Texas	
17. Kentucky		44. Utah	
18. Louisiana		45. Vermont	
19. Maine		46. Virginia	
20. Maryland		47. Washington	
21. Massachusetts		48. West Virginia	
22. Michigan		49. Wisconsin	
23. Minnesota		50. Wyoming	
24. Mississippi			
25. Missouri			
26. Montana			
27. Nebraska			

1. THE FATHER OF PORNOLINGUISTICS

Most theoretical linguists specialize in one field, say syntax, phonology, phonetics, semantics, pragmatics, psycholinguistics, sociolinguistics, or historical linguistics.[1] James McCawley was a generalist. He had an absolute love for language, and he joyfully delved into every aspect of it. Most "dabblers" accumulate a large base of knowledge but rarely impact the fields they study; McCawley contributed profoundly to all the fields he wrote on. His book titles include: *The Phonological Component of a Grammar of Japanese; Grammar and Meaning: Papers on Syntactic and Semantic Topics; Notes from the Linguistic Underground; Adverbs, Vowels, and Other Objects of Wonder; Everything that Linguists have always Wanted to Know about Logic (But were Ashamed to Ask); Thirty Million Theories of Grammar;* and *The Syntactic Phenomena of English.* When he died, he was working on a book on the philosophy of science. At his memorial service, one of his sisters expressed surprise at how many books he'd published; she said that for the past thirty years whenever they'd had dinner together he'd left early saying he had to go home to work on his book, and his relatives had thought, "Poor Jim, he just can't seem to finish that book," not knowing that in his thirty-five year career he published

James McCawley died in 1999. He was an eccentric; he wore dirty jeans, shoulder-length hair, bushy eyebrows that stuck straight up, a walrus moustache, and lamb-chop sideburns. He whistled whenever anybody provided him with an interesting bit of linguistic data (even if the data were provided unwittingly). He stuttered. He never learned to drive and rode his bike to work, even on the most inclement days, when he'd wear a bank robber's ski mask. In the 1960s, he supposedly quit a job in Indiana because he couldn't buy tofu in town. After giving a long, complex answer to a student's question, he was apt to say, "I think I just told you more than I know on this topic."

---

[1] Noam Chomsky, the most famous living linguist, used to work in both syntax and phonology. Legend has it he quit doing phonology so he could devote more time to political writing.

seven academic books (some of them in more than one edition), an untold number of articles, and a non-academic book on reading Chinese restaurant menus in Chinese.

As if Jim's contributions to the established fields of linguistics weren't already enough, we can also credit him with establishing his own field: **pornolinguistics**. He was, by most accounts, the first linguist to write a (quasi)serious article on the grammar of obscenity: "English Sentences Without Overt Grammatical Subject".[2] I parenthetically qualify *serious* because McCawley chose to use a pseudonym for the article, Quang Phuc Dong, even building a back story for his alter ego, such that he was a professor at the South Hanoi Institute of Techonolgy (SHIT), as was another of McCawley's alter egos, Yuck Foo. Nonetheless, the article contains solid linguistic research, as do his subsequent articles in the field. In this chapter, I present some of McCawley's, AKA Quang's, research in pornolinguistics and some of the outgrowth of that research.

2. WHY YOU CAN SAY "FUCK YOU" OR "GO FUCK YOURSELF" BUT NOT "GO FUCK YOU"[3]

I expect at some point in your life you were told by a writing teacher, "Make sure every sentence has a noun and a verb." Like so much advice about language, what teachers say is not quite what they mean. What the teachers don't want are sentence fragments like (1–2).

1. My kingdom for a horse.

2. To be or not to be.

(1) lacks a verb (but has nouns: *kingdom, horse*), while (2) lacks a noun (but has verbs: *be, be*). Therefore, your teacher will tell you they are sentence fragments. But what about (3)?

3. Water, water everywhere, nor any drop to drink.

This sentence has a noun (three, in fact: *water, water, drop*) and a verb (*drink*), but your teacher would still tell you it's a sentence fragment. So's (4).

4. Found a penny.

The thing is, your teacher understood grammar well enough but didn't know how to explain it. Having a noun and a verb is not sufficient. What the teacher really meant was that every sentence should have a **subject** and a **predicate**.

Sometimes, a subject is defined as "who or what is performing the action in a sentence." But this isn't accurate. Consider (5–6).

5. Abigail fucked herself up by snorting too many Pop Rocks.

6. All those Pop Rocks fucked Abigail up.

Your teacher might not appreciate these two sentences; however, they are both perfectly grammatical—and they both have a subject and a predicate. In (5') and (6') the sentences are bracketed to show the subject (marked NP for noun phrase) and the predicate (marked VP for verb phrase).

5' [Abigail]$_{NP}$ [fucked herself up with all those Pop Rocks]$_{VP}$.

6' [All those Pop Rocks]$_{NP}$ [fucked Abigail up]$_{VP}$.

The two sentences describe the same event, but in one case *Abigail* is the subject and in the other *all those Pop Rocks* is the subject. So which is the doer? And which is the doee? Doesn't matter. Not really.[4] Linguists don't define subject that way.

---

[2] I should note that other linguists, such as Otto Jespersen, had discussed taboo language, but they hadn't seen fit to actually look into the grammar.

[3] The ideas and data in this section draw heavily from Quang (1992a).

[4] Note the two sentence fragments. I'm going to hell.

Before I say how linguists define subject, I want to draw a couple trees. Linguists like trees.

7.

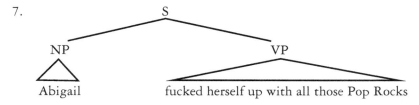

8.

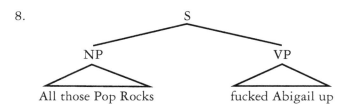

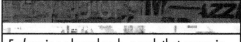

Fuck up is a phrasal verb, a verb that comes in two parts: a verb and a verb particle. The verb particles in phrasal verbs look like prepositions, but they're not. As we discussed in Chapter 2, there are syntactic differences. For example, the question, *Who are you looking up?* is ambiguous between a verb + verb particle interpretation (i.e., 'for whose name are you searching') and a verb + preposition interpretation (i.e., 'up whom are you looking?').

Fuck can be combined with the preposition *up*, not just the verb particle *up*. For example, one can say, "Chris fucked Pat up the poop shoot." This, of course, means something quite different from *Chris fucked up Pat's plumbing*. With the preposition, the literal meaning of *up* is involved. With the verb particle, a new verb with a new meaning is created. In other words, a verb + preposition phrase is compositional—its meaning is composed of the meanings of the two parts. A verb + verb particle has a special meaning, one that is not derivable from the meaning of the two parts.

In **syntactic trees** like these, S stands for sentence, NP stands for noun phrase, and VP stands for verb phrase. An NP consists obligatorily of a noun (N) and optionally of any modifiers of the noun (modifiers can include determiners, adjectives, and prepositional phrases). A VP consists obligatorily of a verb (V) and anything needed to "complete" the verb, which we call the **complement** (for transitive verbs, like *fuck up*, an NP object). A VP can optionally include modifiers of the verb (adverbs and prepositional phrases can be verb modifiers).

For structures like (7) and (8), we draw on the metaphor of family trees, using the terms **mother, daughter,** and **sister.** We define a subject as the NP daughter of an S and a predicate as the VP daughter of an S. Every sentence has a subject and a predicate. Since every subject is an NP and every NP obligatorily has an N, every sentence will have an N. And since every predicate is a VP and every VP obligatorily has a V, every sentence will have a V. Thus, being charitable to writing teachers, we can assume that what they really mean is, "Make sure every sentence has a subject and a predicate."

Of course, a smart student will point out a whole class of English sentences that violate this: imperatives (commands).

9. Do the homework.

10. Stick the homework up your ass.

11. Don't sass me.

12. Go to hell.

(9–12) appear to lack subjects, yet they're complete sentences. So what gives? Well, what would your writing teacher say? She or he would probably say that there's an "understood" subject, namely 'you'. Linguists would say the same thing, only we use a fancier term than "understood." We say there's a **covert subject.** The idea is that (9–12) mean the same thing as (13–16).

13. You do the homework.

14. You stick the homework up your ass.

15. You don't sass me.

16. You go to hell.

In our mental representation of the sentences in (9–12) we have an **underlying** *you,* which is not phonologically realized (i.e., is not pronounced).

There is good evidence to support this idea. Consider sentences like (17–19).

17. I washed *himself/him/*yourself/you/myself/*me.

18. You washed *himself/him/yourself/*you/*myself/me.

19. My dog washed himself/him/*yourself/you/*myself/me.

Note that the *self* form of pronouns (reflexives) are only grammatical when they refer to the same thing as the subject.[5] Note that in (19) both *himself* and *him* are grammatical; however, *him* cannot refer to *my dog* while *himself* has to. With these facts in mind, consider (20).

20. Wash *himself/him/yourself/*you/*myself/me.

If *yourself* is only grammatical when *you* is the subject of the sentence, then we have to assume that the subject of (20) is an underlying *you*.

This argument in favor of an underlying *you* in imperatives is strong, and the consensus in linguistics is that it is correct. In the 1960s, these data were used to argue for syntactic transformations. The idea is that (21) begins with the same underlying structure as (22), given in (23).

21. Stick your finger up your own diaper hole.

22. You stick your finger up your own diaper hole.

23.

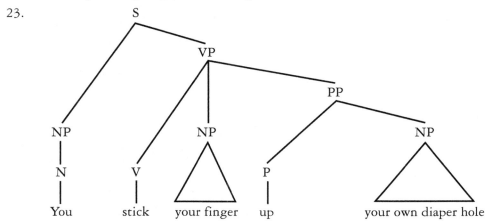

Nothing changes in (23) to produce (22); however, the *you* has to be deleted to produce (21), as shown in (24).

24.

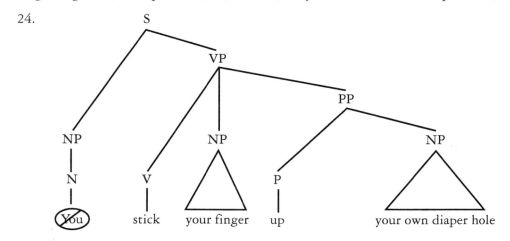

---

[5] This means, of course, that reflexives don't show up as subjects (cf., i–iii).
  i.   *Myself washed the dog.
  ii. *Yourself washed the dog.
  iii. *Himself washed the dog.
You need a separate subject to license the (appositive) reflexive, as in (iv–vi).
  iv. I, myself, washed the dog.
  v.   You, yourself, washed the dog.
  vi. He, himself, washed the dog.

A similar argument is made for (25), which is produced by adding *do* to (23).

25. Do you stick your finger up your own diaper hole?

26.

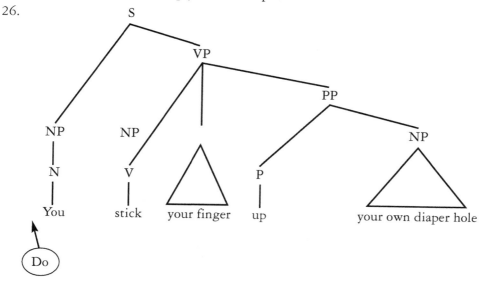

These transformations were fairly well accepted in the 1960s. Today, not all syntacticians believe in the theoretical validity of transformations, and the majority who do have refined the theory so that it no longer resembles the one spelled out here. But everybody agrees that the data need to be explained and that declarative sentences are the basic form from which imperatives and questions are derived. And most everybody agrees that imperatives have an underlying 'you'.

To sum up: Every sentence has a subject. Even sentences that appear not to have a subject have a subject.

One problem with all this: It's wrong. This is where McCawley and his alter ego Quang Phuc Dong come in. At this point, McCawley was still primarily a phonologist and had not published anything on syntax. But he saw a flaw in the received theory. Consider these sentences:

27. Damn my writing teacher.
28. Damn these sentence fragments.
29. Fuck my writing teacher.
30. Fuck sentence fragments.

According to the theory, (27–30) should be underlyingly (31–34).

31. You damn my writing teacher.
32. You damn these sentence fragments.
33. You fuck my writing teacher.
34. #You fuck sentence fragments.

However, I believe you will agree that (31–34) mean something different from (27–30). (31) and (32) only make sense when addressing a deity capable of damning—that is, it would seem they could only be felicitously uttered during prayer—and, moreover, (32) involves a strange theology wherein sentence fragments have souls. (27) and (28) lack such restrictions, and, as we discuss in Chapter 4, they don't even need an addressee. (29) is ambiguous. It can be interpreted as the imperative form of (33), that is, a command to perform intercourse on the speaker's writing teacher. However, it could also be interpreted as an angry malediction against a particular writing teacher. (33) has one primary meaning, which is roughly 'you habitually have sexual intercourse with my writing teacher'. Finally, (30) is a perfectly normal sentence, while (34) is decidedly odd (the # indicates a pragmatically strange sentence, cf. chapter 14). (34) seems to mean 'you habitually have sexual intercourse with sentence fragments', which, at least in my world, is impossible.

In the remainder of this section, we focus on the difference between the *fuck* found in (30) and that found in (33). We'll call the basic one, meaning 'to have sexual intercourse', $fuck_1$. The other one, the one that is part of a malediction, we'll call $fuck_2$. In what remains, we'll see evidence that the two *fucks* have different syntactic behavior and that sentences like (30) are not imperatives. Following Quang's[6] argument, we'll conclude that $fuck_2$ is not even a verb.

Consider the following utterances from *Forgetting Sarah Marshall* (35–37) and *Superbad* (38–42):

35. Fuck everything that moves. Just use a condom.
36. I fucked the housekeeper the other day.
37. I'll just go fuck myself then.
38. She wants to fuck me!
39. Oh, yeah, fuck me, right?
40. Fuck that, we're calling you McLovin!
41. Fuck my life.
42. Fuck you.

(35–38) involve tokens of $fuck_1$, and (39–42) involve tokens of $fuck_2$. It should be obvious that (35), (36), and (38) have $fuck_1$ based on the meaning, and likewise meaning leads us to conclude that (40) and (41) do not have $fuck_1$. However, we can't use meaning entirely, since (39) and (42) have the necessary sort of objects for the 'intercourse' meaning, and, importantly, (37) will probably not be taken to literally involve 'intercourse'.[7]

Moreover, meaning isn't sufficient evidence to posit two different lexical items. One might argue that what we're calling $fuck_2$ is simply a metaphorical or figurative use of $fuck_1$. For example, just because some poets have referred to women's eyes as "stars," we shouldn't assume there are two distinct words $star_1$ and $star_2$, where $star_1$ denotes 'a self-luminous celestial body' and $star_2$ denotes 'eye'. Similarly, we shouldn't automatically assume that $fuck_1$ and $fuck_2$ are two different words just because we find two apparent meanings (for more discussion on polysemy see Chapter 14).

If we can't use meaning alone, how can we distinguish between $fuck_1$ and $fuck_2$? Let's start with (42), a common expression in English. Clearly, this cannot have (43) as its underlying structure because that would lead us to the ungrammatical sentence (44). (Note that (44) ↑ (45)).

43.
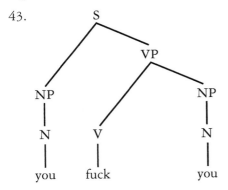

44. *You fuck you.
45. You, fuck you.

This is $fuck_2$. $Fuck_1$ would result in (46), giving us (47) and (48).

[6] There is some inconsistency in the literature in regards to which of Quang Phuc Dong's three names is his family name. Some authors seem to assume that Dong is and others that Quang is. Seeing that Vietnamese names begin with the family name (followed by middle name and then given name), I've chosen to treat Quang as his family name.

[7] Even a contortionist would have difficulty having intercourse with himself.

46.

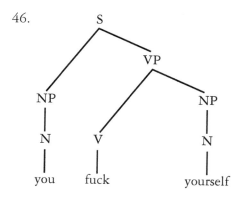

47. You fuck yourself.[8]

48. Fuck yourself.

This is good evidence in favor of positing two lexical items *fuck₁* and *fuck₂*; however, one could argue that the difference isn't in the verb but in the underlying representation. That is, we've assumed that all imperative sentences have an underlying *you*. But what if that's wrong?

Consider, again, (27), repeated here.

27. Damn my writing teacher.

Some have argued that (27) is an imperative where *God* is the underlying subject.[9] So couldn't (42) have an underlying subject other than *you*? It's possible, but unlikely. Consider (49–50).

49. *Go fuck you.

50. Go fuck yourself.[10]

If (42) involves some unspecified underlying subject, why couldn't (49) involve that same subject?

There are other ways that *fuck₁* and *fuck₂* syntactically differ as well. In what follows we will compare the following set of sentences:

51. Write sentence fragments.

52. Fuck me.

53. Fuck you.

54. Fuck sentence fragments.

(51) is a true imperative sentence, and it will serve as a model of how imperative sentences behave. (52) is ambiguous between an imperative and a self-directed malediction, which is to say that (52) could be interpreted either with *fuck₁* or *fuck₂*.[11] (53–54) are only maledictions; they are never true imperatives.

As we see in (49), the maledictive *fuck₂* doesn't go with *go*. However, true imperatives are fine with *go*, as in (55).

55. Go write sentence fragments.

(52) doesn't lend itself well to *go*; however, that has to do with the oddity of using *go* when directing the addressee towards yourself. Note that *come* works fine.

56. #Go fuck me.

57. Come fuck me.

58. Come write sentence fragments.

---

[8] Note that this sentence is ambiguous. We are going for the 'have intercourse with yourself' interpretation, not the 'fuck yourself up' interpretation (e.g., *You fuck yourself every time you forget to study for an exam.*).

[9] In Chapter 4, I argue that this is not a good analysis for sentences like (27).

[10] See footnote 8.

[11] The pronunciation is different: with *fuck₁* the pitch tends to be fairly constant, while with *fuck₂* the pitch tends to fall from a high pitch on *fuck* to a lower pitch on *me*. Also with *fuck₁* heavy stress only falls on *fuck* not *me*, while with *fuck₂* there is heavy stress on both words.

Of course, (57) can only be interpreted as a command or invitation, not a malediction. Neither *go* nor *come* works with (54).

59. *Go/come fuck sentence fragments.

A characteristic of imperatives is that we can precede the imperative with "I order you to . . ." Note that the true imperatives sound fine with this phrase, but not the maledictions (again the 'intercourse' interpretation is the only one available for (61)).

60. I order you to write sentence fragments.

61. I order you to fuck me.

62. *I order you to fuck you.

63. *I order you to fuck sentence fragments.

In a similar vein, one can report what was previously said, as in (64), which describes Abigail uttering (51).

64. Abigail told me to write sentence fragments.

Observe how this works with the other sentences.

65. Abigail told me to fuck her.

66. *Abigail told me to fuck me.[12]

67. *Abigail told me to fuck sentence fragments.

The maledictions can only properly be described using direct quotation:

68. Abigail said, "Fuck me."

69. Abigail said, "Fuck you."

70. Abigail said, "Fuck sentence fragments."

Note that (68) is ambiguous in the same way that (52) is.

Just as you can order somebody to do something using an imperative, you can also use an imperative to order somebody not to do something. For the negation, we precede the imperative with *don't*. Again, we see this works with the true imperatives but not the maledictions.

71. Don't write sentence fragments.

72. Don't fuck me.

73. *Don't fuck you.

74. *Don't fuck sentence fragments.

Often imperatives are considered rude in English. To make them more polite, they can be preceded by *please* or followed by *won't you?* Again, this is not true of maledictions.

75. Please write sentence fragments.

76. Please fuck me.

77. *Please fuck you.

78. *Please fuck sentence fragments.

79. Write sentence fragments, won't you?

80. Fuck me, won't you?

81. *Fuck you, won't you?

82. *Fuck sentence fragments, won't you?

---

[12] *Abigail told me to fuck myself* is a grammatical sentence but is not a fair description of what Abigail said in uttering (53).

Imperatives can be used in quasi-conditional sentences, similar to *if...then* sentences, where the imperative is connected to another sentence with *and*. The imperative describes what the addressee must do in order to ensure the desirable outcome described following *and*. *Or* can be used in a similar way, but this time the second clause indicates what undesirable outcome will occur if the addressee fails to do what is ordered. Unsurprisingly, neither of these types of sentences works with maledictions.

83. Write sentence fragments, and I'll give you a dollar.

84. Fuck me, and I'll give you a dollar.

85. *Fuck you, and I'll give you a dollar.

86. *Fuck sentence fragments, and I'll give you a dollar.

87. Write sentence fragments, or I'll tell your mother.

88. Fuck me, or I'll tell your mother.

89. *Fuck you, or I'll tell your mother.

90. *Fuck sentence fragments, or I'll tell your mother.

Imperatives can be combined together with *and* to give a chain of commands, for example, *Clear the table and wash the dishes.* Here, we'll combine our original sentences with *and eat chocolate out of my belly button.*

91. Write sentence fragments and eat chocolate out of my belly button.

92. Fuck me and eat chocolate out of my belly button.

93. *Fuck you and eat chocolate out of my belly button.

94. *Fuck sentence fragments and eat chocolate out of my belly button.

And is an interesting word because it can be used to combine any two syntactic elements as long as the two elements are of the same grammatical category (i.e., N & N, V & V, Adj & Adj, NP & NP, VP & VP, S & S, etc.). Note that with the imperatives, we can toss in another appropriate verb and it's still a good sentence.

95. Write and diagram sentence fragments.

96. Spank and fuck$_1$ me.

But with the maledictions, a normal verb doesn't work.

97. *Spank and fuck you.

98. *Write and fuck sentence fragments.

However, there is a word that can be combined with *fuck$_2$*, namely *damn*.

99. Damn and fuck$_2$ me.

100. Damn and fuck you.

101. Damn and fuck sentence fragments.

Thus, *damn* is the same type of word as *fuck$_2$*.

Often, we set a specific time or place for the addressee to carry out the order in an imperative. For example, we can tell somebody to do the action tonight or right now, or we can tell them to do the action right here or at their desk. But a maledictive doesn't work this way—it seems to be assumed that it's right now and right here,[13] and adding such modifiers makes for ungrammatical sentences.

102. Write sentence fragments tonight/right now.

103. Fuck me tonight/right now.

104. *Fuck you tonight/right now.

105. *Fuck sentence fragments tonight/right now.

106. Write sentence fragments right here/at your desk.

---

[13] For more on the apparent immediacy involved with swearing, see Chapter 14.

107. Fuck me right here/at your desk.

108. *Fuck you right here/at your desk.

109. *Fuck sentence fragments right here/at your desk.

We can also tell our addressee how to perform the act, e.g., with speed or with care, when we use an imperative. Again, this works with $fuck_1$ but not $fuck_2$.

110. Write sentence fragments quickly/carefully.

111. Fuck me quickly/carefully.

112. *Fuck you quickly/carefully.

113. *Fuck sentence fragments quickly/carefully.

So far we've seen that imperative verbs have certain syntactic characteristics. They can be embedded in larger phrases, negated, conjoined with other imperative verbs, and modified in various ways. Although the maledictive $fuck_2$ resembles an imperative verb, it doesn't behave like one syntactically.

There's a bit more data to consider. This time the data have to do with the sorts of objects[14] $fuck_1$ and $fuck_2$ can combine with. The object of an imperative verb doesn't have to be a specific person or thing. For example, you can tell your friend to have intercourse with a particular linguist, by uttering (114), and you can curse that same linguist by uttering (115). You could also tell your friend to have intercourse with some unspecified linguist, as in (116), but you can't curse an unspecified linguist. You could tell your friend to be promiscuous with (117), but as a malediction it doesn't make sense (118).

114. $Fuck_1$ that linguist—he is good in bed.

115. $Fuck_2$ that linguist—he broke my heart.

116. $Fuck_1$ a linguist—they are good in bed.

117. #$Fuck_2$ a linguist—I hate them all.

118. $Fuck_1$ somebody/anybody—it would do you some good.

119. #$Fuck_2$ somebody/anybody—I hate everyone.

As we've seen before, only $fuck_2$ makes sense with inanimates like sentence fragments. We can curse specific sentence fragments (120–122) but not unspecified sentence fragments (123–125).

120. $Fuck_2$ the sentence fragment that cost me an A.

121. $Fuck_2$ this sentence fragment.

122. $Fuck_2$ these twelve sentence fragments.

123. #$Fuck_2$ a sentence fragment.

124. #$Fuck_2$ any sentence fragment.

125. #$Fuck_2$ twelve sentence fragments.

You could also tell your friend to have intercourse with a certain number of linguists, but this doesn't work with the maledictive $fuck_2$.

126. $Fuck_1$ twelve linguists—the record is eleven.

127. #$Fuck_2$ twelve linguists.

Your high school grammar teacher probably taught you the difference between the definite article *the* and the indefinite determiner (or article) *a/an*. In doing so, you might have gotten the impression that there is exactly one definite determiner and exactly one (or two depending on how you count *a/an*) indefinite determiner. In truth, the possessive pronouns (*my, your, her, their* . . .), and the demonstratives (*this, that, these, those*) are also definite determiners. And, at least according to some analyses, cardinal numbers (*one, two, three* . . .), *some*, and *any* are indefinite determiners. In addition, linguists often argue that NPs that appear to lack any determiner (e.g., *sentence fragments*) have a **null determiner** (Ø), which acts much like *a/an* but is used with plurals and non-count nouns (e.g., *My daughter likes Ø bananas, I filled my bottle with Ø water, Ø rice spilled all over the floor*).

[14] We'll define object in a similar manner to how we define subject and predicate: the object of a verb is the NP daughter of a VP (or alternatively, the NP sister of a V).

From (114–127), it looks like *fuck₂* can only combine with a specified object, not an unspecified object—in grammatical terms, we say a **definite NP** versus an **indefinite NP**. A definite NP is one that has a definite determiner (*the, his, her, my, your, their, its, our, this, these, that, those*), and an indefinite NP is one that has an indefinite determiner (*a/an, some, any, one, two, three, . . .*, and Ø with plurals and non-count nouns).

Unfortunately, things aren't quite so simple. Consider (128–131):

128. #Fuck₂ the first sentence fragment you find.

129. Fuck₂ sentence fragments.

130. #Fuck₂ every sentence fragment.

131. Fuck₂ all sentence fragments.

In (128) *fuck₂* does not combine happily with a definite NP, while in (129) it does combine happily with an indefinite NP. And, although *every sentence fragment* and *all sentence fragments* are similar in meaning, the latter combines better with *fuck₂* than the former. Here's the difference as I see it: there is an immediacy[15] of emotion with the maledictive *fuck₂*, which is to say that whatever you're maligning has to be fully salient in your mind. Typically, this means that definite NPs will work, and indefinite NPs will not, since when you're talking about something specific and familiar (to both you and your addressee) you opt for a definite NP and when you're talking about something unspecific or unfamiliar (to your addressee) you opt for an indefinite NP. However, there are other cases, namely hypotheticals, like *the first sentence fragment you find*. Here, a unique sentence fragment is being discussed, which is why a definite determiner is used, but the speaker does not have a specific sentence fragment in mind. With the bare plural in (129), on the other hand, the speaker is talking about sentence fragments in general, so no specific sentence fragment is in mind; however, now a whole grammatical class is being cursed—that is, the very idea of sentence fragments is being cursed, and that idea is salient in the speaker's mind. The same can be said of (131), but not (130). Why? Because *all* lumps a whole class together and treats it as a unit, while *every* takes each item in the class and treats it separately. (131) curses the whole class of sentence fragments, as does (129); but (130) would curse each sentence fragment separately, and every sentence fragment couldn't possibly be salient in the speaker's mind—indeed a speaker couldn't fathom the limitless[16] number of sentence fragments.

Fuck₁ also has restrictions on the type of NP object it can take. As we've seen, abstract things like sentence fragments don't work with *fuck₁*, and most inanimate objects, such as tables, books, bicycles, etc., don't work, but certain inanimate objects with appropriately shaped orifices are possible, for example, (i):

i. Grant fucked my vacuum cleaner.

Quang (1992b) notes that for some speakers the subject of *fuck₁* must be male when the verb is used transitively, meaning that for these speakers (ii) implies (iii) but (iv) is ungrammatical (% means that a sentence is ungrammatical for some but not all speakers).

ii. Gertrude and Grant fucked.
iii. Grant fucked Gertrude.
iv. %Gertrude fucked Grant.

In an endnote, though, Quang admits to overstating his claim; every speaker accepts (iv) if Gertrude has a strap-on dildo. In informal surveys of my Bad Words and Taboo Terms students, only a small minority find (iv) problematic even sans dildo. For more data, some of it rather graphic, I refer you to Quang (1992b).

Intuitively, we sense there's a difference between saying, "Fuck me!" meaning 'perform intercourse on me' and saying, "Fuck me!" meaning 'woe is me'. What we've seen, though, is that the difference is deeper than just meaning. Although they both look like imperatives, one behaves like a normal imperative, while the other does not. Quang concludes that *fuck₁* is a normal verb and, as such, can be used in both imperative and non-imperative sentences—that is, it can take an overt subject, like *Gertrude,* as in (132) or a covert 'you' as in (133).

132. Gertrude fucked₁ Grant.

133. Fuck₁ Grant.

On the other hand, *fuck₂*, Quang argues, is not a verb at all. It looks like a verb but doesn't act like a verb; he classifies it as a **quasi-verb.**

---

[15] See Chapter 14.

[16] I do not use the word *limitless* carelessly; the number of sentence fragments in any language is literally limitless.

Quang suggests we need to posit a whole new class called **epithets.** Unlike other sentences,[17] which require a subject and a predicate, epithets only require a quasi-verb and an NP. Other English quasi-verbs, according to Quang, are *damn, shit on,*[18] and *the hell with,* as in (134).

134. Damn/shit on/the hell with these false imperatives.

We began with the idea that all sentences have a noun and a verb, saw that this was inadequate, moved to the more accurate hypothesis that all sentences have a subject and a predicate, questioned this hypothesis by pointing out that imperatives seem to lack a subject, rescued the hypothesis by arguing that imperatives have a covert subject, showed that this analysis doesn't work for some imperative-like sentences such as *Fuck you,* then demonstrated that *Fuck you* is not an imperative so the analysis of imperatives is correct, and finally concluded that sentences like *Fuck you* have neither a subject nor a predicate—indeed, they lack a verb. Now, go look up your high school grammar teacher and tell him or her that not all English sentences have a verb—if he or she doesn't believe you, just use (53) as an example.

3. HE'S A FUCKING LINGUIST VS. HE'S FUCKING A LINGUIST

In a tantalizing endnote, Quang (1992a) suggests that the emphatic *fucking* is derived from *fuck₂*. We won't explore that idea so much as explore the different uses *fucking* can be put to. As with *fuck,* we will conclude that there is more than one word involved, and each one has different syntactic restrictions.

But first, some background. The *-ing* suffix in English plays different roles. The first role is the **present participle,** a verb form usually used in combination with another verb (e.g., *be, try, come, hear*).

135. They are singing.

136. She tried bicycling to New York, but failed.

137. He came pushing a wheelbarrow.

138. I heard them arguing about who had to wear the hat.

The present participle can also be used at the beginning or end of a sentence (in what grammarians call a participle phrase).

139. Feeling peckish, the British Secret Service agent ordered bangers and mash.

140. The father of the bride sat through the ceremony, twiddling his thumbs.

Most verbs in English have a present participle form.[19] Here are examples of *fucking* used as a present participle:

141. I heard them fucking through the thin walls of the hotel.

142. They were fucking when the phone rang.

143. Still fucking, he picked up the phone.

Verbs can also be transformed into adjectives by adding *-ing:*

144. I saw the singing girl when I was in Mazatlán.

145. The moving car is the one that hit my bicycle.

146. Look over there—do you see the fucking couple?

---

[17] Quang actually argues that epithets are not sentences. The thing is, though, how Quang defines sentence is different from how your writing teacher defines sentence. For your writing teacher, a sentence begins with a capital letter and ends with end punctuation (period, exclamation point, or question mark). A sentence fragment, then, looks like a sentence in that it begins with a capital letter and ends with end punctuation, but is "incomplete." The epithets, when written, begin with a capital letter and end with end punctuation and are not incomplete, since, as we've seen, they cannot take any additional elements. Thus, by your writing teacher's definition, epithets are sentences.

[18] My dialect lacks the *shit on* quasi-verb. But I trust Quang that for some English speakers it is practically interchangeable with *fuck₂*.

[19] The exceptions are the modal verbs: *can, will, shall, may, must, ought, could, would, should, might.*

The adjective form contributes the same meaning as following the noun with "that is _____-ing".

147. I saw the girl that is singing when I was in Mazatlán.

148. The car that is moving is the one that hit my bicycle.

149. Look over there—do you see the couple that is fucking?

Note that the *fucking* intended in (146) and (149) is derived from *fuck₁* and means 'fornicating'.

In addition to transforming verbs into adjectives, *-ing* can also transform verbs into nouns. Nouns of this type are called **gerunds.**

150. Running is a great way to get in shape.

151. I have no talent for drumming.

152. Teenagers don't realize how seriously fucking should be taken.

So far, we've considered the three *-ing* processes that can be applied to practically all verbs. *Fucking,* however, is unusual in that it has two other functions in the language. The first of these is as a **pause filler.** Among certain people, usually young men, *fucking* has come to replace *um.* Consider the following sentences, the first two lines of *Moby Dick,* and imagine saying them while trying to gather your thoughts:

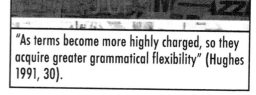

"As terms become more highly charged, so they acquire greater grammatical flexibility" (Hughes 1991, 30).

153. Call me Ishmael. Some years ago—never mind how long precisely—having little or no money in my purse, and nothing particular to interest me on shore, I thought I would sail about a little and see the watery part of the world.

Where can you put *um* in this sentence? Nearly everywhere, right? There are some places, such as between the first two words, where it would sound awkward, but *um* fits in most places. In (153') I've inserted a caret (^) where *um* would sound natural to me.

153' ^ Call me ^ Ishmael. ^ Some ^ years ago — ^ never mind ^ how long ^ precisely — ^ having ^ little ^ or ^ no ^ money ^ in ^ my ^ purse, ^ and ^ nothing particular to ^ interest me ^ on ^ shore, ^ I ^ thought ^ I ^ would ^ sail about a little ^ and ^ see ^ the ^ watery ^ part of the ^ world.

I'm not sure why some places sound better than others, but the point I'm getting to is that *fucking* can fit in the same places as *um.* Also note that a pause filler breaks the normal rhythm and melody of speech. They are said with pauses around them—for example, *Call me . . . um/fucking . . . Ishmael*—and with a lowered voice, often with the nasal sound ([m], [ŋ], or [n]; see Chapter 5) drawn out—of course, I've rarely heard the pause filler *fucking* pronounced with [ŋ], but rather with [n] (written in "eye" dialect as <u>fuckin'</u>). Also the final [n] in the pause filler *fucking* is often quite low, almost a growl—linguists call this growl-like pitch creaky voice.

Throughout this book we return to the fact that taboo words are emotional words. In the case of *fucking* as a pause filler, however, the emotion seems to have been bleached out. Yet its social function as a taboo remains. The people I've known who use *fucking* as a pause

When you're asked to give a typical English word, *um* is not the first one that comes to mind; some people may not even want to call it a word, thinking of it more as a grunt. As we discussed in Chapter 4, though, there are objective ways of thinking about this. First, like all words, *um* is an arbitrary pairing of sound and meaning: only certain sound combinations function as pause fillers in English, for example, [ʌm], [ʌ], [ɑ], [fʌkɪn]. But what is their function? Clearly it's not an informative function but a social one (see Chapter 4). Pause fillers signal that the speaker is thinking about what she will say next and, importantly, that she is not done with her turn. In a conversation, when the speaker stops talking it means that another person can have a turn; pause fillers allow speakers to pause without silence. Second, pause fillers are subject to grammar. While they are not governed by strict syntactic rules (i.e., they can fit nearly anywhere in a sentence), they do follow phonological rules—they must fit into the sound system of the language. Thus, the French pause filler [œ] is not a candidate for an English pause filler, because we don't have this sound. Finally, all languages have pause fillers.

filler are able to regulate their use according to the social situation[20]; in other words, they are aware that, even bleached of its informative and emotional functions, *fucking* still has a social meaning beyond its function as a pause filler.

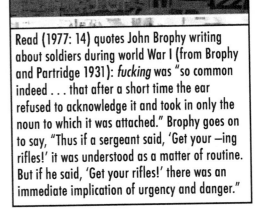

Read (1977: 14) quotes John Brophy writing about soldiers during world War I (from Brophy and Partridge 1931): *fucking* was "so common indeed . . . that after a short time the ear refused to acknowledge it and took in only the noun to which it was attached." Brophy goes on to say, "Thus if a sergeant said, 'Get your —ing rifles!' it was understood as a matter of routine. But if he said, 'Get your rifles!' there was an immediate implication of urgency and danger."

The final *fucking* we'll consider is the emphatic *fucking*, the one Quang suggests is derived from *fuck₂*. This *fucking*, like the pause filler, has been bleached of its informative function, but, unlike the pause filler, it retains its emotional function (see Chapter 14 for more on this). Also like the pause filler, it can fit in all sorts of places in a sentence. Let's consider (153) again, repeated here.

153. Call me Ishmael. Some years ago—never mind how long precisely—having little or no money in my purse, and nothing particular to interest me on shore, I thought I would sail about a little and see the watery part of the world.

This time, instead of the pause filler, insert the emphatic *fucking* wherever it sounds good. Compare your intuitions with mine in (153").

153" Call me ^ Ishmael. Some ^ years ago — never ^ mind how ^ long precisely — having little or no ^ money in my ^ purse, and nothing ^ particular to ^ interest me on ^ shore, I ^ thought I would ^ sail about a ^ little and ^ see the ^ watery ^ part of the ^ world.[21]

So far we've seen that *fucking* can be a verb participle, an adjective, a noun, and a pause filler. But what part of speech is the emphatic *fucking*? Some[22] have assumed the emphatic *fucking* is simply a figurative use of the adjective *fucking*. And, from phrases like *some fucking years, no fucking money, my fucking purse*, and *the fucking world*, this seems like a good hypothesis. However, Quang (1992a) and Bopp[23] (1992) give us some good evidence that the emphatic *fucking* is not an adjective. A normal adjective can be used before a noun that it modifies, and it can also be used after the same noun in a relative clause (*which/who is ____*).

154. a. Turn off that horrible music.

b. Turn off that music which is horrible.

The adjective *fucking* shows the same pattern.[24]

155. a. Keep your eye on that fucking couple.

b. Keep your eye on that couple who are fucking.

But the emphatic *fucking* doesn't work this way.[25]

156. Turn off that fucking music.

157. *Turn off that music which is fucking.

On the other hand, note that a normal adjective can't modify a proper name (unless it's properly part of the proper name, as in *Simple Jack*).

158. *Call me stupid Ishmael.

---

[20] Okay, I'm exaggerating here. I knew some sociopaths in college who were incapable of regulating their speech, especially when overindulging in recreational drugs.

[21] Inserting the emphatic *fucking* between Ishmael's words certainly changes his tone, huh?

[22] "Some" includes the FCC and California Representative Doug Ose—more on this in Chapter 15.

[23] Tina Bopp was a pseudonym adopted by Alice Davison for the purposes of the McCawley festschrift.

[24] You'll have to use your imagination to find an appropriate context for these examples.

[25] Adapting an example by Quang (1992a, 9), Pinker (2007, 360) gives the following data, noting that they are not interchangeable.

i. Drown the fucking cat.

ii. Drown the cat which is fucking.

But as we see in (153"), emphatic *fucking* can. This point may be more apparent in a context where the speaker has been called by a nickname she doesn't like.

159. Don't call me fucking Gertie. Call me fucking Gertrude.

Pinker (2007: 360) gives three more tests showing that emphatic *fucking* is not an adjective.[26]

160. a. That music seems loud.

    b. *That music seems fucking.

161. a. How loud was the music?

    b. *How fucking was the music?

162. a. The very loud music hurt my ears.

    b. *The very fucking music hurt my ears.

Another possibility is that emphatic *fucking* is an adverb, since it can modify adjectives (*fucking long, fucking particular, fucking watery*) just as the adverbs *really* and *very* can, and it can modify verbs (*interest, thought, sail, see*), just as the adverbs *truly, simply, slowly,* and *completely* can. But, as Nunberg (2004) shows, emphatic *fucking* doesn't behave like a normal adverb when modifying an adjective.

163. a. How long was the concert? Incredibly long.

    b. How long was the concert? Very long.

    c. How long was the concert? Fucking long.

164. a. How long was the concert? Incredibly.

    b. How long was the concert? Very.

    c. How long was the concert? *Fucking.

And, as Bopp (1992: 62) shows, it behaves differently from normal adverbs when modifying a verb.

165. a. He slowly sailed around the world.

    b. Slowly he sailed around the world.

166. a. He fucking sailed around the world.

    b. *Fucking he sailed around the world.

As with *fuck₂*, we're left with the problem of what part of speech to call emphatic *fucking*. Bopp (1992), following Quang (1992a), suggests **quasi-adjective** and **quasi-adverb**. These terms, I suppose, are as good as any.

A few final observations. First, as discussed, true adjectives do not modify proper names.

167. *I have to go visit unpleasant Abigail this afternoon.

168. *Rude Grant said he doesn't want to be my friend anymore.

In addition, proper names cannot be preceded by a determiner.[27]

169. *I have to go visit the Abigail this afternoon.

170. *The Grant said he doesn't want to be my friend anymore.

In this way, proper names are like pronouns.

171. *I have to go visit unpleasant her this afternoon.

172. *Rude he said he doesn't want to be my friend anymore.

---

[26] Pinker credits Nunberg (2004) for the tests, but from what I can tell, Nunberg (2004) only gives the first.

[27] There is an exception: when a proper name is preceded by both a determiner and an adjective it's fine.

    i. I have to go visit the unpleasant Abigail this afternoon.

    ii. The rude Grant said he doesn't want to be my friend anymore.

These sentences only make sense when two Abigails or two Grants are under discussion, and the speaker has to differentiate them. In effect, they treat *Abigail* and *Grant* as common nouns, not proper nouns.

173. *I have to go visit the her this afternoon.

174. *The he said he doesn't want to be my friend anymore.

However, there is a difference between proper nouns and pronouns in that the quasi-adjective *fucking* can combine with the former but not the latter.

175. I have to go visit fucking Abigail this afternoon.

176. Fucking Grant said he doesn't want to be my friend anymore.

177. *I have to go visit fucking her this afternoon.

178. *Fucking he said he doesn't want to be my friend anymore.

As for the quasi-adverb, in some ways it seems to most resemble *really* in that it can modify both adjectives and verbs.

179. Gertrude really hates Grant's really ugly toupee.

180. Gertrude fucking hates Grant's fucking ugly toupee.

There is a difference, however, in that *really* can also modify an entire sentence, in which case it has the meaning 'in reality', but emphatic *fucking* doesn't seem to work as a sentential modifier, at least with its typical negative meaning.

181. Really, Gertrude hates Grant's toupee.

182. ??Fucking, Gertrude hates Grant's toupee.

Students in my Fall 2006 Bad Words and Taboo Terms class pointed out, though, that there may be yet another *fucking* in English. Unlike the emphatic *fucking*, which we've been discussing, this one carries a positive emotion. These students demonstrated that positive *fucking* has a different distribution in a sentence from emphatic *fucking*. For example, they found that you could begin an upbeat sentence with *fucking*.

183. Fucking, I get to eat ice cream!

Also, it seems that positive *fucking* can modify a pronoun.

184. I get to dance with fucking her!?

I will leave it as an exercise for you to explore positive *fucking* more deeply.

4. CONCLUSION

In this chapter we have explored in depth the syntax of variants of *fuck*. When we speak, we create sentences without consciously thinking about it, yet the syntactic systems of all languages are mind-bogglingly complex. We've seen in this chapter that swearing, too, follows rules. *Fuck*, depending on its function, fills different places in a sentence, and although it looks like a verb, it doesn't always behave like one. Likewise, its *-ing* form follows different patterns depending on the function.

We have only scratched the surface on the syntax of English—indeed, on the syntax of English swearing. In Chapter 11, we discuss how hard it is to learn the grammar rules of another language, especially the rules surrounding swearing. It is remarkable how easily all speakers of English use such a sophisticated system as English syntax, even from a young age. Moreover, this system is learned by native speakers without ever being taught much of it. In truth, we are taught remarkably little of our syntax—certainly not how to swear—yet we acquire it with little effort as we grow up. Our ability to unconsciously acquire such a sophisticated system from such a young age (most of our syntax is acquired by age six) tells us something about how our minds function and how important language is to our humanness.

REFERENCES

Bopp, Tina. 1992. On Fucking (Well): A Study of some Quasi-Performative Expressions. In *Studies out in Left Field: Defamatory Essays Presented to James D. McCawley,* (eds.) A.M. Zwicky, P.H. Salus, R.I. Binnick, and A.L. Vanek, 61–71. Philadelphia: John Benjamins.

Brophy, John, and Eric Partridge (eds). 1931. *Songs and Slang of the British Soldier: 1914–1918.* London: Scholartis.

Hughes, Geoffrey. 1991. *Swearing: A Social History of Foul Language, Oaths, and Profanity in English.* Oxford: Blackwell.

Nunberg, Geoffrey. 2004. Imprecational Categories. *The Language Log.* http/itre.cis.upenn.edu/~myl/languagelog/archives/000614.html (accessed 7/29/09).

Pinker, Stephen. 2007. *The Stuff of Thought.* New York: Viking.

Quang Phuc Dong. 1992a. English Sentences without overt Grammatical Subject. In *Studies out in Left Field: Defamatory Essays Presented to James D. McCawley,* (eds.) A.M. Zwicky, P.H. Salus, R.I. Binnick, and A.L. Vanek, 3–10. Philadelphia: John Benjamins.

Quang Phuc Dong. 1992b. A Note on Conjoined Noun Phrases. In *Studies out in Left Field: Defamatory Essays Presented to James D. McCawley,* (eds.) A.M. Zwicky, P.H. Salus, R.I. Binnick, and A.L. Vanek, 11–18. Philadelphia: John Benjamins.

Read, Allen. 1977. *Classic American Graffiti: Lexical Evidence from Folk Epigraphy in Western North America.* Waukesha, WI: Maledicta Press.

For the following questions, it's your job to construct sentences, but you are encouraged to solicit grammaticality judgments from native-speaker friends. Simply show them the sentences and ask if the sentences sound "right" to them or not—that is, would they say a sentence like that? Sometimes you may have to construct a context so the sentence makes sense.

1. Intuitively, (i) seems more similar to (ii) than (iii).

   i.   Fuck off!

   ii. Fuck$_2$ you!

   iii. Fuck$_1$ somebody!

   In other words, the *fuck* in (i) seems more similar to *fuck*$_2$ than *fuck*$_1$. Semantically, this is probably correct. However, syntactically *fuck off* may be more similar to *fuck*$_1$. With the same sorts of tests used in the chapter text to show that (ii) is *not* an imperative sentence, demonstrate that (i) *is* an imperative sentence.

2. Explore the differences between emphatic (negative) *fucking* and positive *fucking*. Where can positive *fucking* occur in a sentence as compared to negative *fucking?* Think about different sorts of words (nouns, verbs, adjectives, adverbs, prepositions, determiners[28]) and different sorts of phrases (NPs, VPs, PPs[29]), and determine if positive *fucking* can precede them.

---

[28] See the sidebar on determiners on page 140.
[29] A preposition phrase (PP) consists of a preposition (e.g., *to, with, from, of*) followed by an NP. Examples are: *to the moon, with my best friend, from the sea, of an accidental nature.*

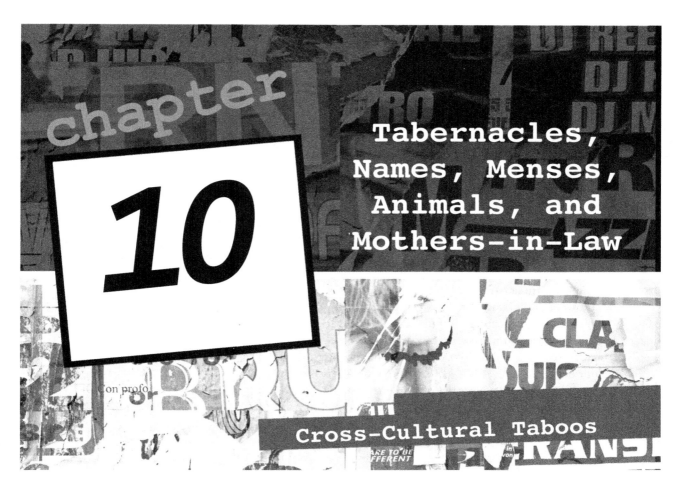

Tabernacles, Names, Menses, Animals, and Mothers-in-Law

Cross-Cultural Taboos

1. INTRODUCTION

When I was on my high school's cross-country team, one of my teammates, Giovanni, was an Italian exchange student. Of course, we all wanted him to teach us how to swear in Italian, and Giovanni was obliging. He taught us *stronzo* and told us it means 'asshole'. He taught us *fica* and told us it means 'pussy'. And he taught us *ficca* and told us it means 'to put it in'.[1]

We thought he'd taught us the worst of the worst. Until one day a friend saw an Italian phrase, *porco Dio,* in an article. From the context, he knew it must be a swear word, so the next day he walked up to Giovanni, and said, "Porco Dio!" Giovanni, a normally unflappable guy, grew very angry. He told us never to say that but refused to tell us what it meant. Needless to say, my friends and I felt cheated. Giovanni had been holding out on us. Here was a word even worse than *ficca,* and Giovanni wouldn't even tell us what it meant. Well, we looked it up and were disappointed to learn it means 'pig God'.

According to Jerrold Sadock (pers. comm), an expert on Greenlandic Eskimo, there is no taboo on scatological or sexual terms in that language. After discussions with native speakers on swearing, he concluded there are only two ways of swearing in Greenlandic Eskimo: one is to use the word *toornavsuaq* 'the devil', and this is probably based on Danish influence; the other is to say "ajorpoq!" very emphatically. When Sadock protested that *ajorpoq* simply means 'it's bad' and people say that all the time, his consultant agreed but said that it's swearing if you say it with the right tone of voice.

---

[1] Imagine Giovanni saying "pussy" and "to put it in" with a thick Italian accent.

I've since learned there are all sorts of 'pig' phrases in Italian. Here's a short list:

- *Porca Madonna*—'pig Madonna'
- *Porca puttana*—'pig whore'
- *Porco Giuda*—'pig Judas'
- *Porca vacca*—'pig cow'

Many years later, my wife and I went on a three-day trek in Thailand led by a gregarious guide named Pira. After years of hearing American tourists exclaim "Oh my God," Pira had taken to saying, "Oh my Buddha." He turned out to be a relatively devout Buddhist, so one of our co-trekkers asked if saying "oh my Buddha" wasn't sacrilegious. He said, "No, it's just funny." Later on the trip, somebody made a joke, not particularly funny, about how maybe someday Pira would become the king of Thailand. He grew uncharacteristically serious, and informed us that the joke was not funny and that we should not talk about the king that way.

I've since learned that it is highly taboo in Thai society to say anything defamatory or insulting about the king. Violations of this taboo are punishable by fifteen years in prison; only recently, an Australian novelist, Harry Nicolaides, was sentenced to three years for insulting the Thai king in his fiction (Mydans & McDonald 2009).

My point in these two anecdotes? Taboos are different from culture to culture. Simple, huh? But interesting.

In this chapter we explore linguistic taboos in various languages, beginning with unusual takes on the following types of taboo words: profanity, scatology, obscenity, appellity, and faunality. First, we look to our neighbor up north, specifically to Québécois French, for church-related swearwords. Next, we explore menstruation taboos in Akan, a language spoken in Ghana. From Africa, we travel to Australia to look at Guugu Yimidhirr, a language in which all words are taboo when a man interacts with his mother-in-law. After this we turn to Chinese and explore some ancient naming taboos. Finally, we consider animal taboos in Ukrainian.

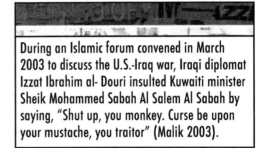

During an Islamic forum convened in March 2003 to discuss the U.S.-Iraq war, Iraqi diplomat Izzat Ibrahim al- Douri insulted Kuwaiti minister Sheik Mohammed Sabah Al Salem Al Sabah by saying, "Shut up, you monkey. Curse be upon your mustache, you traitor" (Malik 2003).

2. TABERNACLE!, HOST!, BAPTISM!, AND CHALICE!

Are you shocked by the title of this section? No? Well, it would be more shocking if said in French—though not in France, where they'd just look at you funny. But in Québec, it would be shocking. The French expressions are: *tabernak, hostie, baptême,* and *câlice.* According to Struck (2006), and confirmed by native Québécois speaker Sylvain Neuvel (pers. comm.), these are the worst words that can be said in Québécois French. Neuvel tells me that other words like *merde* ('shit') don't even feel like swearing to him.

Obviously, these are examples of profanity, which Struck (2006) suggests has the strength it does in Québec because the Catholic Church held such power in this part of the world for so long.

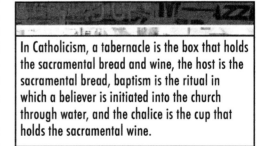

In Catholicism, a tabernacle is the box that holds the sacramental bread and wine, the host is the sacramental bread, baptism is the ritual in which a believer is initiated into the church through water, and the chalice is the cup that holds the sacramental wine.

In contrast, in France, where the Catholic Church lost its power much earlier, swear words tend to be obscene or scatological. Today, though, the Catholic Church has lost some of its hold in Québec. In fact, it seems that many young Québécois French speakers do not know the religious meaning of these words; they only know them as swear words. Struck (2006) describes a campaign in which the Church put up billboards with these words written in large letters; in smaller letters, the religious definition is given. Passersby were initially shocked to see such taboo words posted on billboards.

3. MENSTRUATION: POLLUTION, INDISPOSITION, SECLUSION, TRANSITION, AND PROTECTION

I don't know of any truly taboo words in English for menstruation, but it's a taboo topic. For example, before MGM released Frank Zappa's 1968 album *We're Only In It for the Money,* they cut out the following line from one of his songs: "I still remember Mama with her apron and her pad." MGM censored Zappa because they thought "pad" referred to a 'sanitary napkin', not the waitress' notepad that Zappa had in mind (Zappa & Occhiogrosso 1990, 84).[2]

We can also see the tabooness of menstruation by the number of euphemisms we have for it. For an impressive list of menstruation taboos, see *Aunt Flow's World of Menstruation Euphemisms!* (http://www.starma.com/penis/auntflow/auntflow.html, accessed 5/19/09). Some notable samples from the list can be found in Table 10.1.

TABLE 10.1	
English Euphemisms for Menstruation	
Arts and crafts week at Panty Camp	The nuisance
The Curse	Old Faithful
The dam has burst	On the rag
End of sentence	Seeing red
The gift	Sprung a leak
Girl time	That time of the month
Monthly visitor	Taking Carrie to the prom
Moon time	The visitations
Mother Nature's gift	Weeping womb

Many euphemisms for menstruation are rather imaginative (*arts and crafts week at Panty Camp, Taking Carrie to the prom, end of sentence*); some have notably negative connotations (*the curse, the nuisance*), while others—perhaps in response—are positive (*the gift, girl time*); many refer to its cyclic nature (*monthly visitor, moon time, that time of the month*)—indeed, *period,* now an orthophemism, was originally a euphemism along these lines; some refer to the paraphernalia that accompanies menstruation (*on the rag*); finally, many are metaphoric (*the dam has burst*). We could argue, however, that many of these are impolite, making them dysphemistic rather than euphemistic. For example, *on the rag* is nearly always used negatively, and, in my experience, more by men than women. Even among the polite expressions, there is often a humorous element. This strikes me as similar to expressions for *masturbation,* where there are few, if any, truly taboo terms, but there are many humorous euphemisms, (e.g., *beating the purple-headed yogurt slinger, jerkin' the gerkin, brushing the beaver, clam-bake for one*).

Back to menstruation. Agyekum (2002: 367) argues there are two main perspectives on it: The male perspective, generally negative, views it as "messy, revolting, and polluted—something to be avoided," and the female perspective, generally positive, sees "menstruation as something that portrays the fertility and societal recognition of the female, especially the adolescent." The rest of this section is based on Agyekum's account of language about menstruation in Akan, a language spoken in Ghana.

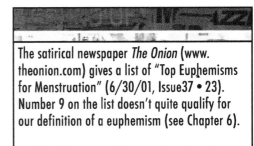

The satirical newspaper *The Onion* (www.theonion.com) gives a list of "Top Euphemisms for Menstruation" (6/30/01, Issue37 • 23). Number 9 on the list doesn't quite qualify for our definition of a euphemism (see Chapter 6).

9. "It's 'that time of the month' where 'I'm not at my best' because 'my vagina is bleeding'"

---

[2] According to Zappa some MGM executive had an image of Zappa's mother "feeding sanitary napkins to people in a restaurant" (Zappa & Occhiogrosso 1990, 84). This just goes to show you we cannot completely control the perlocutionary effect of our utterances (see Chapter 14).

Unlike in English, menstruation in Akan is a serious topic, not to be joked about. The Akan word for 'menstruation' is *kyima,* but it is taboo. Typically, Akan speakers use euphemisms when they have to discuss it. Agyekum lists twenty-five euphemisms, which can be found in Table 10.2. I have divided the expressions according to whether Agyekum classifies them as positive or negative and then according to his subcategories of indisposition, seclusion, fertility/transition, and protection. Expressions marked with '%' are less common and probably not known by the majority of younger speakers.

TABLE 10.2

Euphemisms for 'Menstruation' in Akan

Negative		Positive	
Indisposition	*Seclusion*	*Fertility/Transition*	*Protection*
ɔabu ne nsa 'she has broken her hand'	*ɔnkɔ gya ho* 'she doesn't enter the kitchen'	*Aye ne ho* 'she has shaved herself'	% *ɔahuri asi* 'he has jumped and landed'
ɔnte/ɔnnyina yie 'she is not sitting/standing well'	*ɔako afikyire* 'she's gone behind the house'	*ɔaye bra* 'she's of age'	% *Akoa no abeduru* 'the man has arrived'
ne nsa kɔ n'akyi 'her hand has gone to her back'	*ɔnkɔ ahemfie* 'she doesn't go to the palace'	*ɔakyima/waye asakyima* 'she has flowered'	
% *ɔate kokoniwa* 'she has hurt her toe'	*ɔnkɔ nkonnwafie so* 'she doesn't go to the stool room'	% *ɔbaa no gyamma abere* 'the woman's gyamma fruit is ripe'	
% *ɔaye bafan* 'she has been crippled'	*ɔaba/ ɔkɔ mmaa fie/kuro mu* 'she has come/gone/into women's house'	% *ngo kɔkɔi afo no/aba ne fie* 'red palm oil has soiled her/flowed into her'	
% *bukyia mu afɔ* 'the hearth is wet'	% *ɔako abunkuam* 'she's gone to the parlour of the house'	% *ɔahunu mogya* 'she has seen blood'	
% *aye basaa* 'she is bewildered'	% *ɔnwe bosom so nam* 'she doesn't eat meat from the shrine'	% *ɔakum sono* 'she has killed an elephant'	
% *ɔasunti abu ne nan mu* 'she has stumbled and broken her leg'		% *ɔkɔ po so* 'she has gone to the sea'	

Let's consider each category and subcategory in turn, starting with the negative. From one perspective, the period is negative because it indicates that a couple has failed to conceive a child—though in modern society this is less negative than it used to be, especially for young urban women. The main idea in Akan culture seems to be that a woman's menstrual blood is poisonous, or as Agyekum calls it, pollution. It weakens the woman, but is even more toxic—perhaps even deadly—to a man. This perspective seems to be a patriarchal one, one which "emphasizes men's purity and male superiority in male-dominated societies, like the Akan" (Agyekum 2002, 374).

Going along with this idea of menses as poison, women in Akan are not supposed to perform their regular household duties, such as cooking and, especially, sex. This is for two reasons: first, they are weaker than usual; second, they might contaminate their husbands. Boys and females are apparently not as susceptible to the toxins because a menstruating woman can cook for her children and other women.

The euphemisms in the first column of Table 10.2 reflect the indisposition perspective in that they are all ways of indicating that a woman can't perform certain duties. For example, if the hearth is wet, you can't light a fire, so you can't cook. Likewise, if you're incapacitated in any way, you can't be expected to cook, clean, perform rituals, have sex. Obviously, nobody takes these euphemisms literally. Typically, these are something a woman would say to her husband as explanation for why dinner isn't ready or as a way of fending off his sexual advances (cf. "I have a headache" in English), and the husband knows quite well what she is getting at. Although, from a man's perspective, the period is negative, you can imagine that there are times when an Akan woman might be happy to be relieved of certain duties.

The other side of the poison issue is that a menstruating woman's movements are restricted so she doesn't contaminate people. In earlier times, this was taken so far that she was forced to seek refuge in a special shelter behind the house, hence *ɔako afikyire* 'she's gone behind the house' and *ɔaba/ ɔkɔ mmaa fie/kuro mu* 'she has come/gone/into women's house'. Women no longer retreat to these shelters during their periods; however, they still aren't allowed in sacred places, such as the palace, the temple, or the stool room (yes, the stool room). Agyekum gives the following example from 1994, where a defendant had to explain why a witness didn't show up to testify (2002, 377):

Ɔkyeame:	*Wo danseni wɔ henefa?*
	'Where is your witness?'
Defendant:	*Nananom mesrɛ mo me danseni no se, "ɔmma ahemfie" enti wamma.*
	'Nananom with all my apologies, my witness says that "she does [not] enter the palace" so she could not attend court today.'

The trial was postponed until the witness's period had ended.

Related to the seclusion subcategory is an expression for indicating when a woman's period is over: *mafi* 'I am out [of jail]'.

We've seen the negative side of it; however, there are positives to periods. For one, it marks a girl's transition into womanhood. Agyekum relates the following dialogue between a mother and the village's queen mother (2002, 380):

Mother:	*Nana! Onyame adom wo nana Akyamaa aye bra.*
	'Nana! By the grace of God your granddaughter Akyamaa is of age.'
Queen Mother:	*Ne tiri nkwa. Yɛda Onyame ase.*
	'May she have long life. We thank God.'

The most common ways of describing the transition are to use circumlocutions, as in *ɔayɛ bra* 'she's of age' or *Aye ne ho* 'she has shaved herself'[3]. The other common expression, *ɔakyima/waye asakyima* 'she has flowered', is more metaphoric, as are the other, less common expressions. One in particular is clearly hyperbolic: *ɔakum sono* 'she has killed an elephant', meaning she has so much blood it is like an elephant was slaughtered. It's hard to imagine this is a completely serious expression, despite what Agyekum writes about how serious menstruation is taken in Akan society.

Although it seems that the expressions in the transition/fertility category can all be used to indicate a first period, some can also be used with respect to adult women. The emphasis in this category is primarily on the blood itself, which is not only a sign of transition into adulthood, but also of fertility.

The final category has to do with the power of the menses. Menstrual blood, as we discussed earlier, is considered toxic, but that also makes it powerful. For example, Akans believe it can be used as an antidote to curses, and it can create love charms. Interestingly, it is also pictured as a man (*ɔahuri asi* 'he has jumped and landed'; *Akoa no abɛduru* 'the man has arrived'). Although this menstrual man can be dangerous to other men should they come in contact with him, he is there to protect the woman. Apparently, a woman can use the menstrual man as a shield against unwanted suitors who press for sex. It can even be used to put off her husband, as indicated by the following example (2002, 383):

Wife:	*Kwaku ɛnnɛ deɛ yɛrentumi nkɔ kwan so.*
	'Kwaku, as for today we cannot travel on the road [have sex].'
Husband:	*Adɛn Afua ɛbaa no sɛn?*
	'Afua, what has happened.'
Wife:	*Akoa no abɛduru.*
	'The man has arrived.'
Husband:	*Akoa yi nsoa, ɔkyerɛ ne ho papa.*
	'Oh! As for this man he is very disturbing.'

To sum up this section, I would simply like to observe that taboos and their concomitant euphemisms can tell us a lot about a culture's beliefs and norms. Presently in Akan society, as women gain more status and power,

---

[3] Clearly the shaving refers to pubic hair; however, it's not clear from Agyekum's account whether it is to be taken literally.

many of these euphemisms are no longer applicable. As women begin to work outside the home, they are less and less likely to seclude themselves or to avoid doing work during their periods. Agyekum argues that as women's status rises, the negative view of menstruation loses its hold. In that regard, we might say that American society is somewhat, but not entirely, enlightened with respect to women. Men may not fear menstrual blood, though, judging by our euphemisms, they don't particularly like it.

Yet another English euphemism: *on a losing streak*. This one is most famous in The Rolling Stones' song "Satisfaction." Apparently some censors bleeped Jagger's singing "I'm trying to make some girl," but they didn't even notice what Jagger thought was the dirtiest part, where she tells him to come back next week "'cause you see I'm on a losing streak" (Going to Pot 1966). (Thanks go to Homer Conder (pers. comm.) for pointing out this example.)

4. MOTHERS-IN-LAW

Mother-in-law's Golden Rule for son-in-law:

Never Speak, Even When Spoken To
(adapted from www.quasimother.com/mother-in-law-jokes.html, accessed 2/2/2011)

A man returns home from the night shift and goes straight up to the bedroom. He finds his wife with the sheet pulled over her head, fast asleep. Not to be denied, the husband crawls under the sheet and proceeds to make love to her. Afterward, as he hurries downstairs for something to eat, he's startled to find breakfast on the table and his wife pouring coffee. "How'd you get down here so fast?" he asks. "We were just making love!"

"Oh my God," his wife gasps, "That's my mother up there! She came over early and had complained of having a headache. I told her to lie down for a while."

Rushing upstairs, the wife runs to the bedroom. "Mother, I can't believe this happened. Why didn't you say something?"

The mother-in-law huffs, "I haven't spoken to that jerk for fifteen years, and I wasn't about to start now!"

(Author unknown, found at various sources on the Internet)

Let's get something straight: Me, I like my mother-in-law. The jokes that begin this chapter are examples of mention, not use. They illustrate a common idea that mothers-in-law and sons-in-law do not get along and/or should not speak. This idea has been taken to an extreme in some cultures, where it has become a societal convention. For example, in Guugu Yimidhirr, a language spoken in the northwest part of Australia, it is taboo for a son-in-law to talk to his mother-in-law and vice versa, a taboo whose violation, historically at least, was punishable by death—spearing, apparently (Haviland 1979).

Why should this be? Well, the answer is hinted at in the final of the previous jokes, and to answer it, I'll tell a brief anecdote. In college while studying abroad in Vienna, a friend and I ended up in a strange bar where the waitresses not only delivered drinks to the customers (all of whom were men) but also sat with them. When my friend asked the bartender what the bar was all about, she answered succinctly, *"Sex, eigentlich,"* which translates as 'sex, actually.'[4]

So what's the taboo in Guugu Yimidhirr all about? Sex, actually.

The following discussion of Guugu Yimidhirr is based on Haviland's (1979) description, which is from a man's perspective, and, with apologies to women, this is how we will proceed.

In Guugu Yimidhirr, there are two special types of talk: *guugu-mul* 'without words' and *guya-gurral* 'saying nothing'. Based on the glosses, you would think that these amount to the same thing. You would be wrong. When you are in a *guugu-mul* relationship with somebody, you are without words because you are not allowed to use any with this person.[5] But when you are in a *guya-gurral* relationship with somebody, you are licensed to use

---

[4] The boring ending to this story is that we paid a ridiculous sum for our drinks and left.

[5] In a sense, we could say that, when interacting with this person, all words are taboo words.

any words you like. You can make jokes, even—perhaps especially—obscene jokes. In other words, to 'say nothing' in this culture means to say nonsense.

For the most part, it's your mother-in-law you're in a *guugu-mul* relationship with. No matter what, you cannot speak to her, and she cannot speak to you. The *guya-gurral* relationship is with your grandparents or with your grandchildren; with them, you can be as silly and bawdy as you like.

To understand the Guugu Yimidhirr culture, we have to understand their kinship structure. It would seem that familial relations are based on empirical facts, so you might wonder how they could be culturally determined. After all, relations like mother, father, sister, brother, aunt, uncle, grandfather, grandmother, cousin, niece, nephew, etc. simply represent facts about genetic ties. True. However, it is the choices we make in how we represent these facts that makes kinship a cultural concept. It is a bit like the constellations: the positions of the stars in the sky are facts, but the shapes we make out of these positions are not. For example, in Hungarian, the generic word for 'brother', *fivér*, is rarely used; instead, speakers usually specify 'younger brother', *öcs*, or 'older brother', *bátya*; however, *bátya* is not specifically 'older brother', but also means 'uncle'. We could gloss *bátya* as loosely meaning 'older male relative', a concept that English lacks.[6]

For the speakers of Guugu Yimidhirr, one of the most important classifications is **moiety**, an anthropological term for "[e]ither of two kinship groups based on unilateral descent that together make up a tribe or society" (*American Heritage Dictionary*). What this means: If I'm a member of the Guugu Yimidhirr community, I classify all members of the community according to whether they belong to "my moiety" or "their moiety." My moiety is that of my father's, and it includes his siblings and my siblings; their moiety is that of my mother's, and it includes her siblings and father. You cannot marry within your own moiety; you must seek your spouse from "their moiety." Since you can't marry from within your own moiety, your father and mother have to be from different moieties; furthermore, since moiety is passed down from the father, your mother will always be of a different moiety than you (and your matrilineal grandmother will thus be of the same moiety as you). A basic table of Guugu Yimidhirr kin terms is found in Table 10.3.

Some explanation is warranted. *Yaba* means 'older brother'; *garga* means 'younger brother'; *gaanhaal* means 'older sister'; and *dyin-gurr* means 'younger sister'. *Mugagay* means 'father's older brother', and *biiba* means 'father or father's younger brother'. *Gami* includes anybody of my moiety of the same generation as my grandparents. My ideal bride would be somebody who is my *dyirral*—that

A lot of people are confused by the difference between first versus second cousins, and first cousins versus first cousins once removed. First, second, etc. refer to horizontal distance. Once removed, twice removed, etc. refer to vertical distance (i.e., generational). My first cousin is the child of one of my parents' siblings (same generation as me, and horizontally close). My second cousin is the child of one of my parents' first cousins (same generation as me, but horizontally further away). My first cousin once removed is one of my parents' first cousins or the child of one of my first cousins (one generation away from me, but horizontally close).

is, the daughter of a man who is my *mugur*. *Mugur* would include my mother's brothers and male cousins. My bride should be a *dyirral* not too closely related horizontally—probably no closer than second cousin.

TABLE 10.3				
Guugu Yimidhirr Kin Terms (from Haviland 1979, 214)				
	My moiety		*Their moiety*	
Generation	Male	Female	Male	Female
+2	gami		ngadhi	Babi
+1	mugagay/biiba	biimuur	mugur	Ngamu
0	yaba/garga	gaanhaal/dyin-gurr	gaanyi/dunhu/etc.	Dyirral
−1	yumurr		dyuway	nguudhurr
−2	Gamindharr		Ngadhinil	

---

[6] Of course, when a more specific term is applicable, the specific trumps the general. So your father is your *atya*, not your *bátya*, and your grandfather is your *nagyatya*.

As should be obvious, if my wife has any sisters, they would also qualify as my *dyirral*. In American culture, the relationship between a man and his wife's sisters is a delicate one. If the relationship turns too flirtatious, they all might end up on the Jerry Springer Show. In the Guugu Yimidhirr culture, however, a man can be just as joking and flirtatious with his wife's sisters as he would be with her. In fact, in the traditional culture, polygamy was practiced, and it was common for a man to marry his wife's sister.

The person a man has to be really careful of is his wife's mother, his *biwul*. The reason for this comes back to what we started with: sex, actually. By most people's standards, having sex with your mother-in-law is bad.[7] And, as we all know, talking is the first step towards sex. So, according to Haviland to ensure that a man can never have sex with his mother-in-law, the Guugu Yimidhirr culture has made it taboo for him to talk to her.

In Table 10.1, the shaded terms represent relatives who could become *dhabul*, 'sacred, forbidden, taboo.' A man's mother-in-law is *dhabul*. You don't talk to her. If you absolutely have to communicate something to her, use your child as a proxy. You can talk to your children and so can your mother-in-law—in fact, she can talk obscenely to them, since they're in a *guya-gurral* relationship.

The mother-in-law is the most *dhabul*, but other people are *dhabul*, too. For example, any potential mother-in-law is at least somewhat *dhabul*, so a man should be careful of all his *biimuur* (i.e., mothers of women who are his potential brides). Other *dhabul* kin are his wife's father, *ngadhiina*, and his wife's brother, *gaanyil* (among other terms). With all but the *biwul* 'mother-in-law', a man can speak to his *dhabul* kin, but should use a special vocabulary, *guugu dhabul*.

When using *guugu dhabul*, you should be restrained in your speech, never raising your voice, and not even facing your *dhabul*. You might even want to address your father-in-law's dog instead of addressing your speech directly to him. Most importantly, you want to avoid anything that could lead to a fight, especially with your brother-in-law. If he wants to argue with you, get up and leave. What's likely to lead to a fight? Sex, actually. You don't talk about anything related to sex with your brother-in-law, because you don't want to cause his mind to turn to the kinds of things that you and his sister do behind closed doors. That might anger him, thinking about you and his sister like that. So certainly don't mention any unmentionables like 'penis' or 'vagina'. In fact, don't even say things that might cause him to think of such unmentionables. Like 'axe', for example. Have you ever noticed how phallic axes are? Me neither. But it seems that to a person from this culture it is. So don't, under any circumstances, tell your brother-in-law about your axe, unless you use the more polite term *gadiil-baga;* apparently, the heightened formality of this polite term for 'axe' is enough to circumvent thoughts of penises.

Guugu dhabul has its own very restricted vocabulary, which does not include any terms for sex organs and lacks many common everyday words. For example, the standard variety of the language has at least ten words for 'kangaroo', but *guugu dhabul* has only one, *daarraalngan*.

Finally, there are other people you shouldn't have sex with, particularly your mother and your sisters. These people aren't *dhabul,* and you can talk normally to them, but it's best to avoid mentioning anything related to sex. In fact, you should probably also avoid terms that might metaphorically refer to sex or sex organs, like 'axe', 'stone', and 'hole'.

So next time you find yourself in northwest Australia in a Guugu Yimidhirr village, marrying a local woman, be careful how you talk to your father-in-law or your brother-in-law. Don't say a single word to your mother-in-law. And whatever you do, don't have sex with her.

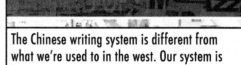

The Chinese writing system is different from what we're used to in the west. Our system is based on a sound-symbol correspondence. Chinese uses ideographs—characters that represent meaning, not sound. It seems that the Imperial Chinese naming taboo was aimed primarily at the written characters; however, since the characters represent words and the words have sounds, it appears that similar sounding words could also be taboo.

5.   THY FATHER'S NAME

When I was a child, there was an unspoken rule in my family and in the families of my friends: You didn't call your parents by their first names. So, of course, behind their backs, we talked about them using their first names—it was very naughty of us. In ancient China, that rule was taken far more seriously.

---

[7] FYI, a British man, Clive Blunden, married his former mother-in-law, Brenda, after a law making such marriages illegal was overturned (http://www.thisischeshire.co.uk/news/1270386.Man_marries_mother_in_law/, accessed 2/2/2011).

TABLE 10.4		
Imperial Chinese Names Whose Taboo Led to New words (Hongxu & Guisen 1990, 70)		
Imperial Names	*Affected Character(s)*	*Substitutes*
Liú Bāng	*bāng* 'state'	*quó*
Liú Ying	*ying* 'full'	*mǎn*
Liú Qǐ	*qǐ* 'open'	*kāi, jīng*
Liú Xiù	*xiùcái* 'scholar'	*maòcái*
Liú Zhūang	*zhūang* 'serious'	*yán*
Yáng Jiān	*jiān* 'solid'	*láo, qù, gāng*

In Imperial China it was forbidden to utter the name of the emperor. "Known as *tiānzi* 'the son of heaven', the Chinese emperor claimed to be the supreme person in the universe and his name was therefore deemed far to sacred to be either pronounced in direct address or referred to in writing" (Hongxu & Guisen 1990, 69). To talk or write about the emperor, one had to use a euphemism: at the beginning of the Qing Dynasty (1644–1911 CE) seventy people were executed for their roles in producing a book in which an emperor's name was written.

This taboo became more and more complex, as emperors began insisting that even parts of their names should not be written (Hongxu & Guisen 1990, 69–70). For example, in one emperor's written name there were two common characters: *shi* 'generation' and *min* 'people'. These two common words had to be replaced with new words, *dai* and *rén,* respectively. In Table 10.4, Hongxu and Guisen give a list of emperor's names, affected characters, and words that had to substitute for the taboo character.

The emperor, obviously, was superior to all his subjects; however, analogous taboos existed in other situations where one person was higher than others. For example, teachers' names could not be uttered by their students, bosses' names by their employees, officials' names by their subjects, fathers' names by their children. So, being that my boss's name is Ed, under Imperial China's laws, I wouldn't have been able to write or say his name. In fact, I wouldn't have been able to talk about special ed, or sex ed, or phys ed, or driver ed, etc. And since my graduate advisor was Jerrold (AKA Jerry), I wouldn't have been able to call a chamber pot a jerry (not that I do—I just like to have the option). Nor could I use words like *norm* or *normal* because my father's named Norman.

You might think I'm being absurd in the previous paragraph; however, Hongxu and Guisen discuss a case where the poet Lǐ Hè was barred from being a candidate for the academic title *Jìnshì* because his father's name had a character that resembled *jìn.*

One last tidbit: the word for 'I', *zhèn,* which was originally used by everybody, was made taboo when it became too closely connected with the emperor (Hongxu & Guisen 1990, 67). That is, it was taboo for everybody but the emperor, making it a remarkably exclusive pronoun, one that could only be used by one living being at a time. Now that the monarchy no longer exists, there's nobody to use *zhèn.*[8]

Students in American universities have to learn to navigate the dos and don'ts of how to address their professors. Some professors want to be called "Dr. So-and-So," some "Professor So-and-So," and some "Mr./Ms. So-and-So." Others want to be called by their first names.

When I began graduate school at the University of Chicago, I was informed that in the Linguistics Department all graduate students were on a first name basis with their professors. However, I later learned it was taboo for undergraduates to refer to their professors by their first names; in many introductory classes, graduate students would ask for their professors' attention by saying, "Jerry . . ." or "Amy . . .", while the undergraduates would have to say, "Mr. Sadock . . ." or "Ms. Dahlstrom . . ."

Things were even more complicated when taking classes in other departments; for example, we had to learn that, in Anthropology, everybody was on a last name basis with their professors. One professor, Michael Silverstein, was affiliated with both the Linguistics and Anthropology Departments, so with him we had to determine whether he positioned himself more as a Linguistics Professor or Anthropology Professor—it turned out it was Anthropology, and we were expected to call him "Mr. Silverstein."

---

[8] Hongxu and Guisen (1990, 67) note that after the monarchy collapsed, presumably making *zhèn* legal for use amongst the hoi polloi, "the word fell out of use completely because no one was so pretentious or socially ignorant as to use an obsolete form which could bring upon him nothing but ridicule and disgrace."

6. DANGEROUS ANIMALS

In modern American English, we have some animal names that are taboo (e.g., *ass, cock, pussy,* and *bitch*). The first is explained in Chapter 7. The middle two appear to be a result of the euphemism treadmill (see Chapters 6 and 7), where they metaphorically refer to body parts until the euphemisms eventually become too closely associated with what they denote and become taboo themselves. We can speculate that the final word became taboo because of its use as a slur, though in special circles (e.g., dog shows), it may still be used orthophemistically.

In older times we probably had more taboos on animal names. Chapter 7 notes that the English word *bear* began as a euphemism, roughly 'brown one'. As we've seen, euphemisms exist in order to avoid taboo words. So let's ask the obvious question: why should the word for 'bear' have been taboo? The taboo seems to have existed in at least two Indo-European language families, namely Germanic and Slavic. In Germanic languages, the modern words for 'bear' tend to come from 'brown', while in Slavic languages, the modern words are derived from 'honey-eater'.

Emeneau (1948) gives two theories on why a word like 'bear' would have been taboo: the first we'll call the hunting theory, the second the demonic theory. The hunting theory holds that hunters didn't say the name for 'bear' because then the bears would hear and know they were being hunted. The demonic theory holds that the bear was a demon in a religious belief system and to utter its name was blasphemous. Emeneau didn't like the hunting theory and advocated the demonic theory. Two years later, Smal-Stocki (1950) dismissed both theories and sketched a theory commonly accepted today: let's call it the word magic theory.

Smal-Stocki, focusing on Ukrainian, notes that the taboo on saying the word for 'bear' is not relegated to the ancient past. Among contemporary[9] Ukranian highlanders, the Ukranian word for 'bear' *medv'id'* is taboo. The word was originally a euphemism meaning 'honey-eater', but via the euphemism treadmill it became taboo itself, so that new euphemisms had to be created, including *vedm'id'* a simple transformation of the sounds (Smal-Stocki 1950, 490). Other euphemisms are *burmylo* 'growler, grumbler', *burč* 'growler', *vujko* 'uncle', *tot* 'that one', *tot staryj* 'that old one', *tot velkyj* 'that big one', *vin* 'he', and *egzekutor* 'bailiff' (for bears' propensity to exact cattle as a "tax" from ranchers). According to Smal-Stocki, the taboo against saying *medv'id'* "exists in Ukrainian without any vestige of a religious or demonic bear cult, and without involving the notion (ridiculous to all hunters) that bears can understand their speech." Instead, the taboo is based on the idea that "the utterance of a name evokes the thing named" (1950, 490).

Under the word magic theory, you don't say the name of a dangerous animal because you don't want to "call" that animal: hence the Ukranian proverb, "*Pro vouka pomouka a vouk u chatu* 'One speaks

---

Word magic, the superstition that words have inherent power, is now the primary explanation for why the names of dangerous animals are sometimes taboo. I use the word *superstition* cautiously, though, because the word has gotten a bad rap. Linguist Jonathon McWhorter dismisses swear words as "a matter of superstition" and goes on to say that "the idea that certain sequences of sounds, which if said make everyone very uncomfortable for reasons that they can't quiet explain, is a very primitive notion" (from *Penn & Teller: Bullshit!,* episode 2-06). I don't take issue with McWhorter's point, so much as the smugness behind it, a smugness belied by his own primitive response when called on to utter the word *cunt* (see Chapter 3).

The truth is words do have power (though not inherent). For example, as discussed in Chapter 14, we can do things with words (e.g., christen, wager, marry, promise, insult, praise, thank, etc.). We also find that "certain sequences of sounds" trigger physiological responses (see Chapters 11 and 12). Moreover, as enlightened as many of us consider ourselves to be, we still indulge in superstitions: I, for example, am forced to knock on wood whenever my wife recklessly says things like, "I never get sick;" modern theater actors do not utter the name of Shakespeare's *Macbeth;* among Wade Boggs' many pre-game rituals, he had to eat poultry (Murdoch 2005); even though we all know that a picture of a baby is not the same as a baby, our aim with a dart declines when a baby's picture is on the dartboard (Hutson 2008); President Barack Obama ritually plays basketball on the day of an election.

One place I've observed word magic used to good effect is among rape survivors. Survivors say they can regain some of their equilibrium after acquaintance-rape by simply naming their rapist. Even if the rapist is never prosecuted or punished and even if the hearers will never meet him, survivors say the act of voicing his name takes power from him.

---

[9] That is, contemporary to Smal-Stocki when he wrote the paper (i.e., 1950). I can't speak for today.

of the wolf and it runs into the house'" (Smal-Stocki 1950, 491). In this way, other dangerous animals are also taboo among highland Ukranians (e.g., *vouk* 'wolf'), which is replaced with circumlocutions, such as 'large dog', 'the insatiable', 'the gray one'.[10] Smal-Stocki also mentions that 'snake', 'hawk', 'fox', and 'wild boar' may be taboo. He relates a couple illustrative anecdotes:

> An old woman told me that *pesky* ['little dog'] used to be the most 'proper' name to use, because if wolves were called by their 'real' names they would multiply rapidly and soon become a danger to peasants and their cattle . . .

> An old man once said to me 'Don't use the word [i.e., *hadyna* ['serpent']]; may it'—and he spat it out—'not often appear!' (Smal-Stocki 1950, 491)

We find this taboo against uttering the "real" name of dangerous animals among many cultures of the world, including East Asia and South America. Presumably, the closer people live to the wilderness, the more likely they are to have such a taboo. Furthermore, Smal-Stocki's word magic theory seems to be a better explanation than to think that uttering these animals' names is a form of profanity or that it is a hunter's superstition, especially given that the taboo is predominantly on dangerous animals and not so much on game animals.

7.   CONCLUSION

We've covered a lot of territory in this chapter: From Italy to Thailand to Canada to China to Ghana to Australia to the Ukraine. There are, of course, many other languages and cultures in the world and, therefore, many more taboos to investigate. For example, my Japanese students have told me that the verb for 'die', especially when used in the imperative, is one of the most taboo words in Japan.[11] I will leave it to you to further investigate the taboos of other languages.

REFERENCES

Agyekum, Kofi. 2002. Menstruation as a Verbal Taboo Among the Akan of Ghana. *Journal of Anthropological Research* 58(3): 367–387.

Emeneau, M.B. 1948. Taboos on Animal Names. *Language* 24(1): 56–63.

Going to Pot. 1966. *Time.* Jul 1, 1966. http://www.time.com/time/magazine/article/0,9171,835889-2,00.html (accessed 6/9/2009).

Haviland, John B. 1979. How to Talk to Your Brother-in-Law in Guugu Yimidhirr. In *Languages and their Speakers,* (ed.) Timothy Shopen, 160–239. Cambridge, MA: Winthrop Publishers.

Hongxu, Huang, and Tian Guisen. 1990. A Sociolinguistic View of Linguistic Taboo in Chinese. *International Journal of the Sociology of Language* 81: 63–85.

Hutson, Matthew. 2008. Election Superstitions. *Psychology Today.* http://blogs.psychologyto-day.com/blog/brainstorm/200810/election-superstitions (accessed 6/1/09).

Malik, Adnan. 2003. Insults fly during Islamic summit. *Oakland Tribune.* March 6, 2003.

Murdoch, Jason. 2005. Superstitious Athletes. *CBS Sports.* http://www.cbc.ca/sports/columns/top10/superstition.html (accessed 6/1/09).

Mydans, Seth, and Mark McDonald. 2009. Novelist Given Three Years for Insulting Thai King. *New York Times.* Jan. 20, 2009. p. A8.

Smal-Stocki, Roman. 1950. Taboos on Animal Names in Ukranian. *Language* 26(4): 489–493.

Struck, Doug. 2006. In French-Speaking Canada, the Sacred is Also Profane. *Washington Post.* Dec. 5, 2008. http://washingtonpost.com/wp-dyn/content/article/2006/12/04/AR2006120401286.html (accessed 10/25/08).

Zappa, Frank, and Peter Occhiogrosso. 1990. *The Real Frank Zappa Book.* New York: Touchstone.

---

[10] In Hungarian, the word for 'wolf' is *farkás,* which is roughly 'the one with the tail'.

[11] Death is yet another taboo type, one we haven't covered in depth in this book. There is a range of ways this taboo can materialize in a language. One common way is for it to interact with names: for some period after a person's death, their name (and any related words) is taboo.

1. Find a willing student in one of your classes who comes from a different language background than you do and interview them on the taboos of their culture and language. In my experience, most international students are willing to talk about this topic, and some will be quick to give you plenty of examples. Others, however, may be reticent and may even deny that there are taboo words in their language. If you explain that you don't just mean the sorts of swearing that are common in America, mostly obscenity or scatology, they may be more likely to give good examples. You may even want to relate some of the examples discussed in this chapter. Doing anthropological linguistics involves not simply asking the right questions, but also getting your interviewees to think about the questions in the right way.

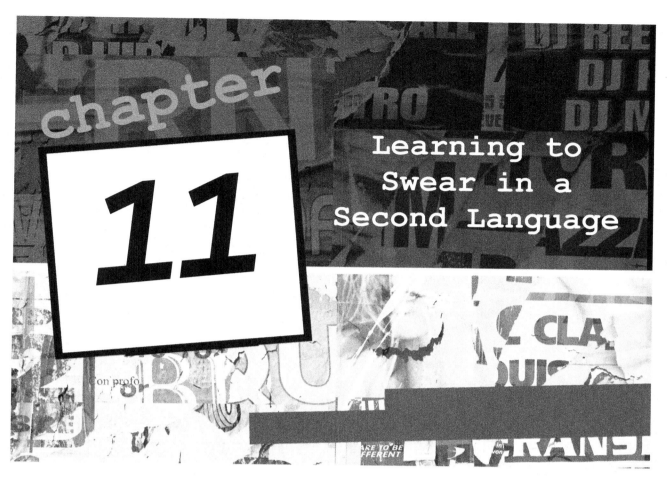

chapter

11

Learning to Swear in a Second Language

1. INTRODUCTION: L1 VS. L2 ACQUISITION

Unfortunately, there's little research about how children acquire taboo words as part of their **first language** (L1). What we do know: children begin using taboo words as soon as they hear taboo words used, often as early as one year old (Jay 2000, 82). As anybody who has been around infants knows, they express anger vocally—but not linguistically; they scream, cry, hit, bite, throw tantrums. But quickly after they begin speaking, toddlers learn to express their anger with words (Jay 2000, 97). Montagu (1967, 70), writing with 1960s masculine bravado, puts it like this: "When [a boy] grows to adolescence, crying and childish naughtiness are abandoned for the more manly forms of conduct; where one formerly wept, one now

Punch cartoon from April 2, 1913 (cited in Montagu 1967, 70):

Old Lady: Why are you crying little boy?
Little Boy: Because I bea'nt old enough to swear.

swears."[1] There's a pattern to how children swear as they grow up: toddlers and children understand that taboo words are used to express emotions of all types (anger, frustration, pain, joy, surprise, fear); toddlers prefer scatology over other types of taboo words; this continues into childhood, when they also begin using slurs as they recognize differences between people; teenagers begin swearing for social purposes as well as expressing emotions (Jay 2000, 82). In Chapter 1, we briefly discuss what types of swearing children acquire and how early. There's not a whole lot else we can say because, simply put, we just don't know much more.

For some reason, there's more research into how speakers acquire taboo words in their **second language** (L2). Maybe folks feel more comfortable studying swearing acquisition in the L2 because they get to look at

---

[1] Apparently, Montagu didn't see swearing as being "womanly." See Chapter 13 for more on perceptions of males' vs. females' swearing.

adults—even scholars are squeamish talking about children's swearing.[2] Nevertheless, the research about **bilinguals'** swearing does tell us something about how we acquire taboo words in our first language. Plus, the research results are pretty interesting.

In Section 2, I briefly memorialize one of my professors from grad school. In Section 3, we look at the differences between swearing in your first language and swearing in your second language. And in Section 4, we look at whether taboo words should be discussed in the second language classroom or not (hint: they should).

2. IN MEMORIUM: KOSTAS KAZAZIS (1934–2002)

The most multilingual person I've ever known was Kostas Kazazis, a linguistics professor at the University of Chicago. He was reputed to speak nearly every language of Europe. His native languages were Greek and French—more on that in a second—but on several occasions I witnessed him turning from person to person at a party and engaging each one in their native language, be it English, Spanish, Portuguese, Norwegian[3], Italian, German, Russian, French, etc. Every summer he would begin learning a new language (the summer before he died he was teaching himself Japanese). One other thing about Kostas: he had a foul mouth. One semester, a student complained he swore too much during lectures, so to placate her he implemented a "swear jar" in which he would drop a quarter every time a bad word slipped out during class—I understand he swore less than usual that semester, but the jar looked pretty full to me. A friend once quipped that as impressive as Kostas' language ability was, he wasn't sure Kostas could do more than swear in all those languages.

I don't know what drove Kostas to learn so many languages, and I certainly can't say how he could manage to do it. But the following story could shed some light on why he chose to swear in them. He grew up in Greece, so Greek was his L1; however, he had a French nanny, who was instructed to never speak to him in anything but French. In this way, French was just as much his native language as Greek. But he learned Greek in a more "normal" way, meaning he picked up a lot from friends and he learned slang and how to swear. His French came from a single adult.

He grew up and went to college in England, where he met a group of students from France. They went out to a bar one evening, and Kostas found that his new French friends laughed at everything he said. It wasn't so much what he said as how he said it. Kostas realized that his father, a rather severe man, had instructed the nanny

"[T]o know another's language and not his culture is a very good way to make a fluent fool of one's self" (Levine & Adelman, 1982, ix, quoted in Khuwaileh 2000, 281).

not just to speak French but to speak "proper" French, reprimanding her if she said anything colloquial. So Kostas, at eighteen years old, spoke fluent French that sounded straight out of a nineteenth century scholarly book.

It was during that evening with the French students that Kostas first realized there was more to speaking a language than just knowing words and how to put them together. You had to know how to speak "properly" and how not to. If he wanted to be a fluent speaker he would have to learn how to swear. So he did—in every language he could.

3. MONOPOLY MONEY: TABOO WORDS IN THE L2

Have you ever traveled to a foreign country? The first thing you do is withdraw some of the local currency. And then, if you're like me, you stare at the strange bills and coins, trying to make a connection to them, telling yourself that it's real money, that it's not Monopoly money. But it's hard to convince yourself, and for a while at least, you throw the money around, spending it more frivolously than you ever would dollars (or whatever your native currency).[4]

For some people, foreign swear words are like that; they throw them around like play money. Dewaele (2004a) found this phenomenon in several responses to a web questionnaire on multilingual swearing that he and Aneta Pavlenko conducted (L1, L2, L3, etc. indicate the order in which the languages were acquired). For exam-

---

[2] Timothy Jay is a notable exception.

[3] Technically it was Swedish he was speaking, but he could fake it well enough that the Norwegian woman understood him.

[4] Thanks go to Rachel Hayes-Harb (2010) for drawing this analogy.

ple, Maureen (English L1, Italian L2) reported that she cannot "hear the weight" of Italian swear words, so she inadvertently hurts people when she swears in that language; Melissa reported that she swears more easily in English (her L2) than in Greek (her L1), saying that she "can't really 'hear' or 'sense' how strong" the words are in English; and Kevin reported that he rarely swears in Finnish (his L1) but "oh shit" or "fuck" often come out "even in quite trivial occasions—they just don't feel that serious to my (or my hearers') ears" (Dewaele (2004a, 213–214). Like Kevin, others claimed to not swear in their L1 but to freely swear in their L2. For example, Maria reported that she cannot swear in Spanish (her L1) because the swear words "are too heavy and are truly taboo for me" (Dewaele 2004a, 214). Some choose to swear in a foreign language so that those around them won't understand and therefore won't be offended. For example, Anne reported that she swears in Russian when in the U.S., while she prefers to swear in English or German when in Russia.

Although swearing may be "easier" in a foreign language, most people prefer to swear in their L1. Dewaele (2004b) found that most participants swear more in their L1 than their L2, and, if they speak multiple languages, more in their L2 than L3, and more in their L3 than L4 or L5. Especially when a speaker is angry, they resort to their first language, where they have the emotional ties. For example, Sandra (German L1, Italian L2) reported, "If I am really angry only German words come into my mind if I use Italian instead I may not use the right measure" (Quoted in Dewaele 2004a, 214). Some participants observed that when they're angry at their significant others, they resort to the L1, even when the partner doesn't understand the language. For example, Erica (Spanish L1, English L2) reported that since her husband doesn't speak Spanish, they always argue in English, but "many times I find myself swearing at him in Spanish" Quoted in Dewaele 2004a, 213). Similarly, Ellen (English L1, Catalan L2) reported that she only uses Catalan with her husband, even when they argue, "although I always use English swear words!" (quoted in Dewaele 2004a, 214).

Why do people swear more in their L1 than their L2? Because swearing carries risks. All of us have said the wrong word at the wrong time—perhaps you slipped and said, "Shit!" in front of your snooty aunt; for me it was jokingly telling a friend to "fuck off" during his wedding reception, in front of his new in-laws, who happened to be born-again Christians. If swearing is risky in your L1, it's even riskier in your L2.

Also, as Dewaele (2004b) discusses, while native speakers may be tolerant of your mispronunciations and grammar errors, they tend to be less tolerant when you swear inappropriately. In fact, native speakers tend to be intolerant of any swearing from a foreigner:

> I personally learned this lesson when using a taboo word in Spanish, my fourth language (L4), in a group discussion with fellow students, [native speakers] of Spanish, at two o'clock in the morning, after consumption of many *tapas* and red wine in one of Salamanca's bars. Although the exclamation *joder* ('fuck') had been uttered several times during the evening, my use of it was greeted by stunned silence. "It sounds funny in your mouth", a friend told me, "you shouldn't use it, it might offend people!" (Dewaele 2004b, 84)

There are at least two issues with regard to swearing in an L2: i) the swear words don't feel as strong; ii) you may unintentionally offend people. I've found there's another hazard: iii) when you are angry and want to be offensive, the locals may simply find your swearing humorous. I don't have more than anecdotal evidence for (ii) and (iii), but there's good empirical evidence for (i).

One thousand thirty-nine multilinguals participated in the online survey conducted by Pavlenko and Dewaele. Their results were clear: participants reported that they perceived the emotional strength of taboo words in their L2 as weaker than in their L1. Moreover, they perceived the strength of taboo words in their L3 as even weaker, and the L4 and L5 as weaker still. Figure 11.1 shows a graph of the mean scores.

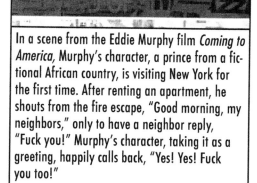

In a scene from the Eddie Murphy film *Coming to America*, Murphy's character, a prince from a fictional African country, is visiting New York for the first time. After renting an apartment, he shouts from the fire escape, "Good morning, my neighbors," only to have a neighbor reply, "Fuck you!" Murphy's character, taking it as a greeting, happily calls back, "Yes! Yes! Fuck you too!"

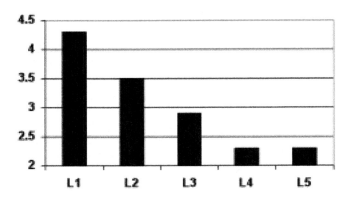

FIGURE 11.1   *Mean scores on perceived emotional force of taboo words in five languages (Dewaele 2004a, 213)*

The following participant's comment sums up speakers' perception that swear words are weaker in their L2:

> Roberto (German L1, English L2, French L3, Spanish L4): I'm pretty much aware of the force of swear words in English, and yet they seem less immediate than swear words in German. (Quoted in Dewaele 2004a, 213)

In other words, consciously speakers may know how strong the emotional meanings of taboo words are in their L2, but they don't feel it at the deep unconscious level that they would in their L1.

Although Dewaele's research is impressive and his results are substantial, it relies on self-report data, and self-report data in linguistics aren't always reliable (see Chapter 13). Fortunately, his research is confirmed by a laboratory study done by Harris, Ayçiçeği, and Gleason (2003). They demonstrated that when people read or hear swear words in their L1, they sweat more than when they read or hear swear words in their L2.

Why look at sweating? It turns out you perspire more when you're agitated, when you're emotionally stimulated—this is called an **autonomic response** (see Chapter 12 for more on what swearing does to our bodies and brains). So researchers hook electrodes up to people's fingertips and run a small current through to see how conductive the fingers are: the more emotion, the more conductive because emotions cause moisture via sweat glands and moisture conducts electricity. When a person hears a swear word like *motherfucker* in their first language, they have an emotional (autonomic) response, which can be measured using the electrodes. The stronger the taboo on the word, the stronger the response, the stronger the current.

The same thing holds for your L2; you are likely to have an autonomic response to swear words in any language you're fluent in. But what Harris et al (2003) showed is that the response is significantly weaker in the L2. They recruited thirty-two native Turkish speakers who were living in Boston to participate in their study (fifteen males, seventeen females). The participants ranged in age from their twenties to their forties; all of them learned English after the age of twelve and had lived in the United States from one to fifteen years. For the study, the participants read words on a computer screen while hooked up to electrodes, as discussed. The list included neutral words (*door*), positive words (*bride, joy*), negative words (*disease, kill*), reprimands (*don't do that, go to your room*), and taboo words (*asshole, breast*) in both English and Turkish. For the taboo words, they consulted with native speakers of each language to ensure that the tabooness strength matched between the two languages.

Like with Dewaele's research, the results are clear: the taboo words in the participants' L1 (Turkish) caused a stronger response than those from their L2 (English). There was a slight difference between the two languages for the positive and negative words and a much larger difference for the taboo words. The most significant difference was for reprimands—but that's not so surprising, since the reprimands are mostly used with children (by parents or teachers), and these speakers all learned English after the age of twelve. Figure 11.2 graphs the results.

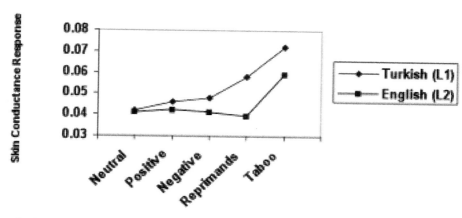

FIGURE 11.2   *The skin conductance response for Turkish (L1) vs. English (L2) words (adapted from Harris et al 2003, 570)*

Notice that in both languages the taboo words cause the greatest autonomic response from the participants. This shows that even in our L2 our bodies respond to the emotional charge of taboo words. As Harris et al (2003, 572) point out, even those participants who claimed to "feel nothing" when hearing or saying a taboo word in English responded more strongly to taboo words than other words. That said, the degree to which speakers respond is significantly lower for their L2 than their L1.

So now let's think about why we don't sense the weight of taboo words in our L2 as much as in our L1. Pavlenko (2008, 156) argues that we have stronger emotional attachments to the language(s) we learn in childhood. For example, some bilinguals choose to use their L2 in psychoanalytic therapy, even when the therapist speaks their first language because the L2 provides a buffer from strong emotions, but documented cases show that a switch to the L1 can trigger a breakthrough in the therapy (Pavlenko 2008, 156). As we acquire a language, we often acquire concepts and words for those concepts simultaneously—this includes words for emotions; moreover, we develop the ability to deal with our emotions at the same time that we learn the words for them.

Our native language vocabulary is emotionally loaded because we acquire the words in social situations that are emotionally loaded. This is especially true for taboo words.

> How is this sense of taboo implanted? Obviously enough, it is the result of training in early childhood, of experiences during the impressionable age, springing from the hushed awe that surrounds these words, the refusal of information concerning them, or the punishment meted out for an inadvertent use of them. There develops a neurosis so ingrained that the will is well-nigh powerless against it. Even when we come to know that there is not a proper basis for the feeling, we are prompted by motivations so deeply planted that we have the reactions in spite of our intellect.   (Read 1977, 10–11)

This is seldom the case for languages learned later in life, which are typically learned in the classroom and from textbooks.

Research shows that this emotional loading in our L1 "infects" related words, so, for example, our early repugnance to the word *poo* can spread to *shit*. Even unrelated words can get infected just by their sound-similarity (see our discussion of *nigger* and *niggardly* in Chapter 7). However, this process does not translate to our L2:

> [L]inguistic conditioning spreads to phonologically and semantically related words of the same language, but not to translation equivalents of another language. Rather one needs to develop such responses anew in the new language. Yet the process of L2 learning in teenage years or in adulthood does not necessarily offer the same opportunities for affective linguistic conditioning as L1 learning in childhood. (Pavlenko 2008, 156–157)

It's not hard to see why we fail to build emotional connections to words when studying a foreign language. Think about the environment we typically learn a foreign language in: a sterile classroom with a teacher lecturing and giving us lists of words to memorize. As Pavlenko (2008, 157) puts it: "Foreign language (FL) classrooms . . . do not offer many opportunities for affective socialization. Rather, lexical development in FL classrooms takes place through the processes of definition, translation and memorization, subserved by declarative or explicit memory." She certainly makes it sound dull and unemotional, doesn't she? Here's a telling response from Pavlenko and Dewaele's survey:

> Pierre (L1 French, L2 Dutch, L3 English, L4 German): I do not feel the emotional load of words in foreign languages. I've only learned them in an "instructed" environment. (Quoted in Pavlenko 2008, 157)

The more that language learners acquire an L2 naturally—that is, immersed in a social situation where the L2 is normally spoken—the more likely they are to create emotional connections to the words of the language, especially the taboo words. Speakers who learn an L2 in a classroom have the least emotional connection to the words of the language, while speakers who learn an L2 through immersion have the most. Speakers who do a combination of the two? They're somewhere in the middle. That's what Dewaele's (2004a) research demonstrates especially with regard to taboo words. The results are shown in Figure 11.3.

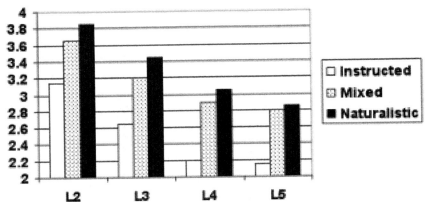

FIGURE 11.3 *Effect of instruction type on perceived emotional force of swear words in five languages (Dewaele 2004a, 217)*

We see a clear pattern in Figure 11.3: for each language learned after the native language, the amount of perceived emotional force of taboo words depends greatly on how the language was acquired.

So what are we supposed to do? Most of us don't have the luxury of simply packing up and moving to a foreign country just so we can immerse ourselves in the language for an extended time. In the next section, we'll discuss what can and should be done in the classroom with regard to L2 taboo expressions.

4. LEARNING A SECOND (OR THIRD, FOURTH, OR FIFTH) LANGUAGE

Hayes-Harb (2010) points out how "tricky" swearing is for native speakers: you have to know when you can swear, who you can swear with, what swearing says about you, what makes swearing appropriate or inappropriate, what taboo words are appropriate or inappropriate to the situation, etc. We all make mistakes and swear inappropriately; maybe you slipped and said "son of a bitch" in front of a friend's young child, or maybe you expressed yourself too vehemently (e.g., said "This is fucked up.") in front of your boss or professor, or maybe you simply used profanity (e.g., "Jesus Christ") that seemed inoffensive to you but offended your addressee. Now, imagine trying to navigate this tricky maze that is "appropriate" swearing in a foreign language.

Not only do the non-native speakers have to navigate the same maze that native speakers do, they have to do so with an incomplete map. As we've seen, they lack some of the native speaker's robust intuitions about the grammar of the language (see Chapter 2), especially when it comes to the tabooness and emotional strength of taboo expressions. They also aren't generally taught about swearing in the classroom—which is where they're used to learning about the L2. On top of that, as we've seen, native speakers may not accept their swearing, even if they do it successfully—many native speakers don't tolerate or don't take seriously foreigners' swearing (Hayes-Harb 2010).

Most of the research done on teaching L2 swearing has focused on learners of English as a Second Language (ESL). Chances are you, yourself, have experience studying a second language, so as you read this you can apply the research from ESL classrooms to whatever language you've studied.

Holster (2005) administered questionnaires to eighty ESL teachers in Auckland, New Zealand. All eighty participants spoke English as their native language, and the questionnaire asked about their teaching practices with regard to swearing and taboo words. Holster found that over two-thirds of her participants do not teach about taboo words in their classrooms.

Several ESL instructors in Holster's survey said they would not discuss taboo words in the classroom because they didn't want to offend their students. This is a real concern; we have to recognize that students may be uncomfortable learning about taboo words. Khuwaileh (2000) interviewed twenty female and twenty male Jordanian students who were studying English. He found that discussing taboo topics and taboo words in the classroom could make it more difficult for the students to learn. For example, when teachers asked the students to write on current issues, including sex-related issues, such as AIDS and contraception, twenty-eight of the forty students would avoid such topics that would "put themselves in a critical position by using impolite words" (quoted in Khuwaile 2000, 286). One female student told him she would never use the words *condom, kissing, homosexual, heterosexual,* etc. Another said: "I even can't look at my teacher's face if he reads words like these written by myself . . ." (quoted in Khuwaile 2000, 287). Another woman said that her "personality, religion, honour and polite [politeness] are more important than the certificate [degree] I work to get. . . ."

On the other hand, instructors may have false preconceptions about their students. For example, one instructor in Holster's study assumed ESL students don't swear in their native language, stating "I'm sure the majority would be uncomfortable being exposed to taboo words" (quoted in Holster 2005, 145). I suppose it's possible this instructor is right . . . but . . . hmm . . . as we've seen elsewhere in this book every culture has some swearing, and most speakers indulge in swearing now and again. Furthermore, as we've seen in Section 3, taboo words in a second language are not as offensive as they are in the native language, so the risk of offense may be overstated. Also, note that the sorts of words that Khuwaile's participants objected to are not generally considered taboo words by native English speakers, again suggesting that teachers shouldn't assume they know what will be offensive to their students.

In fact, instructors may be more concerned about their own sensitivities than their students. For example, one instructor from Holster's (2005) study said that teaching the literal meanings of some taboo words would be uncomfortable, and another said he/she "would feel very uncomfortable" teaching the taboo words because he/she doesn't swear him/herself (Holster 2005, 132–133). In her work with students in a teaching English as a second language program, Hayes-Harb has come across similar statements from student teachers; for example, one of her students told her, "I would never teach my students to use bad language," and another said, "I'm too embarrassed to say those words in front of my students" (quoted in Hayes-Harb 2010).

If the only reason a language teacher avoids the issue of taboo words in class is because they're uncomfortable with the words—well, that's not a good enough reason. Hayes-Harb poses this rhetorical question to her students: Are you teaching your students English or ethics? A clear answer of "ethics" can be found in Holster's survey: "As a Christian . . . , I make it clear to students that using 'God' is an offence to both me personally and to God Himself" (quoted in Holster 2005, 143).

Let's return to the legitimate concern of the students' learning being hampered if the teacher addresses taboo words. One approach that instructors take is to let the students bring up the issue. More than two-thirds of Holster's participants indicated that they would not bring up the topic of taboo words themselves but would be willing to answer any questions their students brought up. One instructor said that he/she does not introduce the topic because students might take offence and does not "model any swear words" for students, but he/she is open to students including taboo words in their answers for how to express things when speaking informally (Holster

2005, 138). Another said that he/she waits for students to bring up the subject of taboo words, and then, depending on how interested other students are, he/she would discuss their meaning. An approach that Hayes-Harb (2010) advocates is setting aside class time in advance to talk about taboo words; this way the instructor can inform students that they will be talking about swearing on such and such a day and allow any students to opt out if they want to.

However, some instructors question why they should devote time to swearing. Some argue that such knowledge isn't necessary to ESL students. One teacher in Holster's study said that teaching taboo words "has no place in the classroom environment" and that learning "decent language" in a foreign language is already difficult, so why "clutter" it with bad words (Holster 2005, 132)? Several others in Holster's study argue that ESL students who want to learn to swear can learn it on the streets. These instructors pointed out that native speakers acquire taboo words without being taught, so ESL learners can too (Holster 2005, 133). There's some truth to what they're saying. As we saw in Section 3, those people who learned their second language in a natural or mixed environment had a better feel for the emotions behind swear words than those who learned it solely in the classroom. That said, I think these instructors are missing the point; teachers may be doing their students a disservice by not teaching about swearing.

We need to make an important distinction: **teaching how** and **teaching about.** Hayes-Harb, for example, does not advocate teaching students how to swear, but she believes ESL teachers should teach students about swearing. Perhaps one of the clearest examples of this distinction comes not from an ESL course, but from a Catholic school in Grosse Pointe Park, Michigan, where the principal, Sister Kathy Avery, required her fifth through eighth grade students to stay after mass so she could instruct them on her "zero-tolerance" policy on swearing; she then read a list of those words that she would not tolerate (AP 2007).[5] Obviously, Sister Kathy Avery did not teach her students to swear—just the opposite—but she did teach them about swearing. Now, I'm not necessarily advocating this nun's proscriptive approach be used in an ESL classroom, but it is a vivid illustration of the difference between teaching how to swear and teaching about swearing.

As we see throughout this book, taboo words and swearing can tell us a lot about a culture. As Mercury (1995, 28) puts it: "I do not mean ESL learners should learn how to swear; rather, learners need to understand what constitutes obscene language in North American contexts, why native speakers choose to use it, and what it signifies sociolinguistically." ESL students could profit from learning about swearing, especially about the social aspects of swearing: when it is appropriate, when it isn't, who it's appropriate with, who it isn't, where it's appropriate, where it isn't, etc. "Obscene expressions can be a veritable gold mine for students of language in their efforts to study the important nonlinguistic variables that largely figure into people's speech behavior" (Mercury 1995, 32). Some of the nonlinguistic variables Mercury has in mind are discretion, setting, and gender. In my experience, ESL learners are fascinated and perplexed by English swearing; quite a few foreign students take my Bad Words and Taboo Terms class and say that it has helped them to better understand Americans.

ESL students will undoubtedly hear taboo words in English, but, as we saw in Section 3, they won't be able to gauge the emotions and the tabooness behind the words for themselves. Dewaele (2008, 173) argues that it is just as important for a student to know a word's emotional charge as it is to know the part of speech. He goes on to argue that misjudging the emotional strength of a word is likely to

> Rachel Hayes-Harb (pers. comm.) related the following incident to my Bad Words and Taboo Terms class. She once announced to a class that there would be a quiz later in the week. That afternoon, she received an e-mail from one of her students who was not a native speaker of English; he wrote, "What the hell is the quiz we have to take?" Her first reaction was anger; fortunately, her linguistic background allowed her to see the student had simply misjudged the social meaning of the *what the hell* construction. She replied to the student, first answering the informative part of his question (she explained what would be on the quiz) and then addressing the social part of his question. First, she complimented him on having acquired a rather complex and difficult grammatical structure and then briefly explained that the construction was OK to use with friends, but not with professors.

be more embarrassing for an L2 speaker than would be grammatical mistakes, like mispronouncing a word or conjugating it wrong. "Nonnative speakers have to recognize insulting speech directed toward them, as well as know what words *not to say* in polite situations" (Jay 2000, 154).

---

[5] She's been labeled a "swearing nun," but that is hardly apt. What she did was not swearing, since, as we discuss in Chapter 1, swearing requires the use of a taboo word, and she merely mentioned the words (see Chapter 3).

Furthermore, the speech that students are exposed to outside the classroom may only be representative of certain contexts. If they generalize too much, they may use taboo words in the wrong situation.

Second language speakers may get a distorted idea of obscene language use due to the influence of movies, hit songs, and popular books where obscene language seems to flow unchecked. Nonetheless, students who are learning conversational English also need to learn what is acceptable or unacceptable in taboo language behavior. Having the opportunity to discuss it affords the learners the chance to understand the importance of the nonlinguistic practices that largely determine its use. (Mercury 1995, 35)

Mercury believes that many ESL speakers misunderstand and misuse taboo words "simply because they are left on their own to learn about [their] use" (Mercury 1995, 31).

As we see in Chapter 12, swearing often acts as an early warning system; when we hear somebody swearing, our bodies automatically prepare for fight or flight. Thus, it's beneficial for an L2 learner to recognize when strong swear words are being used in their presence—or even more importantly, when strong swear words are addressed to them. On the other hand, learners need to know what words may trigger a violent response from others. As we discuss throughout this book, some words are more taboo than others, and how a word is used in a particular context determines how offensive it is. As Holster (2005, 133) writes, "It can be difficult for a L2 learner to gauge the strength of taboo words. For example saying, 'Oh Fuck!' as an expression of frustration is perhaps not as offensive as using the phrase 'You stupid fucking bastard!' as a serious insult."

> When my brother and I were traveling in Romania and learned we were standing in the wrong line for train tickets, my brother exclaimed, "Fuck!" A Romanian in the line, jumping to the ticket agent's defense, shouted, "Fuck you!" He had apparently thought my brother's use of *fuck* was directed at the agent, not at the situation. My brother, acting on reflex, returned the man's invective, and said, "Fuck you!" For a moment, I thought there was going to be a fight—fortunately, we had to sprint across the train station to get in the right line.

Gauging the strength of emotions and what emotions are being expressed is an important part of speaking a language.

In fact, language learners find that sometimes they're put in a situation when they want or even need to know how to swear. Consider the following example from Dewaele and Pavelenko's survey:

Bart (Dutch L1, French L2, English L3): in school we learn how to use French in a polite and friendly way but when I am calling Customer Service of a French company to complain about something and want to sound a bit more severe irritated angry . . . then it is difficult to find that severe irritated angry tone because you are concentrating on French grammar and vocabulary . . . I wouldn't have to do that in Dutch. (Quoted in Dewaele 2004a, 217)

Finally, we can simply take the approach I take in this book: taboo words and swearing are a part of language. If a language teacher is going to teach a language, they ought to teach the whole darned thing. As one instructor in Holster's study put it: Swearing is "a reality of day-to-day life in New Zealand and many other English-speaking countries. It cannot be completely ignored" (quoted in Holster 2005, 131). Another instructor said that an English as a second language teacher's job is "to teach all facets of the English language" (quoted in Holster 2005, 132). And another feared that if students were to learn the words on the street "and to incorporate them into the speech without knowing the proper uses, function, meaning or severity, they could get into trouble" (quoted in Holster 2005, 136).

Some teachers in Holster's study stated yet another reason for not teaching about taboo words and swearing: It's too hard. One instructor admitted not knowing "where to start if I did want to teach about them!" (quoted in Holster 2005, 145). Another thought the traditional approaches to language teaching don't lend themselves to teaching about swearing. Another was quite blunt about his/her reasons for not teaching about taboo words: "It's extremely difficult to teach about taboo words. The appropriate and inappropriate and different contexts of use for swear words are difficult to define. For this reason, I don't teach them in a classroom situation" (quoted in Holster 2005, 137).

What do you think of these excuses? My reaction: Suck it up! Would you accept a similar excuse from a physics teacher (e.g., "It's extremely difficult to teach the Theory of Relativity. For this reason I don't teach it in a classroom situation."). That said, applied linguists need to do further research to come up with best practices for teaching about taboo words and swearing in the L2 classroom. Many linguists have issued a call for such research, including Dewaele, Hayes-Harb, Holster, Jay, and Pavlenko. The field is still in its naissance, but let's hope we'll see more work on it in the coming decades.

5. CONCLUSION

At this point, scholars don't know all that much about how children learn to swear in their L1—all we know is that they do. They swear from early on, practically from when they start speaking. We know a bit more about how folks learn to swear in their L2. Mostly because teachers are too squeamish to talk about swearing in the classroom, learners have to get this knowledge on the streets. In some ways, this naturalistic way of learning about swearing is good insofar as the learners get a better sense of the strength of the words that way. Nevertheless, they will probably never feel the strength of the taboo words like a native speaker does. Furthermore, it's not necessarily practical or advisable for students to learn about swearing entirely from the streets. The chances are that they'll make mistakes, mistakes that could be embarrassing or worse; they may misjudge how angry somebody else is when directing taboo words towards them or they may misuse taboo words and make others think they are angrier than they are. Finally, learning about taboo words and swearing in the classroom may help learners to better understand the culture of the language they're studying; this is probably part of why so many students want to know the swear words first when they beginning studying a new language.

REFERENCES

AP. 2007. Nun Reels off List of Banned Curse Words. *MSNBC.Com.* December 10, 2007. http://www.msnbc.msn.com/id/22179259/ (accessed 10/1/2010).

Dewaele, Jean-Marc. 2004a. The Emotional Force of Swearwords and Taboo Words in the Speech of Multilinguals. *Journal of Multilingual and Multicultural Development* 25(2–3): 204–222.

Dewaele, Jean-Marc. 2004b. Blistering Barnacles! What Language do Multilinguals Swear in?! *Estudios de Sociolinguistica* 5(1): 83–105.

Dewaele, Jean-Marc. 2008. Dynamic Emotion Concepts of L2 Learners and L2 Users: A Second Language Acquisition Perspective. *Bilingualism: Language and Cognition* 11(2): 173–175.

Hayes-Harb, Rachel. 2010. Swearing in a Second Language. Lecture notes.

Harris, Cathrine L., Ayşe Ayçiçeği, and Jean Berko Gleason. 2003. Taboo Words and Reprimands elicit greater autonomic reactivity in a first language than in a second language. *Applied Psycholinguistics* 24: 561–579.

Holster, Dianna. 2005. An Investigation of ESOL Teachers' Attitudes Towards Teaching about Taboo English in the Second Language Classroom. MA Thesis, Auckland University of Technology, Auckland, New Zealand.

Jay, Timothy. 2000. *Why We Curse: A Neuro-Psycho-Social Theory of Speech.* Philadelphia: John Benjamins.

Khuwaileh, Abudullah A. 2000. Cultural Barriers of Language Teaching: A Case Study of Classroom Cultural Obstacles. *Computer Assisted Language Learning* 13(3): 281–290.

Levine, D.R., and M.B. Adelman. 1982. *Beyond Language: Intercultural Communication for English as a Second Language.* New Jersey: Prentice-Hall.

Mercury, Robin-Eliece. 1995 Swearing: A "Bad" Part of Language; A Good Part of Language Learning. *TESL Canada Journal* 13(1): 28–36.

Montagu, Ashley. 1967. *The Anatomy of Swearing.* New York: The Macmillan Company.

Pavlenko, Aneta. 2008. Emotion and Emotion-Laden Words in the Bilingual Lexicon. *Bilingualism: Language and Cognition* 11(2): 147–164.

Read, Allen. 1977. *Classic American Graffiti: Lexical Evidence from Folk Epigraphy in Western North America.* Waukesha, WI: Maledicta Press.

1. Interview two or three foreign students from your college about their experiences with swearing in English. Do they swear in English? If so, how do native speakers react? Have they ever been embarrassed either because they misunderstood when somebody else was swearing or because they misused a swear word?

2. Assuming that language teachers should teach about taboo words and swearing in the classroom, how should they do it? What would you find useful when studying taboo words in a foreign language? How should teachers ensure that students won't be embarrassed or offended by such lessons?

3. If you have any bilingual friends, ask them about their swearing habits. What language do they swear in? Why? Do they feel that taboo words are more emotional in one language than the other?

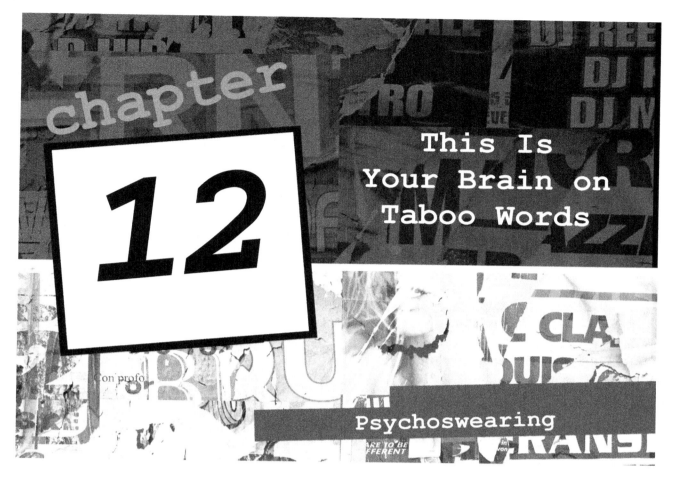

chapter

12

This Is Your Brain on Taboo Words

Psychoswearing

1.   INTRODUCTION: LEFT BRAIN, RIGHT BRAIN

Let's start with a quick personality quiz:

- Are you right- or left-brained?
    a.   Right-brained
    b.   Left-brained
    c.   Who cares?

If you answered (a) then you are random, visual, impulsive, and non-punctual; you gesticulate when you talk, respond to the tone of a person's voice more than their words, recall people's faces better than their names, like background music, and can't sit still while studying. If you answered (b), you are linear, verbal, premeditative, and punctual; you respond to people's words more than their tone of voice, you recall people's names better than their faces, and you like to study with bright lights on. At least so say an array of personality quizzes on the Internet.[1] If you answered (c), well . . . good question.

   Certainly, there is some truth to the idea that the two hemispheres specialize: the left hemisphere analyzes, the right hemisphere recognizes patterns and processes emotions. However, the idea of right-brained and left-brained individuals is probably a nice metaphor and nothing more; I'm no expert on this, but I couldn't find any research showing that artists use the right side of their brain preferentially to the left, nor that logicians use the left preferentially to the right. I think it's safe to say that all normal people use both sides of their brains. That said, linguists have a special attachment to the left hemisphere. Not because linguists fit the stereotype for left-brained people—some linguists do, some don't—but because that's where language is. Sort of.

---

[1] Of course, most of what's on the Internet should be taken with a grain of salt.

2. APHASIA

There are two main areas in the left hemisphere where language is processed: **Broca's area** and **Wernicke's area**. These areas are in the cerebral cortex, our so-called gray-matter, where higher reasoning is done. We humans have a bigger cerebral cortex than other animals, making us smarter. Also we can talk. Broca's and Wernicke's areas are how come we can.

Broca's area handles formal grammatical patterns (syntax, phonology, morphology) and articulation (phonetics). It sends the motor cortex the commands for what our muscles are supposed to do to produce speech, like telling the lungs to release air, the larynx whether or not to spread the vocal folds apart and how much, the tongue where to go, and the lips and velum what to do.

Wernicke's area processes meaning (semantics). It's responsible for choosing words, interpreting them, and deciding what the message is supposed to be.

We've known about these parts of the brain for a long time because doctors noticed that people can lose the ability to speak. One day you might be speaking normally and the next day you can't speak at all, or maybe you can speak but it comes out gibberish, or maybe you can get your words out (usually with difficulty) and communicate but your sentences are ungrammatical, almost like baby talk. This loss of speech is called **aphasia,** and pretty quickly doctors figured out aphasia comes from brain damage, usually from a blow to the head or a stroke. Most people who suffer from aphasia remain intelligent—they just can't speak normally (though, sadly, many people talk to them as though they were children).

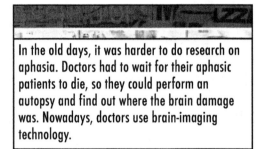

In the old days, it was harder to do research on aphasia. Doctors had to wait for their aphasic patients to die, so they could perform an autopsy and find out where the brain damage was. Nowadays, doctors use brain-imaging technology.

With Wernicke's aphasia (where Wernicke's area is damaged), the person can talk fluently, but nonsensically—because Broca's area is still intact, it can still form sentences and tell the motor cortex to produce them, but the speaker doesn't have control over the meaning because that was the role of Wernicke's area. Ethel Lee Miller (Brain on Strike) relates what it was like visiting her brother-in-law in the hospital right after he suffered a series of strokes:

> Paul's eyes followed my twin sister as she rushed to the side of the bed.
>
> "Paul! Paul, are you all right?"
>
> "Yes, thanks," came his strangely flat reply.
>
> *Whew!* Eileen and I looked at each other. *He's here. He's alive!* Relief. But his right arm didn't move. He couldn't wiggle his toes.
>
> And when we spoke . . .
>
> "Paul, what did the doctor tell you?"
>
> "Yes, thanks."
>
> "Paul, Where is the doctor?"
>
> "Yes, thanks."

Susan Riddle (Breakthrough) describes what it's like to talk to her mother, who has Wernicke's aphasia:

> I would estimate that 95% of what she says is jargon. I try to laugh with her and tell her she is speaking Martian. She can say some of what I call "reflex" phrases, such as: "Hi, how are you?" "Come on in." "I don't want any." "I can't." There are many phrases like this that just come out automatically. However if you ask her a question she cannot respond with an answer. If you ask her to say her name she gets a blank stare. She can play black jack and poker perfectly, but if you ask her to show you a king or a nine, she cannot do it.

Wernicke's aphasia is described as a receptive disorder, where the speaker cannot understand speech, though they can produce (incoherent) speech.

On the other hand, if Broca's area is damaged, the speaker may know exactly what they want to say, but not be able to get it out. Sandi Deranek (Trapped) describes her mother's aphasia like this: "Her mind was playing all the appropriate words and sentences but she could only say three or four words." In many cases of Broca's aphasia, the speech is dysfluent (the speaker seemingly has to force the words out), consists of only content words (i.e., words like nouns, verbs, and adjectives that convey meaning, not function words like prepositions, auxiliary verbs, and articles that show the relation between parts of a sentence), lacks suffixes, and has very simple syntax (e.g., "book good" would mean 'the book is good'). Wheeler E. Hubbard (My Story) describes what it's like to have Broca's aphasia:

> Let me try to explain Aphasia to you. Imagine that you are playing bingo. My brain is like the drum that they turn to pick a number. I have about 2,000 words in my brain. To speak, I have got to go in to the "drum" and find the word that I want, concentrate on it, bring it to my mouth and figure out how to say it, what tense to make it, then get it in the right order in the sentence. Something you take for granted takes all my effort, energy, and concentration to do.

Melba Ashburn (Feelings) describes her speech therapy after a stroke: "During my exercise class I had everyone's attention and I wanted to say 'I will demonstrate.' They waited, but I couldn't say 'demonstrate.'" Broca's aphasia is described as an articulatory disorder, where the speaker can't produce speech but can understand it (although sentences with complex grammar may be difficult to understand).

By definition, aphasics can't speak normally, yet many aphasics can swear fluently: 57% of Wernicke's aphasics and 47% of Broca's aphasics swear (Jay 2000, 38). In fact, some patients with global aphasia, where both Broca's and Wernicke's areas are destroyed—patients who literally can't speak—can swear fluently. Indeed, even individuals with left hemispherectomies (i.e., their whole left hemisphere has been removed) have retained the ability to swear (Landis 2006). So what gives?

Basically, all this talk about where language is processed neglects the distinction we make in Chapter 4 about the three aspects of linguistic meaning: the informative aspect, the effective (social) aspect, and the affective (emotional) aspect. Since linguists have traditionally focused on the informative aspect, they talk about how language is in the left hemisphere.

In a case report, Smith (1966) describes a forty-eight-year-old man, E.C., who was treated for a brain tumor by having his entire left hemisphere removed. Smith describes E.C.'s initial attempts to speak following the surgery: "He would open his mouth and utter isolated words, and after apparently struggling to organize words for meaningful speech, recognized his inability and would utter expletives of short emotional phrases (e.g., 'Goddamit!'). Expletives and curses were well articulated and clearly understandable. However, he could not repeat single words on command or communicate in 'propositional' speech . . ." (468). Smith goes on to explain that E.C. did recover some of his speech abilities over the subsequent seven months. Although E.C. is an isolated case, his ability to speak at all suggests the right hemisphere must play a role in language production. Most strikingly, his ability to swear remained virtually untouched (except he couldn't repeat words on command).

3. LANGUAGE PROCESSING AND THE EMOTIONAL BRAIN

The left hemisphere is better with analysis; the right hemisphere is better with patterns (Van Lancker & Cummings 1999, 96). Plus, the right hemisphere is associated with emotions. It shouldn't be surprising, then, that the informative aspects of speech would be processed predominantly on the left and the emotional and social on the right. After all, the informative aspect requires the brain to analyze the sequence of words (phonologically, morphologically, syntactically), arrive at the information encoded, and evaluate whether the information is true. On the other hand, the social aspect tends to come in preconfigured "constructions"; for example, as we discuss in Chapter 4, the expression *Hi, how's it going?* is nothing more than a greeting with several preconfigured answers: *Fine, and you?; Not bad, how 'bout you?; Good, yourself?;* etc. Likewise, purely emotional expressions tend to be atomic, not parsed into smaller parts (cf. response cries discussed in Chapter 4). The social and emotional aspects, unlike the strictly informative aspect, aren't restricted to words, but are also conveyed by **prosody** (the tone of voice, where stress is put, where pitch rises, where pauses are, etc.). Prosody is processed largely in the right hemisphere (Van Lancker & Cummings 1999, 95).

Consider the simple everyday sentence, "I'm having lunch with my grandmother." This could be stated as a fact, as in (1), where the pitch rises on *grand-* and falls on *mother*. Or as a question, as in (2), where the pitch rises on *mother*. Or it could be a correction, as in (3) where *lunch* is emphasized (perhaps the hearer thought it was dinner). Also the sentence could be uttered with emotion (represented with an exclamation point in (4))—different words will be emphasized and the tone of voice will change depending on the nature of the emotion, excited, annoyed, bored, etc.

1. I'm having lunch with my grandmother.
2. I'm having lunch with my grandmother?
3. I'm having *lunch* with my grandmother.
4. I'm having lunch with my grandmother!

These social (statement vs. question vs. correction) and emotional differences are handled primarily by the right hemisphere, while the word choice, pronunciation, and syntax are primarily handled by the left hemisphere.

So what about taboo words? Where are they processed? Well, swearing is complicated (kind of a theme of this book, isn't it?). Most utterances simultaneously have social, emotional, and informative functions. So do most words. As I argue in Chapter 4, this is especially apparent with taboo words; for example, *pissing* in (5) clearly has an informative function different from *shitting* in (6), but also has an emotional function different from the emotional force of *peeing* in (7) and a social function making it appropriate in different circumstances from *urinating* in (8).

5. Gertrude is behind the bush pissing.
6. Gertrude is behind the bush shitting.
7. Gertrude is behind the bush peeing.
8. Gertrude is behind the bush urinating.

Jay (2000) calls the use of taboo words in the way seen in (5) and (6) **strategic cursing.** Swearing in the form of response cries or invectives (9–12) represent **automatic cursing.**

9. Damn!
10. Shit yeah!
11. Fuck you!
12. Cunt!

Presumably, strategic cursing is mostly processed in the left hemisphere with some interaction with the right hemisphere. Much in the same way we saw with "I'm having lunch with my grandmother," the left hemisphere is responsible for choosing, combining, and articulating the words, but the right hemisphere is responsible for the rhythm and melody of the utterance. The left hemisphere determines the informative meaning, the grammatical form, and how to pronounce the sounds, but the right hemisphere determines the social and emotional meanings. So in (5) and (6), the right brain selected the taboo words for their social and emotional force.

Because taboo words are more emotionally charged than other words—indeed, they are selected because of their emotional charge—the right brain is more active in their selection. So when they're used in response cries, where the informative function is absent, we might imagine that the left hemisphere is to some degree bypassed in their production. Evidence for this is found in people who've suffered damage to the right hemisphere; according to Jay (2000, 37), most people with right hemisphere brain damage do not swear.

Automatic cursing, as the name suggests, is sometimes thought of as involuntary. It's as though these words burst out of us when we're beset by strong emotions. Of course, we know that's not entirely true. Sure, when we're really angry or when we're in pain, people give us more leeway in what we say. When I was twelve, I banged my shin pretty hard and shouted, "Fuck!" Initially, I expected my mom to lay into me for using the word, but to my surprise she simply comforted me. Nevertheless, we all know these response cries are not entirely out of our control; as we grow older, we learn to moderate and even modify what comes out of our mouths, so today if I were to bang my shin, I could preempt the *fuck* from coming out of my mouth, clipping[2] it down to "Fuh" instead.

Like with automatic cursing, at least for some aphasics, the swear words that come out of their mouths are probably not entirely spontaneous and involuntary. They arise from strong emotions, and the aphasic intends them. However, because they don't have an intact speech center in the left hemisphere, they probably cannot transform the swear words. All they have left are these pre-configured forms, and that's all that can come out. Interestingly, we also find that aphasics may have non-taboo pre-configured forms that come out, especially expressions that have a social meaning but hardly any informative meaning, such as greetings and interjections (see Van Lancker & Cummings 1999).

In all of us, these exclamations said under strong emotions—usually negative ones, like fear, pain, or anger—are primal. Indeed, Van Lancker and Cummings (1999) suggest that emotional exclamations are similar to emotional grunts uttered by other primates. Apparently, merely uttering or hearing taboo words taps into our **limbic system,** an older part of our brain whose purpose is to process emotions, especially in situations that would trigger fight or flight.

One way of demonstrating this close connection between taboo words and the limbic system is to measure skin conductance. The idea is that we sweat more when we're emotionally stimulated, so if taboo words tap into our limbic system, then reading them should cause us to sweat, and we can measure this perspiration by testing the skin conductance on a subject's fingers (the more water, the more electricity can flow). LaBar and Phelps (1998) show that taboo words cause higher skin conductance than neutral words. (See Chapter 11 for more on skin conductance and taboo words.)

In particular, one part of the limbic system, the amygdala, has been implicated in taboo word processing. LaBar and Phelps (1998) had normal subjects and subjects with damaged amygdala read a list of neutral and taboo words and then tested their memory for the words. The normal subjects could recall the taboo words better than the neutral words; however, those subjects who had damaged amygdala could not remember the taboo words any better than the neutral words. LaBar and Phelps conclude that the taboo words must trigger an emotional response in the readers, causing the amygdala to enhance the memory for these words, just as the amygdala in animals enhances the memory of emotionally charged events[3]. Building on this idea MacKay et al (2004) hypothesized as follows: emotional events cause the amygdala to bind the event to memory, so the emotional resonance of a taboo word should cause the amygdala to bind the context to memory, making the response time slower for contextual elements, but making those contextual elements easier to remember.

To test their hypothesis, MacKay et al (2004) used the **Taboo Stroop Effect.** When subjects are shown neutral and taboo

If you have any doubts about the primal nature of swearing, track down a video of Michael Richards (the actor who played Kramer on *Seinfeld*) having a meltdown in the middle of a stand-up comedy routine—after being heckled, he repeatedly shrieks "He's a nigger," while pointing at the heckler. Or track down the audio of Mel Gibson's hyperventilating phone call to his ex-girlfriend, Oksana Grigorieva.

Following Pribram (1960), "the behavioral complex" controlled by the Limbic system has been referred to as the 4 Fs: "feeding, fleeing, fighting, and sex." Who says scientists don't have a sense of humor? (Well, okay, there are some humorless scholars who have recast Pribram's 4 Fs as "feeding, fleeing, fighting, and fornicating," but that final F doesn't fit the rhythm of the first three.)

The traditional Stroop Effect is shown using color words and non-color words. Subjects are shown words, one at a time, in different color fonts; they are instructed to call out the color of the font as soon as a new word is shown. Not surprisingly, if a color word, such as *red*, is shown with a non-matching font, such as blue, it takes longer for the subject to respond than if a non-color word, such as *dog*, is shown with a blue font. This demonstrates that, assuming you're literate, you can't help processing the meaning of a word, even when the task at hand doesn't call for it.

The Taboo Stroop Effect refers to a modified version of this experiment where taboo words are substituted for the color words. In this case, subjects take longer to respond with the color of taboo words (e.g., "blue" for *shit*) than they do with the color of neutral words (e.g., "red" for *book*). This demonstrates that extra brain processing is prompted when we read taboo words versus neutral words.

---

[2] See Chapter 6 for a discussion on clipping as a way of creating euphemisms.

[3] If you're a giraffe, it's useful to remember every detail of when you were attacked by a lion at the drinking hole.

words in different font colors, response time for color naming is longer for the taboo words.[4] Like LaBar and Phelps, MacKay et al found that recall was better for taboo words than neutral words, again showing the enhanced memory for emotionally charged words. Moreover, when color was kept consistent by word (e.g., *fuck* is always green, *bastard* is always purple, *sink* is always blue, and *shoe* is always red), memory for color-word matching was better for taboo words than neutral words. Thus, the memory enhancement extends beyond the words themselves to include contextual elements (namely, the color of the words). It follows, then, that the longer response time is caused by the memory processing, and MacKay et al found that response time decreased for taboo words, but not for neutral words, with repetition (i.e., as subjects cycled through the list of words and responded with the font color). In addition, memory for neutral words adjacent in the list to taboo words decreased; in particular, the effect was stronger for neutral words following a taboo word than for neutral words preceding a taboo word (e.g., if the list proceeds, ". . . plate, book, damn, rock . . .", *damn* would be remembered best, then *plate*, then *book*, and *rock* worst of all). Presumably this effect arises because the brain is still committing elements associated with the taboo word to memory, thus leaving fewer resources to the adjacent words. Interestingly, the Taboo Stroop Effect is restricted to contextual (i.e., non-linguistic) aspects of the words: the effect was not found in response times to a purely linguistic task, that of identifying whether they are reading a word or not (non-words, like *mang*, were included in the list for this test). All this supports MacKay et al's hypothesis: "word-specific emotional reactions to the meaning of a taboo word trigger the binding mechanisms that link the taboo word to contextual information" (MacKay et al 2004, 485).

4. TOURETTE SYNDROME

Here's a fun word to use the next time you're at a party: **coprolalia**. It literally means 'shitty chattering'. What it describes: uncontrollable or compulsive cussing. In 1885, Georges Gilles de la Tourette coined this term to describe a symptom of the Marquise de Dampiere. The Marquise was famous for her foul mouth and her uncontrollable swearing. Her favorite phrases: *merde* 'shit' and *foutu cochon* 'filthy pig' or 'fucking pig' (Brown & Kushner 2001, 558). Her condition was first described when she was twenty-six by the well-known French physician Jean Marc Gaspard Itard, who wrote of her:

> In the midst of a conversation that interests her extremely, all of a sudden, without being able to prevent it, she interrupts what she is saying or what she is listening to with bizarre shouts and with words that are even more extraordinary and which make a deplorable contrast with her intellect and her distinguished manners. These words are for the most part gross swear words and obscene epithets and, something that is no less embarrassing for her than for the listeners, an extremely crude expression of a judgment or of an unfavorable opinion of someone in the group. (Itard 1825, 405; cited in Brown & Kushner 2001, 540)

Although for lay-people coprolalia is the defining characteristic of **Tourette Syndrome** (TS), less than fifteen percent of Touretters suffer from coprolalia. TS "is defined by multiple motor and vocal tics lasting for more than one year" (TSA 2007). The tics may be simple or complex. For example, a simple motor tic could be a nose twitch, while a complex motor tic can be as complicated as spinning around and then sitting. Similarly, a simple vocal tic may be a grunt, while a complex vocal tic may involve the repetition of entire phrases. Many Touretters report having a "premonitory urge" before they have to perform a tic (TSA 2007). Other symptoms of TS include invasive, compulsive thoughts.

Although coprolalia is rare among Touretters, it is of particular interest to us given the bent of this book. Before we turn specifically to coprolalia, however, it is useful to consider the taboo nature of many of the tics associated with TS. In a telling moment in the BBC

In the documentary *Talking about Tourette Syndrome*, Dash describes some of the more self-destructive compulsions prompted by his Tourette Syndrome: touching the red-hot burner on a stove, riding a bicycle while looking backwards over his shoulder, running in front of moving cars, and watching movies out of the corner of his eyes (he reports that on one occasion he watched the entire movie this way, giving himself a headache and causing his vision to blur so that he couldn't see straight afterwards).

---

[4] Similarly, LaBar and Phelps (1998) found that subjects took longer to respond to words that they rated as "more arousing."

series *The Mind-Traveler*, Shane, a Touretter, touches the neurologist, Oliver Sacks' ear; when Sacks asks why he did it, Shane responds he did it because he's not supposed to—you're not supposed to touch other people. In the documentary *Talking about Tourette Syndrome*, Dash says that when taking a multiple choice exam, he has the urge to shout out the answer to a question: "A . . . A, A." A Touretter may have to utter his ex-girlfriend's name in front of his present girlfriend (Jay 2000, 66). Although coprolalia is especially rare among Japanese Touretters, Brown & Kushner (2001, 543–544) suggest that an altered tone and pitch may take its place because in Japanese culture speaking in this manner is as taboo as swearing is in other cultures. In addition to coprolalia, there is copropraxia, which involves taboo gestures (e.g., "flipping the bird") rather than taboo words.

We see, then, that coprolalia is simply one among many tics that require Touretters to perform taboo acts. Moreover, by looking at the nature of coprolalic tics, we can see the importance of tabooness. Allan and Burridge (2006, 248) cite two similar cases: in one case, a boy with TS would say "shit" around his parents until the parents stopped reacting with outrage, at which point the tic was replaced by a different one; in the other case, a nine-year-old boy with TS "lost his coprolalia entirely when he was told the words he was uttering were not obscene." Coprolalia, by definition, involves the utterance of taboo words and expressions.

TS is found around the world, and with it coprolalia. As we've seen (see especially Chapters 1, 10, and 13), tabooness is culturally determined, so unsurprisingly the types of words that erupt from coprolalics differ from language to language. We even find differences between American and British English. Singer (1997) culled through reports to find the top coprolalic words in six languages/cultures (see Table 12.1).

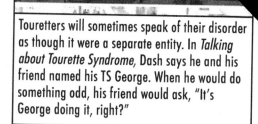

Touretters will sometimes speak of their disorder as though it were a separate entity. In *Talking about Tourette Syndrome*, Dash says he and his friend named his TS George. When he would do something odd, his friend would ask, "It's George doing it, right?"

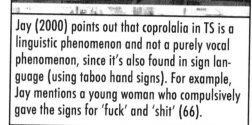

Jay (2000) points out that coprolalia in TS is a linguistic phenomenon and not a purely vocal phenomenon, since it's also found in sign language (using taboo hand signs). For example, Jay mentions a young woman who compulsively gave the signs for 'fuck' and 'shit' (66).

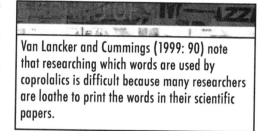

Van Lancker and Cummings (1999: 90) note that researching which words are used by coprolalics is difficult because many researchers are loathe to print the words in their scientific papers.

It might be tempting to associate coprolalic tics with automatic cursing. In both cases, swear words seem to erupt out of the person and the person has only partial control over what comes out. Also, Touretters report that they can transform the words that come out, just as most of us can transform *fuck* into *fudge* before it fully escapes our mouths. Dr. Palmer says that he used to have the tic of saying "fuck!", but he was able to replace it with "look!" (*Talking about Tourette Syndrome*). Still, just as for most people it's less satisfying to shout "fudge!" when angry, some

TABLE 12.1					
Common coprolalic utterances in six countries[5]					
USA	*UK*	*Denmark*	*Spain*	*Hong Kong*	*Japan*
fuck (-er, off)	*fuck*	*kaeft* 'shut up'	*puta* 'whore'	*Tiu* 'fuck'	*kusobaba* 'shit grandma'
shit	*cunt*	*svin* 'swine'	*mierda* 'feces'	*shui* 'worthless person'	*chikusho* 'son of a bitch'
bitch	*bastard*	*fisse* 'vulva'	*cono* 'vulva'	*tiu ma* 'mother fucker'	*omanka* 'female genitalia and breasts'
ass(hole)	*piss*	*kusse* 'vulva'	*joder* 'fornicate'	*tiu so* 'aunt fucker'	
bastard	*sod*	*pik* 'penis'	*maricon* 'homosexual'		
pussy	*cock*	*rov* 'ass'	*cojones* 'testicles'		
prick	*shit*	*pis* 'ass'	*hijo de puta* 'son of a whore'		
dick		*gylle* 'animal feces'	*hostia* 'holy bread'		
cock(sucker)		*sgu* 'by god'			
cunt		*lort* 'shit'			
fart					
nigger					

[5] Adapted from Singer's (1997) Table 1.

rt that a transformed version of their tic may not sat- ... ...ger (1997, 303) suggests that Touretters are often ...substituting another term for a coprolalic one.

...s, however, a big difference between coprolalic erup-...matic cursing: the latter is actual speech. Coprolalic ...ify as use. On the other hand they're not mention either (see Chapter 3). They are, in some ways, outside of language. For example, they aren't said like normal speech: "Although coprolalia entails the utterance of ordinary curse words, these utterances disrupt the patterns of normal speech . . . : the timbre of voice is entirely different from usual speaking tones, and the eruption occurs at grammatical pauses or interstices" (Brown & Kushner 2001, 538). Unlike automatic cursing, which is in response to an external trigger (e.g., something in the environment causes pain, fear, surprise, etc.), a tic is caused by an internal trigger, a message deep in the limbic system telling the person, "Swear!" Touretters sometimes compare their tics to automatic reflexes like blinking.

Blinking is a good comparison because Touretters have some control over their tics just as all of us have some control over how often we close our eyes (unlike, for example, our heart rate). Try this: using a stopwatch (1) blink every 10 seconds for 3 intervals; (2) increase the intervals by 10 seconds and continue for 3 intervals; (3) repeat (2). Eventually you'll reach an interval length where you'll blink unintentionally before the interval is up. Similarly, Touretters say they can hold the tics in for a while, but eventually the TS wins out. As Dr. Palmer puts it, if someone held a gun to his head and told him not to have any tics, he could do it, at least for a while (*Talking about Tourettes*). Eventually, though, he'd have to release the tics, just as you could keep yourself from blinking for a while, but eventually you'd have to blink. The length a Touretter can keep from ticcing differs from individual to individual. In a 1986 episode of NPR's *Weekend Edition*, a radio DJ with coprolalia, reports he can keep from ticcing as long as he's on the air, but as soon as he's off-air he has to let them go. In the documentary *John's not Mad*, John clamps his hand over his mouth to keep himself from involuntarily saying things like *fuck* and *cunt*, and yet even while trying to physically restrain himself, the tics often win out. Thus tics, in general, and coprolalic tics, in particular, are partially controllable.

From our discussion on swearing and the brain, you've probably already guessed that TS is caused by some sort of miswiring or misfiring in the limbic system. On the *Tourette Syndrome—Now What?* message board, a contributor describes it as having too many messengers (dopamine) in the brain: just as if too many messengers were working for a company, some would get bored and cause mischief, some of these brain messengers send unwanted and unnecessary messages to the limbic system (http://tourettesyndromenowwhat.yuku.com/forum/viewtopic/id/1664, accessed 5/28/2010). Presumably, for coprolalics, some of these unwanted messages would be "Swear!" Based on our discussion of coprolalia so far, this seems like a pretty good explanation. However, there's another piece to the puzzle.

From the discussion to this point, you might have the impression that tics are no more tied to the social context than a sneeze is. Much of the time, this is the case. However, not always. We began this discussion by speaking of the taboo nature of some tics, and taboos are intertwined with social context (see especially Chapter 15). Previously, I mentioned a Touretter might compulsively say his ex-girlfriend's name, but only around his present

Recently, while out walking my dog, I saw two men strolling down the street engaged in conversation. As the men conversed, one periodically shouted "fuck you!" at passing cars. As I came nearer, he extended his arm toward me, his middle finger up—while looking away from me, still talking with his friend. What struck me from this encounter was my own reaction: of course, I knew he must have TS and knew that he was not voluntarily swearing or flipping me off, yet my body prepared me for fight or flight, telling me to avoid the man. My mind explained to my body there was nothing to fear and prevented my body from deviating from its course; I decided the most polite thing to do was ignore the man's outbursts, just as his friend was doing. I expect people less familiar with TS respond differently; I expect he's had a tough life.

Hockenberry (1996) describes interviewing Saul Lubaroff, a radio DJ with TS. After watching Lubaroff smoothly complete the news and weather and introduce the next song, Hockenerry witnessed him suddenly convulse and shout "I masturbate!" and "I love you!" and "I smell like come!" Hockenberry, who is in a wheelchair, asked what caused his outbursts; he quotes Lubaroff's answer as follows: "'Tony Tourette is in there. Think of whatever you wouldn't want to do or say. That's what Tony is going to say. If you see a girl with large breasts and dirty hair, what is the one thing you don't want to say? That's what I'm going to say.' Then he looked at me and yelled, 'You're a cripple. You're a cripple!'" (223).

girlfriend (after all, it's not taboo to talk about past loves with people you're just friends with). Some Touretters say their urge to tic is higher when in environments where they have to be quiet and sit still, like during an exam or while watching a movie. Kushner (1999) reports on a Touretter who compulsively shouted "Nigger!" when he met a black person and "There's a bomb on the plane!" while making an airline reservation (cited in Brown & Kushner 2001, 543). In *John's not Mad*, we see John's TS making him say *cunt* when he sees attractive women.

Although coprolalic tics may be compulsive, which is to say they result from an internal trigger, there still may be an external trigger. Confusing, no? Perhaps the best way to see this is to consider our own reactions to a normal situation. Imagine taking a class on gardening. The instructor is teaching how to transplant a flower; he explains that you have to be careful not to break the roots as you remove the old pot, and then, as he tries to show you how to do it, holding up the plant for all to see, the dirt ball falls, taking with it the fragile roots. You'd probably think to yourself, "Idiot!" or even, "Fucking idiot!" But you wouldn't say it, would you? Well, this exact incident can be seen in *John's not Mad*, but John's TS makes him say the phrase the rest of us would just think.

TS may be an inhibitory disorder, and coprolalics cannot suppress their urges to swear. Coprolalia "could be associated with failure to inhibit portions of the limbic minicircuits" (Singer 1997, 303). Speaking of a woman who blurted out "purple nigger" when she saw a black man in a purple track suit, Jay (2000, 6) writes, "Normally, most people with racist thoughts would inhibit racist speech in public. But, the inhibitory mechanism does not work for the Touretter; her brain will not let her suppress the forbidden thoughts."

5. OTHER FORMS OF COPROLALIA

Jay (2000, 64) lists the following disorders whose symptoms can include coprolalia: Tourette Syndrome (discussed previously), obsessive compulsive disorder, aphasia, Alzheimer's Disease (as well as dementia and senility), general paresis[6], frontal-lobe damage, and other tic and seizure-type disorders (epilepsy, encephalitis lethargica with klazomania, and latah).

Obsessive Compulsive Disorder (OCD). OCD and TS are related to some degree. They frequently run in the same families; obsessive thoughts are common among Touretters, and many Touretters are also diagnosed with OCD (Miller 2001, 533). It's imaginable, then, that some obsessive-compulsives could have coprolalia without showing any other tics that would be necessary for a diagnosis of TS. As Jay (2000, 67) points out, however, while saying taboo words may be a compulsive thought (e.g., "the fear of shouting an obscenity in church"), coprolalia is not a recognized symptom of OCD. Jay (2000, 67) mentions one case of an OCD patient who compulsively swore and insulted people, but "[h]is utterances were not automatic and reflexive, but more akin to antisocial impulses that preoccupied his mind as a type of obsessional antecedent to his cursing".

Aphasia. In Section 2, we talked about how people with left hemisphere brain damage can lose the ability to speak fluently, or even to speak at all, yet retain the ability to swear. I suggested in that section that their swearing may be out of frustration, a way to vent their anger and emotion. In that case, we shouldn't call their swearing coprolalia. On the other hand, aphasia can lead to true coprolalia.

Aphasics may swear just as anybody else would—that is, as an emotional response; however, some aphasics may swear uncontrollably, at which point we call it coprolalia. As Jay (2000: 36) puts it:

> It is assumed that a healthy LH [left hemisphere] exercises control over emotional impulsivity. Patients who incur left frontal lobe damage lose their ability to control impulsive thoughts and behaviors, resulting in an emotional storm that has been described (Gainotti, 1972) as a "catastrophic reaction" characterized by anger, aggression, swearing, anxiety, and refusal. Patients' verbal aggression occurs with LBD [left-brain damage] because the facility for cursing remains intact in the RH [right hemisphere] and related substrata and the LH cannot suppress these emotions.

In other words, although it is "normal" for an aphasic to swear when angry (and just imagine how angry you'd be if you couldn't speak), some of their swearing may be "abnormal" in that it may be extreme and exaggerated due to the left hemisphere's inability to put a damper on the emotions.

---

[6] I had to look this one up. It's a brain disorder caused by syphilis.

Alzheimer's Disease, Dementia, and Senility. Aging often leads to uncontrollable swearing. As Jay (2000, 68) writes, "[people] who have had the opportunity to spend time in a nursing home observe that episodes of cursing are quite common there." In advanced stages, Alzheimer's Disease (and dementia and senility) patients may swear even when they've lost the ability to use propositional speech. The website AgingCare.com, which calls itself "The Community for Caregivers," has several threads on swearing among the elderly. In one article, Jacqueline Marcell (My Normally Loving) discusses how, as early Alzheimer's set in, her father, who'd always used some swear words, began using *fuck,* a word he'd never used before (because his wife would have "slapped him silly" if he had), calling his daughter "nothing but a fucking whore," saying she'd never "done a fucking thing" for him and that all she wanted was his "fucking money," and telling her "You can get the hell out of my god-damn house you fucking bitch, that's what you can do!"[7] In the comments section of this article, Quincypopp writes that her mother has started saying "poop" and "poopers" every five to ten minutes, and Jenjilks writes that her father says "Here come [sic] the fat one" when a portly nursing home worker approaches. It is not clear what causes these patients to swear, but it seems that, like Touretters, these patients are unable to inhibit certain commands coming from the limbic system. The symptoms among Alzheimer's and dementia patients may be connected to atrophy or lesions in the frontal lobe (Nagaratnam, Patel, & Whelan 2003).

Frontal Lobe Damage. Phineas Gage is the most famous case of this. He's the guy who got a tamping iron clear through the left side of his head in 1848. Supposedly his personality changed after it, and his friends said he was no longer himself, going from a mild-mannered guy pre-accident to a violent, angry, cussing one after. Unfortunately, most of what we think we know about Gage's personality change is based on poor research and scant factual evidence (MacMillan 2008). Still, as Jay (2000, 69) writes—basing his conclusions on more modern case studies—". . . prefrontal brain damage affects personal, social, emotional, and decision-making abilities needed to monitor when cursing is appropriate in a given social context."

Epilepsy. According to Jay (2000), there is plenty of anecdotal evidence that during seizures epileptics may curse uncontrollably. One documented case is of an epileptic woman who, during a seizure, would involuntarily repeat *damn* (40). In a particularly fascinating case, Caplan et al (1992; cited in Jay 2000, 70) mention a ten-year-old girl with epilepsy who used abusive language uncontrollably—for example, "I'm sorry I did that, you fucking idiot," "I'm sorry I said the F word, you fucking idiot." Doctors removed a cyst from the girl's brain, which was impinging on the amygdala, and afterwards her coprolalia stopped.

Latah. Latah is a "culture-bound syndrome" found in Malaysia and Indonesia. Most people identified with latah are women above the age of forty, and it is marked by prolonged episodes of mimicry, swearing, and outrageous behavior. McLaren and Ringe ("Curious Mental Illnesses") describe latah like this: "Many people, when startled, gasp or swear. But after a few seconds most of us return to whatever we were doing before. For those who suffer from *latah,* however, that jolt of surprise turns into a 30-minute orgy of screaming, dancing, and hysterical laughter, punctuated by shouted obscenities." As described, this could be classified as a form of coprolalia; however, Bartholomew (1994) argues that latah has been misunderstood and misrepresented by outsiders. Based on his observations of an extended family known for having many people with latah, he concludes that most cases are simply habitual reactions to startles, akin to English response cries. Using western definitions of latah, he classified 33 family members, out of his sample of 115, as having a mild case and 4 as a having a severe case. Those with a mild case do not consider themselves to have latah but rather see themselves as doing something similar to swearing. Common utterances (for women over 40) are *Oh! Puki Mak engkau* 'your mother's cunt', *Oh! Puki!* 'oh your cunt', *Oh! Pantat Mak engkau* 'your mother's cunt, pussy, or ass' (332). Of the four severe cases, only one was living, a woman around seventy years old who, when startled, has episodes during which she supposedly loses control, swears, mimics others, and behaves in a sexually provocative manner. However, Bartholomew argues that she is not suffering from any mental or neurological disorder; her episodes are performances which the woman, her startler, and any bystanders participate in.

---

[7] In her article, Marcell does not spell *fuck* or *god-damn,* but writes "f- " for *fuck* and "GD" for *god-damn.*

6. THE USEFULNESS OF SWEARING

Throughout this book, we've seen that taboo words are more emotionally charged than other words. In part, it seems this is because they are associated with taboo things or behaviors (excrement, sex, dangerous animals, deities, etc.). But we've also seen this can't be the full story; after all, for every taboo word, there are non-taboo counterparts with the same informative meaning (*fuck~fornicate; piss~urine; nigger~African American; cunt~vagina*). In the end, we have to conclude that taboo words arrive at their emotional charge partly because they are taboo. In other words, because they are forbidden words, we use them sparingly—only when the situation warrants—and when we do, people react. Thus, over time, an individual is primarily exposed to taboo words in emotionally charged situations, and thereby they become linked to the brain's emotional center, the limbic system. In the end, as we've seen with MacKay et al's study, the taboo words themselves can trigger the brain to identify a new situation as emotionally charged, even in the absence of other cues.

Although taboo words are often maligned, they may be beneficial. It can be useful to have a trigger indicating that an event is fraught with emotion: if somebody's swearing, our limbic system kicks in preparing us for fight or flight, just in case things get dangerous. For example, before most fist fights begin, there's an exchange of invectives.

Although most fist fights may begin with swearing, swearing doesn't necessarily lead to physical violence. As Sagarin (1962, 109) puts it, "There is a release of tension by oral violence, and if this does not in its turn incite further tension leading to physical violence, the release may serve beneficially for the user of the insulting term." Most of the time when anger turns to aggression, the aggression is released verbally, through swearing, not physically (Jay 1992, 108).

Of course, not all swearing is aggressive or aimed at anybody, as we saw in Chapter 4 with response cries. But here, too, taboo words are useful to the user. In an ingenious study, Stephens, Atkins, & Kingston (2009) show that swearing when you stub your toe might actually make you feel better. They had subjects put one hand in ice water and hold it there as long as they could. When subjects were instructed to shout out a swear word (a word "you might use after hitting your thumb with a hammer"), they could keep their hands in the water longer than if they were instructed to shout out a neutral word (a word "to describe a table"). Subjects' heart rates also went up when they swore, and they reported they felt less pain. Stephens et al speculate that swearing taps into the limbic system, causing a fight-or-flight response, which then reduces pain. Or, as they put it, "Neurobiologically, fear may cause amygdala activation of descending pain inhibitory systems" (2009, 1060). Yeah.

If swearing can trigger the fight-or-flight response, then it shouldn't only release anger or inhibit pain, but also trigger adrenaline, amping us up for action: Stephens et al (2009, 1060) mention swearing as a psyching up process in sports, say in a pep talk, where a fight-or-flight response and lessening of pain are beneficial. Time and again, I have had athletes in my Bad Words and Taboo Terms class point out how common it is for them to hear (and use) taboo words while engaged in sports. This includes sports ranging from football to rock climbing. (One rock climber mentioned that her friends commonly tell her to "get the sand out of your cunt" when she is struggling on a climb.)

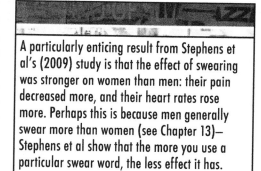

A particularly enticing result from Stephens et al's (2009) study is that the effect of swearing was stronger on women than men: their pain decreased more, and their heart rates rose more. Perhaps this is because men generally swear more than women (see Chapter 13)—Stephens et al show that the more you use a particular swear word, the less effect it has.

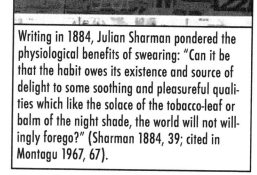

Writing in 1884, Julian Sharman pondered the physiological benefits of swearing: "Can it be that the habit owes its existence and source of delight to some soothing and pleasureful qualities which like the solace of the tobacco-leaf or balm of the night shade, the world will not willingly forego?" (Sharman 1884, 39; cited in Montagu 1967, 67).

7. CONCLUSION

In this chapter, we've seen our brains process taboo words differently from other words. Because of their emotional load, taboo words trigger more right brain processing than do neutral words. Moreover, while most language processing happens in the cortex, the higher brain, swearing—especially automatic swearing—is processed by the limbic system in the middle brain. The reason taboo words are different from other words is because they are more emotionally loaded. Taboo words are commonly used when people are angry, afraid, or in pain, so the words become associated with these negative emotions by our brains. As a result, simply hearing or uttering the words can trigger a fight-or-flight response in our limbic system. Because the right hemisphere is primarily responsible for processing emotions, taboo words are catalogued by this side of the brain.

People who have suffered from left hemisphere brain damage may not be able to access much of their former linguistic knowledge, but because taboo words are cross-referenced by both hemispheres (in the left hemisphere for their informative meaning and their grammatical form, and in the right hemisphere for their emotional and social meaning), they are often still able to swear. On the other hand, if the damage occurs in the right hemisphere, chances are the person will not swear.[8] Some kinds of damage to the left hemisphere can cause uncontrollable swearing.

Certain brain disorders, most notably Tourette Syndrome, Alzheimer's disease and dementia, as well as left hemisphere brain damage can lead to uncontrollable swearing, coprolalia. With these conditions, the brain receives a command from the limbic system (namely, "Swear!") which, in normal individuals, would be inhibited by the left hemisphere, but due to a brain disorder or damage is left unchecked.

Swearing is a linguistic universal, found in every known language, so we should expect that it has an evolutionary purpose. We have adapted swearing to tap into our emotional brain, using it as an alert system to prepare ourselves for danger, to release anger, to suppress pain, and to pump ourselves up for action.

REFERENCES

Allan, Keith, and Kate Burridge. 2006. *Forbidden Words: Taboo and the Censoring of Language.* Cambridge: Cambridge University Press.

Ashburn, Melba. Feelings After a Stroke. http://www.aphasia.org/aphasia_community/in_their_own_words.html (accessed 7/14/2010).

Bartholomew, Robert E. 1994. Disease, Disorder, or Deception? Latah as Habit in a Malay Extended Family. *The Journal of Nervous and Mental Disease* 182(6): 331–338.

Brown, Kate E., and Howard I. Kushner. 2001. Eruptive Voices: Coprolalia, Malediction, and the Poetics of Cursing. *New Literary History* 32: 537–562.

Caplan, R., Y. Comair, D.A. Shewmon, L. Jackson, H.T. Shugani, and W.J. Peacock. 1992. Intractable Seizures, Compulsions, and Coprolalia: A Pediatric Case Study. *Journal of Neuropsychiatry* 4: 315–319.

Deranek, Sandi. Trapped in Your Own Mind. http://www.aphasia.org/aphasia_community/in_their_own_words.html (accessed 7/14/2010).

Gainotti, G. 1972. Emotional Behavior and Hemispheric Side of the Lesion. *Cortex* 8: 41–55.

Hockenberry, John. 1996. *Moving Violations: War Zones, Wheelchairs, and Declarations of Independence.* New York: Hyperion.

Hubbard, Wheeler E. My Story. http://www.aphasia.org/aphasia_community/in_their_own_words.html (accessed 7/14/2010).

Itard, Jean M.G. 1825. Mémoire sur quelques functions involontaires des appareils de la locomotion, de la préhension et de la voix. *Archives Générales de Médecine* 8: 405.

Jay, Timothy. 1992. *Cursing in America: A Psycholinguistic Study of Dirty Language in the Courts, in the Movies, in the Schoolyards, and on the Streets.* Philadelphia: John Benjamins.

Jay, Timothy. 2000. *Why We Curse: A Neuro-Psycho-Social Theory of Speech.* Philadelphia: John Benjamins.

---

[8] I suspect that such individuals would know the words but wouldn't be able to process their social and emotional meaning.

Kushner, Howard I. 1999. *A Cursing Brain? The Histories of Tourette Syndrome.* Cambridge, Mass: Harvard University Press.

LaBar, K.S., and E.A. Phelps. 1998. Arousal-Mediated Memory Consolidation: Role of the Medial Temoporal Lobe in Humans. *Psychological Science* 9: 490–493

Landis, Theodor. 2006. Emotional Words: What's so Different from Just Words? *Cortex* 42:823–830.

MacKay, D.G., M. Shafto, J.K. Taylor, D.E. Marian, L. Abrams, and J. Dyer. 2004. Relations between emotion, memory, and attention: Evidence from taboo Stroop, Lexical Decision, and Immediate Memory Tasks. *Memory and Cognition* 32(3): 473–488.

MacMillan, Malcolm. 2008. Phineas Gage: Unraveling the Myth. *British Psychological Society* 21(9): 828–831.

Marcell, Jacqueline. My normally loving but now slightly demented father is suddenly using the worst possible profanity. How should I handle it? http://www.agingcare.com/Answers/112079/My-normally-loving-but-now-slightly-demented-father-is-suddenly-using-the-worst-possible-profanity.htm (accessed 7/15/2010).

McLaren, Carrie, and Alexanra Ringe. Curious Mental Illnesses Around the World. *Stay Free,* 21. http://www.ibiblio.org/pub/electronic-publications/stay-free/archives/21/mental_illness.html (accessed 2/2/1011).

Miller, Ethel Lee. Brain on Strike. http://www.aphasia.org/aphasia_community/in_their_own_words.html (accessed 7/14/2010).

Miller, James. 2001. The Voice in Tourette Syndrome. *New Literary History* 32: 519–536.

Montagu, Ashley. 1967. *The Anatomy of Swearing.* New York: The Macmillan Company.

Nagaratnam, Nages, Ilesh Patel, and Clair Whelan. 2003. Screaming, shrieking and muttering: the noisemakers amongst dementia patients. *Archives of Gerontology and Geriatrics* 36: 247–258.

Pribram, Karl H. 1960. A Review of Theory in Physiological Psychology. *Annual Review of Psychology* 11: 1–40.

Riddle, Susan. Breakthrough. http://www.aphasia.org/aphasia_community/in_their_own_words.html (accessed 7/14/2010).

Sagarin, Edward. 1962. *The Anatomy of Dirty Words.* New York: L. Stuart.

Sharman, Julian. 1884. *A Cursory History of Swearing.* London.

Singer, Carlos. 1997. Coprolalia and other Coprophenomena. *Neurologic Clinics* 15(2): 299–308.

Smith, Aaron. 1966. Speech and other functions after left (dominant) hemispherectomy. *Journal of Neurological Psychiatry* 29: 467–471.

Stephens, Richard, John Atkins, and Andrew Kingston. 2009. Swearing as a Response to Pain. *Neuroreport* 20: 1056–1060.

TSA. 2007. Tourette Syndrome Association. What is Tourette Syndrome? http://www.tsa-usa.org/Medical/whatists.html (accessed 5/24/10).

Van Lancker, D., and J. Cummings. 1999. Expletives: Neurolinguistics and neurobehavioral perspectives on Swearing. *Brain Research Reviews* 31: 83–104.

1. Using a presentation program (such as PowerPoint, Keynote, or Impress), create your own Taboo Stroop Test. Come up with 5 common taboo words and 15 common neutral words. All words should be one-syllable long and 4 to 5 letters in length (yes: *fuck, cock, bitch, door, light, bath;* no: *pussy, motherfucker, bastard, table, computer, mountain*). Assign one of five colors to each word (red, blue, green, yellow, orange), and type a single word in each slide of the presentation, making the font the right color for the word (make sure the background is white). The first slide of the presentation should have the title "Stroop Test"; follow that slide with 10 of the neutral words, insert one blank slide, and arrange the remaining 10 slides in random order.

   Find several volunteers and give them the test individually (make sure not to use children or anybody who might be overly offended by the taboo words). Position the volunteer so that they can see the slideshow on your computer. While they are looking at the title slide, explain what their task will be—that is, they will see a word written in a particular font color, and they are to say the color out loud. Tell them you will give them the test in two sets. Go through the first ten words, manually moving on to the next slide as soon as the volunteer has successfully said the word. Pause when you get to the blank slide. Ask the volunteer if they are ready for the next set, and when they are, continue with the test. After the subject has finished with the test, close the program. Give the subject a pen and paper and have them write as many words from the test as they can remember.

   - Did your subjects take a noticeably longer time to say the color of the taboo words than the neutral words?
   - Were your subjects able to recall the taboo words on the list better than the neutral words?

1.   INTRODUCTION

Do women swear more or less than men? How about senior citizens versus twenty-somethings? Middle-class versus upper-class versus working class? Educated versus uneducated? Does your racial or ethnic background affect your swearing?

You probably have some guesses about all of these. But what good's a guess? All of these are empirical questions, which is to say the answers lie out there in the world and are discoverable via the scientific process. However, as we'll discuss, it can be tricky to do good research to definitively answer these questions about swearing.

Questions relating to how linguistic behavior breaks down along social lines fall under a branch called **sociolinguistics,** so we'll call the sub-branch that we'll be investigating **socioswearing.** Because gender's effect on swearing has been discussed more than any other sociolinguistic variable, we'll concentrate on men's vs. women's swearing.

In Section 2, we hypothesize that men swear more than women, we consider ways of testing the hypothesis, and we examine the existing evidence for and against the hypothesis. In Section 3, we look at reasons why men and women may have different swearing habits. In Section 4, we look at slurs for men and women and what they tell us about society.

2.   MEN'S VS. WOMEN'S SWEARING

2.1   *Formulating the Hypothesis*

In seminal works by Jespersen (1922), Trudgill (1974), and Lakoff (1975), the observation was made that women use "bad language" less frequently then men. I imagine that's what you would have guessed. The problem: none of them really examined this idea closely, nor did they base their observations on good empirical research (cf. Coates 1993 and Stapleton 2003 for discussion). As Stapleton (2003, 23) puts it, "much (socio)linguistic writing on 'gender and swearing' has relied on folklinguistic beliefs and conceptions with little reference to empirical data." Despite PhDs and publishing contracts, without data, a scholar's guess isn't worth more than anyone else's.[1] One thing everybody agrees on: Most people believe that women swear less than men.

Let's state our hypothesis succinctly:

HYPOTHESIS: Women swear less than men.

Stated like this, it might not sound so bold, but it is. Let's assume we know what *swear* means. You might also think we know what *women* and *men* mean; however, things are more complicated than we commonly believe. For example, do we define these terms sociologically or biologically? That is, when we say "women" and "men" are we thinking of gender or sex? Gender is defined culturally, and sex anatomically and genetically: In terms of gender in Western society, a woman is thought to be delicate, emotional, and intuitive, while a man in is thought to be strong, unemotional, and logical; in terms of sex, a woman has a vagina and two X chromosomes, while a man has a penis and an X and a Y chromosome.

Of course, we know that gender stereotypes are neither universal nor fully accurate (and perhaps not even statistically accurate). Not all men and women fit the stereotypes, and cultures may have different stereotypes. Plus there's the problem of groups who fall outside our typical definitions, for example, females and males in drag and so-called "bull dykes" and "twinks." Will such sub-groups pattern with "women" or "men" or neither?

It's simpler to use sex, not gender, when defining women and men.[2] This is the tradition in sociolinguistic work. To emphasize we're talking sex not gender, scholars often frame things in terms of "females and males" instead of "women and men." So we should rephrase our hypothesis as follows:

HYPOTHESIS: females swear less than males.

Our hypothesis as it stands now is too broad; it'll be nearly impossible to demonstrate. Let me put it this way: how would we go about testing it? To do it adequately, we'd have to investigate the swearing habits of a representative cross-section of people from every corner of the world. To say the least, this would be a massive undertaking, especially considering there are just shy of seven thousand languages in the world (Harrison 2007, 3), and we'd have to identify what qualifies as swearing in each language in our sample.

Let's make this easier on ourselves, and revise our hypothesis:

HYPOTHESIS: English-speaking females swear less than English-speaking males.

Easier, right? Sure. That doesn't mean it's easy, though. How many people speak English? According to Ethnologue, more than 500 million worldwide, with more than one hundred countries having sizable populations of speakers. That's a lot of samples, even if we take just a representative cross-section. But, anyways, let's give it the old college try.

How do we begin?

2.2 *Collecting Data*

To test our hypothesis that English-speaking females swear less than English-speaking males, we need data. What kind of data? Well, linguistic data, naturally. More specifically, we want spontaneous conversations. Spontaneous because much of our swearing is unplanned and, moreover, much of it is automatic (see Chapters 1 and 12). Conversation (as opposed to letters, chats, e-mails, blogs, etc.) because people swear more when speaking than writing.

How do we get these data from spontaneous conversations? Optimally, we'd want to follow folks around for an extended period of time, recording everything they say. And we'd want to do this with enough people from enough backgrounds to get a good cross-section of English. Simple, huh? Right. I don't know about you, but I don't have that kind of time (not to mention the fact that most people feel uncomfortable being followed around by a nerd who wants to record everything they say).

---

[1] I do not want to dis Jespersen, Trudgill, or Lakoff in making this point. They are all fine scholars, and I admire their work in general.

[2] Again, however, things aren't as simple as we typically like to think. According to the Intersex Society of North America, around 1 in 100 people are born with "bodies [that] differ from standard male or female" (ISNA). It's more difficult to say how many people qualify as **intersex** ("a general term used for a variety of conditions in which a person is born with a reproductive or sexual anatomy that doesn't seem to fit the typical definitions of female or male"), but it is significant (ISNA). Our conceit that there are exactly two sexes may be more cultural than biological.

But let's imagine we have lots of volunteers who help us record. We've got hours and hours and hours and hours and hours of recorded data. Now what? We need to have a way to search through the recordings and pick out the swearing, and we have to identify which of the swearers are male and which are female. Someday, we might have computer technology that could do that, but we don't yet. Today, the only way to make linguistic data searchable is to put it into writing, which means now we've got to transcribe all that spoken language into written form, and we need to create tags for every utterance indicating whether the speaker is female or male—more work (every hour of speech takes several hours to transcribe). In fact, something like this has been done for British English; the name for it is the British National Corpus, and we'll discuss it in a bit (Section 2.3).

A **corpus** is a searchable database of naturally produced utterances (either written or spoken—but most often written). There are now several linguistic corpora available. Most corpora tag each utterance with useful information, for example, about the speaker/writer, when and where it was uttered, the level of formality, etc. The corpus may also tag lexical items in the database, making it possible to search on grammatical category as well as words or strings of words. For a list of corpora, see the LINGUIST List's list (www.linguistlist.org/sp/Texts. html #173).

Corpus research is relatively new in linguistics; it certainly wasn't available to Otto Jespersen in the 1920s nor Peter Trudgill and Robin Lakoff in the 1970s. Corpora have had a major role in linguistic research beginning in about the 1990s. One benefit for us: you can search on specific naughty words from a huge number of utterances, and you can break them down by sex of speaker/writer. A downside for us: most of these corpora are composed of written utterances, not spoken—because it's easier to compile the written sources.

Another downside for corpus research, one that is shared by other types of studies: the **observer's paradox**. In a nutshell, a researcher can affect what they're studying simply by observing it. This can be a problem for all scientific endeavors, but it's especially problematic when studying human subjects. I'm sure you can see why this would be a problem for research on swearing: if you're conscious you're being observed—even if you don't know why—you may swear less (or maybe more, who knows?) than you normally would. In the British National Corpus, which we discuss in Section 2.3, all the subjects knew they were being recorded.

So why not record folks surreptitiously? For example, why not hide a tape recorder in a café and record the conversations that happen there? Well, as my colleague Ed Rubin would say, "You could do that, but it would be wrong." Also, if you do a study like that, you wouldn't get it published. The thing is, researchers have a history of doing immoral studies in the name of science (e.g., studies conducted on concentration camp inmates by Nazi scientists during World War II and the syphilis study conducted on African Americans by the U.S. Public Health Service from 1932–1972), so in 1979 the Belmont Report was issued by the National Commission for the Protection of Human Subjects of Biomedical and Behavioral Research; this report set the standards for ethical research on human subjects. One of the basic principles set forth is **respect** (Belmont Report 1979). Researchers have to respect their human subjects, and that means the subjects have to be told they're being studied, as well as the risks of participating, so they can make an informed consent. Today, any researcher affiliated with an American university has to have their human subject research approved by the university's Review Board before they can begin. As much as we might want to record people surreptitiously, ethically (and professionally) we just can't.

There are other methods for collecting swearing data besides recording conversations. Another approach, one that has been around for some time, is to do surveys. You can interview individuals and ask them about their cussing practices. For example, you could ask, "Do you swear (a) often, (b) sometimes, (c) never?" Or for individual swear words, you could ask, for example, "Do you use *shit* (a) often, (b) sometimes, (c) never?" Then you could compile the surveys and see what percentage of men answered with (a) and which percentage of women. This is easier and faster than recording people.

Large-scale linguistic surveys have been done in the United States. The most ambitious is the *Linguistic Atlas of the United States and Canada,* a multi-decade project only partially complete, portions of which have been published in book form (e.g., McDavid & Kurath 1961). Another ambitious project is Labov, Ash, and Boberg (2005). However, both of these projects focus on pronunciation, not language use. There are no large-scale surveys of cussing as far as I know.

There are some problems with the survey approach. For one thing, men and women may have different perceptions of what it means to swear or use a word "often." In my experience, it's better to be specific with such questions, asking instead, for example, "Do you use *son of a bitch* (a) daily, (b) weekly, (c) seldom, (d) never?" But there's a bigger problem: How much can you trust these data? It's well-known among linguists that speakers are not conscious of their linguistic habits; people will often tell you that they "never" use such and such a word, yet if you listen to them speaking you're likely to catch them using the very word they say they never use. So when you collect self-report data on word usage, the data don't really tell you how much people use a word, but how much they think they use a word.

Rather than self-report data, some studies have asked subjects to report how often they hear a word used. According to Jay (1992) such word frequency estimations for non-taboo words correlate well with other methods for estimating word frequency. He concludes that "if one believes that these previous reports using nontaboo words were accurate, then one must accept that these ratings of taboo words are also accurate . . ." (Jay 1992, 142). I'm not convinced. Even if we accept that the data for non-taboo words is accurate, the data for taboo words may be inflated because, as it turns out, we have a better memory for taboo words than we do for non-taboo words (see Chapter 12).

The most extensive study I know of on swearing habits is collected in Jay (1992), but it is hardly an exhaustive study. As Jay, himself, notes:

> Gender in most studies refers to white men and white women. Also, heterosexual identity is assumed in many gender studies . . . Obviously, a broader sample of ethnic, homosexual, and lower-economic groups is needed to draw valid conclusions about gender differences and cursing.
> (Jay 2000, 168)

What Jay is getting at is a logistical problem. The people who conduct academic research are generally academics in academic institutions. When they (or their students) conduct a survey, the subjects are more often than not undergraduate students. This is because students are convenient: easy to find and easy to entice into participating (occasionally by offering extra credit or money or even a cookie[3]). Like it or not, American university campuses are not a representative cross-section of the United States; the student body is disproportionately white and middle class.

In examining the research that had been performed, Jay (2000, 166) concluded, "men curse more often than women; men use a larger vocabulary of curse words than do women; and men use more offensive curse words than do women." However, given our previous discussion, we should amend his observations by replacing each token of "men" and "women" with "white, heterosexual, middle-class, English-speaking men" and "white, heterosexual, middle-class, English-speaking women," respectively. Moreover, as Jay (2000, 167) notes, "the frequency gap between men's and women's swearing is decreasing." So who knows how long these observations will hold true?

In fact, not everybody agrees with Jay's conclusions. McEnery (2006, 34) writes: "[I]t is still, in my opinion, a widely held folk belief in Britain that men swear more often than women. This is not the case." In the following section, we discuss specific data about men's and women's swearing.

2.3   Examining the Data

In this section we'll examine evidence for and against the hypothesis that English-speaking females swear less than English-speaking males. Some of the evidence comes from observational studies, some from corpus studies, and some from surveys.

Jay (1992) presents research from two studies on children's swearing habits. In the first study, he had six student assistants (three female, three male) log all the swearing incidents they heard from children (they hung around places like stores, ball games, playgrounds, swimming pools, schools, etc.). The student researchers carried index cards with pre-printed information slots for information: "the sentence or expression used, speaker's age and sex, the target's age and sex, and the ages and sex of any other people in the setting . . . the physical location and the manner in which the word was spoken" (Jay 1992, 36). Note that they did this surreptitiously to avoid the observer's paradox.[4] From the data collected in this study, Jay concluded that "boys produce more dirty words in public than do girls and... this trend may begin as early as the age of 5 years" (37).

The data for Jay's second study was collected by Peter Hall. Hall, a camp counselor in the summer of 1987, collected examples of taboo word usage by campers; he did so by logging every instance he heard on an

---

[3] Seriously, a cookie. I can't tell you how many studies I participated in as a student just to get a snack, though I've always preferred donuts to cookies.

[4] Jay's researchers did not have to inform their subjects of what they were doing because neither their autonomy nor their privacy were violated. People are aware that when in public they will be overheard; where there's no expectation of privacy, we can observe people without any ethical qualms. Moreover, no identifying information was written down about the subjects. However, it would have been unethical had Jay's students been surreptitiously tape-recording conversations because while we expect people might overhear our public conversations, we don't expect them to record them.

index card pre-printed with categories such as "speaker age and sex, target age and sex, the utterance including taboo words, the volume . . . and pragmatic function" (Jay 1992, 62). The campers were aged from 4 to 14 with slightly more males than females. Most of the campers were from Massachusetts and were middle class. In the data collected for this study, boys used taboo words more than four and a half times as often girls. In particular, boys used *fuck* more often: twenty-one times as often (Jay 1992, 64).[5] However, Jay notes that the sample size is small and that the observer was male (70).

It may be relevant that the observer was male because, as Jay (1992, 123) suggests: "Both male and female speakers are more likely to swear in the company of same sex companions." Hughes (1992, 294–295) points out that few studies have looked at all female speech when they are in all-female groups, and that studies on women's swearing may be skewed if they are conducted by male interviewers. This latter point, of course, is part of the larger problem of the observer's paradox.

On the other hand, Coates (2003) found a different pattern. Over several years, Coates collected spontaneous conversations (with the participants' consent), transcribed them (i.e., wrote them down), and put them into a corpus. Some of the conversations were between all males, some between all females, and some mixed. Coates found that people do swear differently depending on the gender of the participants, but it's different than we might expect. In Coates' corpus of stories told by males to males, men used *fuck* (in all its forms) a total of 72 times; in stories told in mixed company, speakers used it 12 times; and in stories told by females to females, nobody used it at all. Notably, females accounted for more than half the *fucks* used in mixed company (Coates 2003, 173). Thus, it seems that men swear a lot with men, and they tone it down when women are present, while women don't swear much with women, and they tone it up when men are present. As Coates (2003, 148) puts it: "In fact, male and female speakers are both sensitive to the perceived norms of the other gender in their use of taboo language in mixed talk: while the all-male sub-corpus contains much taboo language and the female sub-corpus virtually none . . . , the mixed sub-corpus contains far less taboo language in the narratives produced by male speakers, and far more in the narratives produced by female speakers." Class discussions in my Bad Words and Taboo Terms class confirm this trend: female students report that they feel more comfortable swearing with their male friends, while male students report that they feel less comfortable swearing with their female friends.

Like Coates (2003), McEnery and Xiao (2004) conducted a corpus-based study on the use of *fuck* by men and women. For their study, they used the British National Corpus (BNC), which has 100 million words used by British English speakers in all sorts of sources, both spoken and written, all of them collected from the end of the twentieth century. Most of the BNC is written (90%), but since we're looking at swearing, we're more interested in the spoken part—McEnery and Xiao found that *fuck* (in all its forms) occurred far more often (twelve times as often) in the spoken component as in the written component. The spoken part of the corpus is transcribed from informal conversations (meant to include a wide demographic of speakers) and other spoken sources, including business meetings, government meetings, and radio call-in shows. The speakers are classified in the corpus by age, gender, and social class.

McEnery and Xiao (2004) searched the spoken part of the BNC for tokens of *fuck*. They then looked specifically at how often males and females were found using the word. Male speakers used *fuck* (in all its forms) more than two times as often as women—but *fucked* and *fucks* were not significantly different. Interestingly, there was a difference in how often men and women use *fuck*, but not in how they use it; in other words, men used *fuck* (in all its forms) more often than women, but both sexes used *fuck*, and, moreover, they used the same forms of the word (*fuck, fucking, fucks, fucked, fucker(s)*) to the same degree. For both men and women, the most common form of *fuck* was *fucking* (about three-fourths of the usage), next was *fuck* (about one-fifth), then *fucked, fucker(s),* and *fucks* (accounting for the remaining 5% or so).

When McEnery and Xiao (2004) looked at age, they found that people on the young end of the spectrum (15–34 years old) used *fuck* the most—this was especially true for males in their teens and early twenties. Those in their late thirties to early forties and those over sixty used it the least, especially the females.

It's interesting to note that there's a bell curve for how much more males use *fuck* over females when we track it across the age groups; the difference in rate of usage is lowest at the two extremes (0–14 years old and over 45 years old), and peaks in the middle (15–24 years old): for age group 0–14, males used *fuck* around one-and-a-half times as often as females; for 15–24, around seven times as often; for 25–34, around fifteen times as often; for

---

[5] That was easy math; boys used it 21 times, and only one girl used it only 1 time.

35–44, around four times as often; for 45–59, around one-and-a-half times as often; and for 60+, the difference is not significant because so few senior citizens use *fuck* in the corpus.

Let's try to explain these data relating to age and gender. First, we see that young people swear. No news there, right? In part, adolescents and young adults define themselves by how they speak, and they are testing the boundaries of what is acceptable. But there's another issue involved: young people aren't so concerned with their careers—most don't have any. But once people get into their late twenties through their late forties, they need to worry about "being professional"; they strive to rise up in the world, so they censor themselves in order to appear more like the class they want to belong to.[6] Women in that age group may be more sensitive than men, in part because it's more acceptable for men to swear than women (more on this in Section 3). Once you get older, though, you feel more established and more comfortable with where you are in society, so swearing picks up again. (We can explain why the 60+ age group didn't use *fuck* much by observing that it is a more stigmatized term for that generation than for other generations—see Chapter 7).

When McEnery and Xiao (2004) broke down males and females by social class, they found an interesting phenomenon: both males and females in the upper-middle class (the BNC classifies this as "lower management") used *fuck* the least, but males used it almost eighteen times as often as females; males in the lower-middle class (classified by the BNC as "skilled manual") used it by far the most of any group—more than seventy times (!) as often as females from that class; at the two extremes, we see a good deal of usage, and the difference between males and females is lower, males using *fuck* about twice as often as women for both upper class ("higher management") and lower class ("semi-skilled or unskilled"). The lower-class women used *fuck* almost as often as the upper-class men and nearly three times as often as the upper-middle-class men.

Again, we can explain this in terms of advancement or "social striving." As we discussed, women may be more sensitive to their public image and their social status than men. The middle classes want to be more like the upper class, so they censor their speech (see footnote 4). The upper class is the class that everybody else is striving to be, so they don't have to concern themselves with striving. And lower-class workers generally don't have much hope for advancement, so they, most of all, don't give a crap about how they're perceived. Indeed, we see that the lower-class women swear as much as or more than the men of the other classes.

This latter point is confirmed by a small qualitative study (i.e., not enough data to run statistics on) conducted by Hughes (1992). Hughes looked at a group of six lower-working-class women in Ordsall, Salford, "an inner-city, deprived area of Britain." She found that, contrary to common belief about female speech, these women swore extensively. One of her participants said, "It's not swearing to us, it's part of everyday talking" (1992, 296). All of her participants reported using obscenity and scatology sometimes or often (e.g., *bleeding/er, balls, cunt, dick/head, fuck/ing, prick, shit/e, twat*); all of them reported using *shite* often, and all but one reported using *fuck/ing* often; for each of *balls, prick,* and *twat,* there was only one woman who reported not using it, and for *cunt* there were two. In contrast to obscenity and scatology, the women avoided profanity, "the use of which would be paid for after death" (298): five, four, and three women reported never using *Christ, Jesus,* and *God,* respectively, and none reported using these words often.[7]

Although we should be wary about generalizing from a qualitative study like Hughes', research that looks at a small group of people can uncover things that large-scale studies like McEnery and Xiao's corpus study cannot. Another qualitative study is Stapleton's (2003) research into the swearing habits of a group of young Irish friends.

Stapleton's (2003) data come from a study done in a local pub found in a "small, but relatively cosmopolitan Irish town," where she looked at a group of young men and women who met twice a week to drink together. She conducted the study over the course of two to three months during summer break from university (most of the group members were college students). There were fifteen men and fifteen women in the group, all of them white, Irish, middle-class, educated, and twenty-two to thirty years old. All but two members were heterosexual. She interviewed each participant at the pub over coffee for on average of thirty minutes, and she also recorded normal group conversations over the course of the summer. Stapleton was a member of the group of drinkers, which meant they were comfortable with her, but it also means they were intimately familiar with her and her research.

---

[6] This is an example of what linguists call hypercorrection. When speakers try to "pass" as a member of a prestigious group, they will try to talk like members of that group, but they often overshoot the mark. In this case, middle-class speakers perceive upper-class speakers as not swearing much, so they censor their own swearing to the point that they actually swear less than the upper-class speakers.

[7] *Bloody* was the only non-profanity that none of the women reported using often, and although Hughes doesn't comment on the status of *bloody,* it's possible that these women perceive the word as profane. See Chapter 7 for more on the etymology of *bloody.*

In fact, she notes that members had increased awareness of swearing because of the interviews, and her research became a common topic of conversation within the group. Once again, we see the observer's paradox rearing its head: we can only speculate how much Stapleton's research affected the group members' swearing habits.

During interviews, Stapleton (2003) gave the participants a questionnaire with a list of common taboo words (see Table 13.1) and asked them which words were obscene.

Mostly, the men and women in her study agreed on what words are obscene, except for the female body part terms *cunt, fanny* (which means 'vagina' in Irish English), and *tits,* with many more women than men finding them obscene.

Stapleton (2003) also asked her subjects which words they regularly use when socializing (see Table 13.2). Note that Stapleton's data counts as self-report. That is to say, these numbers don't reflect actual usage, only how participants perceive their own usage. Moreover, Stapleton asked subjects whether they "regularly" use a particular word, and it's possible that different subjects had a different standard for what qualifies as regularly.

The majority of participants from both sexes reported using all of the words regularly, with the exception of *cunt, fanny,* and *tits;* just as more women found them obscene, fewer women reported using them regularly. Only one woman reported using *cunt* regularly, two women reported using *fanny* regularly, and five women reported using *tits* regularly (compared to thirteen, twelve, and fifteen men for each word, respectively).

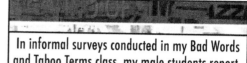

In informal surveys conducted in my Bad Words and Taboo Terms class, my male students report using *tits* more frequently than my female students, and my female students report using *boobs* more frequently than my male students.

Stapleton asked her subjects whether they believed that some words are more appropriate for men than women; all but one of the men said yes, and only three women did. "When probed as to the particular 'words' in question, 'female anatomy' was by far the most salient category mentioned by the respondents" (2003, 27). She goes on to say that men in her study believe that "really obscene" words belong to men, but the women "do not share this view" (27). Some of the women recognized that society views male and female swearing differently, but they distinguished between what society finds acceptable and what they personally find acceptable.

TABLE 13.1		
Numbers of Women and Men Who Judged Each Expletive to be 'Obscene' (adapted from Stapleton 2003, 26)		
Word	*Women*	*Men*
arse	4	2
bastard	5	3
bitch	2	2
bollocks	5	4
cock	8	5
cunt	15	8
fanny	14	6
fuck	8	7
prick	0	0
screw	5	4
shag	4	3
shit/shite	4	4
tits	10	0
wanker	1	0

TABLE 13.2		
Numbers of Women and Men Who Regularly Use Each Expletive (adapted from Stapleton 2003, 26)		
Word	*Women*	*Men*
arse	11	15
bastard	15	15
bitch	14	15
bollocks	12	15
cock	9	13
cunt	1	13
fanny	2	12
fuck	12	13
prick	15	15
screw	10	14
shag	13	15
shit/shite	14	15
tits	5	15
wanker	14	15

On the whole, we can't say that the female subjects in Stapleton's study swore less than her male subjects. It seems that all of her subjects swore regularly. However, we can say that the men used stronger taboo words than the females did. McEnery (2006) found the same thing in his corpus research of British swearing using the BNC.

McEnery discovered that when we consider all the bad words in the BNC, females are just as likely to swear as males. However, there are fifteen words that distinguish female swearing from male: *god, bloody, pig, hell, bugger, bitch, pissed, arsed, shit,* and *pissy* are more likely to be used by females (in descending order of likelihood), and *fucking, fuck, Jesus, cunt,* and *fucker* are more likely to be used by males (in descending order of likelihood). In other words, at least for British English, McEnery found that men and women swear about equally, but men choose stronger taboo words. As McEnery (2006, 35) puts it: Taboo words "are a marker of distinction between males and females, but the distinction is marked quantitatively with a small set of word forms and is more generally marked qualitatively, with males drawing more typically from a stronger set of words than females."

Stenström (1991) also found that females tended to use words that were less taboo than males did. In her corpus of thirty-four face-to-face conversations and five telephone conversations, she found that the female speakers used terms relating to heaven (*God, heaven, Christ, Jesus, goodness,* etc.) and euphemisms, while the males used terms relating to hell (*bloody, hell, damn, devil,* etc.) and sex (*fucking, bastard, sod, buggered,* etc.).

2.4   *Revising the Hypothesis*

To sum up the findings, there is some evidence that men swear more in public than females. Jay (1992: 123) is unequivocal in this regard: "[I]n public males produce more dirty words than do females." However, he also speculates that males and females may swear at the same frequency in certain settings (142). We've seen some evidence that males swear less when around females, and females swear more when around males. Also, depending on the age and social class of the speakers, males' and females' swearing habits are more or less distinct; at the high and low ends of the age scale and of the class scale, the differences are less exaggerated. Finally, we've seen that our initial hypothesis is inaccurate. A more accurate hypothesis is as follows:

HYPOTHESIS: On average, English-speaking females swear the same amount as English-speaking males; however, females use terms that are less taboo than males do.

3.   WHY DO MEN AND WOMEN SWEAR DIFFERENTLY (ASSUMING THEY DO)?

One thing we can all agree on, it seems, is that our society perceives women as swearing less than men. In my Bad Words and Taboo Terms class, when I ask students whether they think "a) men swear more than women, b) women swear more than men, c) men and women swear the same amount," the vast majority say (a), a small minority say (c), and hardly anybody says (b). Because society sees women as swearing less than men, "swearing inevitably acquires different meanings, and thereby functions differently for female users" (Stapleton 2003, 23).

We can go a step further: if men are perceived to swear more, then we can conclude that it is more acceptable for men to swear than for women. Thus, when women swear, they will be judged more harshly. Jay (1992, 188) concludes from his research that for most people females' swearing is more offensive than males'. Similarly, Stapleton (2003: 22) writes:

> A woman in my Bad Words and Taboo Terms class said that she was once told by a male: "I fucking hate it when girls swear. It's not feminine."

> While breaching a taboo inevitably entails certain consequences for the speaker, such consequences will be intensified by the speakers positioning within the prevailing (gender) hierarchy. This process is clearly exemplified in differential attitudes to female/male swearing. . . , whereby women's use of obscenity is likely to be evaluated more negatively than that of their male counterparts.

I suppose this leads to a vicious circle: because men's swearing is more acceptable and they are not judged harshly, they swear more; because women's swearing is less acceptable and they are judged harshly, they swear less. The more men swear, the more acceptable it is; the less women swear the less acceptable it is. End of story? Nah.

Students in my Bad Words and Taboo Terms class have hypothesized that women may swear less because girls are more strongly punished for swearing than boys are. Informal studies the class conducted proved inconclusive; however, Jay (1992, 32), citing Berges et al (1983), says parents are more lax with boys' swearing than girls'. It would be interesting to study this in more depth to see whether this holds true more than twenty-five years later.

A long-standing hypothesis is that women are more class conscious than men, so they may avoid stigmatized speech (e.g., non-standard grammar) more than men do. Taboo words "carry strong connotations of lower socioeconomic groupings and/or working class culture" (Stapleton 2003, 22). In Section 2.3, we saw evidence that this hypothesis may be true when we examined sex together with social class.

Another hypothesis is that women and men swear for different reasons. Risch (1987, 358) suggests that swearing for females may not be so much about masculinity vs. femininity, but about public vs. private. "[S]wearing frequently signals intimacy or trust between female speakers. In certain situations, it may be read as an act of solidarity or even affection, between women friends" (Stapleton 2003, 23). But Coates (2003, 105) observes that taboo language also helps create solidarity among men.

Stenström's (1991) research led her to conclude that "women typically use expletives[8] to give feedback" (243), while men mostly use them to emphasize their points. McEnery (2006) similarly found that females tend to use exclamations more than males do, and males tend to use emphatics more than females do (see Chapter 1 for the distinction between exclamations and emphatics).

Fine and Johnson (1984) found that the main motives for swearing were to express anger and emphasize feelings, followed by relieving tension and habit. Stapleton (2003) also found that anger was a common motive for swearing among her subjects, and although traditionally anger is more appropriately expressed by men than women, in her study an equal number of men and women (ten out of fifteen each) reported they swore when angry. Like Fine and Johnson, she also found many of her subjects reported swearing for reasons of emphasis (thirteen men and eleven women gave this reason). But the most common reason reported was for entertainment reasons, either when telling a story or a joke (all of the men and all but two of the women gave this as a reason).

Stapleton (2003) did find differences between the sexes with regard to motives for swearing, though. One of the most commonly reported motives for men was out of habit. Women, on the other hand, were more likely to report that they swore because it showed intimacy or trust (twelve women gave this as a reason and no men did). Six of the women said that swearing was part of their personality, while no men did—this shouldn't be surprising since sixteen out of fifteen (!) men reported they swore because it's expected.

Another place where Stapleton (2003) found a difference was with regard to the use of female body part terms, especially *cunt* and *fanny*. Almost all the participants reported they avoid *cunt* and *fanny* at least sometimes, and most of the women reported they avoid those words all the time. But the men's and women's reasons for avoiding the terms were different. All the women said they avoid the terms because they are sexist or offensive, while only eight of the men gave that reason—the other seven reported avoiding certain terms because they didn't want to appear sexist. In particular, it seems the men avoided using the terms in front of women because they didn't want the women to think they were sexist—but in front of other men . . . well, as Stapleton puts it: "words such as 'cunt' and 'fanny' tend to be used only in the context of all-male interaction (a phenomenon described by nine men), thereby marking these as specifically 'masculine' terms." In addition, nearly all the men in the study said these words were "more acceptable for men than women" (2003, 31).

The Tabooness Survey was designed in part to test another hypothesis: males and females have different perceptions of tabooness. More specifically, men may view swear words as less taboo than women do. If that is the case, men perceive swearing as less of a taboo violation than women do. This could go a long way toward explaining why men swear more in public and why they use stronger taboo words. Although, as I discuss in Chapter 1, the Tabooness Survey is skewed towards residents of Utah, our conclusions from it are probably applicable to the rest of the country. Jay (1992, 147) says that correlations across the country are very high with respect to tabooness.

When we average all of the women's ratings on swear words on the Tabooness Survey and we average all of the men's ratings, we find that women were 0.4 points higher than men (4.0 vs. 3.6).[9] Women were 0.2 points higher than the men for the average ratings on the sentences (3.4 vs. 3.2).[10] Thus we find that women do, in fact,

---

[8] Stenström uses the term "expletive" for taboo words used for their emotional force, not their informative meaning, that is, taboo words used in emotive swearing.

[9] These averages do not include ratings for orthophemisms, such as *feces, African American, vagina*, etc.

[10] These averages do not include reverent uses of religious terms, such as *Jesus Christ had disciples*.

perceive swearing as more taboo than men do. These results are confirmed by a British study conducted by the Advertising Standards Authority, British Broadcasting Corporation, Broadcasting Standards Commission, and the Independent Television Commission (ASA 2000). This study surveyed a large cross-section of the UK on the severity of different swear words and concluded "In all cases women find the words far more offensive than do men..." (ASA 2000, 10).

Finally, we can return to a question we pondered in Section 2.1. Should we be looking at gender or sex? Most researchers have tacitly assumed that men swear more than women due to cultural factors, meaning that it is a matter of gender, not sex. But could something biological be at play? Perhaps testosterone makes men swear. I haven't seen any research pursuing this or related hypotheses. We do know, however, that men's and women's bodies respond differently to swearing (see Chapter 12). However, that is probably an effect not a cause—that is, men's bodies respond differently because they swear more, not they swear more because their bodies respond differently.

4. SLURS FOR MEN AND WOMEN

In Chapter 1, we discussed slurs extensively. In Chapters 7 and 15, we find that racial slurs are the most taboo words in today's English. In this section, we focus on sexual slurs, those slurs specifically aimed at either males or females and those aimed at homosexuals.

We have plenty of inoffensive, generic terms for referring to a man: *man*[11], *guy, dude, fellow, chap, bloke*. But there are few good counterparts for referring to a woman. *Gal? Dudette? Lady? Girl?* For many people, *woman* is about the only word they'll use. As Hughes (1991, 214) puts it: "[I]n contrast with the semantic field of 'man', there are remarkably few neutral terms for 'woman'." On the other hand, there are lots and lots of derogatory terms for women. As Sutton (1995, 279) writes, "Researchers have pointed out that in English there are many more negative terms for women than for men—a quick look in a thesaurus will confirm that . . ." In her own research with Berkeley undergraduates, Sutton (1995) found a higher percentage of negative words for women than positive (and the positive words tended to focus on attractiveness to men).

On the other hand, James (1998) argues that slurs for men are more common than slurs for women. Through brainstorming and observation, her students came up with one-and-a-half times as many derogatory terms for males as females: 343 for males and 206 for females (James 1998, 401).

We got similar results in an informal study conducted in the Spring 2010 Bad Words and Taboo Terms class at the University of Utah. In this study, students were separated by sex into two groups, men and women, and each group was tasked with coming up with the ten most common slurs for males and the ten most common slurs for females in name-calling. The lists were then collected and collated. As a class, we discussed each term to decide whether or not it really qualified. For example, *manwhore* was dismissed because the males said it didn't qualify as a slur since most of them considered it positive, and *milf* was dismissed on two accounts: it isn't intended as an insult by users (though many of the female students found it offensive) and it wouldn't be used in name-calling (e.g., one wouldn't say, "You milf!"). In the end, we collected sixteen commonly used words for men and twelve for women. However, in the results listed in Tables 13.3 and 13.4, I have omitted one of the terms for women, *dirty slut*, because it was too similar to another term, *slut*. This gives us sixteen and eleven name-calling terms used for men and women, respectively.

Once we collected the lists of slurs, students were asked to rate each term for offensiveness when it is used in the frame "You _____!" as an insult (i.e., not jokingly or affectionately) on a scale of 1–7 (1=inoffensive, 7=extremely offensive); and for each term they were asked whether they used it (in any capacity, including jokingly and affectionately) daily, weekly, occasionally, or never. A total of thirty native English speakers participated in this survey: fourteen males, sixteen females.[12] Tables 13.3 and 13.4 give the offensiveness ratings and Tables 13.5–13.8 give the frequency of use estimations.

The usage estimates may not reflect actual usage patterns in the population as a whole. First, as we discussed in Section 2.2, these are self-report data, so not necessarily representative of use. Second, by the time they took this survey the participants had attended nearly a semester's worth of lectures on swearing and they had read a great deal on the topic; these students were undoubtedly more aware of issues surrounding slurs than average speakers. That said, there are some interesting trends.

---

[11] Duh!

[12] Some students did not give ratings and estimations for every part of the survey, so the numbers will vary for each sub-part of the survey.

TABLE 13.3		
Offensiveness Ratings for Male-Referential Slurs Used in Name-Calling		
Slur	*Female Average (n=16)*	*Male Average (n=14)*
tool	2.2	2.3
ass	2.9	2.8
cock	3.4	2.9
dumbass	3.1	3.0
dumbshit	2.9	3.1
prick	3.3	3.1
douche	3.3	3.1
dick	3.5	3.1
bastard	3.4	3.3
pussy	3.8	3.5
asshole	3.3	3.6
douchebag	3.3	3.6
son of a bitch	3.8	3.7
cocksucker	4.6	4.2
fucker	5.0	4.4
fag	4.4	4.5

TABLE 13.4		
Offensiveness Ratings for Female-Referential Slurs Used in Name-Calling		
Slur	*Female Average (n=16)*	*Male Average (n=13)*
bimbo	2.6	2.6
trick	2.7	2.5
skank	3.1	3.6
hooker	3.2	3.4
dyke	3.8	4.3
ho	3.9	3.2
twat	4.1	3.8
slut	4.1	4.4
whore	4.1	4.5
bitch	4.4	5.1
cunt	6.1	5.8

TABLE 13.5				
Frequency of Use for Female-Referential Slurs by Females (n=16)				
Slur	*Daily*	*Weekly*	*Occasionally*	*Never*
bimbo	0% (0)	0% (0)	19% (3)	81% (13)
trick	0% (0)	6% (1)	6% (1)	88% (14)
skank	0% (0)	19% (3)	38% (6)	38% (6)
hooker	0% (0)	19% (3)	19% (3)	62% (10)
dyke	0% (0)	6% (1)	6% (1)	88% (14)
ho	6% (1)	25% (4)	31% (5)	38% (6)
twat	0% (0)	6% (1)	13% (2)	81% (13)
slut	6% (1)	37.5% (6)	37.5% (6)	19% (3)
whore	13% (2)	25% (4)	31% (5)	31% (5)
bitch	44% (7)	6% (1)	44% (7)	6% (1)
cunt	6% (1)	0% (0)	13% (2)	81% (13)

TABLE 13.6

Frequency of Use for Female-Referential Slurs by Males (*n*=12)

Slur	Daily	Weekly	Occasionally	Never
bimbo	0% (0)	8% (1)	8% (1)	83% (10)
trick	0% (0)	8% (1)	8% (1)	67% (8)
skank	17% (2)	8% (1)	25% (3)	50% (6)
hooker	0% (0)	17% (2)	33% (4)	25% (3)
dyke	0% (0)	0% (0)	33% (4)	67% (8)
ho	8% (1)	8% (1)	50% (6)	33% (4)
twat	0% (0)	8% (1)	42% (5)	50% (6)
slut	17% (2)	17% (2)	50% (6)	8% (1)
whore	17% (2)	8% (1)	58% (7)	17% (2)
bitch	58% (7)	17% (2)	25% (3)	0% (0)
cunt	17% (2)	25% (3)	17% (2)	42% (5)

TABLE 13.7

Frequency of Use for Male-Referential Slurs by Females (*n*=16)

Slur	Daily	Weekly	Occasionally	Never
tool	19% (3)	13% (2)	31% (5)	38% (6)
ass	38% (6)	31% (5)	31% (5)	0% (0)
cock	0% (0)	6% (1)	50% (8)	38% (6)
dumbass	19% (3)	50% (8)	13% (2)	19% (3)
dumbshit	6% (1)	13% (2)	44% (7)	31% (5)
prick	0% (0)	6% (1)	63% (10)	31% (5)
douche	25% (4)	13% (2)	44% (7)	13% (2)
dick	19% (3)	44% (7)	31% (5)	6% (1)
bastard	0% (0)	19% (3)	75% (12)	6% (1)
pussy	0% (0)	25% (4)	31% (5)	44% (7)
asshole	13% (2)	50% (8)	38% (6)	0% (0)
douchebag	31% (5)	25% (4)	25% (4)	19% (3)
son of a bitch	13% (2)	13% (2)	50% (8)	25% (4)
cocksucker	0% (0)	6% (1)	31% (5)	10 (63%)
fucker	19% (3)	25% (4)	13% (2)	38% (6)
fag	0% (0)	19% (3)	19% (3)	56% (9)

If we combine the numbers for "daily" with those for "weekly" and the numbers for "occasionally" with those for "never," we get a sense of which slurs are used frequently and which are used rarely (Tables 13.9 on page 205 and 13.10 on page 206).

Not only do we find more slurs for men than women in this study, we also find that the slurs for men received higher frequency estimates than those for women. More than half of the males reported frequently using eight of the slurs for men (*dumbass, ass, asshole, dick, douchebag, fucker, douche,* and *pussy*), and more than half of the females reported frequently using five of the slurs for men (*dumbass, ass, asshole, dick,* and *douchebag*). Of the terms

Table 13.8

Frequency of Use for Male-Referential Slurs by Males (*n*=13)

Slur	Daily	Weekly	Occasionally	Never
tool	8% (1)	15% (2)	23% (3)	46% (6)
ass	54% (7)	15% (2)	23% (3)	0% (0)
cock	15% (2)	31% (4)	23% (3)	31% (4)
dumbass	38% (5)	31% (4)	8% (1)	15% (2)
dumbshit	31% (4)	15% (2)	31% (4)	23% (3)
prick	0% (0)	23% (3)	46% (6)	31% (4)
douche	31% (4)	46% (6)	0% (0)	23% (3)
dick	31% (4)	31% (4)	23% (3)	15% (2)
bastard	23% (3)	23% (3)	46% (6)	8% (1)
pussy	31% (4)	31% (4)	23% (3)	15% (2)
asshole	46% (6)	31% (4)	23% (3)	0% (0)
douchebag	31% (4)	38% (5)	15% (2)	15% (2)
son of a bitch	31% (4)	8% (1)	54% (7)	8% (1)
cocksucker	8% (1)	15% (2)	46% (6)	31% (4)
fucker	54% (7)	8% (1)	23% (3)	8% (1)
fag	8% (1)	38% (5)	23% (3)	31% (4)

Table 13.9

Frequency of Use For Female-Referential Slurs (combined data)

Slur	FEMALES		MALES	
	Frequently	Rarely	Frequently	Rarely
dyke	6%	94%	0%	100%
bimbo	0%	100%	8%	92%
twat	6%	94%	8%	92%
trick	6%	94%	8%	75%
hooker	19%	81%	17%	58%
cunt	6%	94%	42%	58%
skank	19%	75%	25%	75%
ho	31%	69%	17%	83%
whore	38%	62%	25%	75%
slut	44%	56%	33%	58%
bitch	50%	50%	75%	25%

TABLE 13.10

Frequency of Use For Male-Referential Slurs (combined data)

Slur	FEMALES		MALES	
	Frequently	Rarely	Frequently	Rarely
prick	6%	94%	23%	77%
cocksucker	6%	94%	23%	77%
cock	6%	88%	46%	54%
tool	31%	69%	23%	69%
son of a bitch	25%	75%	38%	62%
bastard	19%	81%	46%	54%
dumbshit	19%	75%	46%	54%
fag	19%	75%	46%	54%
pussy	25%	75%	62%	38%
douche	38%	56%	77%	23%
fucker	44%	50%	62%	31%
douchebag	56%	44%	69%	31%
dick	62%	38%	62%	38%
asshole	62%	38%	77%	23%
ass	69%	31%	69%	23%
dumbass	69%	31%	69%	23%

for men, only *prick* had no participants reporting that they used it daily. In contrast, with the exception of *bitch*, the slurs for women received low frequency estimations—less than half of the students reported using any of the slurs for women (except *bitch*) frequently. In fact, there are five terms for women which so few students reported using that we may question whether they should be considered "common" slurs for women: *dyke, bimbo, twat, trick,* and *hooker.* No students reported using these terms daily.

Bimbo and *trick* received a relatively low offensiveness rating of 2.6 (across both men and women). *Twat* and *dyke,* on the other hand, received a relatively high average rating of 4.0—interestingly, males found the latter term more offensive than females (4.3 vs. 3.8).

On the other hand, *dyke* isn't unusual in being rated higher by males; males rated most of the female-referential terms as more offensive than the females did; the exceptions were *cunt, ho, twat,* and *trick.* A similar pattern was found for the male-referential terms, where the women generally rated them higher than the males, the exceptions being *tool, douchebag, asshole, dumbshit,* and *fag.*

> "Calling a man a *dick* is something of a standard insult term; one even finds it on television in mutated forms, such as *duckweed* and *dickwad.* But one will never hear a woman called a *cunt* on television" (Sutton 1995: 280).

Seeing that the slurs for men are reported to be used more than those for women, it is not surprising that the slurs for men were also rated as less offensive in general. Only three of the sixteen slurs for men were rated an average of 4 or higher: *fucker, fag,* and *cocksucker.*[13] More than half the slurs for women were rated an average of 4 or higher: *cunt, bitch, whore, slut, twat,* and *dyke.*[14]

---

[13] Receiving average ratings of 4.7, 4.4, and 4.4, respectively.

[14] Receiving average ratings of 6, 4.7, 4.3, 4.2, 4.0, and 4.0, respectively.

When we look at the personal characteristics targeted by the slurs for women and men in these lists, an interesting pattern emerges: most slurs for women target sexual promiscuity, while most slurs for men target unpleasant behavior.

- Slurs for women
  - Sexual promiscuity: *slut, whore, skank, ho, bimbo, trick, hooker*
  - Unpleasant behavior: *bitch, cunt, twat*
  - Homosexuality: *dyke*

- Slurs for men
  - Unpleasant behavior: *ass, asshole, bastard, cock, cocksucker, dick, douche, douchebag, fucker, prick, son of a bitch, tool*
  - Intelligence: *dumbass, dumbshit*
  - Weakness: *pussy*
  - Homosexuality: *cocksucker,*[15] *fag*

This pattern is confirmed by others' research. Sutton (1995) found that the largest number of slang terms for women that her students could come up with targeted promiscuity, which does not even seem to be a category for men—as Sutton observes: "A man who has sex often is to be admired; a woman, despised" (1995, 287). Jay (1992, 80) notes that slurs for men "indicate general disgust with the wrongdoer's behavior . . ." and say less about what the behavior is than do slurs for women. In a study by James (1998) where she collected slang terms for men and women, the category "mistreats others" is the largest category for male-referential terms, much larger than the equivalent for women (108 terms vs. 28 terms).

James (1998) assigned seven categories to female-referential terms and seven to male-referential terms:

Male-Referential Terms

1. 'mistreats others (non-sexually)' (108 terms): e.g., *asshole, bastard, motherfucker, prick*

2. 'stupid' (91 terms): e.g., *bonehead, boner, butt-head, doofus, shit-for-brains, yutz*

3. 'weak in character/like a woman/homosexual'
   a. 'weak in character/like a woman' (28 terms): e.g., *cuntlapper, mama's boy, pussy, sissy, wuss*
   b. 'homosexual' (38 terms): e.g., *bum-packer, cock-lover, femme, girly-man, nancy-boy*

4. 'sexual behavior offensive to women' (35 terms): e.g., *creep, dog, horndog, lecher, stud, swine, womanizer*

5. 'socially inept' (18 terms): e.g., *brainiac, doofus, dork, dweeb, geek, reject, schmo*

6. 'lack of accomplishment, especially ability to earn a living' (16 terms): e.g., *boozehound, bum, deadbeat, loser, wastecase, wino*

7. 'Physically weak' (10 terms): e.g., *beanpole, pipsqueak, shrimp, wimp*

Female-Referential Terms

1. 'promiscuous/prostitute/sexually aggressive' (62 terms): e.g., *ho, hootchie, hussy, Lolita, skag, skankslut, whore*

2. generally demeaning/diminishing (the terms under (a) are considered more demeaning than those in (b)):
   a. 'sex object' (28 terms): e.g., *bearded clam, beef, cunt, gash, hole, pie, piece of ass*
   b. general terms for women (12 terms): *babe, blouse and skirt, bombshell, broad, chick(ie), dame, skirt*

---

[15] I've included *cocksucker* in both the "unpleasant behavior" and "homosexuality" categories. I think most speakers today use it in the former sense; however, we have to recognize that it comes from a homosexual slur originally.

3. 'unattractive' (33 terms): e.g., *cow, dog, porker, pruneface, thunderthighs*
4. 'mistreats others' (28 terms): e.g., *ballbreaker, ballbuster, battleaxe, bitch, biter, cunt, shrew, twat, witch*
5. 'brainless' (20 terms): e.g., *airhead, Barbie, bimbo, bubbleheadditz, hairbrain, space-cadet*
6. 'masculine/lesbian' (11 terms): e.g., *Amazon, bush pig, butch, cuntlicker, dyke, lesbo, lezzie*
7. 'sexually cold/unavailable' (11 terms): *cockteaser, cold fish, fag hag, feminaut, ice queen, pricktease(r), prude*

James observes that most of the male categories (five out of seven) target incompetence "either in character or in mental or physical abilities," but most of the female categories (again, five out of seven) target sexuality (403).

In James' classification, the categories "stupid" for males and "brainless" for females are similar; however, the terms for unintelligent women suggest they have nothing in their heads, while the terms for men suggest they have something other than brains in there (James 1998, 404). In her corpus, there were four-and-a-half times as many terms for unintelligent men as for unintelligent women (417). She suggests that it is considered worse in society for a man to be unintelligent than for a woman (405).

James (1998) argues that we can look at what terms of abuse are used against men and women to get a sense of how society views the genders. For example, slurs that attribute feminine traits to men are more offensive than slurs that attribute masculine traits to women (James 1998, 404): *bitch* is generally defined with the adjective *dominant, pushy,* or *bossy,* but these terms are never used with *bastard* or *prick.* More generally, James argues that sexually oriented slurs reflect a masculine viewpoint with regard to men and women:

> In general, female-referential and male-referential derogatory terms reflect a construction of gender by which males are evaluated primarily in terms of the extent to which they can function as competent masters of every situation, which in turn has much to do with gaining and maintaining status in the eyes of other males. Females, on the other hand, are evaluated primarily in terms of how well they conform to heterosexual male needs and desires, including being attractive, faithful to one man, of average intelligence, and docile and supportive. (James 1998, 406)

The exception to this "male-centered view of the world," she notes, is the male-referential category "sexual behavior offensive to women" (James 1998, 404).

We might expect women to chafe at such a male-centric system of values; James (1998, 407) notes that some scholars claim "women may resist using these [female-derogatory] terms to criticize other women." However, her research doesn't bear this out except with the "sex object" terms. In other words, women target women with the same slurs that men do, with the exception that they seldom use terms like *piece of meat, hole, bearded clam, gash,* etc.

Although James (1998, 408) suggests that women largely accept the "male-biased construction of femininity expressed through these derogatory words for women," she notes that some women viewed assertive terms, namely *bitch* and *ballbuster,* as positive. *Bitch,* especially, has been "reclaimed" by women as a symbol of strength. During the lead-up to the 2008 Democratic primaries, Tina Fey made the following comments about Hillary Clinton: "Maybe what bothers me the most is that people say that Hillary is a bitch. Let me say something about that. Yeah, she is. So am I . . . You know what? Bitches get things done . . . Bitch is the new black!" (*Saturday Night Live,* Feb. 23, 2008). Similarly, Sutton (1995, 288) found that among her subjects (college students), *bitch* and *ho* could be terms of affection between women (but not coming from a man).

In an in-class survey, Sutton (1995) asked her female students if they used *bitch* and *ho,* and if so, whether they were positive or negative. Out of the thirty women surveyed, twenty said the words were always negative and they would only use them as insults; two said the words were negative and they did not use them, but among friends, no offense would be taken; six said they used *bitch* as "joke insults"; eight said *ho* was not insulting. One female student said of *ho,* "When talking about women it's negative, but when talking to women it's a joke" (288). Sutton concludes that *ho* and *bitch* are similar to *nigga,* in that it's okay for in-group members (females and African Americans, respectively) to use it, but not for out-group members. Baldwin (2009, ii) also argues that *bitch* "is becoming to women what the 'N-Word' has become to Blacks."

Some have observed that the same is true for homosexual slurs—that is, they can be used by homosexuals but not by heterosexuals.[16] Here, we specifically are looking at homosexual terms that are used as generic slurs

---

[16] There seems to be some disagreement here. I have heard members of the GLBT community argue that terms like *dyke* and *queer* (and, to a lesser extent, *fag*) can, and should, be used by everybody so long as they are used positively.

for men and women (i.e., not specifically directed at members of the GLBT community). James' (1998) study found that this was an especially common practice with slurs for men, and she gives this example observed by one of her student researchers: A man angered by a driver in a parking lot said, "You wouldn't want to wait for me to go through, would you, faggot?" (James 1998, 417).

This pattern may exist with female-directed slurs, too, but it is not nearly as prevalent. Historically in English, there have been more and worse slurs for male homosexuals than for female homosexuals. "Not only is the male field [for homosexuals] far larger, virtually every word in the field is far more virulent and contemptuous than any in the female equivalent" (Hughes 1991, 230).

A similar conclusion was reached in a study conducted over two semesters in my Bad Words and Taboo Terms class. During the Spring and Fall semesters of 2009, students divided into two groups: men and women. Each group came up with as many name-calling slurs as they could for members of the opposite gender. Once each group had collected their lists, the men, as a group, rated the male-directed slurs for offensiveness, and the women, as a group, rated the female-directed slurs for offensiveness (in other words, each group rated the list that the other group had compiled). Offensiveness ratings were again on a scale of 1–7 (1 = inoffensive, 7 = highly offensive). Across the two semesters, a total of forty-eight for derogatory terms for males were collected. Of these, only a handful were rated 4 or higher: *assfucker, faggot, punk-ass bitch, fudgepacker, cocksucker, cumguzzler,* and *pussy.* Notice that all of these but *pussy* are derived from homosexual slurs.[17] See Table 13.11 for the scores.

In total, more than one-quarter (13) of the male-directed slurs were derived from homosexual slurs: *fruitcake, fag, shitstabber,*

"I was arrested, as you know, for using taboo, derogatory . . . vulgate [audience members applaud] Whew! what does that applause mean? Taboo, derogatory . . . 'Hooray, he was arrested.' That's hard to figure out. There were three kind of words or references. One was to a vulgate term [*cocksucker*]—that they assumed related to a homosexual. That's funny how they picked it up. Because I don't know if they're hip to it, that's not only a homosexual practice, but the practice of every good wife, who is contemporary."

(Lenny Bruce, *Live at the Curran Theater,* 1961)

TABLE 13.11		
Offensiveness Ratings for Homosexual-Derived Slurs for Men		
Slur	Spring 2009 rating	Fall 2009 rating
assfucker	n/a	6
punk-ass bitch	5	n/a
faggot	6	4
fudgepacker	n/a	4
cumguzzler	4	n/a
cocksucker	4	n/a
queer	n/a	3.5
homo	3	n/a
ball-licker	n/a	3
flamer	n/a	2.5
shitstabber	n/a	2
fag	2	n/a
fruitcake	n/a	1.5

17 Moreover, *pussy* received very different ratings across the two semesters, which was unusual compared to other terms on the list.

TABLE 13.12		
Offensiveness Ratings for Homosexual-Derived Slurs for Women		
Slur	*Spring 2009 Rating*	*Fall 2009 Rating*
carpetmuncher	4	n/a
dyke	5	1.5
lesbo	2	n/a
rugmuncher	1	n/a
carpetlicker	n/a	0.5
muffdiver	n/a	0

flamer, ball-licker, homo, queer, cocksucker, cumguzzler, fudgepacker, faggot, punk-ass bitch, and *assfucker.*[18]

In contrast to the male-directed slurs, the female-directed slurs had fewer terms derived from homosexual slurs; out of fifty-five total terms only six were homosexual slurs: *carpetmuncher, dyke, lesbo, rugmuncher, carpetlicker, muffdiver.*[19] Furthermore, these tended to be rated low on the offensiveness scale. Despite instructions that 1 was the lowest rating, the women of Fall 2009 rated *muffdiver* a 0 and *carpetlicker* 0.5. Only *dyke* and *carpetmuncher* received scores of 4 or higher, and *dyke* was rated considerably lower by the spring class vs. the fall class. Table 13.12 gives the ratings.

One thing we find with slurs for men and women is that the respective sexes don't always agree on what the terms mean. For example, during both the spring and fall semesters of the previous study, the women proposed *manwhore* as a slur, and both semesters the men protested that it was not a slur. For the women, the word had negative connotations, for the men, positive. Other studies have found differences in how the sexes define terms. For example, James (1998, 408) found men and women had different meanings for *slut:* 'sexually promiscuous' for women and 'sexually promiscuous, dirty, and undesirable' for men. She also found that, for women, *slimeball* and *sleazeball* refer to sexual predators, while, for men, they are simply general slurs for men who mistreat others. Likewise, she found that *stud* may refer to a cheater for women, but to a "sexual athlete" for men (James 1998, 409). One of her students observed the following conversation:

When I was in college, one of my closest friends was Rachel, who happened to be a lesbian. One day I was in the cafeteria looking for an empty seat, when Rachel waved me over to sit with her and her friends, who were all lesbians. Shortly after I sat down, Rachel spotted a classmate and got up to ask him if she could borrow his class notes. She returned looking befuddled. "When I asked him what he thought of our professor, " she said, "he was like, 'she's all right, but I think she's a carpetmuncher.'" Rachel hadn't known how to respond, so she hadn't said anything to him. "I guess he doesn't know I'm a lesbian, or he wouldn't have said that, but still . . . That's a pretty ugly word."

"I know," one of Rachel's friends said, "and it's not even accurate. I mean, it's not like we *always* do it on the floor."

> Male: Some people might say I'm a stud.
>
> Female: A stud!?
>
> Male: You know, good in bed.
>
> Female: Oh, I thought you meant that you have a lot of girlfriends.
>
> Male: Oh no.

(*quoted in James 1998, 409*)

---

[18] I left *teabagger* off of this list because *teabagging* is one of those sexual practices that is not specific to a particular sexuality. There's also that whole confusion of whether a teabagger is someone who engages in the sexual practice or is a member of the Tea Party Movement.

[19] It might seem that this study is counterevidence to the observation that there are more slurs for men than women; however, my feeling is that the men in my class were simply more competitive, trying to come up with more terms for women than the women could for men. In the end, they were scraping the bottom of the barrel, listing words that most of the women were unfamiliar with (e.g., *carrot peeler, cookie bumper, knobgobbler, sackgulper, clamjammer*), as well as terms that seemed outdated (e.g., *succubus, harlot, Jezebel, streetwalker*).

Even though we speak of terms as being "slurs for males" or "slurs for females," many terms can be used for both sexes. It's interesting to note that in the studies by the Bad Words and Taboo Terms class, *douchebag* is male-referential, while James (1998) puts it in the female-referential category, though she admits that it was more ambiguous than most. In fact, James found that all terms in her study could be used for either sex. She goes on to suggest that this may be a recent innovation: "Although no firm data exist as to the extent to which derogatory terms could be used for the non-preferred sex in the usage of previous generations of speakers, older speakers have often expressed surprise to me that terms such as *slut* would be used for men or *dick* for women" (1998, 411).

For what it's worth, women in Risch's (1987) study said that *bitch, slut,* and *whore* could be used as slurs for men. When we look at the history, terms that are presently used as slurs for women began life as derogatory terms for either sex: *bitch* and *harlot* were originally applied to both men and women (Hughes 1991, 209). Read (1977), quoting Eric Partridge, reports that among World War I soldiers, *cunt* was used to refer to men and inanimate objects. In British English today, it seems that *cunt* is often directed at men: McEnery (2006) reports that "*Cunt* is directed exclusively at males by females" (38), and males direct *cunt* predominantly at males, though they also direct it at females.

In sum, slurs for men and women can tell us a lot about our culture's view of the sexes. Most slurs for men are based on disrespecting others. The most offensive slurs for men are derived from homosexual slurs. Most slurs for women are based on promiscuity. The most offensive slurs for women are derived from obscenity for female genitalia. There are differences in how the sexes use slurs, as well. Women may use certain terms for women (especially *bitch*) jokingly or affectionately, but men are not "allowed" to use these terms in the same fashion. Also, men and women may not agree on what the slurs mean when they're applied; men may view certain terms (e.g., *manwhore, milf*) as compliments, while women view them as derogatory, and there may be nuance differences between the meanings of the terms (e.g., men include 'dirty' or 'undesirable' in the meaning of *slut*, while women think of it as just meaning 'promiscuous').

5. CONCLUSION

Although it is commonly believed (even by linguists) than men swear more than women, at least for English speakers, it is more accurate to say that men tend to swear more in public than women. In general, men and women probably swear about the same amount, but men tend to use stronger taboo words and women tend to use weaker ones. These differences between males' and females' swearing may be more or less prominent depending on age and social class.

Regardless of the reality, if men are perceived to swear more and if it is more acceptable for men to swear, it is a different social act when a man swears and when a woman swears. Men and women swear for different reasons: men tend to use swearing to express their emotions, to emphasize points, and out of habit, while women tend to use swearing as feedback in a conversation and to create intimacy among friends. Both sexes swear while telling stories or jokes. Men may swear more in public and use stronger taboo words because they tend to perceive swear words and swearing as less taboo than women do. Another reason may have to do with biology; however, there is little evidence to demonstrate this as of yet.

One place where our society's values and prejudices can be seen is in the slurs we use for the sexes. Slurs for men tend to target disagreeable behavior in general, while slurs for women tend to specifically target promiscuity. Furthermore, slurs for women tend to be more offensive than those for men; this is most obvious when we compare the slurs for men derived from male genitalia, *cock* and *dick,* with a slur for women derived from female genitalia, *cunt*—there is no doubt that *cunt* is far more taboo and offensive than *cock* and *dick.* The most severe slurs for men are derived from homosexual slurs (e.g., *cocksucker, fag(got)*), but homosexual-derived slurs are less common for women and less offensive.

There is some evidence that men and women use the same slurs but have different meanings for them—for example, *manwhore* may be negative for women and positive for men. Also it's more acceptable for a woman to use a female-directed slur affectionately than it is for a man to do so.

REFERENCES

ASA. 2000. Delete Expletives? Electronic file accessible from http://www.asa.org.uk/Resource-Centre/Reports-and-surveys.aspx (accessed 8/13/2010).

Baldwin, Martina. 2009. *What's up, Bitch? Women's Use of a Derogatory Word.* Unpublished masters thesis, California State University, Fullerton.

Belmont Report. 1979. Ethical Principles and Guidelines for the Protection of Human Subjects of Research. http://www.hhs.gov/ohrp/humansubjects/guidance/belmont.htm#xethical (accessed 8/18/2010).

Berges, E.T., S. Neiderbach, B. Rubin, E.F. Sharpe, and R.W. Tesler. 1983. *Children & Sex: The Parents Speak.* New York: Facts on File.

Coates, Jennifer. 1993. *Women, Men and Language: A Sociolinguistic Account of Gender Differences in Language.* New York: Longman.

Coates, Jennifer. 2003. *Men Talk: Stories in the Making of Masculinities.* Malden, MA: Blackwell.

Coyne, James C., Richard C. Sherman, and Karen O'Brien. 1978. Expletives and Woman's Place. *Sex Roles* 4: 827–35.

Ethnologue. English. http://www.ethnologue.com/show_language.asp?code=eng (accessed 11/14/08)

Fine, Marlene G., and Fern L. Johnson. 1984. Female and Male Motives for Using Obscenity. *Journal of Language and Social Pscyhology* 3: 59–74.

Harrison, David. 2007. *When Languages Die: The Extinction of the World's Languages and the Erosion of Human Knowledge.* New York: Oxford University Press.

Hughes, Geoffrey. 1991. *Swearing: A Social History of Foul Language, Oaths, and Profanity in English.* Oxford: Blackwell.

Hughes, Susan E. 1992. Expletives of Lower Working Class Women. *Language in Society* 21(2): 291–303.

ISNA. http://www.isna.org (accessed 11/14/08).

James, Deborah. 1998. Gender-linked Derogatory Terms and their Use by Women and Men. *American Speech* 73(4): 399–420.

Jay, Timothy. 1992. *Cursing in America.* Philadelphia: John Benjamins.

Jay, Timothy. 2000. *Why We Curse.* Philadelphia: John Benjamins.

Jespersen, Otto. 1922. *Language: Its Nature, Origin and Development.* London: Allen and Unwin.

Labov, William, Sharon Ash, and Charles Boberg. 2005. *The Atlas of North American English: Phonetics, Phonology, and Sound Change.* The Hague: Mouton de Gruyter.

Lakoff, Robin. 1975. *Language and Women's Place.* New York: Harper and Row.

McDavid, Hans and Raven I. Kurath. 1961. *The Pronunciation of English in the Atlantic States: Based Upon the Collections of the Linguistic Atlas of the Eastern United States.* Ann Arbor: University of Michigan Press.

McEnery, Anthony. 2006. *Swearing in English: Bad Language, Purity and Power from 1586 to the present.* New York: Routledge.

McEnery, Anthony, and Zhonghua Xiao. 2004. Swearing in Modern British English: The Case of *fuck* in the BNC. *Language and Literature* 13(3): 235–268.

Read, Allen 1934. An Obscenity Symbol. *American Speech* 19(4): 264–278.

Read, Allen. 1977. *Classic American Graffiti: Lexical Evidence from Folk Epigraphy in Western North America.* Waukesha, WI: Maledicta Press.

Risch, Barbara. 1987. Women's Derogatory Terms for Men: That's Right, "Dirty" Words. *Language in Society* 16(3): 353–358.

Stapleton, Karyn. 2003. Gender and Swearing: A Community Practice. *Women and Language* 26: 2, 22–33.

Stenström, Anna-Brita. 1991. Expletives in the London-Lund Corpus. In *English Corpus Linguistics: Studies in Honour of Jan Svartvik,* (eds.) Karin Aijmer and Bengt Altenberg. New York: Longman.

Sutton, Laurel A. 1995. Bitches and Skankly Hobags: The Place of Women in Contemporary Slang. In *Gender Articulated: Language and the Socially Constructed Self,* (eds.) Kira Hall and Mary Bucholtz. New York: Routledge.

Trudgill, Peter. 1974. *Sociolinguistics.* Harmondsworth: Penguin.

1. Design a study to determine whether or not girls are punished more harshly for swearing than boys are.

2. In your opinion, what are the four most commonly used slurs for men and for women? Give your list of eight slurs to ten friends (five women, five men) and have them define each term. Are there differences between the ways that the sexes define the terms?

3. Survey your friends (aim for an equal number of male and female subjects) as to whether there are any swear words they think are more appropriate for men to use and whether there are any they think are more appropriate for women to use. If so, which words are appropriate to which sex? Do your male and female friends agree?

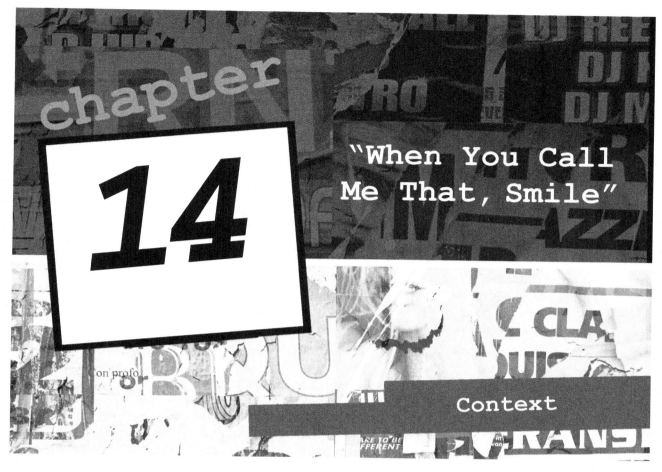

"When You Call
Me That, Smile"

Context

1.   INTRODUCTION: IT DEPENDS ON THE CONTEXT

"It depends on the context." People say this all the time. And they're right. *It* does depend on the context. In fact, *it* is one of those words that requires a context to be understood. Consider (1).

1.   Give it to me.

Nothing remarkable about this sentence. I'm sure you've said and heard it many times. However, what *it* refers to is different with each context. And once we bring context into our discussion of meaning, we are in the domain of **pragmatics.**

To some degree, whenever we interpret what somebody has said, we draw on the context. Consider the following sentence, already discussed in Chapters 4 and 6.

2.   You want to go get some shit to eat?

As I indicate in Chapter 4, (2) was uttered in the University of Utah's student union building by a male roughly twenty years old, and it was addressed to three males about the same age as the speaker. Given that context, how should we interpret the referent of "shit" in (2)? Should we take the word in its core meaning of 'feces'? That is, should we infer that the speaker is a coprophagist and is inquiring of his compatriots whether they would like to join him in his coprophagy? Unlikely.[1]

More likely, given this context, he was using *shit* to mean 'something'. On the other hand, in another context, as, for example, a bit of dialogue in a short story about dung beetles, the "shit" in (2) could refer to 'feces'. *Shit* depends on the context.

---

[1] According to Fossey (1983, 46), "The eating of excrement occurs among most vertebrates, including humans, who have certain nutritional deficiencies." Beck & Frohberg (2005) found cases of coprophagia among people with mental disorders, especially mental retardation and schizophrenia, but only one case in a non-psychotic adult of normal intelligence, and he was alcoholic and severely depressed. Seeing that the utterer of (2) was apparently well nourished, of average intelligence, and non-psychotic, it's highly unlikely that he was a coprophagist.

Assuming that the young man who uttered (2) is not a coprophagist, then why would he ask his friends if they "want to go get some shit to eat"? For that matter, why do potheads refer to potent marijuana as "good shit"? And why is it an insult to say (3) but a compliment to say (4)?

3.   You're a piece of shit.

4.   You're the shit.

To some degree, we have to say that *shit* is ambiguous. For example, the expression in (4), *be the shit*, is an idiom meaning 'really good', and, as an idiom, speakers simply memorize the meaning of this expression.[2] The context helps to disambiguate ambiguous sentences.

Moving on, right now I'd like to talk about the Old West. Gun slingers. Cattle rustlers. Poker games. If you watched any of HBO's *Deadwood,* you likely got the impression that the wild west was rife with taboo words. And it probably was. But not with the ones used on the show. Not *fuck, asshole, cocksucker,* and *motherfucker.* As Geoffrey Nunberg puts it:

> The words those "Deadwood" characters would actually have used had religious overtones rather than sexual or scatological ones. They would have peppered their speech with "goddamn," "Jesus," and particularly "hell," a word that 19th-century Americans were famous for using with a dazzling virtuosity—"a hell of a drink," "What in hell did that mean?," "hell to pay," "The hell you will," "hell-bent," "Hell, yes," "like a bat out of hell," "hell's bells," and countless others.[3] (http://people.ischool.berkeley.edu/~nunberg/deadwood.html, accessed 8/19/08)

But what about slurs? If they didn't say "motherfucker" or "cocksucker" what did they say? For that, we can go to Owen Wister's novel, *The Virginian,* published in 1902 and based on Wister's travels in Wyoming during the 1880s and 1890s. Wister (or his publisher) was too squeamish to actually print the full version of what he called "a term of heaviest insult." What was this horrible slur? Wister gives it as "You're such a son-of-a———." Fill in the blank.

What shocks Wister's city dude of a narrator is that the Virginian, a rough cowpoke with a six-shooter on his belt, doesn't take offense the first time this "term of heaviest insult" is used against him. The term is used by the Virginian's friend Steve, and Wister's narrator observes (pp. 10–11):

> I had expected that the man would be struck down . . . I had marveled to hear it come so unheralded from Steve's friendly lips. And now I marveled still more. Evidently he had meant no harm by it, and evidently no offence had been taken. Used thus, this language was plainly complimentary.

Later in the chapter, however, the narrator is witness to another incident in which the Virginian is slurred with this same term, this time in a tense poker game. Trampas, the novel's villain, is introduced in the scene. He and the Virginian are strangers, and Trampas, as a character observes, "don't enjoy losin' to a stranger." Trampas has been goading the Virginian throughout the game, and the tension has risen:

> It was now the Virginian's turn to bet, or leave the game, and he did not speak at once.
>
> Therefore, Trampas spoke. "Your bet, you son-of-a———."
>
> The Virginian's pistol came out, and his hand lay on the table, holding it unaimed. And with a voice as gentle as ever, the voice that sounded almost like a caress, but drawling a very little more than usual, so that there was almost a space between each word, he issued his orders to the man Trampas:—
>
> "When you call me that, *smile!*" (p. 21)

A few paragraphs later, the narrator observes:

> Once again I had heard applied to the Virginian that epithet which Steve so freely used. The same words, identical to the letter. But this time they had produced a pistol . . . So I perceived a new example of the old truth, that the letter means nothing until the spirit gives it life. (p. 22)

---

[2] In the same way, speakers simply have to memorize that *spill the beans* means 'divulge a secret' and *kick the bucket* means 'die'.
[3] See Chapter 1, Section 2.1 for a longer list of *hell* expressions.

More prosaically, the primary difference between the two name-callings in Wister's novel is in the speakers' intentions. As a part of the context, speaker **intentions** are a big part of pragmatics. When we talk about the **pragmatic meaning** of a sentence, we need to consider all aspects of the context: what was said, who said it, who they said it to, who else was there, where they said it, when they said it, how they said it, why they said it, etc.

2. PRAGMATICS DEFINED (SORT OF)

Many linguists have given definitions for pragmatics, and none is completely satisfactory. The standard definition is "the study of language use," but that definition is too broad and would include **anthropological linguistics** (see Chapter 10), **sociolinguistics** (see Chapter 13), and possibly **psycholinguistics** (see Chapter 12). I like Kent Bach's (1999, 74) definition: "[S]emantic information pertains to linguistic expressions, whereas pragmatic information pertains to utterances and facts surrounding them." I like this definition, but that doesn't mean you have to. Rather than trying to explain why it's a good definition we'll follow another approach suggested by Bach (1999, 65): "The distinction between semantics and pragmatics is easier to apply than to explain."

In Chapters 2 and 4, we discussed semantic meaning. I argue that semantic meaning has three components: informative, emotional, and social. Semantic meaning relies on the arbitrary linguistic conventions of the language (see Chapter 5). When we study semantics, we look at the linguistic meaning of words and sentences (propositions in semantic terminology).

The object of study in pragmatics is the **utterance**. An utterance, simply put, is what is produced when a person uses a linguistic expression. Thus, every sentence of this book you're reading counts as an utterance. Including that last one—and this one. Whoa.[4] Dude![5] Utterances are when a speaker takes the tools of the grammar and lexicon and puts them to use in creating speech or writing.

Sentences are grammatical objects; they are the output of a mental grammar. Utterances are pragmatic objects; they are the output of language use. Both sentences and utterances have meaning, and, obviously, an utterance's meaning is directly related to the meaning of its sentential counterpart. However, a basic tenet of pragmatics is that **sentence meaning** underspecifies **utterance meaning**. To see this, consider (5).[6]

5. I haven't had breakfast yet.

What do you understand (5) to mean? Do you understand it to mean that the speaker has never had breakfast? Ever? A more likely interpretation would be that the speaker meant she hadn't had breakfast yet that day. On the other hand, (6) is more likely to have the 'ever' interpretation.

6. I haven't had sex yet.

Grammatically, the two sentences are similar, yet we interpret them differently. Why? Pragmatics. In interpreting (5–6) we bring in non-linguistic knowledge to understand the most likely interpretation. In our society, it is commonly understood that people have breakfast each morning, so we interpret (5) to pragmatically mean 'I haven't had breakfast yet today'. But it is not commonly understood that people have sex each morning.

Of course, we can construct a context in which (6) could have the 'today' interpretation. Imagine your friend Abigail has told you that she and her husband have made a pact that for a month they will have sex every morning before they get up. You phone Abigail to see if she wants to meet you at the farmer's market in fifteen minutes, and her answer is (6), in which case you will understand her to mean 'I haven't had sex yet today', not 'I haven't had sex yet in my life'.

We could construct all sorts of other contexts that will lead to all sorts of other interpretations. The point is that the sentence itself can only take us so far; we need the context to help us fully interpret an utterance. And a big part of the context is the speaker's intentions.

Our understanding of (5) and (6) comes from our ability to mind-read. I don't mean ESP. I mean we make calculated guesses as to what's going on in a person's mind. When a stranger approaches you on a street corner and asks (7), you know "yes" would be an insufficient answer.

7. Do you know what time it is?

---

[4] Utterance.

[5] Ditto.

[6] Examples (5–6) adapted from Horn (2005).

When asked this question, you calculate that the stranger doesn't care about your knowledge so much as your ability to impart that knowledge to him. That is, you read into this simple question to arrive at the idea that the stranger wants to know the time.

But the speaker may have quite different intentions in a different context. This time, imagine you're hosting a party, there is loud knocking at your door, you open it to find your next door neighbor, and she utters (7). This time, you can be pretty confident your neighbor knows the time and her intention is for you to become aware of the time, realize it is late, and conclude you should be quieter.

In yet another context, we may infer that (7) is a rhetorical question. For example, if it were spoken by the host of a radio show, it may be the set-up to announce the next segment of the show.

We humans are pretty good mind readers. Most of the time we can calculate a speaker's intentions. We don't even notice when we get it right. It's when we miscalculate that we remark on it.

Returning to example (2), repeated here, we know the speaker's friends didn't interpret the utterance literally.

A few years ago I was chatting with a friend in a coffee shop when a man walked up to us carrying a chess board. He said to my friend, "Do you play chess?" My friend said she did. We both expected the man to then ask if she wanted to play a game. But instead, he went to the next table and asked the same question, listened to the answer, and proceeded to the next table. The patrons in the shop exchanged confused glances with each other, looked at the man, and collectively shook their heads. I never learned what his intentions were, and that's why I remember the incident.

2. You want to go get some shit to eat?

Instead, the friends calculated what he meant: that he was asking them if they wanted to get food to eat; that he was asking if they wanted to join him in getting food to eat; that he was making light of the suggestion by choosing the word *shit*; that he was probably commenting on the quality of food they were likely to find; etc.

3. SPEECH ACTS

Recall in Chapter 4 we discussed the three communicative functions of language: informative, social, and emotional. The idea is that there are conventional linguistic means for communicating each of these. For example, "Ouch!" is a conventional way of expressing pain. As we discussed, the word itself doesn't have any informative or social functions, which is to say that in a speaker's mental lexicon, *ouch* is linked only to the emotion 'pain'. However, when the word is used, it can convey information (e.g., 'you are standing on my foot') and may act as a demand that requires a social response (e.g., 'step off my foot'). This information and demand are not built into *ouch*, since we can use the word without them being communicated. Again, it depends on context and the hearer's ability to read the speaker's intentions.

We don't usually think of talking as being an active pursuit. However, utterances themselves are acts—social acts. Just as you can physically perform social acts by, say, shaking hands, waving, patting a person on the back, flipping the bird, even slapping a person across the face with your suede glove, you can perform these same acts with words: *it's a deal, hi, good job, fuck you, I challenge you to a duel.* When we use language to perform an act, we call it a speech act. Some speech acts can be seen in (8–12).

8. I promise to never use a naughty word again.

9. I bet you ten bucks you can't go a whole day without cussing.

10. I now pronounce you husband and wife.

11. I do solemnly swear (or affirm) that I will faithfully execute the office of President of the United States, and will to the best of my ability, preserve, protect and defend the Constitution of the United States. (Article II, Section I of the US Constitution)

12. On my honor, I affirm that I have neither given nor received inappropriate aid in the completion of this exercise. (The University of Oklahoma Student Association Integrity Pledge)

In these examples we can see that speech acts have real-world consequences. When you promise something, you are obligated to carry through on the promise. When you bet, you must pay the stake if you lose. When a judge or properly ordained spiritual leader utters (10), two people transition from being unmarried to married. In the right circumstances, (11) marks the peaceful transfer of power in the United States. And (12) reinforces the assumption that a University of Oklahoma student has not cheated on an assignment. Note that in each case, the subject of the sentence is *I* and the main verb is in simple present tense: *promise, bet, pronounce, swear, affirm.* We call these **speech act verbs.** When used as in sentences (8–12), these speech act verbs simultaneously describe and perform the speech act; in other words (8) is a promise, (9) is a bet, (10) is a pronouncement, (11) is an oath, and (12) is an affirmation.

We don't have to use the speech act verbs to perform the relevant acts, though. (13–17), in the right contexts, can be the same sorts of speech acts as (8–12).[7]

13. I will be there to pick you up at the airport.

14. Ten bucks says nobody breaks two hours in the marathon this year.

15. And the winner of this year's *Professor Potty Mouth Award* is Abigail Yuasa.

16. I will uphold my duties as *Professor Potty Mouth* to the best of my ability.

17. I am not now, nor have I ever been, affiliated with a law enforcement organization.

In fact, some speech acts do not allow speech act verbs, for example, compliments and insults (# indicates that an utterance is pragmatically odd):

18. #I insult you that you smell like a goat.

19. #I compliment you that you have nice teeth.

Regardless of whether or not an utterance contains a speech act verb, all utterances are speech acts. Even utterances that do nothing more than state a fact or an opinion are speech acts. Although we rarely compose statements of fact or opinion with speech act verbs, we can:

20. I opine that regardless of whether an utterance contains a speech act verb, all utterances are speech acts.

21. I assert that even utterances that do nothing more than state a fact or an opinion are speech acts.

22. I state that although we rarely write such sentences with speech act verbs, we can.

Austin (1962) divides a speech act into three aspects: **locution, illocution,** and **perlocution.** The locution is the form of the utterance; it includes the grammatical representation of the sentence, how loud it is said, the tone of voice, etc. The illocution is the social purpose of the utterance: a request, a statement, an order, an apology, an expression of thanks, a christening, a promise, a threat, a greeting, a farewell, a proposal, an oath, an epithet, an insult, etc. Finally, we have the perlocution, which is the effect an utterance has on its recipient. For example, when you say, "Ouch!" the perlocutionary effect may be for your friend to step off your foot. However, perlocutions are less predictable than locutions or illocutions; if your friend is sadistic, she might simply smile when you say, "Ouch!"

Location comes from the Latin word *loquī* 'to speak'; thus the locution is the result of speaking. For our purposes, it is anything that can be described with the lexicon, phonetics (including pitch and loudness), and the core modules of grammar (phonology, morphology, syntax, and semantics). Austin added the prefix *in-* 'in' to create illocution; thus the illocution is what is produced in saying the locution (i.e., the intended speech act). Finally, perlocution incorporates the prefix *per-* 'by'; the perlocution is what is produced by saying the locution (i.e., the effect on the hearer).

Some illocutions are entirely formulaic, which is to say there's only one possible locution. For example, the Presidential Oath of Office for the United States is spelled out in the Constitution. When swearing in Barack Obama, Chief Justice Roberts misplaced an adverb, so he later re-administered the oath to Obama with the correct wording (Shear 2009).

Insults, in contrast, are valued for their innovation. Nevertheless, there may be a formulaic aspect to them, as with "Your Mama" jokes (e.g., *Your Mama's so bony skeletons dress up as her for Halloween*), where the "Your Mama's so . . ." part is fixed and the challenge is to find a new way to finish the insult (see Chapter 1, Section 4.2.3).

---

[7] Some specific contexts, such as the swearing in of the President of the United States, require a speech act verb. See the side bar on page.

When you stub your toe and say one of (23–27), your intent may be to vent emotion, which is to say, the illocutionary act is an exclamation.

23. Motherfucker.

24. Damn.

25. Fuck.

26. Son of a bitch.

27. Shit.

Around some people, say a concerned friend, the perlocutionary effect may be to offer sympathy or to ask if you're all right. Around others, however, the perlocutionary effect may be to take offense at the choice of words. Just as context is important in reading a speaker's intentions, it's equally important in determining how a recipient may respond to an utterance.

Because sentence meaning underspecifies utterance meaning, we communicate more than we say. In previous chapters, we've already seen how versatile taboo words can be. Depending on the context, each sentence in (23–27) can convey a wide range of informative, social, or emotional functions at the level of pragmatic meaning.

Now assume that (23) was uttered by Grant in close proximity to Gertrude after knocking over a cup of coffee. We can make certain guesses about Grant and Gertrude, simply based on this skeletal context. Because Grant chose to use a taboo word instead of a more neutral term, Gertrude is, most likely, an adult. This guess doesn't come from any linguistic knowledge. It comes because we are aware of social practices in the English-speaking world. Moreover, Grant and Gertrude are probably not strangers. How do we know this? Again, it's based on our extra-linguistic knowledge of social practices. You can test your own intuition to see whether it aligns with mine. Finally, in all probability, Grant and Gertrude are peers or Grant is in a position of power over Gertrude.

Notice that I keep hedging by saying, "most likely," "probably," and "in all probability." In pragmatics, we can't speak in absolutes. When we discuss grammar, we can say that a linguistic expression is grammatical or not, but when discussing pragmatics,

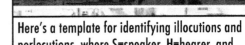

Here's a template for identifying illocutions and perlocutions, where S=speaker, H=hearer, and L=locution:

Illocution: In saying L, what was S doing?
Perlocution: After hearing L, what did H do?

For example, if L is "I'll fuck you up," we could answer the questions as follows:

Illocution: In saying "I'll fuck you up," S was threatening H.
Perlocution: After hearing "I'll fuck you up," H was frightened.

This is one possibility. We could imagine, however, that H is not easily frightened, in which case a more likely perlocution might be for H to threaten or even attack S. That is, the second part could be:

Perlocution: After hearing "I'll fuck you up," H slapped S.

One more example: If L is "Your shit stinks" we might get:

Illocution: In saying "Your shit stinks," S was stating a fact.
Perlocution: After hearing "Your shit stinks," H was insulted.

Or

Illocution: In saying "Your shit stinks," S was informing H.
Perlocution: After hearing "Your shit stinks," H flushed the toilet.

it's impossible to say definitively that a given utterance, tied to a given context, is appropriate or inappropriate.

Imagine different scenarios for why somebody might utter one of (23–27), and for each scenario consider how old you think the individuals are and what their relationship is. In my experience, people are generally more careful how they speak in front of children, strangers, and superiors than they are in front of adults, friends, peers, and inferiors. More to the point, people are more likely to swear in front of adults, friends, peers, and people socially below them. This is a hypothesis. Of course, a hypothesis should be tested on data. I will leave it as an exercise to design a test for the hypothesis.

Let's consider (27), repeated below, in some detail.

27. Shit.

In some contexts, it could be used to simultaneously convey information and a warning, roughly, 'look out, there's fecal matter right there'. This illocution might be in a context where the hearer is in imminent danger of treading on said fecal matter. In another context, while still being informative, it might lack the warning aspect while still communicating 'there's fecal matter right there'. This might be in a context where the speaker is a supervisor and the hearer is a worker assigned to clean a park. In this context, (27) would not only be informative but also be illocutionarily a reprimand.

Note that in both of these situations, the speaker chose to use a taboo word, instead of, say, *poo*. This choice conveys something as well. It carries with it the emotional weight discussed in Chapter 4, and additionally a social meaning; not only can we infer something about the relationship between the speaker and hearer of (27), as we did previously, but I think we can see that *you missed that bit of poo* is less of a reprimand than *you missed that bit of shit*.

Of course, (27) may lack any informative function. It could simply be an exclamation or response cry (see Chapter 4). But, then, the response cry could be used strategically to convey further pragmatic information. For example, (27) could be uttered while trying and failing to complete a difficult task. In such cases, the meaning 'feces' is not involved at all, only the emotional meaning. Yet, often in such situations, the speaker intends for the hearer to recognize that she is having troubles with the task and, moreover, wishes the hearer to help her. Thus, (27) could be an indirect request for help. This indirect approach is useful because it allows a speaker to make a request "off the record" (see Chapter 6 on indirectness as a strategy for preserving face).

When a speaker performs a speech act through non-conventional means, we call it an **indirect speech act**. In contrast, a **direct speech act** (or just **speech act**) uses conventional means to convey a social function. In Chapter 4, we talked of words having a conventional social function. Other aspects of language also have conventional social functions, namely intonation and sentence structure. A rising intonation at the end of a sentence conveys a question, which has the social function of requesting information. Similarly, an imperative sentence typically has the social function of ordering or requesting an action, as with (28–30):

28. Clean your room.

29. Help me.

(28) is probably an order and (29) is probably a request. But let's consider (30).

30. Fuck me.

As an imperative, it would seem that (30) should act as a request on the part of the hearer to perform a particular sexual act on the speaker. As we've seen, however, the context in which a sentence is uttered can affect what is communicated. Certainly, there are occasions when (30) is a request. Not always, though. The first time I heard (30) used as a non-request, it was spoken by an English man. A bunch of us were cliff-jumping into a mountain lake. The Brit had never swum in a snow-fed lake before, and when he surfaced after his jump, he shouted (30). Clearly, he did not intend it as a request or an order. See Chapter 9 on the different uses of *fuck me*.

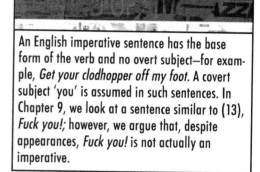

An English imperative sentence has the base form of the verb and no overt subject—for example, *Get your clodhopper off my foot*. A covert subject 'you' is assumed in such sentences. In Chapter 9, we look at a sentence similar to (13), *Fuck you!*; however, we argue that, despite appearances, *Fuck you!* is not actually an imperative.

Finally, we should discuss the difference between **tabooness** and **offensiveness**. As I argue throughout this book, tabooness is a semantic phenomenon, part of the social meaning of a word or expression. In Chapter 6, we argue that offensiveness is a pragmatic phenomenon. In the present terms, offensiveness is part of the perlocutionary effect of an utterance. Of course, we can estimate that the more taboo the locution is, the more likely the utterance is to be offensive. However, some utterances that tend to be offensive, like "Shut up!," do not contain any taboo words. And, depending on the context, uttering a taboo word may not be offensive. If tabooness is part of our mental grammar, and offensiveness is part of pragmatics, then we should expect that people will have more similar intuitions about which words are taboo than about which words are offensive. This is an empirical question, one that warrants further research.

4. POLYSEMY

Polysemy is a subtype of homophony (see Chapter 2), sometimes described as one word having several meanings. But when we say that a word has several meanings, what we really mean is that, over time, a single word has evolved into multiple words, each with different meanings. Intuitively, we know the words are related, but the meanings are different enough to warrant calling them different words. Take, for example, the different meanings of *light:* i) "electromagnetic radiation to which the organs of sight react, ranging in wavelength from about 400 to 700 nm and propagated at a speed of 186,282 mi./sec (299,972 km/sec), considered variously as a wave, corpuscular, or quantum phenomenon" (http://dictionary.reference.com/browse/light, accessed 6/16/09), as in *the sun gives off light;* ii) 'a source, typically electrical, of light [in sense (i)]', as in *turn on the light;* and iii) 'a source of fire', as in *do you have a light?* All of us recognize the relation between these three words; they are not like *pen* meaning 'a writing utensil using ink' and *pen* meaning 'a fenced in area for keeping domestic animals', which are totally unrelated. Yet the three *lights* are different enough to call them different words.

We've seen examples where taboo words have taken on a meaning or meanings different from the original: *shit* in (2); *son of a bitch* in Wister's text; certain uses of (23–27); and *fuck* in (30). It seems that taboo words are especially open to transformation. We could argue that these words are polysemous. For example, we could say that there are three different words with the sound form /ʃɪt/: $shit_1$, $shit_2$, and $shit_3$. $Shit_1$ denotes 'fecal matter', $shit_2$ denotes 'stuff', and $shit_3$ has no informative meaning, only social and emotional meanings. Examples (31–33) illustrate the three posited *shits,* and (34) incorporates them all into one *shit*-filled sentence.

31. Even Natalie Portman's $shit_1$ stinks.

32. Get your $shit_2$ together, we're going camping.

33. $Shit_3$!

34. $Shit_3$, if there weren't so many toys and balls and $shit_2$ in the yard, maybe I'd have seen the dog $shit_1$ before I stepped in it.

This is the approach advocated by Geurts (2007, 211), who uses *bastard* as an example: "like nearly all words *bastard* is polysemous, i.e. it has several related senses. The word *bastard* was initially used for persons born out of wedlock. From this meaning, its primary expressive sense ('unpleasant and/or despicable person') was derived, which in its turn spawned further senses."

I both agree and disagree with Geurts. Let's start with where I agree. Yes, there is a great deal of polysemy in language, and taboo words are no different in this regard. Chapter 9 demonstrates that there are at least two *fucks* in English and several *fuckings*. Moreover, I certainly agree that *bastard* has at least two senses: $bastard_1$ means 'child born out of wedlock' and $bastard_2$ means, as Geurts indicates, 'unpleasant and/or despicable person'. In Chapter 2 I quote Herman Jolly singing, "Just 'cause your mom and dad got wed doesn't mean that you can't be a bastard." Likewise, we can imagine saying of somebody, "his parents might not have been married but he's not a bastard."[8]

Where I disagree with Geurts is with respect to the "further senses" he mentions at the end of his quote. Here, he has in mind cases where *bastard* can be used affectionately, cases where it can be applied to inanimate objects, and cases where it is merely an exclamation, as in (35–37), respectively.

35. [In the comments to a blog where the author announces he has a new nickname] Am I still good calling you bastard? You know it is from the heart.
   (http://easyfiend.blogspot.com/2009/05/call-me-knee-bone.html, accessed 6/16/09)

36. I used to be someone, once, before the bastard internet shattered all my dreams
   (http://littleredboat.co.uk/?p=2376, accessed 6/26/09)

37. [Said after hitting thumb with hammer] Son of a fuck bastard.
   (From King Missile's "Pain Series 2 Hammer Thumb")

This is where I disagree with Geurts. The problem is that taboo words in general can be used affectionately, as in (38–41),[9] and figuratively, as in (42–44).

38. You one smart motherfucker.
   (from *Pulp Fiction*)

39. We miss you crazy shithead!
   (http://serrifth.deviantart.com/art/OZYMANDIAS-STAAAAMP-115084059, accessed 6/16/09)

---

[8] Interestingly, I find it harder to imagine somebody uttering a sentence that uses the original sense while denying the later one (e.g., (i)).
   i. He may be a bastard, but he's not unpleasant or despicable.
   (i) works best for me in the context of dialogue in a historical novel taking place at a time when the original sense would have been more commonly used.
[9] Also cf. Steve's utterance from *The Virginian* discussed at the beginning of the chapter.

40. You'll never know, you wonderful bitch, how grateful I am for this night . . .
   (Miller 1994, 15)

41. Damn fine coffee! And hot!
   (Agent Cooper, *Twin Peaks*)

42. Life's a bitch and then you die.

43. Yesterday at midnight, I thought it was hot as hell, went to check the AC, and guess what, it's 80 degrees and the motherfucker stopped working.
   (http://www.srtforums.com/forums/f348/anybody-electrician-377293/, accessed 6/24/09)

44. The iPhone is a piece of shit, and so is your face.
   (http://www.thebestpageintheuniverse.net/c.cgi?u=iphone, accessed 6/24/09)

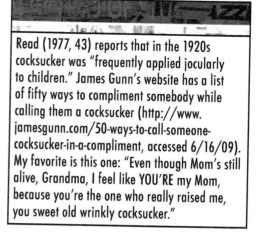

Read (1977, 43) reports that in the 1920s cocksucker was "frequently applied jocularly to children." James Gunn's website has a list of fifty ways to compliment somebody while calling them a cocksucker (http://www.jamesgunn.com/50-ways-to-call-someone-cocksucker-in-a-compliment, accessed 6/16/09). My favorite is this one: "Even though Mom's still alive, Grandma, I feel like YOU'RE my Mom, because you're the one who really raised me, you sweet old wrinkly cocksucker."

Simply saying the words are polysemous strikes me as a cop-out. It misses a generalization.

There is a principle of science widely used in linguistics: **Occam's Razor.** In a nut-shell, Occam's Razor tells us the simplest solution is the best one. More specifically, in pragmatics this has been cast as "[s]enses are not to be multiplied beyond necessity" (Grice 1989, 47). What this means: Don't assume polysemy unless you have to.

Let's start with the affectionate uses. In Potts' (2007) semantic analysis of taboo words (what he calls "expressives"), he characterizes them as negative; however, he acknowledges that they can be used positively at times. He has no real solution to this problem, and Geurts' suggestion of polysemy is offered as one. Keeping Occam's razor in mind, let's see if there's another solution.

The fact is that this is not unique to taboo words—for example, non-taboo negative words, like *idiot*, *dummy, ugly, ridiculous,* etc. can be used the same way.

45. *The Complete Idiot's Guide to Clear Thinking*
   (by LoCicero, LoCicero, & LoCicero, published by Alpha)

46. *English Grammar for Dummies*
   (by Woods, published by For Dummies)

47. MY UGLY (by ugly I mean adorable) LITTLE PUSSY![10]
   (http://www.youtube.com/watch?v=5pwwseWL5x8, accessed 6/23/09)

48. Bands nominated for Mercury Prize see ridiculous jump in sales
   (http://www.prefixmag.com/news/bands-nominated-for-mercury-prize-see-ridiculous-j/21673/, accessed 6/23/09)

These strike me as being ironic uses of the words. If we were to posit polysemy every time a word is used ironically or sarcastically, our lexicon would expand dramatically. On the other hand, if we recognize that any negative word can be used positively (and any positive word negatively), we simply need a way of accounting for irony/sarcasm. It is beyond the scope of this book to dig into such an account, so we'll leave it with this: most positive uses of taboo words can be captured with a generalization rather than positing polysemy, and that generalization will almost certainly appeal to the context of use.

The same observation can be made for figurative uses (49–51), and again, the phenomenon is not unique to taboo words. For example, *girl* in (49), *fiám* 'my boy' in (52), and *baby* in (51).

49. OMG! Frank Lampard is SUCH a girl . . .
   (http://www.heatworld.com/Article/6071/OMG!+Frank+Lampard+is+SUCH+a+girl%E2%80%A6, accessed 6/23/09)

---

[10] FYI, this is the title of a video of a cat.

50. *Kedves Fiám.* 'my dear boy'
   [Hungarian term of endearment—Erika Sólyom (pers. comm.) once told me her grandmother used to say it to her]

51. This baby is black I'll tell ya, it's a dark ugly thing.
   (Utah State Senator Chris Buttars, said in reference to a pending state bill, 2/12/08)[11]

Finally, we should address yet another point made by Potts (2007): taboo words lack any descriptive or propositional meaning. In Chapter 4, we said something similar when we observed that taboo words are often used without any informative function. Potts takes this further than we do, though, arguing that taboo words always lack informative meaning and have only an emotional ("expressive" in his terms) meaning—that is, the speaker[12] feels negatively towards something/somebody. This seems to be a fair analysis of at least some uses of taboo terms.

52. My son-of-a-bitch car won't start.

53. This piece of shit isn't worth a god-damn penny.

54. What a shitty situation!

55. Who in the hell asked you?

56. I've got to take the GR-fucking-E tomorrow.

If we remove the taboo expressions from (52–56), we get:

52' My car won't start.

53' This isn't worth a penny.

54' What a situation!

55' Who asked you?

56' I've got to take the GRE tomorrow.

The revised sentences still have the same informative meaning as the originals, but they lack oomph.

In my opinion, though, Potts takes this too far when he argues that taboo words lack informative meaning. Jay and Janschewitz (2007, 218–219) offer (57) and (58) to show that there can be a clear informative meaning to taboo words. Expanding on these examples, we can add (59) and (60).

57. The shitty little boy . . .

58. The little shitty boy . . .

59. I don't want to buy such a shitty diaper next time.

60 I don't want to change such a shitty diaper next time.

In (57) and (59), we're likely to get an emotional, non-informative meaning for *shitty* (i.e., the speaker has negative feelings towards the little boy or diaper), while in (58) and (60) we're likely to get a literal, informative meaning for *shitty* (i.e., the little boy needs his diaper changed/the diaper is full of excrement). As I suggested in Chapter 4, highly emotional terms can have their informative meaning bleached out of them, as in (52–56), (57), and (59). The syntax can sometimes help us to determine when a term is being used purely to express emotions, as with (52), (55), (56) and (57), but most of the time we have to rely on the context.

In sum, although taboo words may have a wide range of uses, we should not automatically assume that each use of a term is a different sense. That is, we should not assume that taboo terms are wildly polysemous. First of all, certain non-taboo terms show similar patterns of usage. And second of all, applying Occam's razor, we should look for a generalization to account for the uses. In this case, the generalization will appeal to the context and, therefore, will be pragmatic.

Of course, we don't want to exclude the possibility of polysemy. Many words, including taboo words, are polysemous. However, polysemy should be posited only when no other explanation is plausible. In Chapter 7, we discuss the case of *gay*, which diverged into two words—one meaning 'happy' and the other 'homosexual'—and

---

[11] Buttars apologized for the remark later that afternoon, noting that people might find it racist. Many groups subsequently called for his resignation.

[12] Potts notes that in some contexts it is not the speaker's feelings that are expressed but some other salient individual's.

today may be diverging into yet another word meaning 'lame' or 'uncool'. Spears (2006) argues that *nigger* has now diverged into two words: one commonly spelled *nigger* and the other commonly spelled *nigga.*

> The first one nowadays (the historical period and communities one speaks of are always important) is primarily a term of abuse leveled at those of African descent. It carries great psychological baggage, and its use can cause serious bodily harm. *Nigga,* spelled thus, to distinguish it, is highly versatile in terms of use, ranging from invective to term of endearment. (Spears 2006)

Not all scholars agree with Spears that *nigger* and *nigga* are separate words (see Asim 2007), but I think we could make a good case for it, simply based on public perception alone. For example, in 2005, Damon Wayans tried to trademark *nigga* to use on a clothing line (Cadenhead 2006).[13]

This brings us to our next point: whether or not *nigga* is a different word than *nigger,* we have to recognize it is still a taboo word. It may be less taboo than *nigger,* but it is taboo insofar as it is unacceptable for certain people in the speech community to use it. For some (but by no means all) African Americans, *nigga* is acceptable when used by an African American but only rarely acceptable when used by people of other races, especially whites (see Chapter 1 for further discussion). Pavlenko (2008) explains this phenomenon in terms of the "affective valence" being reversed in certain contexts:

At least as early as the 1930s, *nigger* was used affectionately among African Americans, but they objected to its use by whites. Lucius Harper, managing editor of the *Defender* wrote in 1939: "It is a common expression among the ordinary Negroes and is used frequently in conversation between them. It carries no odium or sting when used by themselves, but they object keenly to whites using it because it conveys the spirit of hate, discrimination and prejudice" (quoted in Mencken 1962, 626).

> [O]ne of the greatest taboo words of the English language, the n-word, would undoubtedly elicit strong reactions and very negative ratings from participants in any experiment. And yet this term does not function exclusively as a racial slur, it may also signal brotherhood in hip-hop lyrics or in friendly banter between African-American males, where it acquires a positive valence. What matters, then, is not only the word per se but who utters it and with what intent. Similarly, as we go about our daily lives, we may perceive words like *table* or *argument* as neutral. But if we hear the same seemingly neutral words on a street of a far-away city when we have been away from our native language for weeks or months, they may elicit a very emotional response of surprise and nostalgia. This differential perception of the same words suggests that words may have more than one emotional dimension, and that the contexts in which they are uttered may shape, rather than simply trigger, the perception of their affective valence and emotional force. (Pavlenko 2008, 200)

I would be reaching beyond my expertise as a linguist (and as a white person), if I were to discuss the merits of African Americans using *nigga.* However, I will speak to white people using it. Over the years, I have had students argue that if it is OK for African Americans to use *nigga,* it should be OK for white people. In my experience, those who argue this most vociferously are young white males. According to their argument it is a matter of justice: "If it is OK for one, it is OK for all." However, it strikes me the argument is tainted by a sense of entitlement: "If it is OK for one, it is OK for me." At this point, I am undoubtedly reaching beyond my expertise—so be it.

I have also heard white people argue that they should be able to say anything as long as their intentions are good. This ignores the complexity of language use. As discussed, Austin (1962) postulated the three aspects of an utterance: the locution, the illocution, and the perlocution. The locution represents the grammatical structure of the words uttered and their linguistic meaning. The illocution represents the intentions behind the utterance: its purpose and the speech act it represents (compliment, request, greeting, advice, statement, threat, etc.). And the perlocution represents the recipient's response to the utterance. Those who argue that intentions are sufficient ignore the conventional aspects of meaning inherent in the locution and the recipient's role in interpreting the utterance. We cannot ignore the fact that *nigga* is a slur (part of its conventional meaning). And we cannot ignore the fact that people are offended by the word, even by its mere utterance, even when they know the offense

---

[13] The judge denied the copyright, saying that "immoral or scandalous" trademarks are prohibited (Cadenhead 2006), so the judge might not have seen *nigger* and *nigga* as separate words.

was unintended—it taps into a part of our brain that resists rationalization. Nonetheless, we've seen that context can subvert this offense; in certain situations, uttered by certain individuals, we consider something inoffensive that would be offensive if uttered by anybody else in any other situation. This is analogous to physical displays of affection; a kiss from one person at the right moment is welcomed, but coming from another person or coming at the wrong time, it is repulsed. See Chapter 15 for more on the importance of illocutions and perlocutions, as well as linguistic conventions.

Finally, we should conclude by observing that taboo words are more flexible than other words—they have a wider range of possible uses. This is an important observation; however, we shouldn't stop at the observation. Just as prosecutors in a murder trial look for a motive, linguists look for an explanation. Why are taboo words so flexible? Here, I think Potts (2007) is on the right track: it almost certainly has to do with their emotional function. Because these words are more emotionally expressive than other words, they are prone to being used in contexts where none of their other functions are relevant. But there is probably more to it. In the next section, we'll see how closely tied taboo words are to the context they're used in.

5.   INDEXICALITY

Imagine you are walking along the beach, a bottle washes up on shore, and inside you find a piece of paper with (61) written on it.

61. After I got it from him, I forgot to send it to you.

What would we need to know to determine whether (61) is true or false? Well, among other things, we need to know who "I" refers to, what "it" refers to, who "him" refers to, and who "you" refers to. All that we can gather without context is that, assuming (61) is true, a certain somebody received a certain something from a certain male somebody and forgot to send it to a certain third party. This kind of context-independent information—that *he* refers to a male entity, *it* refers to a (typically) non-human entity, etc.—is the purview of semantics. The rest of it, the actual **reference** of the terms belongs to pragmatics.

Words like *this, that, I, you, they, here, now,* and *today* are called **indexicals.** *Indexical* comes from the Latin word for 'point'. The idea is that, unlike most words, the main function of indexicals is to point at something in the context. When I say "you," I linguistically point at whoever I'm speaking to. When I say "I," I linguistically point at myself.

Just as indexicals are inextricably connected to the context in which they're uttered, Potts (2007) argues that taboo words are, too. As we've observed many times, taboo words are attached to emotion—but not just any emotion. It's (generally) the speaker's emotion that's indicated, and, more specifically, the speaker's emotion at the time of the utterance. Consider (62a–c):

62. a   Abigail's bringing her asshole of a boyfriend.
    b   #Abigail's bringing her asshole of a boyfriend, but I don't think he's an asshole.
    c   #Abigail's bringing her asshole of a boyfriend, but I think he's a nice guy.

When a speaker utters (62a) she is, in part, expressing her own negative feelings towards Abigail's boyfriend. The word *asshole* doesn't simply point to a negative feeling, it points to the speaker's negative feeling at that moment. Even if *asshole* is part of reported speech, the assumption is that the negative feeling belongs to the speaker of the present sentence, not the speaker of the reported sentence. In other words, when a speaker utters (63a), he expresses his own feelings towards Abigail's boyfriend, not Abigail's feelings.[14]

63. a   Gertrude said Abigail's bringing her asshole of a boyfriend.
    b   # Gertrude said Abigail's bringing her asshole of a boyfriend, but I don't think he's an asshole.
    c   # Gertrude said Abigail's bringing her asshole of a boyfriend, but I think he's a nice guy.

---

[14] As always, we need to distinguish between use and mention. Sentence (i) is far different from (63a).
  i Gertrude said Abigail's bringing her "asshole of a boyfriend."

Also, we can see that the emotion is tied to the moment of utterance. In (64a), by uttering "bitch," the speaker is expressing her feelings at the moment she utters the sentence, regardless of the fact that the rest of the sentence is about the past.

64. a   I used to hate that bitch.

     b   I used to hate that bitch, but now I just don't care about her.

     c   #I used to hate that bitch, but now I don't think she's a bitch.

     d   #I used to hate that bitch, but now I think she's really nice.

This connection to the context of utterance seems to be true of taboo terms in general (see 65–68).

65. I broke my fucking foot yesterday.

66. My boyfriend was such a bastard.

67. If I've told you once, I've told you a hundred times to mind your own damn business.

68. That shithead just cut me off.

Also notice that when taboo words are used to express emotion, the emotion doesn't have to be directed at what it is syntactically attached to. For example, in (69) the speaker probably isn't angry at his foot.

69. You're standing on my fucking foot.

Like indexicals, taboo words index (i.e., point to) an aspect of the context—in this case the speaker's emotions. As I suggested earlier, Potts (2007) goes so far as to argue that this is the extent of what they do, that they have no informative meaning. Back to *bastard*, Potts argues that calling somebody a bastard does not describe the person, but rather expresses the feelings the speaker has towards that person. According to his analysis, this should be true of any of our terms of abuse, and the difference between each term will be in the amount of negative emotion expressed.

70. a   That bastard Carmine ate my donut.

     b   That son of a bitch Carmine ate my donut.

     c   That shithead Carmine ate my donut.

     d   That cocksucker Carmine ate my donut.

     e   That motherfucker Carmine ate my donut.

Potts further observes that when you negate an utterance such as (70), the negative emotions still go through:

71. a   That shithead Carmine did not eat my donut, but I still don't like him.

     b   #That shithead Carmine did not eat my donut; therefore, I think he's a nice guy.

72. a   It's not true that that shithead Carmine ate my donut, but I still don't like him.

     b   #It's not true that that shithead Carmine ate my donut; therefore, I think he's a nice guy.

And even when you express such a sentence as merely a possibility, you are still committed to the negative feelings.

73. a   Maybe that motherfucker Carmine ate my donut, and maybe he didn't.

     b   #Maybe that motherfucker Carmine ate my donut, and maybe I think he's a nice guy.

Potts is onto something; however (there had to be a however, didn't there?), it's an overstatement to say these words have no informative meaning. The examples that Potts (2007) chooses and the examples we've considered stack the deck. In most of these cases, the slurs are used **referentially** (i.e., to refer to an individual). On the other hand, if the slurs are used **descriptively** (i.e., to describe an individual), their informative meaning is more obvious.

74. a   Gertrude said Abigail's boyfriend is an asshole—but I don't think he's an asshole.

     b   Gertrude said Abigail's boyfriend is an asshole—but I think he's a nice guy.

75. a   I used to think she was a bitch, but now I don't think she's a bitch.

      b   I used to think she was a bitch, but now I like her.

76. a   Carmine ate my donut; therefore, he is a shithead.

      b   Carmine didn't eat my donut; therefore, he is not a shithead.

77. Maybe Carmine is a motherfucker and ate my donut, or maybe he didn't know the donut was mine, in which case he's not a motherfucker.

I suppose we could argue that in all these cases an emotion is being indexed, but it's not necessarily an immediate emotion, one that is true of the speaker at that particular moment. Additionally, examples like (76) and (77) show that these terms must have informative meaning because otherwise one couldn't define rationale for determining if somebody is or is not a shithead or a motherfucker.

Nonetheless, Potts' analysis does seem to fit some words. For example, we could argue that the emphatic *fucking* (as distinct from the 'intercourse' *fucking*),[15] has no informative meaning, and that it immediately indexes the emotion of the speaker (see 78–80).

78. How fucking pathetic is that?
    (http://mama.indstate.edu/users/bones/WhyIHateWebLogs.html, accessed 6/29/09).

79. You want to succeed in Business and in Life? Do it fucking now.
    (http://seoblackhat.com/2007/01/29/do-it-fucking-now/, accessed 6/29/09)

80. My favorite moments from you and your friends are when you send me the "I love you virus" or the e mails I get with the jokes that are so not fucking funny I wanna snap your neck like a twig.
    (http://www.se7en-x.com/oops/, accessed 6/29/09)

6.   CONCLUSION

In this chapter, we've moved towards a vision of language and communication where we need to distinguish two types of meaning: semantic meaning and pragmatic meaning. Semantic meaning comes from the sentence itself—the words and how they're combined together. It's purely linguistic, and our ability to understand the semantic meaning of a sentence is based entirely on our knowledge of the language it's coded in. Pragmatic meaning comes from the uttering of the sentence in a particular place, at a particular time, by a particular person, to one or more other particular persons. Non-linguistic knowledge—better said, extra-linguistic knowledge—helps us to take the linguistic meaning of an utterance and arrive at a pragmatic meaning. Our knowledge of society is important (how people interact), as is our knowledge of psychology (how people think), and our knowledge of the world (physical laws, as well as what is physically present during the utterance). The social, psychological, and physical surroundings of an utterance constitute the context, allowing us to contextualize an utterance and make sense of it.

We've seen that uttering a sentence is a special kind of social act, a speech act, which has real-world effects (perlocutionary effects). Swearing can liven up a speech act, adding emotion to it, or it can be a speech act on its own (an exclamation). Because taboo words have unique perlocutionary effects, we find they are only appropriate in certain contexts. We also find people using taboo words innovatively, applying them in contexts where their semantic meaning is bizarre based on what we know about the world. In such cases, we don't interpret the words literally—sometimes to the extent that we understand the words to have no informative meaning whatsoever. Finally, we observe that taboo words may (sometimes) belong to a special class of words, indexicals, words that straddle the border between semantics and pragmatics, whose function is to point at aspects of the context; in the case of taboo words, they index the speaker's emotions.

---

[15] Here, we're on safe ground saying that there are two distinct *fuckings*. See Chapter 9 for syntactic arguments in favor of analyzing *fucking* as polysemous.

REFERENCES

Asim, Jabari. 2007. *The N Word: Who Can Say it, Who Shouldn't, and Why.* New York: Houghton Mifflin.

Austin, J.L. 1962. *How to do Things with Words.* Oxford: Clarendon.

Bach, Kent. 1999. The Semantics-Pragmatics Distinction: What It Is and Why It Matters. In *The Semantics-Pragmatics Interface* from Different Points of View, (ed.) K. Turner, 65–84. Oxford: Elsevier.

Beck, D. A., & Frohberg, N. R. (2005). Coprophagia in an Elderly Man: A Case Report and Review of the Literature. *International Journal of Psychiatry in Medicine* 35(4): 417–427.

Cadenhead, Rogers. 2006. Actor Tries to Trademark 'N' Word. *Wired,* 2/23/2006. http://www.wired.com/science/discoveries/news/2006/02/70259 (accessed 10/3/2010).

Fossey, Dian. 1983. *Gorillas in the Mist.* New York: Houghton Mifflin Co.

Geurts, Bart. 2007. Really Fucking Brilliant. *Theoretical Linguistics* 33(2): 209–214.

Grice, Paul. 1989. *Studies in the Ways of Words.* Cambridge, MA: Harvard University Press.

Horn, Laurence. 2005. The Border Wars. In *Where Semantics Meets Pragmatics,* (eds.) Turner et al., 21–48. San Diego, CA: Elsevier.

Jay, Timothy, and Kristin Janschewitz. 2007. Filling the Emotion Gap in Linguistic Theory: Commentary on Potts' Expressive Dimension. *Theoretical Linguistics* 33(2): 215–221.

Mencken, H.L. 1962. *Supplement One: The American Language.* New York: Alfred A. Knopf.

Miller, Henry. 1994. *Under the Roofs of Paris.* New York: Grove Press.

Pavlenko, Aneta. 2008. Bi- and Multilingualism as a Metaphor for Research. *Bilingualism: Language and Cognition* 11(2): 197–201.

Potts, Christopher. 2007. The Expressive Dimension. *Theoretical Linguistics* 33(2):165–198.

Read, Allen. 1977. *Classic American Graffiti: Lexical Evidence from Folk Epigraphy in Western North America.* Waukesha, WI: Maledicta Press.

Sheer, Michael D. 2009. Obama Sworn in Again, With Right Words. *Washington Post.* 1/22/09, p. A04.

Spears, Arthur K. 2006. Perspectives: A View of the 'N-Word' from Sociolinguistics. *Diverse Issues in Higher Education— Online.* July 13, 2006.

Wister, Owen. [1902] 1956. *The Virginian.* New York: Pocket Books.

1. Why is it that *You're a piece of shit* is, in most contexts, an insult, while *You're the shit* is, in most contexts, a compliment? Is your explanation a grammatical one or a pragmatic one? What other uses of *shit* are there? Do these different uses represent different semantic meanings, or are they better explained by appealing to the context of utterance?

2. In this chapter, I put forth the hypothesis that people are more likely to swear in front of peers or people who are socially lower. How could we test this hypothesis?

3. How much does context affect whether a taboo word will offend a recipient or not? For example, does it matter if the word is used primarily for its informational meaning or its emotional meaning? Are people more likely to be offended by (i) or (ii)? (iii) or (iv)?
   i   Grant fucked his job interview.
   ii   Grant fucked his job interviewer.
   iii. Gertrude has a cunt.
   iv. Gertrude is a cunt.
   Come up with similar pairs. How could you empirically determine which one is more offensive?

4 Think of another taboo word, like emphatic *fucking,* that has no informative meaning, only emotional. Is there a polysemous form of the word that does have informative meaning? If so, how can you be sure that it is polysemy?

1. INTRODUCTION

Discussions of censorship often turn political, with strong views from either side on what is the proper role of government and other institutions with regard to the freedom of speech. While I have political views of my own, that is not the point of this book, where I have no political agenda, only a linguistic one: this book is intended to investigate the linguistics of swearing. That said, it is impossible to talk about taboo words without talking about censoring language—they go hand in hand.

Whenever we prohibit any sort of behavior, whether our own or somebody else's, we act as a **censor.** Usually, though, we reserve the word for those who are empowered by an institution to censor others. Allan and Burridge (2006: 27) give the following broad definition for **censoring of language,** which includes both acts of institutional censoring and self-censoring:

> The **censoring of language** is the proscription of language expressions that are taboo for the censor at a given time, in contexts which are specified or specifiable because those proscribed language expressions are condemned for being subversive of the good of some specified, specifiable or contextually identifiable community.

For specifically governmental or institutional censoring, they reserve the word *censorship,* which they define as follows: "institutionalized suppressions of language by powerful governing classes, supposedly acting for the common good by preserving stability and/or moral fibre in the nation" (Allan & Burridge 2006: 24).

In this chapter, I have little to say about self-censoring. Here, we are more interested in acts of censoring that are directed against somebody else. We all, in effect, act as censors on each other by our explicit or implicit reproof of what others say; by tacitly or vocally objecting when somebody uses a word in our presence, we participate in the censoring of language. This is how words achieve their tabooness; tabooness is a societal agreement on which words should be censored. However, we discuss this sort of censoring enough elsewhere in this book. In this chapter, we focus on censoring of language that comes from above, by some authority (whether self-proclaimed, appointed, or elected). Such authorities see it as their role to protect "the common people" from exposure to bad words.

Of course, many object to authorities of any kind censoring language. Notably, Milton, one of the greatest poets of English, the writer of *Paradise Lost*, was a vocal opponent of censorship, writing: "as good almost kill a Man as kill a good Book; who kills a man kills a reasonable creature, God's Image; but hee who destroyes a good Booke, kills reason it self, kills the Image of God, as it were in the eye" (Milton 1644, 4; quoted in Allan & Burridge 2006, 18).

Many of us trust our own sense to discern the difference between Milton's "good Booke" and drivel that we should not read over some authority's sense of which is which. As Ernst and Seagle (1928, 13; quoted in Allan & Burridge 2006, 19) put it: "CENSORSHIP in action has little to recommend it. Suppression is a sordid, unhappy sport. The legal chicanery brings out the worst in every one concerned . . . To act the rôle of the censor develops a lack of honesty more anti-social than any amount of sexual excess." Many would argue that the marketplace, not the government, should determine what is to be avoided. If a book, movie, or play contains language that you do not wish to read or hear, you are not obliged to be in the audience.

On the other hand, language is not something we choose to process or not. When we are exposed to speech or writing in a language we know, we can't help but understand it (see Chapter 12). So some see it as government's role to ensure that we are not involuntarily contaminated by offensive language. Aristotle explained this role as follows:

> [T]here is nothing that the legislator should be more careful to drive away than indecency of speech; for the light utterance of shameful words leads to shameful actions. The young especially should never be allowed to repeat or hear anything of that sort. A freeman if he be found saying or doing what is forbidden, if he be too young as yet to have the privilege of reclining at the public tables, should be disgraced and beaten, and an elder person degraded as his slavish conduct deserves. (Aristotle c. 350 BCE, *Politics*, Book VII; quoted in Allan & Burridge 2006, 12)

Even Milton agreed that not all speech should be allowed:

> I mean not tolerated popery, and open superstition, which as it extirpates all religious and civil supremacies, so itself should be extirpated . . . that also which is impious or evil or absolutely against faith or manners no law can possibly permit that intends not to unlaw itself.[1] (Milton 1644; quoted in Fish 1992, 232)

Many see it as government's role to protect us from ourselves with regards to language. As Allan and Burridge (2006, 13) put it: "The censorship of profanity and blasphemy supposedly guards against [a citizen's] moral harm." Biblical law takes a particularly hard line on profanity. When a man is taken to Moses for having "cursed the name of the Lord," God tells Moses:

> This man has cursed me! Take him outside the camp and have the witnesses lay their hands on his head. Then command the whole community of Israel to stone him to death. And warn the others that everyone else who curses me will die in the same way, whether they are Israelites by birth or foreigners living among you. (Leviticus 24, 14–16)

Censoring obscenity is supposed to protect us from our baser instincts: "The censorship of pornography supposedly guards against [a citizen's] moral harm, and perhaps physical danger, by someone stimulated to rapine action by exposure to the excitement of pornog-

The word *sadism* is derived from the Marquis de Sade's last name.

raphy" (Allan & Burridge 2006, 13). Now, this might strike you as hyperbole—would somebody really commit rape after being exposed to obscenity? Well, Shattuck (1996) argues that the Marquis de Sade's graphic descriptions of rape, murder, and cannibalism in his writings influenced the crimes of three serial killers, including Ted Bundy (cited in Allan & Burridge 2006, 22). Yeah, kind of a reach, huh? Allan and Burridge think so, too.

---

[1] Fish (1992, 231) summarizes this passage as Milton saying, "of course, I didn't mean Catholics, them we exterminate."

In Section 2, we focus on the history of governmental censorship in England and America. In Section 3, we look at censorship in dictionaries. In Section 4, we look at censorship with respect to the First Amendment to the U.S. Constitution. In Section 5, we look at censorship of film, television, and radio. In Section 6, we consider PC language; we do not have the space to do justice to this topic, so we focus on speech codes on college campuses.

2. THE HISTORY OF CENSORSHIP IN ENGLAND AND AMERICA

The English language has a long history of censorship. Hughes (1991, 43) quotes from a law dating back to the seventh century, the Laws of Hlothhere and Eadric, kings of Kent, no 11: "If anyone in another's house calls a man a perjurer, or shamefully accosts him with insulting words, he is to pay a shilling to him who owns the house, and six shillings to him to whom he spoke that word, and to pay twelve shillings to the King." Hughes notes that this is the same fine as for stealing a cup. Note that insulting a person (calling somebody a perjurer was one of the worst insults you could make at the time) was seen not only as an offense to the person accused, but also to the host who had welcomed the offender.

Four to five hundred years later, Henry I (1068–1135) instituted incremental fines for swearing near the royal residence (cited in Hughes 1991, 59):

duke	40 shillings
lord	20 shillings
squire	10 shillings
yeoman	3 shillings, 4 pence
page	a whipping

These fines were based on what the swearer could afford to pay, not on the seriousness of the offense. Across the English Channel, things were even stricter; Saint Louis of France (1214–70) had swearers branded on the face so they would remember their crime (Montagu 1973, 111; cited in Hughes 1991, 60).

Until the Renaissance, censorship was primarily against profanity—so-called "loose swearing," where people made insincere oaths or used religious terms as emotives. The Renaissance brought the first organized secular censorship (Hughes 1991, 102); the "Master of the Revels" was designated by the Crown in 1574 to oversee and censor plays, primarily to censor anything that might jeopardize the monarchy.

It wasn't until 1606 that censorship against taboo words was part of the Master of the Revels' purview—probably because Queen Elizabeth, who died in 1603, was an avid swearer (Hughes 1991, 103). Here's the 1606 "Acte to Restraine Abuses of Playes":

> If . . . any person or persons doe or shall in any Stage play, Interlude, Shewe, Maygame or Pageant jestingly or pro-phanely speake or use the holy name of God or of Christ Jesus, or of the Holy Ghoste or of the Trinitie . . . [They] shall forfeite for every such Offence by him or them committed Tenne pounds. (3 Jac. I. c. 21; quoted in Hughes 1991, 103)

We would be underestimating human inventiveness if we assumed that playwrights ceased being vulgar and used only polite language simply because the Master of the Revels was watching over their shoulders. As Hughes (1991, 106) puts it: "The censorship and institutionalized fines served, as they usually do, to encourage circumlocution through enforced ingenuity." For example, Shakespeare used foreign words for obscene puns, as in this language lesson from

In 1623, the English government instituted a law against profanity that would apply to all citizens: "For as much as all profane Swearing and Cursing is forbidden by the Word of GOD, be it therefore enacted by the Authority of the then Parliament, that no Person or Persons should thenceforth profanely Swear or Curse, upon Penalty of forfeiting one shilling to the use of the Poor for every Oath or Curse" (21 Jac. I. c. 20; quoted in Hughes 1991, 105). Those who refused to pay or were unable to pay were led to the stocks if they were over twelve years old and were whipped if they were younger.

Henry V (III. iv. 55–8; cited in Hughes 1991.107), in which Shakespeare plays on the similarity in sound between English *foot* and *gown* and French *foutre* ('fuck') and *con* ('cunt'):

> Katherine   *Comment appelez vous le pied et la robe?*
> ['How do you say the foot and the gown?']
> Alice   *De foot, madame; et* le coun.
> [the English words are pronounced with a thick French accent]
> Katherine   *De foot, et* le con? *O Seigneur Dieu! ces sont mots de son mauvais, corruptible, gros, et impudique, et non pour les dames d'honneur d'user.*
> ['De foot and le con? Oh God! these are bad-sounding words, corruptible, gross, and impudent, and not for women of honor to use']

Shakespeare's character Pistol also uses *foutre:* "A foutra for the world . . ." (Henry IV, part II, V. ii 98; quoted in Hughes 1991, 107).

It's interesting to note that the King and the Master of the Revels did not always agree on what should be censored. In 1634, Charles I overruled some of his edits, as noted in the Master's journal:

> This morning . . . the kinge was pleasd to call mee into his withdrawinge chamber to the win-dowe, where he went over all that I had croste in Davenant's playe-booke and allowing of *faith* and *slight* to bee asseverations only, and no oaths, marked them to stande, and some other few things, but in the greater part allowed of my reformations . . . The kinge is pleasd to take *faith, death, slight,* for asseverations, and no oaths, to which I doe humbly submit as my masters judge-ment; but, under favour, conceive them to be oaths, and enter them here to declare my opinion and submission. (quoted in Hughes 1991, 117–118)

Although Shakespeare's work was censored during his own time, in 1818, Thomas Bowdler took it upon himself to do it again. He produced an edition of Shakespeare's works in which "Those words and expressions are omitted which cannot with propriety be read aloud in a family" (quoted in Hughes 1991, 243). As Hughes (1991, 244) puts it, "Generally speaking, Bowdler retains the violence but excises the sex."[2]

Laws against swearing have lasted longer than we care to think. In Scotland, the death penalty remained on the books for blasphemy until 1825 (Hughes 1991, 247). In 1914, there was a big to-do in London over whether the censors would allow *bloody* to be uttered in George Bernard Shaw's play *Pygmalian.* The night before the play's opening, London's *Daily Sketch* debated whether Mrs. Patrick Campbell, the actress playing Eliza Doolittle in *Pyg-malian,* would utter "Walk? Not bloody likely!" as it was scripted—the paper, itself, did not print the word, though (cited in Hughes 1991, 186). In the end, Campbell did utter it, and the controversy died down quickly thereafter. Theatrical censorship in England was only abolished in 1968 (Hughes 1991, 191). In February 1990, after ninety-four soccer fans in Sheffield, England were crushed to death, Lord Justice Taylor issued a report rec-ommending a prohibition on "obscene and racist chanting" at soccer games (cited in Hughes 1991, 246).

Here in the States, we have our own history of censorship. General George Washington issued the following order in 1776, before there even was a United States:

> The General is sorry to be informed that the foolish and wicked practice of profane cursing and swearing, a vice heretofore little known in an American army, is growing into fashion. He hopes the officers will, by example as well as influence, endeavor to check it . . . and that they and the men will reflect, that we can have little hope of the blessing of Heaven on our arms, if we insult it by our impiety and folly. . . . (quoted in Norman 1956, 110)

Perhaps the most prominent of our censorship laws was the **Comstock Act** of 1873, which forbid, among other things, printed material containing taboo words to be sent through the U.S. Postal Service. The law reads:

> That no obscene, lewd, or lascivious book, pamphlet, picture, paper, print, or other publication of an indecent character, or any article or thing designed or intended for the prevention of con-ception or procuring of abortion, nor any article or thing intended or adapted for any indecent or immoral use or nature, nor any written or printed card, circular, book, pamphlet, advertisement

---

[2] The same could be said of present-day "edited for television" movies.

or notice of any kind giving information, directly or indirectly, where, or how, or of whom, or by what means either of the things before mentioned may be obtained or made, nor any letter upon the envelope of which, or postal-card upon which indecent or scurrilous epithets may be written or printed, shall be carried in the mail, and any person who shall knowingly deposit, or cause to be deposited, for mailing or delivery, any of the hereinbefore-mentioned articles or things, or any notice, or paper containing any advertisement relating to the aforesaid articles or things, and any person who, in pursuance of any plan or scheme for disposing of any of the hereinbefore-mentioned articles or things, shall take, or cause to be taken, from the mail any such letter or package, shall be deemed guilty of a misdemeanor, and, on conviction thereof, shall, for every offense, be fined not less than one hundred dollars nor more than five thousand dollars, or imprisoned at hard labor not less than one year nor more than ten years, or both, in the discretion of the judge. (42nd Congress 1873, 599)

Mencken (1947, 30) writes: "The passage of the Comstock Postal Act in 1873, greatly stimulated the search for euphemisms. Once that amazing law was upon the statute-book and Comstock himself was given the inquisitorial powers of a post-office inspector, it became positively dangerous to print certain ancient and essentially decent English words." He goes on to write in a subsequent book that magazines and newspapers:

> . . . may be barred from the mails, and hence subjected to ruinous loss, at the fiat of a Postmaster General who maintains a bureau of snoopers and smut-snufflers for harassing them. In the proceeding against *Esquire* in 1943–44 these dogberries actually objected to its use of such perfectly harmless words as *backside, behind* and *bawdy-house*. It is thus no wonder that American newspapers, with few exceptions continue to use the euphemisms inherited from the Victorian age. . . . (Mencken 1962, 646)

He continues this passage with an example from a New York paper which, as a practice, avoided the word *rape*, and so described how the assailant "dragged her down the cellar-steps, beat her with an iron pipe, and then assaulted her" (quoted in Mencken 1962, 646).

The etymologist and lexicologist Allen Read's writing was widely censored because of his fascination with taboo words. In 1934, Read wrote a scholarly article about the etymology and usage of *fuck*, in which the word is never written, not once in its fifteen pages. All he can do is describe it as "the word that has the deepest stigma of any in the language" (Read 1934, 264) and "the most disreputable of all English words" (267). A year later, he had to go to Paris to privately publish his book on bathroom graffiti because it could not be published in the United States. The book was not published in the U.S. until 1977, forty-two years after the initial printing, when Reinhold Aman persuaded Read to let him publish it—Aman had been searching in library after library for the "pioneering and frequently quoted work" (Read 1977, Afterword). Even so, the book had to be published by an obscure press that specializes in scholarly research on the linguistics of taboo words.

Pinker 2007 (324–325) lists the following prominent acts of censorship by our government:

- In 1921, a magazine excerpt from James Joyce's *Ulysses* was declared obscene by an American court, and the book was banned in the United States until 1933.

- D.H. Lawrence's *Lady Chatterley's Lover*, written in 1928, was not published in the United Kingdom until 1960, whereupon Penguin Books was prosecuted (unsuccessfully) under the Obscene Publications Act of 1959.

- *Lady Chatterley* was also banned in the United States, together with Henry Miller's *Tropic of Cancer* and John Cleland's *Fanny Hill*. In a series of court decisions reflecting the changing sexual mores of the 1960s, the bans were overturned, culminating in a Supreme Court ruling in 1973.

- Between 1961 and 1964, the comedian Lenny Bruce was repeatedly arrested for obscenity and banned from performing in many cities. Bruce died in 1966 while appealing a four-month sentence imposed by a New York court, and was finally pardoned by Governor George Pataki thirty-seven years after his death.

- The Pacifica Radio Network was fined in 1973 by the Federal Communications Commission for broadcasting George Carlin's monologue "Seven Words You Can Never Say on Television." The Supreme

Court upheld the action, ruling that the FCC could prohibit "indecent" language during hours when children might stumble upon a broadcast.

- The FCC fined Howard Stern's popular radio program repeatedly, prompting Stern to leave broadcast radio in 2006 for the freedom of satellite radio. Many media experts predicted that it would be a tipping point in the popularity of that medium.

In 1998, Timothy Boomer, the so-called cussing canoeist, was arrested in Michigan for repeatedly using *fuck* in front of women and children (Bradsher 1999). Boomer was canoeing the Rifle River when he capsized. He then shouted "fuck" repeatedly—according to witnesses anywhere from 25 to 70 times (Associated Press 1999). A woman, Tammy Smith, was also in the river with her five-year-old son and three-year-old daughter (Bradsher 1999). Two deputies arrested Boomer once he reached the shore. The law he was charged with violating was 102 years old and few Michiganders were aware it existed. The case went to trial, and in 1999 Boomer was convicted, fined $75, and ordered to work four days in a child-care program; he appealed and three years later the law was ruled unconstitutional (Simon 2002).

In 2003, Bono, the lead singer of U2, caused a scandal when, on live TV, he said, "This is really, really fucking brilliant" (see Section 5.2). That same year, Representative Doug Ose of California tried to ensure that Bono's utterance would be illegal by introducing the following bill to Congress (HR 3687):

A BILL

To amend section 1464 of title 18, United States Code, to provide for the punishment of certain profane broadcasts, and for other purposes.

Be it enacted by the Senate and House of Representatives of the United States of America in Congress assembled, That section 1464 of title 18, United States Code, is amended—

(1) by inserting '(a)' before 'Whoever'; and

(2) by adding at the end the following:

'(b) As used in this section, the term 'profane', used with respect to language, includes the words 'shit', 'piss', 'fuck', 'cunt', 'asshole', and the phrases 'cock sucker', 'mother fucker', and 'ass hole', compound use (including hyphenated compounds) of such words and phrases with each other or with other words or phrases, and other grammatical forms of such words and phrases (including verb, adjective, gerund, participle, and infinitive forms).'.

Pinker (2007, 360) notes, however, that Ose's bill would have failed to target Bono's utterance "because it fails to specify the syntax of Bono's expletive properly" (in Chapter 9 we discuss the part of speech that *fucking* belongs to). Others have pointed out that had Ose's bill passed, it would have been illegal to read the bill over the airwaves. In fact, the FCC has no interest in specifying which words are illegal—we'll discuss this more in Section 5.2.

3.   CENSORSHIP IN DICTIONARIES

Read (1934) spends an entire section looking at which English dictionaries throughout history have and which have not included *fuck*. The first dictionary to give an entry for the word was *Etymologicon Linguæ Anglicanæ,* published in 1671 by Thomas Henshaw (268–269). Several dictionaries that followed did not include it, though one lexicographer criticized previous dictionaries as being too "stufft with obscenity not to be named" (quoted in Read 1934, 269). The next dictionary to include the word was published by a schoolteacher; as Read describes it, "His piety had to struggle with his linguistic sense, and the latter won . . ." (269). But, for the most part, the eighteenth century was a censorious one, where dictionaries did not include taboo words.

In the middle of the eighteenth century came Samuel Johnson's *Dictionary.* Johnson, himself, was famous as a moralist; however, there is some anecdotal evidence that he may have been more vulgar in private than he was in public (see Read 1934). Hughes (1991, 144) quotes Johnson as saying that of life's greatest pleasures first was ". . . fucking and second was drinking." In publishing his *Dictionary,* however, Johnson's public face prevailed; he did not include swear words—with the exceptions, perhaps, of *bloody* and *bum* (Read 1934, 271).

Many of the dictionaries that followed Johnson's were intended for schools, so they omitted taboo words, seeing them as inappropriate for youth to see. One lexicographer, George W. Lemon, explained the policy as follows:

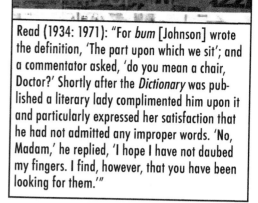

Read (1934: 1971): "For *bum* [Johnson] wrote the definition, 'The part upon which we sit'; and a commentator asked, 'do you mean a chair, Doctor?' Shortly after the *Dictionary* was published a literary lady complimented him upon it and particularly expressed her satisfaction that he had not admitted any improper words. 'No, Madam,' he replied, 'I hope I have not daubed my fingers. I find, however, that you have been looking for them.'"

> Permit me to close my observations, with mentioning only one thing more, in which the reader will intirely agree with me; viz. in censuring without reserve that total want of decency and decorum, which compilers of many dictionaries, and etymologies, have shewn, in first of all collecting, and then afterwards explaining, tho' in Latin, and sometimes in plain English, many words which they must unavoidably have met with, and which are to be found in every language under the sun, but which convey such ideas of indelicacy, as would have been much more prudent, and commendable in those writers interely to have omitted, instead of endeavouring to trace their etymology, and explain their meaning, which wanted no explanation; for, from objects, and from words of obscenity and turpitude, not only the eyes and ears, but even the thoughts and imaginations too, ought to be kept pure and untainted. (Lemon 1783; quoted in Read 1934, 271)

Lemon's policy highlights the difference between his approach and that taken by other lexicographers. The difference lies in the distinction between **prescriptivism** and **descriptivism** (see Chapter 2).

The approach by many lexicographers, Lemon among them, has been prescriptivist. In other words, they see their jobs as listing the "correct" way to use words—as well as the "correct" words to use. Samuel Johnson, Jr. summarized this approach in the first American dictionary: he saw his purpose as providing children with the words "without which no person can either write, or speak our language with purity or elegance" (Johnson 1798; quoted in Read 1934, 272). Most American dictionaries have fallen under the prescriptivist paradigm. As Read puts it, "From the earliest times in America there has been a sharp division between the Puritans and the roistering, hearty backwoods element. The former have always prevailed as far as printing is concerned" (272).

In practice, the American lexicographer Noah Webster was a studious follower of the prescriptivist approach—none of his dictionaries were to include *fuck* in his lifetime (Read 1934, 273). In fact, Webster felt that Samuel Johnson had gone too far, saying he had "transgressed the rules of lexicography beyond any other compiler, for his work contains more of the lowest of all vulgar words, than any other now extant, Ash excepted" (Webster 1807; quoted in Read 1934, 273).

The Ash referred to by Webster in the above quote was a British lexicographer who followed the descriptivist approach. In other words, Ash saw his job as listing and describing all of the words used in the language, regardless of whether they were "proper" or not. Ironically, Webster gives one of the most succinct descriptivist explanations of a lexicographer's job: "The business of the lexicographer is to collect, arrange and define, as far as possible, *all* the words that belong to a language, and leave the author to select from them, at his pleasure, and according to his own taste and judgment" (Webster 1817; quoted in Read 1934, 274).

The most famous dictionary in the descriptivist tradition is the *Oxford English Dictionary* (see Chapter 7), the first parts of which were published in the late nineteenth century. Read (1934, 274) describes the project as follows: "Here was a work, conceived in a scientific spirit, whose aim, presumably, was beyond that of supplying youthful minds with elegant words." Although James Murray and Henry Bradley, the original editors, saw the job of a lexicographer as being decidedly descriptivist in nature, they ultimately bowed to pressure, and the first edition left out those terms that were too taboo by the standards of the day (cf. Hughes 1991, 161). As Read (1934, 274) scathingly writes, "It is to the lasting shame of Murray and Bradley that their linguistic sense was not strong enough that they could dissociate themselves from the warped outlook of the age."

The *Oxford English Dictionary,* as did many other dictionaries, eventually chose to include *fuck* among other taboo words. It's interesting to note that in the 1970s, as the editors were preparing the second supplement to the dictionary, they were petitioned to omit racial slurs—this time they did not bow to pressure (see Chapter 7). In contrast, though, the *Webster's Dictionary,* always more prescriptivist in nature, did omit racial slurs: in 1970, *Webster's New World Dictionary* omitted *dago, kike, wop,* and *wog.* The editor-in-chief, David B. Guralnik, wrote in the Forward

(p. viii): "It was decided in the selection process that this dictionary could easily dispense with those true obscenities, the terms of racial or ethnic opprobrium, that are, in any case, encountered with diminishing frequency these days" (quoted in Hughes 1991, 241).

To bring us up to the twenty-first century, we can consider the case of the Ninjawords dictionary application for the iPhone. In 2009, Apple required Ninjawords to remove all "objectionable" words before it could be sold on Apple's iTunes App Store (Beaumont 2009). There is some debate about what words Apple required Ninjawords to remove; one of the co-creators claimed that they included *shit* and *fuck* (Myslewski 2009), but a spokesperson for Apple said they censored "other more vulgar terms than those found in traditional and common dictionaries, words that many reasonable people might find upsetting or objectionable;" he went on to cast these words as "offensive 'urban slang' terms" (quoted in Myslewski 2009).

4. CENSORSHIP AND THE FIRST AMENDMENT: WHAT SPEECH IS NOT FREE?

The First Amendment to the United States Constitution reads in part: "Congress shall make no law . . . abridging the freedom of speech, or of the press . . ." But according to Fish (1992), the freedom of speech is not—cannot be—absolute. There will always be exceptions:

> When the pinch comes (and sooner or later it will always come) and the institution (be it church, state, or university) is confronted by behavior subversive of its core rationale, it will respond by declaring "of course we mean not tolerated _____, that we extirpate"; not because an exception to a general freedom has suddenly and contradictorily been announced but because the freedom has never been general and has always been understood against the background of an originary exclusion that gives it meaning. (Fish 1992, 233)

And, of course, Congress has abridged the freedom of speech. The Supreme Court recognizes four constitutional restrictions on free speech: that which poses an imminent danger, defaming or libelous speech, fighting words, and obscene speech (Jay 1992, 196).

The first of these restrictions, imminent danger, was originally about censoring anti-war speech during the build-up for World War I—this is the famous case where Justice Holmes spoke of "falsely shouting fire in a theater and causing a panic" (Jay 1992, 196). This type of censorship is not relevant to our present discussion, nor is the restriction on defamatory or libelous speech.

The restriction on fighting words dates back to the 1940s. The idea is that some words are so inflammatory that a normal person couldn't help but respond violently to them. Jay (1992) discusses in some depth how difficult it can be to prove in court that fighting words were used. Fighting words have four key pillars (Gard 1980; cited in Jay 1992, 200–201):

1. The expression must be "an extremely provocative personal insult."
2. The expression must "have a direct tendency to cause immediate violent response by the average recipient."
3. The utterance must be made to the target's face.
4. The utterance must "be directed to an individual and not to a group of people."

Obviously, fighting words typically consist of slurs. We'll discuss fighting words in more depth in Section 6.

Our final category of restricted speech is obscenity—but not in the sense that we use the term in this book. The original legal definition for obscenity came from Hicklin's 1873 test: "Whether the tendency of the matter charged as obscenity is to deprave and corrupt those whose minds are open to such immoral influences, and into whose hands a publication of this sort may fall" (quoted in Jay 1992, 198). This test is now considered outdated, and most current obscenity laws grew from a 1957 case, *Roth v. United States*:

1. The dominant theme of the material as a whole appeals to a prurient interest in sex,
2. the material is patently offensive as it affronts contemporary standards relating to descriptions of sexual matters, and
3. the material is utterly without redeeming social importance. (quoted in Jay 1992, 198)

The comedian Lenny Bruce, on his 1969 *Berkeley Concert* LP (recorded in 1965), describes the law in far more colorful language:

> An illiterate view of the law is that what's obscene is dirty screwing and fancy screwing, and if a guy can tear off a piece of ass with class then he's cool. But if the author depicts factory workers who are not experts with stag shows, then it's obscene, which is just nonsense . . . Here's how it works . . . In 1933 . . . when *Ulysses* tried to come into the country, you dig, and the customs and tariffs people said, "Uh uh, you can't bring your book in, it can't come into the country, it's obscene." So these people said, "No, we want the book to come in, and we want to knock off the injunction to restrain." So they moved forward, and the judge said "Okay, I'm going to read this book, but I'm not going to apply this Hickman rule anymore." The Hickman rule says that we should judge this book by the part, the portion of it, to the guy who gets horniest quickest, the most corruptible mind in the community. "I think," said this judge, "we should apply the average man, the reasonable man, the man with normal average sex instincts to aim that test . . . the man with the normal average sex instincts, to that cat." Then they add the balance. Contemporary, to his average age, so to the guy with average sex instincts, to his average age, his society, that's how we'll test it. So that means, that at rule, when any judge has to judge any work, he always has to apply that rule first. Now that was cool . . . Now it goes: They say, "Well we've got to narrow it because what's happened here there's a lot of works of art that may get people horny." And there's a Los Angeles ordinance now in 1961 that this guy got busted on, and the judge said, "I don't need any art critics. I know what's obscene." But the judge didn't know in that local court that that wasn't the question the guy was asking. He said, "This ordinance is unconstitutional because it doesn't have *knowingly* in it." And that's the principle of the whole American law system: your intent. "So how could I know it, schmuck, when these people told me on the book jacket that it was art?" So the intent has to be there.

Bruce died in 1966, a year after the performance this monologue is taken from; he was broke from years of fighting one obscenity charge after another. Today, we don't find comedians being arrested for the words they use. Arguably in large part because of Bruce's legal fights, further changes were made to the legal definition of obscenity in 1973. In the *Miller* case, the criteria laid out in *Roth v. United States* were revised as follows:

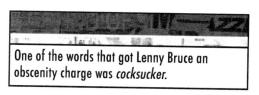

One of the words that got Lenny Bruce an obscenity charge was *cocksucker.*

1. The average person, applying contemporary community standards, would find the work, taken as a whole, appeals to the prurient interest in sex; and

2. The work depicts or describes, in a patently offensive way, sexual conduct specifically defined by the applicable state (or federal) law; and

3. The work, taken as a whole, lacks serious literary, artistic, political, or scientific value. (quoted in Jay 1992, 199)

These are roughly the three pillars that the FCC bases its present obscenity restrictions on (see Section 5.2).

5.   CENSORSHIP IN FILM, TV, AND RADIO

In this section we'll be looking at two different types of censors, one imposed by an industry upon itself, the other imposed on an industry by the U.S. government. The first is the Motion Picture Producers and Distributors Association (often called "The Hays Office"), which regulated what could and could not be put into movies during much of the twentieth century. The other is the FCC, which regulates what can and cannot be put into programs broadcast over the airwaves.

5.1 Censorship of Movies

America has never had the equivalent of a Master of the Revels for our film industry, at least not one appointed by the government. Throughout most of its history, our film industry has been self-regulated in order to avoid governmental interference. Early on, they created the so-called "Hay's Office," whose job it was to censor movies.

In 1922, the Motion Picture Producers and Distributors Association (MPPDA) was created with Will Hays, the Postmaster General at the time, as the president, where he remained until 1945—the MPPDA was commonly known as the "Hays Office." In 1927, sound was introduced, which lead the MPPDA to publish its list of eleven "don'ts,"[3] including the ban of the following words: *God, Lord, Jesus, Christ, hell, damn, gawd,* and "every other profane and vulgar expression however it may be spelled" (see the list that follows).

Resolved, That those things which are included in the following list shall not appear in pictures produced by the members of this Association, irrespective of the many [sic] in which they are treated.

1. Pointed profanity—by either title or lip—this includes the words "God," "Lord," "Jesus," "Christ" (unless they be used reverently in connection with proper religious ceremonies), "hell," "damn," "Gawd," and every other profane and vulgar expression however it may be spelled;

2. Any licentious or suggestive nudity—in factor in silhouette; and any lecherous or licentious notice thereof by other characters in the picture;

3. The illegal traffic in drugs;

4. Any interference [sic] of sex perversion;

5. White slavery;

6. Miscegenation (sex relationships between the white and black races);

7. Sex hygiene and venereal diseases;

8. Scenes of actual childbirth—in fact or in silhouette;

9. Children's sex organs;

10. Ridicule of the clergy;

11. Willful offense to any nation, race or creed.
(http://www.digitalhistory.uh.edu/historyonline/film_censorship.cfm, accessed 7/7/2010)

Three years after the list of "don'ts," the Hays Office issued the Production Code, which issued several working principles that included these choice tidbits about vulgarity and obscenity:

Vulgarity

The treatment of low, disgusting, unpleasant, though not necessarily evil, subjects should be guided always by the dictates of good taste and a proper regard for the sensibilities of the audience.

Obscenity

Obscenity in word, gesture, reference, song, joke or by suggestion (even when likely to be understood only by part of the audience) is forbidden.
(http://productioncode.dhwritings.com/no4ind.php, accessed 9/27/2010)

In 1934, the following lines were added about profanity:

Profanity

Pointed profanity (this includes God, Lord, Jesus, Christ—unless used reverently—Hell, S.O.B., damn, Gawd), or other profane or vulgar expressions, however used, is forbidden.
(http://productioncode.dhwritings.com/no4ind.php, accessed 9/27/2010)

---

[3] There were also twenty-five "be carefuls."

In 1939, the code was revised to include this passage:

Pointed profanity and every other profane or vulgar expression, however used, is forbidden.

(1) No approval by the Production Code Administration shall be given to the use of words and phrases in motion pictures including, but not limited to, the following:

> Alley cat (applied to a woman); bat (applied to a woman); broad (applied to a woman); Bronx cheer (the sound); chippie; cocotte; God, Lord, Jesus, Christ (unless used reverently); cripes; fanny; fairy (in a vulgar sense); finger (the); fire, cries of; Gawd; goose (in a vulgar sense); "hold your hat" or "hats"; hot (applied to a woman); "in your hat"; louse; lousy; Madam (relating to prostitution); nance, nerts; nuts (except when meaning crazy); pansy; razzberry (the sound); slut (applied to a woman); SOB.; son-of-a; tart; toilet gags; tom cat (applied to a man); traveling salesman and farmer's daughter jokes; whore; damn; hell (excepting when the use of said last two words shall be essential and required for portrayal, in proper historical context, of any scene or dialogue based upon historical fact or folklore, or for the presentation in proper literary context of a Biblical, or other religious quotation, or a quotation from a literary work provided that no such use shall he permitted which is intrinsically objectionable or offends good taste).

(2) The following words and phrases are invariably deleted by political censor boards:

> Bum (in England)
>
> Bloody (in England)
>
> "Cissy" or "Sissy" (in England)
>
> Gigolo (in England)
>
> Poisons (specific names of) (in United States)
>
> Punk (in England)
>
> Sex appeal (in England)
>
> Sex life (in England)
>
> Shag (in British Empire)
>
> Shyster (in England)
>
> "Stick 'em up" (in United States and Canada)

(3) The following words and phrases are obviously offensive to the patrons of motion pictures in the United States and more particularly to the patrons of motion pictures in foreign countries and, therefore, should be omitted:

> Chink (Chinese)
>
> Dago (Italian)
>
> Frog (French)
>
> Greaser (Mexico and Central America)
>
> Hunkie (Hungarian)
>
> Kike (U.S. and England)
>
> Nigger (U.S.)
>
> Spic (Mexico and central America)
>
> Wop (Italian)
>
> Yid (U.S. and England)
>
> (http://productioncode.dhwritings.com/no4ind.php, accessed 9/27/2010)

Note the exception given at the end of part 1 of this passage: *damn* and *hell* are forbidden "excepting when the use of said last two words shall be essential and required for portrayal, in proper historical context, of any scene or dialogue based upon historical fact or folklore, or for the presentation in proper literary context of a Biblical, or other religious quotation, or a quotation from a literary work provided that no such use shall he permitted which is intrinsically objectionable or offends good taste." They had to add this exception because *Gone With the Wind* violated the code with its oft-quoted "Frankly, dear, I don't give a damn," but was ultimately approved (Hughes 1991, 199)—they added the exception in order to retroactively justify their approval.

From today's perspective, the use of *damn* in *Gone With the Wind*, seems pretty mild. And it seems hard to believe the Hays Office sweated about it at all. Yet we find even milder words that the Office did censor. In 1942, the Office ordered a producer to replace *louse* with *stinkbug*, and the Office supposedly frowned on the word *belch* (Mencken 1962, 644).

Due to competition with TV, films became more risqué, while TV remained a family medium, partly because of the pressure from advertisers, which film did not have (Hughes 1991, 199). In the 1950s and 1960s the code was condensed substantially, and by 1968, the code was done away with entirely (http://productioncode.dhwritings.com/no4ind.php, accessed 9/27/2010). Today, we have the rating system imposed by the Motion Pictures Association of America (MPAA, the present name of the MPPDA), where movies are assigned G, PG, PG-13, R, NC-17, or X ratings (initially there were only G, R, and X).

5.2   *The FCC*

It might seem we have a modern-day equivalent of the Master of the Revels in the Federal Communications Commission (FCC); however, that would be overstating things. Unlike the Master, who censored speech prior to a play being approved, the FCC only censors speech after the fact. Indeed, the FCC does not even monitor programs; instead, they respond to citizen complaints. Partly, I suppose, this is a practical approach in that it would be impossible for a government organization to monitor everything that is broadcast over the airwaves.

In an episode of the Fox cartoon series *Family Guy*, there's a musical number about the "fellas from the freakin' FCC."

The FCC was founded in 1934 by the U.S. government to regulate communication through the airwaves, wire, satellite, and cable. It is composed of five commissioners appointed to five-year terms by the President and confirmed by the Senate (FCC). Its responsibilities go far beyond those of being a censor, though it is the latter role that has brought upon it so much hatred in recent years. Two songs released in 2004 express some vitriol against the FCC: Steve Earle's song "F the CC" features the prominent line, "Fuck the FCC" and Eric Idle's "FCC Song" features the line "Fuck you very much the FCC."

In Section 4, we discussed how the Supreme Court has ruled that obscenity is not protected by the First Amendment. Thus, the FCC has the right to levy fines against any broadcast medium that airs anything, including language, that rises to the level of obscenity:

> [T]o be obscene, material must meet a three-prong test: (1) an average person, applying contemporary community standards, must find that the material, as a whole, appeals to the prurient interest (i.e., material having a tendency to excite lustful thoughts); (2) the material must depict or describe, in a patently offensive way, sexual conduct specifically defined by applicable law; and (3) the material, taken as a whole, must lack serious literary, artistic, political, or scientific value. (FCC)

Taboo words are not generally taken to rise to the level of obscenity today, so they are considered protected speech. Nevertheless, the Supreme Court has determined that the FCC can regulate the use of taboo words during a certain time span during the day, the period from 6:00 am to 10:00 pm, when children are most likely to be watching. From 10:00 pm to 6:00 am, the FCC recognizes a **"safe harbor"** when network television and radio stations are free to broadcast any words short of obscenity (as defined previously).[4]

---

[4] The Safe Harbor only applies to stations that broadcast over the airwaves. Cable and satellite media are not regulated for speech as of now—unless it rises to the FCC's definition of obscenity.

The FCC has defined two types of speech that they regulate outside of the safe harbor: **indecency** and **profanity**.

> Material is indecent if, in context, it depicts or describes sexual or excretory organs or activities in terms patently offensive as measured by contemporary community standards for the broadcast medium. In each case, the FCC must determine whether the material describes or depicts sexual or excretory organs or activities and, if so, whether the material is "patently offensive." (FCC)

Notice that indecency for the FCC subsumes our two categories of obscenity and scatology and then adds the characterization "patently offensive."

Profanity for the FCC seems to be something of a catchall, so as to include under their enforcement taboo words that are not obviously indecent under their definition, but that they still want to regulate.

> "Profane language" includes those words that are so highly offensive that their mere utterance in the context presented may, in legal terms, amount to a "nuisance." In its Golden Globe Awards Order the FCC warned broadcasters that, depending on the context, it would consider the "F-Word" and those words (or variants thereof) that are as highly offensive as the "F-Word" to be "profane language" that cannot be broadcast between 6 a.m. and 10 p.m. (FCC)

Notice that the FCC's definition of "profanity" is far different from ours and has nothing to do with religious taboos. From their discussion, we can infer the term applies primarily to obscenity (in our sense, not theirs). This category is apparently intended to circumvent arguments that *fuck* and its variants are not always indecent in that its informative meaning is sometimes bleached away, leaving only its emotional and social meaning; if *fuck* can be used non-sexually (and it clearly can be) then one could make the case that it is not indecent, since indecency is defined as sexual or excretory language.

The Golden Globes Awards order referred to in the definition for profanity was given in 2004 (FCC, File No. EB-03-IH-0110). In a 2003 live broadcast of the Golden Globes Awards on NBC, Bono, the lead singer for U2, said during his acceptance speech, "This is really, really fucking brilliant!" Initially, the FCC determined that because *fucking* was used as an intensifier absent any sexual meaning, it was not indecent. However, they shortly after reversed this finding, observing, "We recognize NBC's argument that the 'F-Word' here was used 'as an intensifier.' Nevertheless, we believe that, given the core meaning of the 'F-Word,' any use of that word or a variation, in any context, inherently has a sexual connotation, and therefore falls within the first prong of our indecency definition" (FCC, File No. EB-03-IH-0110). As for the "patently offensive" part, they decided that in the context of the awards show it was. In earlier decisions, however, the FCC had decided that fleeting instances of expletives were not indecent and only repeated utterances would be prosecuted; their decision in this case marked a departure. Because this was a new policy they chose not to penalize NBC, but put all stations on notice that they would begin penalizing even fleeting instances of indecent or profane language.

Although the FCC has, in no uncertain terms, indicated that *fuck* and its equivalents are likely to lead to a penalty, the FCC does not (unlike the Production Code discussed in Section 5.1) list those words they consider profane. Indeed, they maintain that they should not do so. In their "Frequently Asked Questions" section, they respond to whether or not certain words are always restricted:

> No. Offensive words may be profane and/or indecent depending on the context. In the Golden Globe Awards Order, the FCC stated that it would address the legality of broadcast language on a case-by-case basis. Depending on the context presented, use of the "F-Word" or other words as highly offensive as the "F-Word" may be both indecent and profane, if aired between 6 a.m. and 10 p.m. (FCC)

The FCC recognizes that context affects how offensive the use of a word is[5]: **"In making obscenity, indecency, and profanity determinations, context is key.** The FCC staff must analyze what was actually aired, the meaning of what was aired, and the context in which it was aired" (FCC). For this reason, they have intentionally kept their definitions of obscenity, indecency, and profanity vague. For example, they have determined that the use of *fuck* in Oliver Stone's movie *Saving Private Ryan* was not profane given the WWII context of the movie; on the other

---

[5] See Chapter 14 for more on context.

hand, they determined that it was profane when used in Martin Scorsese's documentary *The Blues: Godfathers and Sons.*

Another reason the FCC does not list words that are indecent or profane is that even euphemisms or double entendres can rise to the level of indecency. For example, they decided that the "Candy Wrapper" song was indecent when played on KB-FM, San Diego, CA. The song uses the brand names of popular candy bars to depict a sexual encounter (e.g., ". . . she immediately went down on my Tootsie Roll . . ."). The FCC determined that the sexual meaning was inescapable and the song "pandered" to the audience.

The most recent Supreme Court hearing on the reach of the FCC was *FCC v. Fox* (2008). As we saw, the Golden Globes Awards order marked a shift in the FCC's policy towards fleeting expletives. Two similar cases against Fox Television led to Fox appealing the FCC's decision to the Supreme Court. First in the 2002 and then in the 2003 Billboard Music Awards shows broadcast live on Fox, the FCC determined that fleeting expletives had violated their decency rules; in 2002, Cher said "Fuck 'em" and in 2003 Nicole Richie said, "Have you ever tried to get cow shit out of a Prada purse? It's not so fucking simple." Fox argued that the FCC was being "arbitrary and capricious." In the end, the court decided in favor of the FCC. For us, however, it's enlightening to look at the issues raised during the hearing. In particular, two issues are relevant to discussions elsewhere in this book.

It's interesting to note that the FCC recognizes the difference between use and mention qua quotation (see Chapter 3).

> **CHIEF JUSTICE ROBERTS:** [I]f you had a news report about Nicole Richie and the Cher exhibits, they—they could use the actual language, even though they can't during the—the awards shows?
>
> **GENERAL GARRE:** Yes. And, similarly, if there were a news report about the argument today in this Court and there were reports about the actual language used, that's right.
>
> (*FCC v. Fox,* transcripts)

We also find the justices discussing the process of semantic weakening (see Chapter 7).

> **JUSTICE STEVENS:** Isn't it true that—isn't it true that that is a word that often is used with—with no reference whatsoever to the—the sexual connotation?
>
> **GENERAL GARRE:** It can be—it certainly can be used in a non-literal way. It can be used in a metaphorical way, as Cher used it here, to say "F them" to her critics . . .
>
> **JUSTICE STEVENS:** You think it's equally—it's equally subject to being treated as indecent within the meaning of the statute regardless of which meaning was actually apparent to everybody who listened to it?
>
> **GENERAL GARRE:** I wouldn't say equally, Justice Stevens, but what we would say is that it can qualify as indecent under the—under the Commission's definition, because even the non-literal use of a word like the F-Word, because of the core meaning of that word as one of the most vulgar, graphic, and explicit words for sexual activity in the English language, it inevitably conjures up a core sexual image.
>
> **JUSTICE SCALIA:** Which is, indeed, why it's used.
>
> (*FCC v. Fox,* transcripts)

I find it gratifying to see Supreme Court justices grappling with one of the major ideas that we discuss in this book—though I'm not sure I agree with Scalia's point. As we see in other chapters, it is possible for a word to remain taboo while the original informative meaning is lost for the users of the word; perhaps the best example is shown in Chapter 10 with the Québécois French word *tabernak,* one of the most taboo words in the language, but one that lacks a denotation for many speakers. It strikes me that some words are offensive not because of their "core meaning," but because, simply put, they are taboo, and tabooness is a linguistic convention. On the other hand, I am agnostic as to whether or not such words, regardless of why they are taboo, arise to the level of a "nuisance."

6. POLITICAL CORRECTNESS: SPEECH CODES ON COLLEGE CAMPUSES

Allan and Burridge (2006, 92) suggest that the present use of **politically correct** (PC) began self-mockingly among 1960s liberals (e.g., "Is that fruit salad politically correct?"), but it was soon co-opted by the right as true mockery. As I stated at the beginning of this chapter, I am approaching censorship from an apolitical stance. Likewise, I use *politically correct* apolitically.

Although PC language clearly relates to taboo language—indeed its goal is to make certain terms taboo—we cannot discuss PC language in its entirety in this chapter—the scope would be far too large; moreover, other books have trod this territory well (cf., for example, Hughes 2010). Instead, we focus on slurs, which have become more and more taboo since the 1980s and more and more politically incorrect. In particular, we focus on **hate speech** prohibitions on college campuses.

In the late 1980s and early 1990s, many American universities adopted **speech codes** that prohibited hate speech. Here are some representative examples of such speech codes:

- The University of Michigan speech code prohibited individuals from:
  "stigmatizing or victimizing" individuals or groups on the basis of race, ethnicity, age, marital status, handicap, or Vietnam-era veteran status. (Smith 1995, 241)

- The University of California, Berkeley speech code:
  "Fighting words" are those personally abusive epithets which, when directly addressed to any ordinary person are, in the context used and as a matter of common knowledge, inherently likely to provoke a violent reaction whether or not they actually do so. Such words include, but are not limited to, those terms widely recognized to be derogatory references to race, ethnicity, religion, sex, sexual orientation, disability, and other personal characteristics.

  "Fighting words" constitute "harassment" when the circumstances of their utterance create a hostile and intimidating environment which the student uttering them should reasonably know will interfere with the victim's ability to pursue effectively his or her education or otherwise to participate fully in University programs and activities.[6] (quoted in Lakoff 2000, 111)

- The University of Pennsylvania prohibited speech that:
  1. is directed at an identifiable person or persons; and
  2. insults or demeans the person or persons to whom the behavior is directed, or abuses a power relationship with that person, on the basis of his or her race, color, ethnicity, or national origin, such as (but not limited to) by the use of slurs, epithets, hate words, demeaning jokes, or derogatory statements; and
  3. is intended by the speaker or actor only to inflict direct injury on the person or persons to whom the behavior is directed, or is sufficiently abusive or demeaning that a reasonable, disinterested, observer would conclude that the behavior is so intended; or occurs in a context such that an intent only to inflict direct injury may reasonable be inferred. (quoted in Kors & Silverglate 1998)

- To be a violation of the University of Wisconsin's speech code:
  a comment, epithet or other expressive behavior must: (a) be directed at an individual; (c) demean the race, sex, religion, color, creed, disability, sexual orientation, national origin, ancestry or age of the individual; and, (d) create an intimidating, hostile, or demeaning environment for education, university-related work, or other university-authorized activity. (Smith 1995, 244)

- The speech code at Central Michigan University forbade:
  any intentional, unintentional, physical, verbal, or nonverbal behavior that subjects an individual to an intimidating, hostile or offensive educational, employment or living environment by (c) demeaning or slurring individuals through . . . written literature because of their racial or ethnic affiliation; or (d) using symbols, epitaphs [sic] or slogans that infer [sic] negative connotations about an individual's racial or ethnic affiliation. (quoted in Smith 1995, 253)

---

[6] Lakoff (2000, 111) describes this code as "both about as clear as it could be and full of murk" (111).

The basis for such campus speech codes is that hate speech creates a hostile environment, one where a student or a group of students feel so oppressed that their ability to study is jeopardized. In effect, these students feel excluded from normal university life—silenced, so to speak. Fish sees a trade-off here; either way somebody will be silenced:

> And when someone observes, as someone surely will, that anti-harassment codes chill speech, one could reply that since speech becomes intelligible only against the background of what isn't being said, the background of what has already been silenced, the only question is the political one of which speech is going to be chilled, and, all things considered, it seems a good thing to chill speech like "nigger," "cunt," "kike," and "faggot." (Fish 1992, 244)

Not surprisingly, many people oppose such codes. Most opposition has come from the right, arguing for the sanctity of the freedom of speech (Lakoff 2000 highlights the irony insofar as the right has sponsored the majority of censorship legislation). For a time, at least, those from the left who objected to such speech codes were afraid to speak out; Hentoff (1992, 217) mentions that a liberal professor at the University of Buffalo Law School spoke to him about his opposition to the school's speech code only on the condition of anonymity because he feared being labeled a racist.

One liberal and vocal opponent to speech codes was George Carlin, who while sympathetic to the spirit that leads people to prohibit hate speech, was against the codes themselves:

> And, by the way, when it comes to these liberal language vandals, I must say I agree with their underlying premise: White Europeans and their descendants are morally unattractive people who are responsible for most of the world's suffering. That part is easy. You would have to be, uh, visually impaired not to see it. The impulse behind political correctness is a good one. But like every good impulse in America it has been grotesquely distorted beyond usefulness.
>
> Clearly, there are victims, but I don't agree that these failed campus revolutionaries know what to do about them. When they're not busy curtailing freedom of speech, they're running around inventing absurd hyphenated names designed to make people feel better. Remember, these are the white elitists in their customary paternalistic role: protecting helpless, inept minority victims. Big Daddy White Boss always knows best. (Carlin 1997, 163)

Carlin's final line echoes a statement made by a black student at debate on whether Harvard Law School should prohibit hate speech. After a white student had defended speech codes, saying that without them black students would be pushed away from college campuses, the black student rose and "said that the white student had a hell of a nerve to assume that he—in the face of racist speech—would pack up his books and go home" (Hentoff 1992, 219). He concluded by saying: "It is more racist and insulting to say that to me than to call me a nigger" (quoted in Hentoff 1992, 219).

However, this black student may have been an exception in opposing speech codes. In Hentoff's experience traveling across the country attending such debates, most black students supported speech codes (Hentoff 1992). On the other hand, Hentoff found that some of the black student organizations that supported speech codes were simultaneously inviting speakers such as Louis Farrakhan, Kwame Touré, Steve Cokely, and Dr. Khallid Abdul Muhammad, who were all notorious for making anti-Semitic remarks during their speeches.

> Carlin (1997, 160): "I want to be really clear about one thing: as far as other people's feelings are concerned—especially these 'victim groups'—when I deal with them as individuals, I will call them whatever they want. When it's one on one, if some guy wants me to call him a morbidly obese, African-ancestored male with a same-gendered sexual orientation I'll be glad to do that. On the other hand, if he wants me to call him a fat nigger cocksucker, then that's what it will be. I'm here to please."

According to Lakoff (2000), much of the opposition to speech codes is based on unsupported anecdotal evidence.

> The same stories are trotted out again and again . . . But there is a distinct urban-folklore coloration to many of these tales: they often turn out to be third-party anecdotes ("my brother's friend heard from someone who teaches there . . .") that, when tracked down, either cannot be ver-

ified, are much milder than reported, or involved additional factors that explained the "unreasonable" p.c. stance. (Lakoff 2000, 97)

Regardless of whether we personally agree with speech codes or not, there is a separate question to ask: are they constitutional? As it turns out, the answer is probably no.

The legal basis for these codes rests on the "fighting words" exception to the First Amendment, outlined by the Supreme Court decision of *Chaplinsky v. New Hampshire:* "There are certain well-defined and narrowly limited classes of speech, the prevention and punishment of which have never been thought to raise any Constitutional problem. These include . . . the insulting or 'fighting' words—those which by their very utterance inflict injury or tend to incite an immediate breach of the peace" (quoted in Lakoff 2000, 106).[7] Lakoff goes on to explain that the legal concept of fighting words is based on two of government's responsibilities to its citizens: to protect them from injury and to keep the peace (106–7). The first justification would imply that words can injure, and Lakoff writes that later opinions have struck that justification down. The second has proved quite dicey (see Section 4). The idea is that some words are so powerful that the addressee's only reasonable response is to resort to violence, or, as Lakoff suggests, the violence is as reflexive as kicking your leg when a doctor taps your knee with a hammer. It seems quite a burden on the prosecution to demonstrate that going berserk was a reasonable and/or reflexive reaction to the defendant's use of certain words, no matter how taboo the words.

Some have argued that hate speech inflicts psychological damage (Lakoff cites Matsuda et al 1993), but Lakoff (2000) argues that this kind of injury is not covered by *Chaplinsky v. New Hampshire.* Thus, psychological injury can't be used as a constitutional argument in favor of prohibiting hate speech.

All this raises the question: is verbal violence on a par with physical violence? Most, I believe, would say no. As Lakoff (2000, 107) puts it: "Most people given the choice between a vile epithet and a punch in the nose would opt for the former." Yet, deep down, even as we deny the power of words, we realize that they can wound.

We teach our children the proverb "Sticks and stones may break my bones, but words will never harm me." Do we offer this saying as truth or as wishful magic: believe it and the pain will go away? Probably we would not be so quick to teach our children these words if we did not fear that the opposite was true. In our natural desire to save our children from pain, we encourage them to deny their feelings. But denial doesn't make it so. (Lakoff 2000, 104)

But how do we identify such wounds? And, more importantly, how do we identify which words do the wounding? Do we compile a list of "wounding words"? We can't. Simply put, there is no such list because what is wounding to one is not to another and what is wounding from one is not from another; when words are put to use, they can mean many different things: "a word that would shock and intimidate a woman uttered by a strange man on a dark street at night might be a delightful expression of intimacy between her and someone she loves and trusts. African Americans can call one another 'nigger' with relative impunity under specific conditions, but a white person cannot do the same" (Lakoff 2000, 105).

Although we can't simply list what words are forbidden and although any speech prohibitions are necessarily vague (see section 5.2, where we discuss the necessary vagueness of the FCC's phrasing), according to Smith's (1995) survey of the several cases where campus speech codes have been contested in court, in every case the courts have determined that the codes are unenforceable because they are too vague.

Here's an illustrative example of how difficult it can be to identify hate speech. I attended the University of Montana, a predominantly white college, where the student body was relatively (by Montana standards) liberal. Saying the word *nigger*—especially for a white student—was unacceptable, not because of any speech code, but because those who heard it would not have tolerated it. Some white students in my dorm began using a sort of secret code in order to "use" *nigger* covertly; they called African Americans "sheriffs," a reference to a line from the movie *Blazing Saddles,* "The sheriff is a nigger." So, in this context, does saying, "sheriff" qualify as hate speech? At what point would it qualify? We'll return to this example shortly.

One approach to the question of when speech qualifies as hate speech is to consult the addressee; if the addressee perceives a word as offensive enough to qualify as hate speech then it's hate speech. This appears to be the approach taken by the University of Pennsylvania administration in the infamous "Water Buffalo Incident." In 1993, a predominantly black sorority held a celebration on the University of Pennsylvania campus; the cele-

---

[7] See Section 4 for more on the prohibition of fighting words.

bration was loud—singing and stomping were involved—and annoyed some students in a dormitory who were try-ing to study; one of those studying students was Eden Jacobowitz, who shouted, "Shut up, you water buffalo!" (Kors & Silverglate 1998). Shortly after the incident, Jacobowitz was charged with violating the school policy on hate speech (see the University of Pennsylvania speech code quoted earlier).

Jacobowitz said that he had not intended his slur racially, that he was simply referring to the noise the sorority sisters were making, he refused to apologize to the sorority sisters for anything other than shouting at them, and he refused to settle with the university. Five months later a hearing was held, where Jacobowitz applied for dismissal of the case; the panel then set a date for ten days later to present a procedural report. In the wake of intense media scrutiny, the sorority sisters withdrew their charges against Jacobowitz.

From a linguistic perspective, this incident is troubling in that the administration had no real evidence that *water buffalo* was a racial slur; the administration's judicial inquiry officer, Robin Read, claimed that *water buffalo* was clearly a racial slur directed at blacks because water buffalo are "primitive, dark animals that lived in Africa" (quoted in Kors & Silverglate 1998). But this statement shows geographic ignorance on Read's part—water buffalo live in Asia, not Africa. A query to LINGUIST List, the world's largest linguistics listserv, asked if anybody knew of *water buffalo* being used as a racial slur; the answer was a resounding no. Dan Ben-Amos, an Israeli scholar, after being briefed on the incident, asked if Jacobowitz spoke Hebrew; it turns out that the Hebrew word for 'water buffalo', *behema*, is slang for 'oaf'. Moreover, Jacobowitz had attended a yeshiva, where the word was thrown around all the time: between students and from teachers and rabbis to students. In the end, the admin-istration was left with only one argument: *water buffalo* was a racial slur because the sorority sisters perceived it as one. In a letter to Read, Jacobowitz wrote that he disagreed with her "that it was important to take the women's interpretation of my words and the pain that they inflicted upon them into account" (quoted in Kors & Silvergate).

If we are to take the concept of hate speech seriously, we need to consider both sides of the linguistic circuit—both the speaker and the hearer—as well as the larger society. As we discuss in Chapter 14, we need to distinguish between the **illocutionary effects** and the **perlocutionary effects** of an utterance. The illocutionary effects refer to what sort of speech act is intended (e.g., a greeting, a command, a compliment, an insult, or even harassment). The perlocutionary effects refer to how the recipient responds to the utterance (e.g., returning a greet-ing, complying with a command, offering thanks, being offended, or striking out violently). We also need to think about linguistic conventions; speakers can produce an illocution through conventional linguistic means or through non-conventional means—for example, a speaker can offend a person directly by saying, "Fuck off!", which is a con-ventional insult, or they can offend a person indirectly by saying, "How about you buy yourself a dictionary, look up the word *fuck,* and then look up the word *off?*", which is a non-conventional insult.

We have to consider all three components when identifying hate speech. If we just focus on the perlocu-tionary effects (i.e., on whether the recipient is offended), we have a situation like the one at University of Penn-sylvania, where the slur was neither intended racially, nor conventionally associated with race, but because the recipients believed it to be a racial slur, it was considered hate speech by the administration. On the other hand, we can't focus entirely on the speaker's intentions either. At Central Michigan University, a basketball coach was suspended and later fired for calling an assistant coach and several players (both black and white) "niggers" (Smith 1995, 252). Although everybody agreed that the coach did not intend to offend any of his athletes with his utter-ance of *nigger*—indeed, the black players later told the Athletic Director that they had not been offended—we have to recognize that this is a highly charged word, that is, highly charged via linguistic conventions—especially when used by a white person, and it is likely to offend many hearers, regardless of the speaker's intentions. For this reason, many people choose not to utter the word, even when merely mentioning it; hence the creation of forms like *the n-word* and *n***er*. At the same time, most people would agree that instances of mention should be exempt from speech code prohibitions, as, perhaps, should be "affectionate" uses of slurs.

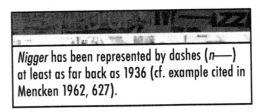

Nigger has been represented by dashes (*n*—) at least as far back as 1936 (cf. example cited in Mencken 1962, 627).

Finally, let's return to my dorm-mates' use of *sheriff* to refer to African Americans; we don't need to delve deeply into their intentions[8] to realize that, no matter how obnoxious and juvenile, this couldn't qualify as hate speech because nobody in the larger community could decode it (i.e., *sheriff* = *nigger* through a line from a movie).

---

[8] In truth, I don't think this cadre of students were particularly racist, so much as they derived pleasure from surreptitiously breaking a taboo and getting away with it. If they had been students in the 1920s perhaps they would have developed an in-group code for *fuck* instead.

The linguistic conventions were not there; as Butler (1997, 20) defines it, "hate speech is an act that recalls prior acts, requiring a future repetition to endure" (quoted in Lakoff 2000, 101). If *sheriff* had caught on in the larger community, eventually it could have risen to the level of hate speech, but at that point *sheriff* would no longer be code, it would be a slur in its own right.

In the end, if we apply rigorous linguistic criteria, it may be possible to semi-objectively define what qualifies as hate speech. It wouldn't be easy, but I expect it's possible. This seems to be Lakoff's (2000) point of view. But just because it's possible doesn't mean that speech codes that prohibit hate speech would stand up against the First Amendment—Smith (1995) does not believe they would, but Fish (1992) thinks they should. Nor does it mean that such speech codes are advisable, irrespective of the constitutionality. Few scholars are willing to argue that hate speech is good, but many are willing to say that prohibiting it is less good. Nevertheless, when we look outside the U.S., many nations have decided to outlaw hate speech; the U.S. may be unique among Western industrialized nations in not having any proscriptions against hate speech (Smith 1995, 228).

7. CONCLUSION

In this chapter we've seen that censorship is an endemic part of our culture, beginning early on and continuing to this day. We all censor language from time to time, either our own or somebody else's, but this chapter has focused on censoring that comes from above, from an authority—either appointed, elected, or self-proclaimed.

Many of the challenges faced by censors relate directly to issues we discuss in other chapters. One of the challenges we've seen with censorship is in defining what should be censored. We've seen that such definitions invariably end up being vague because the censors recognize the need to consider context (see Chapter 14) when deciding if an utterance should be censored; a simple word list has not proven useful in proscribing speech. Furthermore, censors have debated whether it's the meaning of the words or the words themselves that warrant censor (see Chapters 1 and 4). We've also seen that issues of use versus mention are important (see Chapter 3). Although even mentioning taboo words is often censored, most censors recognize that it is typically more offensive to use a taboo word than to mention it. The use/mention distinction is especially important with scholarly work; we've seen that linguistic research has been censored in the past when it looks too closely at taboo words. Furthermore, we've seen a debate among lexicographers about whether dictionaries are meant to be descriptive and thus should include all words, even taboo words, or they should be prescriptive and only include those words deemed "proper" (see Chapter 2).

Chances are you can think of plenty of cases and types of language censorship not covered here. Everybody I talk to brings up another instance. I could have gone on and on and on. But for the sake of relative brevity, I censored myself.

REFERENCES

Allan, Keith, and Kate Burridge. 2006. *Forbidden Words: Taboo and the Censoring of Language*. Cambridge: Cambridge University Press.

Associated Press. 1999. Cussing Canoeist Convicted in Michigan. *LA Times*, June 12, 1999.

Beaumont, Claudine. 2009. Apple bans dictionary from App Store over swear words. *The Telegraph*, August 6, 2009. http://www.telegraph.co.uk/technology/apple/5982243/Apple-bans-dictionary-from-App-Store-over-swear-words.html (accessed 10/24/2010).

Bradsher, Keith. 1999. Canoeist Goes to Court, Fighting for Right to Curse. *The New York Times*, June 3, 1999.

Butler, Judith. 1997. *Excitable Speech: A Politics of the Performative*. New York: Routledge.

Cadenhead, Rogers. 2006. Actor Tries to Trademark 'N' Word. *Wired*, 2/23/2006. http://www.wired.com/print/science/discoveries/news/2006/02/70259 (accessed 8/11/2010).

Carlin, George. 1997. *Brain Droppings*. New York: Hyperion.

Ernst, Morris L., and William Seagle. 1928. *To the Pure: A Study of Obscenity and the Censor*. New York: Viking.

FCC. Frequently Asked Questions. http://www.fcc.gov/eb/oip/FAQ.html (accessed 2/4/2011).

Fish, Stanley. 1992. There's No Such Thing as Free Speech and It's a Good Thing, Too. In *Debating P.C.: The Controversy Over Political Correctness on College Campuses,* (ed.) Paul Berman, 237–245. New York: Laurel.

Forty-Second Congress. 1873. Session III. Ch. 258.

Gard, S.W. 1980. Fighting Words as Free Speech. *Washington University Law Quarterly* 58(3), 531–581.

Hentoff, Nat. 1992. "Speech Codes" on the Campus and Problems of Free Speech. In *Debating P.C.: The Controversy Over Political Correctness on College Campuses,* (ed.) Paul Berman, 215–244. New York: Laurel.

Hughes, Geoffrey. 1991. *Swearing: A Social History of Foul Language, Oaths, and Profanity in English.* Oxford: Blackwell.

Hughes, Geoffrey. 2010: *Political Correctness: A History of Semantics and Cuture.* Malden, MA: Wiley-Blackwell.

Jay, Timothy. 1992. *Cursing in America: A Psycholinguistic Study of Dirty Language in the Courts, in the Movies, in the Schoolyards, and on the Streets.* Philadelphia: John Benjamins.

Johnson, Samuel, Jr. 1798. *A School Dictionary, being a Compendium of the Latest and most Improved Dictionaries.* New Haven, CT: Edward O'Brien.

Kors, Alan, and Harvey Silverglate. 1998. *The Shadow University: The Betrayal of Liberty on America's Campuses,* Chapter 1, The Water Buffalo Affair. New York: Harper Perennial. http://www.shadowuniv.com/excerpts-wb1.html (accessed 8/27/2010).

Lakoff, Robin Tolmach. 2000. *Language War.* Berkeley, CA: University of California Press.

Lemon, George W. 1783. *English Etymology, or a Derivative Dictionary of the English Language.* London: G. Robinson.

Matsuda, Mari, Charles R. Lawrence III, Richard Delgado, and Kimberlé Williams Krenshaw. 1993. *Words that Wound: Critical Race Theory, Assaultive Speech, and the First Amendment.* San Francisco: Westview Press.

Mencken, H.L. 1947. *The American Language: An Inquiry into the Development of English in the United States.* New York: Alfred A. Knopf.

Mencken, H.L. 1962. *Supplement One: The American Language.* New York: Alfred A. Knopf.

Milton, John. 1644. *Aereopagitica.*

Montagu, Ashley. 1967. *The Anatomy of Swearing.* New York: The Macmillan Company.

Myslewski, Rik. 2009. Apple denies censoring App Store swear words. *The Register,* Music and Media, August 6, 2009. http://www.theregister.co.uk/2009/08/06/apple_denies_dictionary_censorship/ (accessed 10/24/2010).

Norman, Arthur N.Z. 1956. Army Speech and the Future of American English. *American Speech* 31(2): 107–112.

Pinker, Stephen. 2007. *The Stuff of Thought: Language as a Window into Human Nature.* New York: Penguin Group.

Read, Allen. 1934. An Obscenity Symbol. *American Speech* 19(4): 264–278.

Read, Allen. 1977. *Classic American Graffiti: Lexical Evidence from Folk Epigraphy in Western North America.* Waukesha, WI: Maledicta Press.

Shattuck, Roger. 1996. *Forbidden Knowledge: From Prometheus to Pornography.* New York: St. Martin's Press.

Simon, Stephanie. 2002. Cussing Canoeist Wins Michigan Appeal/Court Rules Swearing Ban Violates Free Speech. *LA Times,* April 2, 2002.

Smith, Stephen A. 1995. There's Such a Thing as Free Speech: And It's a Good Thing, Too. In *Hate Speech,* (eds.) Rita Kirk Whillock & David Slayden, 226–266. Thousand Oaks, CA: Sage.

Webster, Noah. 1807. *A Letter to Dr. David Ramsay, of Charleston, S.C., respecting the Errors in Johnson's Dictionary, and other Lexicons.* New Haven, CT: Oliver Steele & Co.

Webster, Noah. 1817. *A Letter to the Honorable John Pickering.* Boston: West and Richardson.

1. How do different newspapers handle censorship? Do they make a distinction between use and mention? For example, do they have a different policy for what words a journalist can use versus words that are quoted? Look at several newspapers' coverage of Mel Gibson's telephone conversations with his girlfriend; when discussing or quoting what he said, do they print the taboo words? Which newspapers do and which don't? Is there a difference between online news sources and traditional newspapers?

2. The University of Utah's Student Code prohibits the following behavior:

   Physical or verbal assault, sexual harassment, hazing, threats, intimidation, coercion or any other behavior which threatens or endangers the health or safety of any member of the University community or any other person while on University premises, at University activities, or on premises over which the University has supervisory responsibility pursuant to state statute or local ordinance. (http://www.regulations.utah.edu/academics/6-400.html, accessed 9/24/2010)

   Does your college or university have a similar code? What would constitute a verbal assault that "threatens or endangers the health or safety" of another person? Is such a code enforceable when applied to speech?

3. Should a dictionary's purpose be descriptive or prescriptive? What arguments could be mounted for either side?

INDEX